SPIRIT AND METHOD

T&T Clark Systematic Pentecostal and Charismatic Theology

Series editors
Daniela C. Augustine
Wolfgang Vondey

SPIRIT AND METHOD

Pentecostal Theology and the Pneumatological Imagination

Edwin Rodríguez-Gungor

LONDON • NEW YORK • OXFORD • NEW DELHI • SYDNEY

T&T CLARK
Bloomsbury Publishing Plc, 50 Bedford Square, London, WC1B 3DP, UK
Bloomsbury Publishing Inc, 1385 Broadway, New York, NY 10018, USA
Bloomsbury Publishing Ireland, 29 Earlsfort Terrace, Dublin 2, D02 AY28, Ireland

BLOOMSBURY, T&T CLARK and the T&T Clark logo
are trademarks of Bloomsbury Publishing Plc

First published in Great Britain 2024
Paperback edition published 2025

Copyright © Edwin Rodríguez-Gungor, 2024

Edwin Rodríguez-Gungor has asserted his right under the Copyright,
Designs and Patents Act, 1988, to be identified as Author of this work.

For legal purposes the Acknowledgments on p. x constitute
an extension of this copyright page.

Cover design by Anna Berzovan
Cover image © naqiewei/GettyImages

All rights reserved. No part of this publication may be: i) reproduced or transmitted
in any form, electronic or mechanical, including photocopying, recording or by means
of any information storage or retrieval system without prior permission in writing from
the publishers; or ii) used or reproduced in any way for the training, development or
operation of artificial intelligence (AI) technologies, including generative AI technologies.
The rights holders expressly reserve this publication from the text and data mining
exception as per Article 4(3) of the Digital Single Market Directive (EU) 2019/790.

Bloomsbury Publishing Plc does not have any control over, or responsibility for,
any third-party websites referred to or in this book. All internet addresses given in this book were correct
at the time of going to press. The author and publisher regret any inconvenience caused if addresses
have changed or sites have ceased to exist,
but can accept no responsibility for any such changes.

A catalogue record for this book is available from the British Library.

Library of Congress Cataloging-in-Publication Data
Names: Rodriguez-Gungor, Edwin, author.
Title: Spirit and method : Pentecostal theology and pneumatological
imagination / by Edwin Rodriguez-Gungor.
Description: New York : T&T Clark, 2023. | Series: T&T Clark systematic
Pentecostal and charismatic theology | Includes bibliographical references and index.
Identifiers: LCCN 2023023914 (print) | LCCN 2023023915 (ebook) | ISBN 9780567712004 (hardback) |
ISBN 9780567712059 (paperback) | ISBN 9780567712011 (pdf) | ISBN 9780567712042 (epub)
Subjects: LCSH: Pentecostalism. | Gifts, Spiritual.
Classification: LCC BR1644 .R6244 2023 (print) | LCC BR1644 (ebook) | DDC 269/.4–dc23/eng/20230914
LC record available at https://lccn.loc.gov/2023023914

LC ebook record available at https://lccn.loc.gov/2023023915

ISBN:	HB:	978-0-5677-1200-4
	PB:	978-0-5677-1205-9
	ePDF:	978-0-5677-1201-1
	eBook:	978-0-5677-1204-2

Series: T&T Clark Systematic Pentecostal and Charismatic Theology

Typeset by Integra Software Services Pvt. Ltd.

For product safety related questions contact productsafety@bloomsbury.com.

To find out more about our authors and books visit www.bloomsbury.com
and sign up for our newsletters.

For Kevin Webb

There is a friend who sticks closer than a brother.
Pr. 18:24

CONTENTS

Acknowledgments — x
Abbreviations — xi

Chapter 1
INTRODUCTION
Presuppositions — 3
Structure and Flow — 5

Chapter 2
PENTECOSTAL *QUA* PENTECOSTAL
Introduction — 9
The First Essential: Rooted in Revivalism — 14
    The Numinous — 15
    The Predispositions of the Numinous — 17
    The Numinous Awe — 19
    Why Revival Is Privileged over Rational Theology — 22
    Revival's Commitment to Incomprehensibility — 26
    Revival Keeps Theological Reflection in Check — 28
The Second Essential: Mysticism — 30
    A Constructivist Mysticism — 33
    Christian/Pentecostal Mysticism — 34
The Third Essential: The Pneumatological Imagination — 38
Evidences of Genuine Pentecostalism — 45
    Evidence 1: Affection — 46
        Affection as Motivation — 49
        The Difficulty with Affection — 50
    Evidence 2: A Priority of Love — 51
    Evidence 3: Theological Openness — 56
    Evidence 4: Jesus-Centered and Missional — 61
Conclusion — 62

Chapter 3
THE RELIGIOUS RATIONAL INFLUENCE WITHIN
EARLY AMERICAN PENTECOSTALISM
Introduction — 67
The Rational Theological Gestalt in Pentecostalism — 71
    The Role of Scripture — 73
    Apostolicity — 77
Conclusion — 80

Chapter 4
THE RATIONAL PHILOSOPHICAL INFLUENCES WITHIN EARLY PENTECOSTALISM

Introduction	83
Intellectual History	86
The Philosophy Influencing Early Pentecostalism (c. 1900–25)	92
The Challenge of Theological Liberalism	95
Pentecostalism's Overreaction	97
A Dangerous Detour	99
Exiting Fundamentalism	99
The Longing to Belong	103
Conclusion	104

Chapter 5
A RETURN TO PENTECOSTAL *QUA* PENTECOSTAL

Introduction	107
A Second Copernican Revolution	109
Postmodernism	115
A Return to Mystery	116
Pentecostals as Metamoderns	120
Conclusion	122

Chapter 6
IN SEARCH OF THE BUTTERFLY

Introduction	125
Why New Theological Methodologies?	127
Theology	129
Theological Methodology	132
The Pneumatological	135
Pneumatological Theology	137
The Spirit of Life	140
The Spirit of Truth	144
Interdisciplinary	145
Doxastic Logic	149
Knowledge through Story	152
The Spirit of Love	160
Theological Pluralism	161
The Spirit of the Wind	164
The Surprising	165
The Wild Goose	169
Epistemological Crises	171
Conclusion	176

Chapter 7
DOING THEOLOGY FROM A PNEUMATOLOGICAL IMAGINATION: A PNEUMATOLOGICAL THEOLOGICAL METHODOLOGY

Introduction	177
Imagined Worlds	179
World of Enchantment	179
A World Unfinished	181
World of Relationality	184
World of Dialectic Tension	187
The "Be's" of the PTM	189
Be Converted	189
Be Prayerful	190
Be Scriptural	191
Be Historical	194
Be Philosophical	196
Be Ecumenical	199
Be Discerning	201
Discerning the Evil	202
Discerning the Good	204
The Complexity of Discernment	205
Discernment Requires Time	206
Be Provisional	207
Conclusion	208

Chapter 8
EPILOGUE

Summary and Contributions	211
Further Tasks	213
Bibliography	217
Index	230

ACKNOWLEDGMENTS

This project is a modified version of my PhD thesis titled "In Search of the Butterfly: Toward a Pneumatological Theological Methodology." I came into the academy later in life and doing this work is the fulfillment of a life-long dream for me. I remain desperately grateful to Gail, my wife of forty-seven years, for her willingness to create space in the midst of our busy life for me to engage in it.

I want to acknowledge the immense support and encouragement of my friends and colleagues: Kevin Webb; Dr. F. Russel Hittinger, III; Fr. Brent Sharpe; Fr. Paul Paino; and the whole Diocese of St. Anthony family. I feel especially grateful to Dr. Chris E. W. Green, who served me through this academic process as both friend and supervisor. His expertise, patience, and clear thinking afforded me the joy of learning a pedagogy that has transformed my thinking life.

The voices and contributions of my fellow Bangor University PhD students, as well as the insights and encouragement of the Associate Director of the Centre for Pentecostal and Charismatic Studies, Dr. John Christopher Thomas, also proved deeply helpful and constructive in my study. Additionally, I acknowledge the many scholars who helped me frame my study. By standing on the shoulders of their work, I was able to "see" what I never could have seen otherwise. I am especially indebted to Rudolf Otto, Nancey Murphy, Clark Pinnock, Amos Yong, L. William Oliverio Jr., Veli-Matti Kärkkäinen, and Gerald O'Collins. This village of voices brought immeasurable insight that helped me write and revise what appears on these pages—I alone am responsible for its faults.

I express my sincere gratitude to Wolfgang Vondey and Daniela Augustine, the editors of the Systematic Pentecostal and Charismatic Theology series. Their unwavering support and encouragement were invaluable to me during the entire publishing journey. I would also like to extend my thanks to the dedicated staff at Bloomsbury for their professionalism and meticulous efforts in bringing this work to fruition.

My final word of thanks goes to God. My journey of faith has been full of delight and hope, along with a good mix of ambiguity, contradiction, and uncertainty. Yet, the Christian story still captures and delights me (and I believe it most of the time). So, as I submit these thoughts, I offer *Deo gratias*: Father, Son, and Spirit.

ABBREVIATIONS

DPCM	Burgess, Stanley M., and Gary B. McGee, eds., *Dictionary of Pentecostal and Charismatic Movements* (Grand Rapids, MI: Zondervan, 1988).
IVP	InterVarsity Press
JPT	*Journal of Pentecostal Theology*
NIDPCM	Burgess, Stanley M., and Eduard M. Van Der Maas, eds., *The New International Dictionary of Pentecostal and Charismatic Movements* (Grand Rapids, MI: Zondervan, 2002).
Pneuma	*Pneuma: The Journal of the Society for Pentecostal Studies*

BIBLICAL TRANSLATIONS

BST	*Bible Speaks Today*
ESV	*English Standard Version*
GNV	*Good News Version*
KJM	*King James Version*
NASB	*New American Standard Version*
NIV	*New International Version* (All verses quoted will be in NIV unless otherwise noted.)
NKJV	*New King James Version*
NRSVA	*New Revised Standard Version, Anglicized*

Chapter 1

INTRODUCTION

Some may wonder why a theologue should make the Spirit, whose work is often surprising and disorienting,[1] central to the pragmatic work of developing a theological methodology as the title, *Spirit and Method,* suggests. All theology speaks of God, but a pneumatological theology, as this project sets out to explore, focuses specifically on the Holy Spirit and insists from beginning to end that theological reflection and methodology should be infused with the experience of God vis-à-vis the Spirit. This is the pneumatological, which, as we will see in what follows, includes the non-rational aspects that encounter with God afford (e.g., humility, awe, a creature-consciousness, mystery, etc.). This focus on the Spirit in theological activity, however, carries some legitimate concern.

Jürgen Moltmann avers, "From the very beginning, the personhood of the Holy Spirit was an unsolved problem, and the problem is as difficult as it is fascinating."[2] Augustine reflected on the difficulty one encounters when speaking about the Spirit—the problem being that the Spirit "withdraws from us into mystery even more than Christ."[3] The concern here is that a theologian must find a way to speak of the Spirit—who must be spoken of largely using obtuse, nonpersonal personal words and phrases like divine energy, wind and fire, inward assurance and mutual love, etc.—along with a theological process that proceeds by rational argument and erudite reflection. At first glance, giving priority to the Spirit in our theologizing may seem contradictory, if not oxymoronic. Hence, doing pneumatological theology is a double-edged sword. On one side there is the danger of trying to put too fine

---

1. The scriptures are replete with examples of this. For example, see John 3:5-8; Acts 2:1-4, 10:9-23, 16:6-8; 1 Cor. 12-14; etc.

2. Jürgen Moltmann, *The Spirit of Life: A Universal Affirmation* (Minneapolis, MN: Fortress Press, 2001), loc. 264–7, Kindle.

3. Augustine, as interpreted by Joseph Ratzinger, "The Holy Spirit as *Communio*: Concerning the Relationship of Pneumatology and Spirituality in Augustine," *Communio* 25 (Summer 1998): 324; accessed May 17, 2022, http://www.communio-icr.com/files/ratzinger25-2.pdf, quoted in Veli-Matti Kärkkäinen, *Pneumatology: The Holy Spirit in Ecumenical, International, and Contextual Perspective* (Grand Rapids, MI: Baker Publishing Group, 2018), 5.

a point on *who* the Holy Spirit is and *how* the Spirit informs theological activity; and on the opposite side, the theological reflections fostered in the wide spaces the Spirit confers can be too broad and open to be considered traditional theology.

Pentecostals are suited to lead the way for the church-catholic here. Privileging the Spirit within the theological enterprise has always been central and innate to pentecostalism, and pentecostals have done so in large part while staying tethered to Christian orthodoxy and careful thought. Hence, this writing dives deeply into the pentecostal heart and mind to develop and construct a pneumatological theological methodology (PTM), the purpose of this book. The pentecostal priority for a deep encounter with the Spirit has always been considered critical and antecedent to the process of discursive theologizing. The goal excited in the pentecostal heart is not first that which emerges from theology, rational morality, or teleology; it does not draw its energy from postulates. It has roots in the hidden depths of the pneumatological. But why the need for a PTM?

It is easy to recognize the pace of profound upheaval unfolding in the modern world and the disorientation it can cause to those of us tethered to the ancient world with its sacred stories (viz., the Bible). Theological methodologies carefully developed and wisely used can prevent us from defaulting immediately to a reactive and polemical stance against change, giving us space to respond to unexpected discoveries in faithful, lifegiving, and loving ways. I contend in this writing that a methodology that privileges the presence and guidance of the Holy Spirit is best suited to navigate through such shifts. In the past two decades or so, pneumatological studies have exploded on the theological scene.[4] Anglican Alister McGrath asserts, "The rise of the charismatic movement within virtually every mainstream church has ensured that the Holy Spirit figures prominently on the theological agenda. A new experience of the reality and power of the Spirit has had a major impact upon the theological discussion of the person and work of the Holy Spirit."[5]

Today's rapidly changing world demands theological responses that are fresh and not anachronistic, which is why theologians are affirming that examining our theological methods is "an urgent matter of attention" in the church.[6] My purpose here is to broadly articulate such a method that is rooted in what is pentecostal *qua* pentecostal[7] and built from a pneumatological imagination—or an imagination

---

4. Kärkkäinen, *Pneumatology*, 10.

5. Alister McGrath, *Christian Theology: An Introduction*, 5th ed. (Oxford: John Wiley & Sons, 2011), 227, quoted in Kärkkäinen, *Pneumatology*, 2–3.

6. Paul L. Allen, *Theological Method: A Guide for the Perplexed* (London: T&T Clark International, 2012), 228.

7. Throughout this project I use the small letter "p" pentecostalism to refer to global pentecostals from all times and places, and I will use the capital "P" Pentecostal to refer specifically to North American classical Pentecostals who emerged in the twentieth century and formed into Pentecostal denominations. The morphology is not as clear as I make it seem in this writing, and inconsistencies do exist. Such, however, is the limitation of language.

that sees the order of things (ontology) and the order of knowing (epistemology) mediated through the eternal Spirit and the God-breathed Word, as called for by Amos Yong.[8] In essence, this work is a "pneumatology of quest."[9] Its uniqueness is in its pentecostal theologizing that affords holding in tension: the *What is?* question over against the *What if?* question. I contend that a theologizing that houses this dialectic approach will give the theologian a relevant voice in the twenty-first century.

Presuppositions

Several presuppositions undergird the structure and flow of the argument presented herein. First, it takes the position that though pentecostalism holds a host of variegated theologies, experiences, and practices,[10] there exists a set of shared essentials and distinctives that are universal and have been present since its inception.[11] Walter Hollenweger considers the spirituality of early pentecostalism as representing the heart, not the infancy of the movement.[12] This indicates that though the movement has developed in numerous ways, there is a pentecostal spirituality that was in full bloom at its onset and continues to the present in all its various forms and contexts.

Second, there are many "pentecostalisms" that have emerged around the world,[13] which one should not reduce by assigning the right of primogeniture to the views and values of pentecostals in the North America.

Third, pentecostal spirituality is primarily a universal, essential concern of engagement with the pneumatic through devotion to God's Spirit.[14] However, the task of theological reflection on the meaning of that engagement (viz., pneumatology) proves susceptible to a swirl of intellectual shifts both religious

---

8. Amos Yong, *Spirit-Word-Community: Theological Hermeneutics in Trinitarian Perspective* (Eugene, OR: Wipf & Stock Publishers, 2002).

9. Ibid., 8.

10. See Chris E. W. Green, "Pentecostalism," in *The Cambridge Companion to American Protestantism*, ed. Jason Vickers and Jennifer Woodruff (New York: Cambridge University Press, 2022), 461–78.

11. This is explicated in Chapter 2.

12. Walter J. Hollenweger, *The Pentecostals: The Charismatic Movement in the Churches* (Peabody, MA: Hendrickson, 1988), 551.

13. See Daniel Castelo's discussion of the diversity of forms found within global pentecostalism. He, along with many others, claims, "there are many Pentecostalisms." Daniel Castelo, *Pentecostalism as a Christian Mystical Tradition* (Grand Rapids, MI: William B. Eerdmans Publishing Company, 2017), xvii. Another helpful rendering of the complex forms of pentecostalism is found in Allan Heaton Anderson, *An Introduction to Pentecostalism*, 2nd ed. (Cambridge, UK: Cambridge University Press, 2014), 1–7.

14. Kärkkäinen, *Pneumatology*, 6.

and philosophical in nature. One must take the influence of these religious and philosophical forces into account.

Fourth, there is a pneumatological renaissance[15] afoot in the modern world of theologizing—due in large part to the rise and spread of the pentecostal/charismatic movement—that is beginning to counter the "forgetfulness of the Spirit"[16] present in many communities of faith. This "renaissance" always privileges the pneumatic, which gives rise to what Yong calls a *pneumatalogical imagination*.[17]

Fifth, any PTM needs to be radically committed to the scripture. For pentecostals, as for other orthodox Christians, nothing can carry the same authority as sacred text, which must be seen as the guide for all belief and practice. That said, this project welcomes an interdisciplinary, multilateral approach to theology. I argue that a theological method should seek to analyze, synthesize, and harmonize the shared themes and ideas found in theology with other outside disciplines (e.g., philosophy, history, psychology, etc.).

Sixth, theological assertions should remain provisional, with all theological decisions and positions remaining open to at least nuanced revision. Human beings are always, in Gerald O'Collins's words, "short of the final vision of God."[18] For now, St. Paul tells us, we only "see through a glass, darkly"; we only "know in part"; and it will only be *then* that we shall really "know even as" we are known—when we see him "face to face" in the eschaton (1 Cor. 13:12, KJV). Theologizing requires theologues to remain modest, provisional, and apophatic in what they say and claim.

Seventh, the impulse toward unity and cooperation serves as a central value to a Spirit-filled people; this should signal the welcome of ecumenism. Hence, during the whole time of writing, I had an eye on the larger church. I contend that the *us*-ness of faith remains critical to a theological methodology inspired by the Spirit. Theologians need one another—irrespective of what denomination or theological stream one comes from. Listening to voices less known from the history of the church or from those in communities one is unfamiliar with enriches an individual's theological thinking. This project assumes that carrying an ecumenical resonance serves as one of the final tests for the viability of any proposed theologoumena, as well as any proposed theological method.

Eighth, pentecostals with their "radical countercultural identity,"[19] when truest to their convictions, have always lifted their voices in a prophetic way to the world. Articulating a theological methodology rooted in what is pentecostal could offer

---

15. Ibid., 2.
16. Ibid., 7.
17. Yong, *Spirit-Word-Community*, 133.
18. Gerald O'Collins, *Rethinking Fundamental Theology: Toward a New Fundamental Theology* (Oxford: Oxford University Press, 2011), 336 Reproduced with permission of Oxford Publishing Limited through PLSclear.
19. Cheryl Bridges Johns, "The Adolescence of Pentecostalism: In Search of a Legitimate Sectarian Identity," *Pneuma* 17, no. 1 (Spring 1993): 4.

clear, Spirit-directed ways of faithfully speaking for God in this historical moment into the circumstances of local and global contexts of the church-catholic and her future.

Structure and Flow

Academic inquiry usually advances through the rigorous analysis of a limited topic, where the researcher seeks a rich, contextualized understanding of a particular context through the intensive study of particular cases. This kind of knowledge is idiographic—found in the particulars. This project, however, does not use that methodology. It makes no claim to being a thoroughgoing historical-critical study of pentecostalism, nor does it offer an ethnographic analysis of specific cultural understandings of pentecostals. It attempts, rather, to be something of a performance (rather than mere description) of how authentic pentecostal spirituality supervenes the theological enterprise where theologians are driven (like Moses or Isaiah or those on the Day of Pentecost in Acts 2) to wonderment and awe that transcend the distinctions ordinarily made between subject and object—where one becomes a knower of that which one seeks more passionately to know.

Therefore the approach used in this book is broad and draws upon many interlocutors from various disciplines across time. Because I imagine an overarching heuristic theological methodology that can embody a pentecostal spirituality, this broader, exploratory, and multi-disciplinary approach seems better suited here. Such an approach can reveal higher-level concepts and theories not unique to a particular participant or setting. Generalizing with this process remains more complicated and, perhaps, controversial; at first blush the process may even seem a bit helter-skelter, but the methodology is intentional. In a broad approach, tendencies and opportunities may appear that are not always found in a *gestalt*.

The limitations of this approach are obvious. Each of the major disciplines I brush up against (from science to psychology, philosophy, history, and theology) are broadly sketched, which will alert specialists in those areas that a non-specialist has entered their field. This is not an attempt at an apology because no author should apologize for a new contribution. These comments are meant to guide the reader into the kind of goal I had in mind while producing this work. My goal is to articulate a theological methodology deeply rooted in a pneumatological foundation and imagination, fueled by wonderment. Pointillism in art would be a corollary to this approach.

This is precisely what pentecostal academicians like Cheryl Bridges Johns call for in asking pentecostal theologians to offer "educational paradigms that better reflect a Pentecostal worldview ... [where] all things relate to the whole of unity that is in God."[20] She writes:

---

20. Cheryl Bridges Johns, "Athens, Berlin, and Azusa: A Pentecostal Reflection on Scholarship and the Christian Faith," *Pneuma* 27, no. 1 (Spring 2005): 144.

The Pentecostal emphasis upon the systemic relational unity of all things and the transrational nature of knowledge point us in the direction of a new unifying culture of *paideia*. Pentecostals could offer to higher education a way beyond the fragmentation of the curriculum inherent within the Berlin model. The Pentecostal vision of "The Good" that unifies the fields of study would not be formulated within a static deterministic historical worldview. Rather, it would offer a systemic, open, and highly interdisciplinary worldview grounded in a robust theology of creation. Herein lay the possibilities of a synergy of the human spirit with that of the Creator Spirit and an emerging "Christian mind" that participates in trinitarian relationality.[21]

Clark Pinnock's work, *Flame of Love: A Theology of the Holy Spirit*,[22] might be considered a precursor or predecessor to this project. Pinnock resources a wide swath of voices from popes to mystics, poets, scientists, historians, psychologists, philosophers, litterateurs, and theologians—and from premodern, modern, and postmodern contexts—to bring fresh nuances of understanding to the theology of the Spirit. Though some critiqued this methodology because of what seemed the odd miscellany of his sources and the inchoate shape of his arguments, it seems clear that his work yielded new orientations and helpful perspectives, which in turn opened new lines of conversation.

Given the assumptions that guide this study, the argument begins (Chapter 2) as an imaginative construal (or model) that seeks to define pentecostal *qua* pentecostal—utilizing a framework to investigate and build from its idiosyncratic shape. This construal is far from a wish for a definitive description. It is rather a welcoming of a splash of fragments, accents, and paths that seemed precious to me among the many others I researched.

Chapter 3 begins to examine the influences—both religious and secular—present at the onset of the development of North American classical Pentecostalism as a model of how pentecostalisms around the globe are susceptible to forces native to their contexts. Religiously, pentecostals reflected the theological hermeneutics of faith communities that came before them which impacted their orthodoxy, orthopraxy, and orthopathic expectations. This chapter traces how American Pentecostals portaged their deep Wesleyan-Holiness and Keswick theological influences and expectations—already known and familiar to them—into their theologizing.

Chapter 4 examines the philosophical, political, cultural, economic, and sociological forces that deeply impacted the early theological work within the pentecostal ethos of North America. Pentecostal people may be "Spirit-filled," but they are also just everyday people too, influenced along with everyone else by the forces that surround them. These forces (or leanings) limited the open and

---

21. Ibid., 145.
22. Clark Pinnock, *Flame of Love: A Theology of the Holy Spirit* (Downers Grove, IL: IV Press, 1996).

generous impulse within pentecostalism over time, and the evidence suggests that American Pentecostals (along with many theological conservatives) were unwittingly taken captive by the strictures of modern thought, practice, and habits of the heart.

Chapter 5 is devoted to exploring how the huge shifts in science and philosophy began to afford an intellectual path for North American pentecostals to recapitulate the priorities and thought that were critical to what is definitively or recognizably pentecostal. The chapter examines how these pentecostals engaged with and were influenced by (both negatively and positively) the various *zeitgeists*: premodernism, modernism, and postmodernism.[23] It also shows how those philosophical constructs did not dominate them long. The evidence supports the claim that pentecostalism is inherently a movement born out of time, which means it ultimately transcends philosophical considerations and cultural forces. I am suspicious (though it is beyond the scope of this research) that pentecostalisms around the world carry this same penchant.

Chapter 6 resources Yong's schema of the *pneumatological imagination*[24] to sketch out the rationale for a theological methodology that would remain tethered to the foundational pneumatological essentials of pentecostalism, while launching into second-level intellectual theologizing that is distinctively pentecostal and "glocal" in nature.[25] It addresses the *Why?* of any new methodology and what one should consider warranted in a pneumatocentric methodology. The chapter examines the pneumatological renaissance currently happening in the world of theology and the opportunity afforded by that renaissance to the pentecostal theologue.

Chapter 7 is devoted to constructing a particular kind of *PTM* that utilizes the sensitivities and values explicated throughout this book. It proffers a kind of thought experiment with a set of imagined *worlds* in which theology takes place in particular ways that favor what is pentecostal. Though one could imagine many kinds of PTMs, I attempt to concretize a path for others to examine and possibly employ.

---

23. I am aware that some in the academy are skeptical of using sweeping periodizations or broad epistemes (viz., *zeitgeists*) to refer to perceived global patterns, which they see as "narrow and selective groupings of Euro-American cultural production." See Jason Ananda Josephson Storm, *Metamodernism* (Chicago: University of Chicago Press, 2021), 12. Storm prefers the term *metamodernism* (versus premodernism, modernism, or postmodernism), not to describe a new zeitgeist or periodization, but to put forward a particular scholarly model or paradigm (in a way inspired by Hegel's dialectic) to follow philosophical and cultural moments on which the dialectic advances. Ibid., 6.

24. Yong, *Spirit-Word-Community*.

25. The term "glocalization" has been offered to combine the emphasis of both local and global concerns without biasing the moment's global pluralism against the movement's local embeddedness. See Wolfgang Vondey, *Pentecostalism: A Guide for the Perplexed* (New York: T&T Clark, 2012), 24–5.

The study concludes (Chapter 8) by describing contributions of this writing to the theological methodology of pentecostal theologues and extends an invitation to those theologians to engage in further research. The hope is that the outline drawn out in these pages will be useful and stimulating, and that it will provide pertinent, penetrating elements to understanding how pentecostals do theology in a pentecostal way.

An important note to bear in mind is this author's "come-from." I write as a self-identified pentecostal (though not a classical Pentecostal), which means I am deeply invested in all-things-Spirit. The personal involvement of an author in their research does raise important hermeneutical questions.[26] However, Belden Lane asserts that, though it may do so reluctantly, "the academy continues to probe the permeable boundaries between critical scholarship and lived experience."[27] I dare to wander a bit between those boundaries as I offer this project to the reader.

---

26. Though this is generally recognized as a limitation, Dorothy Sölle, *The Window of Vulnerability* (Minneapolis: Fortress Press, 1990), 35, claims that this should not be seen as problematic. She writes, "I consider the separation of the personal from the professional, of one's own experience from reflections that then vaunt themselves as 'scientific' philosophical-theological thought, to be a fatal male invention, the overcoming of which is a task for any serious theology that intends to be a theology of both women and men."

27. Belden C. Lane, *The Solace of Fierce Landscapes: Exploring Desert and Mountain Spirituality* (New York: Oxford University Press, 1998), 5.

Chapter 2

PENTECOSTAL *QUA* PENTECOSTAL

Introduction

What exactly does it mean to be pentecostal and why should pentecostalism inform theological methodology? In this writing, I intend to address those questions while resisting the reductionist urge to produce a single account of pentecostalism that quashes the significant diversity of the global movement or to concretize its essences in ways that overshadow the freedom and adaptability of its spirituality.

In the North American context, pentecostalism erupted with the famous Azusa Street Revival in Los Angeles in the early twentieth century (1906–9). Thousands of individuals began having powerful religious experiences with lingering biblical phenomena associated with the promise of scripture and the power of the Holy Spirit. Although it cannot be said that pentecostalism began at Azusa,[1] after the revival in Los Angeles, what became known as the "pentecostal movement" spread from there like wildfire from culture to culture and from denomination to denomination across the globe. Some estimate that pentecostalism had spread to as many as fifty nations by the end of the first decade of the twentieth century.[2] To date, according to the World Christian Database, at least one-quarter of the world's 2 billion Christians claim to have encountered a pentecostal experience, aligning themselves "as members of these lively, highly personal faiths, which emphasize such spiritually renewing 'gifts of the Holy Spirit' as speaking in tongues, divine healing and prophesying."[3] These sort of phenomena continue to echo through pentecostalism as a whole; though the interpretation and understanding of pentecostal experiences are certainly not univocal—they afford a potpourri of beliefs and practices that have emerged and continue to emerge.

---

1. Jürgen Moltmann, "Preface," in *The Spirit in the World: Emerging Pentecostal Theologies in Global Contexts*, ed. Veli-Matti Kärkkäinen (Grand Rapids, MI: William B. Eerdmans Publishing Company, 2009), ix.

2. Allan H. Anderson, *To the Ends of the Earth: Pentecostalism and the Transformation of World Christianity* (Oxford: Oxford University Press, 2013), 2.

3. "Spirit and Power—A 10-Country Survey of Pentecostals," *Pew Research Center*, October 5, 2006, accessed May 2, 2022, http://www.pewforum.org/2006/10/05/spirit-and-power-a-10-country-survey-of-pentecostals3/.

As the movement expanded globally, groups did not simply mirror the same theological constructs and religious priorities of their early North American Pentecostal predecessors.[4] In fact, it may be a mistake to think of pentecostalism as a movement that began in the United States, though certain forms of the movement certainly did emerge there. Pentecostals in other cultural contexts have not always reflected the same theological hermeneutics as the classical Pentecostals of North America. Cultures have disparate theoretical concepts, expressions, and priorities that show up in their values, community involvement, political orientation, and theologizing. Emerging pentecostalisms within other cultures (e.g., Latin America, Africa, Asia, etc.) carry the worldviews and values of those cultures, which predisposes their theological reflection to be done through their own native hermeneutical lenses. Hence, the term "pentecostal" has grown to designate a variety of groups, but at least until recently has been generally defined in three broad ways by North American scholars: (1) Classical Pentecostals, which in some contexts split into Wesleyan Holiness and Finished Work expressions and gave rise to a number of Pentecostal denominations, including the Assemblies of God, the Church of God, and the Church of God in Christ; (2) the Charismatic Movement, which dawned in the early 1960s and found expressions within mainline churches (viz., Roman Catholic, Lutheran, Greek Orthodox, Episcopalian, etc.); and (3) Neo-Pentecostalism (or Neo-Charismatic), largely non-denominational and largely indigenous churches considered the "Third Wave" of pentecostalism.[5]

Even with these categories, however, nuances of difference abound, making it difficult to arrive at some definition or description of global pentecostalism. As Allan Anderson explains:

> Because of the great diversity within Pentecostal and Charismatic churches, it is very difficult to find some common unifying features or distinctiveness by which they might be defined. It is an extremely precarious task in the first place, as it gives the one who attempts it the responsibility to see that justice is done to those who might not fit precisely into this definition. Pentecostals have defined themselves by so many paradigms that diversity itself has become a primary defining characteristic of their identity.[6]

Truly, when one examines the landscape of pentecostalism, it seems virtually impossible to overstate the diversity one finds. Chris Green avers, "Some have argued 'Pentecostal' should be taken as a noun, not an adjective. But they do not agree on what constitutes authentic Pentecostalism or what belongs to its

---

4. See Veli-Matti Kärkkäinen, ed., *The Spirit in the World: Emerging Pentecostal Theologies in Global Contexts* (Grand Rapids, MI: William B. Eerdmans Publishing Company, 2009).

5. See Peter D. Hocken, "Charismatic Movement," in *The New International Dictionary of Pentecostal and Charismatic Movements*, ed. Stanley Burgess and Eduard M. Van Der Maas (Grand Rapids, MI: Zondervan, 2002), 477–519.

6. Anderson, *An Introduction to Pentecostalism*, 2.

essence—and there seems to be no way to arrive at a consensus."[7] Those who claim to be a part of the pentecostal tradition carry so many theological, experiential, and practical disparities that many believe it is not possible to identify or describe an essence of pentecostalism that captures that which is pentecostal. The problem is if pentecostalism is demarcated by certain theological markers, experiences, or practices—*which* group's theology or experience or practice should be established as the standard? The multiplicity and diversity of pentecostalism will mean that we will always have a host of pentecostal theologies, experiences, and practices.

All of this leads to the fundamental query: *Does the global pentecostal movement carry any shared essentials and distinctives that are unique?* I am convinced that the answer is *yes*. However, to begin to identify what makes pentecostalism pentecostal, a shift must happen from searching for a simple taxonomic list of similarities to a more complex process of understanding. Throughout the scope of this writing, I proffer a process flexible enough to explain what pentecostalism is while accounting for the many pentecostalisms that have emerged. This is no small task, as Green reports:

> There are also serious—and, in some cases, seemingly irreconcilable—differences amongst Pentecostals on doctrinal formulation, theological method, the interpretation of Scripture, ecclesial authority, institutional structure, religious ethos, devotional and liturgical practices, ethical commitments, ecumenical and inter-religious engagement, political identification and participation, etc. Over time, some of these differences widen and deepen and others fade into relative insignificance as new problems, seemingly more insistent and menacing, emerge.[8]

Despite this fair assessment, I feel convinced that one *can* identify essences and distinctives that, despite difference, are sufficient to show how all expressions of pentecostalism are part of a coherent whole.

What I attempt here entails an imaginative construal (or model) that seeks to make sense of the data in a way that enables further investigation.[9] This writing seeks to construct a model to facilitate an understanding of the birth and development of pentecostalism (asking *What exactly is pentecostalism? What is its identity? Why does it exist?*), along with some underlying reasons for its idiosyncratic shape (asking *Why do pentecostals look the way they do?*). This approach seeks not only to examine pentecostals as sources of information in themselves, but also to account for the process of development (the *story*) that has led to what

---

7. Green, "Pentecostalism," 5.
8. Ibid., 3.
9. For more on how building models prove effective for interpreting complex data, see Ian Hacking, *Representing and Intervening: Introductory Topics in the Philosophy of Natural Science* (Cambridge, UK: Cambridge University Press, 1983), 210–19.

could be identified as pentecostal. This demands we look not only at the religious dimensions embedded within the emergence of pentecostalism (explored more specifically in Chapter 2), but to the anthropological, philosophical, and historical influences as well. The sources I draw from are varied. In this chapter I engage with interlocutors who are more "outside" observers (*not* confessional scholars), whose interest rests in anthropology and general religious studies, as well as with scholars and practitioners who are insider participants who live and speak from within the pentecostal experience. My hope is to host a kind of "round table" to hear from scholars of religion, pentecostal academicians and practitioners, to garner insight into the essence of pentecostalism. Surprisingly, the research shows that both insiders and outsiders have similar observations that suggest traits of a coherent whole.

I begin with what pentecostals hold as central to their narrative—the deep work of God within the human heart, which is often referred to as *revival*.[10] What comes to be known as pentecostalism emerges from revivals—which some identify as non-rational, pneumatocentric experiences (explicated below) that later evolve into a mosaic of hermeneutics, as well as idiosyncratic beliefs and practices through second-level rational theologizing. The research suggests that some often describe the pentecostal movement with characteristics that emerged *after* the addition of rational human reflections to raw pneumatological experiences. Central to this project is the insight that one can see the idiosyncratic characteristics arising after these experiences as secondary aspects of the movement, not necessarily essential to it. Throughout this work I have asserted that the primary or essential aspects of what makes pentecostalism pentecostalism are signaled by less obvious pneumatological traits (explored herein).

The goal of this chapter is to shed light on the critical essence of pentecostalism shared by pentecostals of all stripes at all times, along with the effects one should expect when participating in that essence.[11] Though this list may not be exhaustive, I explicate what I see as three key essentials of pentecostalism: (1) it

---

10. I use the term "revival" as a catch-all phrase to describe the priority of the pentecostal experience with the living God, along with a specific kind of mysticism that is explored below. Not all revivalism focuses on experience or would be mystical in nature, but I focus on those forms of revival concerned with *who God is* and how *experiencing* God is the reason for the existence of the church. See Grant Wacker, *Heaven Below: Early Pentecostals and American Culture* (Cambridge, MA: Harvard University Press, 2001); Castelo, *Pentecostalism*; Harvey Cox, *Fire From Heaven: The Rise of Pentecostal Spirituality and the Reshaping of Religion in the Twenty-First Century* (Cambridge, MA: De Capo Press, 1995); and Peter D. Neumann, *Pentecostal Experience: An Ecumenical Encounter* (Eugene, OR: Pickwick Publications, 2012).

11. "Essence" is being used here in the Aristotelian sense in that it corresponds to the kind of a thing signified or expressed by its definition (*viz.*, its genus and differentia). See Aristotle, *Metaphysics*.

is rooted in *revivalism*; (2) it is a specific kind of *mysticism*; and (3) it carries a *pneumatological imagination*. Of course, what one finds as an emphasis or focus within pentecostalism will be held as a conviction (in one form or another) by all Christians, yet it seems for pentecostals that these distinguishing essentials incur unusual importance and centrality, which I believe gives this deeply variegated movement a recognizable coherence. In this chapter I also give some examples of how these essences reify within the pentecostal ethos.

A note of warning is appropriate here. Imagine a lepidopterist on an expedition to the Amazon to collect butterfly species for her collection and study. She wanders into the rainforest and comes upon a host of beautiful, colorful butterflies of various species, both old and new, flitting about. They rise and fall gently, effortlessly, and the lepidopterist finds it surprisingly delightful to follow them and watch. Then, one lands on her shirt sleeve, and she captures and immobilizes it with an aerial net. She recognizes the butterfly as part of the iconic genus of the Amazon rainforest, the blue morphos (*Morpho peleides*). She gently grabs and squeezes the specimen by the thorax between her thumb and forefinger with the wings folded over the back until it has no more life. She immediately takes out a spreading board covered in balsa wood, with adjustable grooves perfectly suited for butterfly specimens. She proceeds to pin the butterfly down. She can now examine the butterfly with a magnifying glass much more closely—measuring its large wingspan—which measures over six inches. She knows these are one of the "brush footed" butterflies because they have only four functional legs, and she examines the legs carefully as they lie lifeless on her specimen board. She can study it carefully because she is not distracted by its glorious flight. Indeed, something has been gained by its capture, but something has also been lost—maybe something greater than what was found. Dead things are not nearly as interesting as living ones. She can make more sense of the structure of the *Morpho peleides* for its capture, but the wonder engendered by its life and flight is gone.

This is precisely the danger of this project. In my quest to explore and discover what is pentecostal, a grave danger exists of being too specific or aggressive in my attempt to "pin down" pentecostalism. It is my conviction that one must study pentecostalism the way one studies a fluttering butterfly. The moment you try to catch it, there is a danger of killing it. Trying to pin it in the display case for further study destroys the experience of observing the butterfly in flight. True, a lifeless species under a microscope yields knowledge, but the wonder of life is gone. In this writing I am searching for the soaring butterfly that is pentecostalism—to enjoy and to remain in amazement of it—not to capture and immobilize it with a net or squeeze it by the thorax until it has no more life, only to pin it to a theological "spreading board" for other theologues to scrutinize.

This danger is also why I have chosen *not* to focus on any particular uniqueness of different traditions within the pentecostal family (such as classical Pentecostalism) in any totalizing way. I am convinced that, though identifying such distinctions can prove helpful, particularities can also cause the loss of common family resemblances. I thus use, in pentecostal scholar Wolfgang Vondey's words, a "search for fundamentals"[12] that can be used heuristically within a theological methodology that privileges what is essentially pentecostal.

The First Essential: Rooted in Revivalism

Revival—or more specifically the experience of God—was the Big Bang of the whole pentecostal narrative. Though something more is meant when one speaks specifically of "pentecostal revival," it is accurate to claim that the term can be used generally to describe what is understood as the immediate and primary work of Christian conversion within *any* culture throughout time. But where do revivals spring from, and what is their essence? Even the term *revival* seems a second-level reflection on something more profound and raw.

A step toward understanding the essence of revival (and pentecostalism by extension) is afforded as we ask a broader question regarding the essence of religion itself. Psychological anthropologist and historian Anthony Wallace asserts that "religion is a universal aspect of human culture."[13] He estimates that over 100,000 various religions have been imagined and practiced over the scope of human history. Wallace contends that all religions carry four basic characteristics: (1) they have *an individual expression*—it must be personal as each person involved finds some basic connection with it; (2) they contain *an aspect of the supernatural* (or is shamanistic) where the religion paves the way for healings, guidance for life, authoritative ethics, addressing chaos, etc.; (3) they *provide communal connection*—where beliefs and practices are shared and affirmed; and 4) they are *ecclesiastical*—where a centralized organization or structure is promoted that protects the faith from becoming too individualistic or too shamanistic.[14] When examining pentecostalism, one can clearly see it housed these characteristics in various degrees.

It is significant to claim that revivalist movements like pentecostalism hold a universal nature of religion. It suggests that on some intrinsic level, religious experiences are central to what it means to be human. But *why*? Why would some claim that religious experiences are native to the human experience? Is there some embedded "God-gene" in the human race that predisposes us to spiritual/mystical experiences, as suggested by geneticist Dean Hamer?[15] Or are such experiences initiated in the human soul directly by God? For insight into these questions, and into the essential qualities of revival/pentecostalism itself, it is

---

12. Vondey, *Pentecostalism*, 26.

13. Anthony F. C. Wallace, *Religion: An Anthropological View* (New York: Random House, 1966), loc. 224, Kindle.

14. Wallace, *Religion*, loc. 1025–5192, Kindle.

15. Dean Hamer, *The God Gene: How Faith Is Hardwired into Our Genes* (New York: Random House, 2005).

helpful to resource the work of anthropologist and religious studies' scholar, Rudolf Otto (1869–1937).[16] It should be noted that Otto is an outsider to pentecostal concerns, and his interests are primarily anthropological as he traces the primitive development of religion through an evolutionary lens. (Young-earth pentecostals may find this off-putting, but there is much good to garner here.) In his project, *The Idea of the Holy*,[17] Otto devotes the majority of his writing juxtaposing the difference between the rational and non-rational (or supra-rational) aspects of religion, and that juxtaposition will give us our first clue as to why I am making the claim that revival is one of the essences of pentecostalism.

The Numinous

In trying to describe or explicate *any* religious idea, rational thought is required. But embedded within the testimonies of those who claim to have had divine encounters, we discover an aspect of religion that is deeper and more primitive than what is rational (this holds true with testimonies within the pentecostal tradition). It appears the essence of divine encounter (viz., revival) is prerational and pretheological, and it carries an innocence (like that of a child). The biblical record opens with Adam and Eve encountering God in Eden with only the most primitive instruction. The pinnacle of the narrative was that they were in the Garden *with God*. As the biblical text progresses beyond the creation narrative, story after story is told of God's interaction with human beings *before* the development of any formal religious ideas or concepts appear. In many stories there were individuals (sometimes called "holy pagans"[18]) who lived outside the religious structures established by Israel's law or the prophets (or later Christian teaching), yet their lives are flooded with the activity of the Spirit.[19]

The simplicity of faith within the transformative encounters with the holy (that naturally lead to later reflection and rational theological discourse) initially are

---

16. It should be noted that there are many criticisms of Otto. See Gerard van der Leeuw, *Religion in Essence and Manifestation: A Study in Phenomenology* (New York: Harper & Row, 1963).

17. Rudolf Otto, *The Idea of the Holy: An Inquiry into the Non-Rational Factor in the Idea of the Divine and Its Relation to the Rational*, trans. John W. Harvey (London: Oxford University Press, 1958).

18. See Pinnock, *Flame of Love*, 198.

19. These include believing men and women recorded in scripture: Abel, Enoch, Noah, Lot, Job, Daniel (Cf. Ezek. 14:14), Melchizedek, Abimelech, Jethro, Rahab, Naaman, Ruth, the Magi, and Cornelius—individuals who were known as those in right relationship with God outside the religious customs/practices of Jewish or Christian salvation lines. These individuals form what some refer to as the "holy pagan tradition." See Amos Yong, *Beyond the Impasse: Toward a Pneumatological Theology of Religions* (Ada, MI: Baker Academic, 2003), 113.

not freighted with deep rational or theological thought (though some modicum of rationality is always present[20])—the prerational and pretheological preponderate. James K. A. Smith, following the insights of Steven Land and Amos Yong, argues that the pentecostal experience emerges first as prerational and pretheological. Smith claims that pentecostals "express a certain 'other-worldliness' or 'ardent supernaturalism'" that privileges the prerational/pretheoretical over the rational/theoretical.[21] "From a Pentecostal view," he asserts, "when the pretheoretical/theoretical distinction is conflated, faith—which is not theoretical but precedes theory—is forced into a theoretical mode and eventually becomes equated with theological propositions or formulations."[22] Smith suggests that the faith that emerges in revival is an integration of pretheoretical commitments with simple theological understandings that do not necessarily carry intellectual sophistication—they need only be childlike.

Otto insists that it is problematic when one views religion primarily or exhaustively through a constructive or rational lens. He claims this mistake comes easily because theologues generally begin religious themes using sacred text, and the rational element inherent in that process occupies the foreground.[23] Intrinsic to language itself (the use of words and concepts) is the emergence of a copious rationality. Otto holds that the problem is, attaching rational attributes to an unseen, living God does not afford a broad enough view of what one would know as a deity. He claims that in our theologizing, the "nature of God is thus thought of by analogy with our human nature of reason and personality,"[24] thus reducing God to anthropomorphic limitations.[25] Though these attributes may prove essential to the discussion of God (and may even have emerged from sacred texts), they exist as *synthetic* attributes constructed through a human hermeneutic and, as such, serve simply as predicates to a fuller picture. Otto views theological language as inappropriate when addressing the non-rational, ineffable, suprarational aspects of God, which require a comprehension on a deeper level and of a different kind than mere ideas and concepts. Additionally, he argues (as we will see later pentecostals and theologians from other traditions also argue) that a deep encounter with the holy is antecedent and a critical experience for any theologian who wants to effectively theologize. Otto does not suggest that non-rational encounters are beyond rational consciousness but asserts that in the religious experience, the non-rational always antecedes the rational. Here, Otto

---

20. To be expanded in what follows.
21. James K. A. Smith, "Scandalizing Theology: A Pentecostal Response to Noll's *Scandal*," *Pneuma* 19, no. 2 (Fall 1997): 227.
22. Ibid., 232.
23. Otto, *Idea of the Holy*, 2.
24. Ibid., 1.
25. Otto echoes Ludwig Feuerbach here. See Ludwig Feuerbach, *The Essence of Christianity*, trans. George Eliot (Amherst, NY: Prometheus Books, 1989).

claims, "[W]e come up against the contrast between rationalism and a profounder religion."[26]

To explicate what Otto considers "profounder" in religion, he reframes the sense of the word *numinous* from the Latin word, *numen*. The term *numen* literally means a "nod of the head"[27] and began to be associated with spiritual power in ancient Rome. The Romans believed that the forces behind the movement of inanimate objects and various other non-human phenomena around them came from the nod of the gods. *Numen* began being used in common parlance to recognize divine forces expressed toward objects, places, or phenomena when those forces could not be readily explained by natural forces. The term was resourced by English speakers during the 1600s as well, as by Otto in the early twentieth century, to describe the essence and phenomenology of faith.[28] Otto uses the term "numinous" to explore the category of "the holy," which he feels is the thing peculiar about the sphere of religion. He pushes back from the ordinary usage of the holy, claiming, "[W]e have come to use the words 'holy,' 'sacred' (*heilig*) in an entirely derivative sense, quite different from that which they originally bore."[29] He is careful to distinguish the idea of the holy from the Kantian notion of the "perfectly moral will,"[30] which couches holiness as a purely human "imperative upon conduct and universally obligatory"[31] action. For Otto, the holy has its root in the divine and stands "above and beyond the meaning of [human] goodness."[32]

The Predispositions of the Numinous

The term "numinous" becomes Otto's place-marker to describe the moment a person experiences what he considers to be the *extra* within "the holy." The numinous stands for a state of mind which is "*sui generis* and irreducible to any other" category—though he contends that the numinous "cannot be strictly defined"[33]—and uses it to frame what he sees as essentially inexplicable. For Otto, the numinous is an a priori potential within human beings that, if one allows oneself to be guided by, will erupt into a transformational consciousness of the divine.

This brings us to the anthropological dimension of Otto's argument. Otto's articulation of the numinous is a heuristic term that helps to explain the potential

---

26. Otto, *Idea of the Holy*, 2.
27. H. J. Rose, *Primitive Culture In Italy* (London, UK: Methuen & Co. Ltd., 1926), 44–5.
28. Alondra Yvette Oubré, *Instinct and Revelation: Reflections on the Origins of Numinous Perception* (London: Taylor & Francis, 2007).
29. Otto, *Idea of the Holy*, 5.
30. Immanuel Kant, *Groundwork of the Metaphysics of Morals*, trans. and ed. Mary Gregor and Jens Timmerann (Cambridge, UK: Cambridge University Press, 2012).
31. Otto, *Idea of the Holy*, 5.
32. Ibid., 6.
33. Otto, *Idea of the Holy*, 7.

every human being has to experience the holy (viz., revival). William James (1842–1910), considered a leading thinker of the late nineteenth century, had been influenced by Otto. James held that the numinous penchant arises in human beings as a fact central to the human existence.[34] Though the numinous in Otto's description is not exactly synonymous with revival, its descriptions match those given through the testimonies of many revival participants. Otto claims that numinous experiences are possible for *all* because intrinsic to the numinous itself is the presence of predispositions or propensities that nudge human beings into a quest for the knowledge of God:

> They are seen as propensities, "predestining" the individual to religion, and they may grow spontaneously to quasi-instinctive presentiments, uneasy seeking and groping, yearning and longing, and become a religious *impulsion*, that only finds peace when it has become clear to itself and attained its goal. From them arise the states of mind of "prevenient grace."[35]

Arguably, the predisposition afforded by the numinous, when contextualized within Christianity, is captured in Augustine's famous line from *The Confessions*: "Thou hast made us for thyself, O Lord, and our heart is restless until it finds its rest in thee."[36] The *restlessness* of Augustine can be understood as analogous to the "impulsion" created by Otto's numinous. And on Otto's account, it is an a priori knowing which can be linked to texts like: "[God] has made everything beautiful in its time. He has also *set eternity in the hearts of men*" (Eccl. 3:11, emphasis added).[37] Or to Paul's assertion in Romans 1 that "what may be known about God is plain to them, because God has made it plain to them. For since the creation of the world God's invisible qualities—his eternal power and divine nature—have been clearly seen, being understood from what has been made, so that men are without excuse" (vv. 19-20). We also find the recognition of this untaught capacity for knowing God in Martin Luther:

> The knowledge of God is impressed upon the mind of every man by God, under the sole guidance of nature all men know that God is—without any acquaintance with the arts or sciences; and this is divinely imprinted upon all men's minds. There has never been a people so wild and savage that it did not believe that there is some divine power that created all things.[38]

---

34. William James, *The Varieties of Religious Experience: A Study in Human Nature, Being the Gifford Lectures on Natural Religion Delivered at Edinburgh in 1901–1902* (New York: Longmans, Green, and Co., 1902).

35. Otto, *Idea of the Holy*, 115 (emphasis original).

36. Augustine, *Confessions*, 2nd ed., trans. F. J. Sheed (Indianapolis, IN: Hackett Publishing Company, 2006), Ch. 1:1.

37. All verses quoted herein will be from the NIV unless otherwise noted.

38. Luther, *Table-Talk* (Wei. V. 5820), quoted by Otto, *The Idea of the Holy*, 139.

Otto views the numinous as a raw, internal impulse present a priori in the soul of every human being, which the Gospel writer, John, seems to acknowledge as he claims that God "gives light to every man" (John 1:9). This is a claim that *every* person born on this planet has the innate potential to recognize the divine (viz., the numinous). It suggests that the basis of *all* religious impulse is this intrinsic knowing of eternity and capacity to perceive the holy. But that does not mean all people *will* or that they will do so *rightly*. Again, from the Christian perspective, Romans 1 suggests that each person only has the *potential* to recognize the holy, and, accordingly, that that potential requires acknowledgment, openness, and right judgment to become a fully Christian experience. However, when this impulse is unguided by the gospel of Christ, it can be escorted by other religious constructions (as in Acts 17 where worshippers build an "altar to an unknown God" or Acts 14 where worshippers of Zeus try to give Zeus credit for what God had done through Christ).

Otto argues for the ongoing work of God (or Spirit) in the lives of *all* human beings through the phenomenon of the numinous. Yong speaks along similar lines of the ubiquitous potential for all to encounter the Spirit: "The Holy Spirit is being poured out universally (Acts 2:17) means that whatever else we as human beings might be up to, we do not live apart from the Spirit of God nor can we escape the Spirit's presence and activity (cf. Ps. 139:7-12)."[39] Yong is not suggesting that all people everywhere *will* experience God's presence, only that it is possible, which agrees with what Otto contests.

Otto is clear that the predispositions inspired by the numinous may be dim and easily ignored, though he claims they lie a priori within the human heart. Otto is *not* claiming (as Christian theists would) that the primitive numinous impulse is essentially Christian. He is claiming that it is merely an impulse intrinsic to the spirit of human beings by which they can recognize and receive "supra-sensible" information or truth.[40] The numinous, then, is a raw, internal impulse present a priori in the soul of every human being that can erupt into a transformational consciousness of the divine. In its most archaic sense/phase, it closely resembles the Greek concept of "enthusiasm" (ενθουσιασμός), where a human being is caught up or possessed by the divine. In this primitive sense, it is the Dionysian impulse that symbolizes the escape from reason, which can only be attributed to the action of the gods.[41]

The Numinous Awe

Otto insists that when describing the numinous, it proves more fruitful to speak of a consciousness rather than a construct or system (viz., an articulated religion).

---

39. Yong, *Beyond the Impasse*, 131.
40. Otto, *Idea of the Holy*, 104.
41. Several authors suggest that the Dionysian impulse is associated with the roots of human spirituality and helps to explain the quest that lies at the foundation of the precursors to human religions. See Rosemarie Taylor-Perry, *The God Who Comes: Dionysian Mysteries Revisited* (New York: Algora Publishing, 2003).

This "consciousness" is a blend of seeing and feeling (or "affection"). In its most primitive state, it manifests by giving the human person an awareness of being creaturely and of having a sense of dependence upon something *otherly*—the divine. It could also be said that the numinous manifests a consciousness of awe or wonder, captured by a Latin phrase used by Otto, "*mysterium tremendum*" ("awe inspiring mystery").[42] Otto references Schleiermacher's claim that an encounter with the divine (or with the holy) creates a unique "feeling of dependence."[43] Otto calls this feeling a "creature-consciousness," and claims "it is the emotion of a creature, submerged and overwhelmed by its own nothingness in contrast to that which is supreme above all creatures."[44] He insists that this feeling is beyond any possible conceptual explanation, which makes it non-rational (though not irrational). This is Otto's description of an encounter with a perceived deity or "Other" where one feels self-depreciation in the presence of an overwhelming, absolute Being; this encounter cannot be expressed in words but only "suggested indirectly through the tone and content of a [person's] feeling-response to it."[45]

Otto's use of *mysterium tremendum* as an element of the numinous suggests there is a sense of urgency about it, along with a kind of disorienting chaos. He contends that as the numinous breaks into experience, an encounter with the one universal transcendental Reality is realized—of which the experience itself offers the proof of such a Reality.[46] From the initial inklings afforded by the numinous, through to the erupting moment when the holy is experienced, the numinous remains in the domain of being indescribable—beyond any construct or system. Hence, the numinous cannot be taught; it can only be realized existentially. It is not difficult to see how language like this comports well to any description of the pentecostal experience—especially with the presence of tongues, as "no one understands" what is being spoken because the one who speaks with tongues "speaks mysteries" (1 Cor. 14:2).[47]

The concept of the numinous helps when describing what is found scattered throughout the biblical record—from Genesis where Abraham speaks in the presence of the God and says, "Now that I have been so bold as to speak to the Lord, though I am nothing but dust and ashes" (Gen. 18:27) to Isaiah who in the face of the "holy" cried, "Woe to me! I am ruined! For I am a man of unclean

---

42. Otto, *Idea of the Holy*, 12.

43. Otto (*Idea of the Holy*, 9) likes Schleiermacher's phrase, "feeling of dependence," but feels Schleiermacher is not as exacting as he should be with his understanding of "dependence." See Georg Behrens, "Feeling of Absolute Dependence or Absolute Feeling of Dependence? (What Schleiermacher Really Said and Why It Matters)," *Religious Studies* 34, no. 4 (1998): 471–81.

44. Otto, *Idea of the Holy*, 10.

45. Ibid.

46. The numinous affords a new kind of epistemology, to which I return below.

47. For more on glossolalia, see Randal H. Ackland, *Towards a Pentecostal Theology of Glossolalia* (Cleveland, TN: CPT Press, 2020).

lips, and I live among a people of unclean lips, and my eyes have seen the King, the LORD Almighty" (Isa. 6:5) to Luke's description of Peter meeting Jesus and falling to his knees as he cried out, "Go away from me, Lord; I am a sinful man!" (Lk. 5:8) to the Mount of Transfiguration where the apostles fall to the ground (Mt. 17:6) to John on Patmos falling to the ground before the risen Christ "as though dead" (Rev. 1:17).

Otto's argument of the pre-rational and pre-dispositional nature of the numinous toward religious experience helps to explain how revivals can spread like wildfires (which was certainly true of the global pentecostal revival), though those involved did not understand all its theological ramifications. It is as if revival is more "felt" than "reasoned." Hence, a revival moment (or *awakening*) opens the way for people to understand the gospel without full understanding or complete intellectual proofs. Otto asserts that missionary efforts around the world support the notion that numinous encounters with God can awaken the human heart when only laconic instruction was given for conversion. Otto cites how the numinous created a "co-witnessing spirit" that powered the adventures from missionary efforts of his day all the way back to the story of the Apostle Paul's conversion:

> As evidence of the way in which this inward principle—this co-witnessing spirit within us—works, prompting, interpreting, and sending out intimation and surmise, I have found the information of a keenly observant missionary from a remote field very instructive. He told me that he had found it a constant matter for fresh astonishment to see how a presentment of the Word so inadequate, which could only hint at its meaning in a difficult foreign tongue and had to work with alien conceptions—could yet at times win so surprisingly deep and inward an acceptance. And he said that here too the best results always were due to the responsive apprehension that came out of the hearer's heart half-way to meet the presented truth. Certainly it is only in this fact that we have a clue to the understanding of the problem of St. Paul. Persecutor of the Church as he was, the intimations he had of the being and meaning of Christ and his Gospel must have come to him piecemeal, in fragmentary hints and caricature. But the spirit from within forced upon him the acknowledgement to which he succumbed on the way to Damascus.[48]

In summary, Otto's articulation of the numinous helps to explain what pentecostals describe as the transformative pentecostal revival. The *mysterium tremendum* is germane to what pentecostals would say is essential to their spiritual experience (though they would use different words). The awe experienced in many of the early pentecostal revivals was so pervasive that many reports existed of how it forced many to prostrate themselves on the floor. Pentecostal outsider and Harvard scholar, Harvey Cox, reports, "At one midwest revival the 'weight of glory' was so heavy the people could not even remain seated but had to sprawl full length

---

48. Otto, *Idea of the Holy*, 162.

on the floor."[49] Many described the revival moment as an encounter with "a glory so bright they could not bear it."[50] Rickie Moore, speaking as an insider, speaks of how the pentecostal narrative introduces "a vibrant, dynamic community ... forged and propelled forward in the fire of Pentecost. ... [this experience was a] sustained, continuing, growing, erupting revelatory dynamic ... [where] awe came upon everyone."[51]

Why Revival Is Privileged over Rational Theology

According to Otto's morphology, the mystical encounter (viz., the numinous) inherently pushes any intellectual pursuit and rational analysis into the background, subjugating serious theological reflection to moments of raw encounter with God. Otto goes on to affirm that this is the experience of the holy where one senses "deepest worship" or a gentle "tranquil mood" to a "burst into sudden eruption up from the depths of the soul," which "lead to the strangest excitements, to intoxicated frenzy, to transport and to ecstasy."[52] Rational religion does not precipitate such experiences. What Otto is describing is, for the pentecostal, the peculiarity of *revival*—though technically, at this very primitive stage it would *not* be developed enough to be called pentecostalism. Another stage is necessary—a stage of rational reflection that employs a process that frames the non-rational into rationality so one can perceive or describe the experience as reality (though, as we will see below, that reflection could be happening nearly concurrently with the non-rational experience).

The point is that revival (and I am using this term interchangeably with the experience of God) is *not* something that resides solely (or even primarily) in the intellect or reasoning faculties of human beings. Revivals cannot be exhaustively explicated (though they can contain rational activity). It is the task of theology to apprehend, understand, and speak of God in rational terms. Contrariwise, revivals are more accurately explained as moments of experience that happen at a level deeper than ideas or concepts happen. The goal excited in revival is not first that which emerges from theology, rational morality, or teleology; it does not draw its energy from postulates. It has roots in the hidden depths of the Spirit himself. Therefore, revivals are more (lived) existential moments than (thought or spoken/written) theological constructs. They are the place where one encounters the *presence* of God. It is one thing to theologically construct ideas and concepts about a reality beyond the senses, it is quite another to *experience* that reality. In the pentecostal ethos, there must be an *encounter* with the divine. Revival is not a

---

49. Cox, *Fire from Heaven*, 69–70.

50. Ibid., 69.

51. Rickie D. Moore, "Revelation: The Light and Fire of Pentecost," in *The Routledge Handbook of Pentecostal Theology*, ed. Wolfgang Vondey (New York: Taylor & Francis Group, 2020), 53–62, 58.

52. Otto, *Idea of the Holy*, 12.

product of rational reflection, but the experience of inklings of a Reality fraught with mystery and momentousness. Those who speak of the experience sometimes describe it as coming "suddenly," like the wind on the Day of Pentecost in Acts 2. It turns out that a religious *moment* of this kind is ultimately ineffable. Trying to explain it solely in rational language is a bit like trying to expound the category of "the beautiful" with words. Something more is needed.

Otto insists that trying to define and classify the numinous using a theological system or structure is rather to miss it completely (if not to destroy it). A numinous moment is not something to be grasped by setting it within distinct conceptual limits or by giving it exact characteristics or theological forms. True, cultural and religious structures and forms are *always* present, no doubt.[53] Yong affirms that though faith has a pretheoretical aspect to it (so that it is not restrained by reason), it is not *entirely* pretheoretical. He writes, "Is not faith a much more complex integration of imagination, interpretation, theory and the pursuit of responsibility in the experimental process?"[54] Though Yong holds to a pretheoretical element to faith, he concludes, "Human beings are never only 'pretheoretical,' but through and through thinking animals."[55] However, the numinous/revival/experience *itself*, using Otto's morphology, is not bound by intellectual distinctions, but is pretheoretical, prerational, and prestructural. It is wrapped in mystery and a sense of the irrational because it challenges the reasonable (or what is reasonably expected) by going against the grain of reason, affording naked trust, paradoxical belief, and the acceptance of metaphysical belief-claims in the minds of the faithful (e.g., eschatological and apocalyptic expectations, an expectation of the miraculous, etc.[56]).

The claim here is not that revival experiences cause a person to disengage the rational mind completely but that the primary concern in the moment of renewal is antecedent to reason. Certainly, pentecostals are not against rational thought. The very concept of faith in God, whose characteristics include purpose, good will, supreme power, and selfhood, are definite concepts which necessitate the use of

---

53. Pentecostals certainly had deep expectations for specific outcomes (i.e., glossolalia, miracles, etc.) when revival sentiment arose, and one can make the strong case that those expectations affected revival participants causing a predilection toward certain outcomes. However, based on my research, I would claim that those predilections were actually additions (or, in Aristotle's morphology, *accidents*) to the revival experience—not the essence of it, which would suggest that not *everything* associated with pentecostalism (particularly in the North American context) needed to be so.

54. Amos Yong, "Whither Systematic Theology? A Systematician Chimes in on a Scandalous Conversation," *Pneuma* 20, no. 1 (Spring 1998): 87.

55. Ibid.

56. For more background on this, see Neumann, *Pentecostal Experience*; Wacker, *Heaven Below*; Cox, *Fire from Heaven*; Anderson, *An Introduction to Pentecostalism*; and *The Routledge Handbook of Pentecostal Theology*, ed. Wolfgang Vondey (London: Routledge, Taylor and Francis, 2020).

reason. Christianity is a rational religion—arguably with more unique clarity and abundance than many other world religions care to articulate. However, the case can be and has been made that rational descriptions (dogmas or doctrines) are not, properly speaking, the essence of the Christian *faith* (nor of pentecostalism proper); rather these things derive from it. Faith is the miracle that emerges when one has an encounter with the divine or infinite—rational thoughts (like dogmas) are the reflections we make on that miracle. Yong affirms that theology itself is a "cognitive enterprise" that is "a product of reflection on the human situation, ... a strictly second-hand affair that proceeds in abstraction from first-hand experience."[57] Smith expresses that this is exactly the case in the pentecostal world as well: "A Pentecostal paradigm locates faith in pretheoretical existence and experience. Theology, on the other hand, is a theoretical investigation of faith as a mode of reality."[58] This is why revival is more pretheoretical or non-rational at its inception than rational, and why pentecostals do not (insofar as they are true to their spirituality) prioritize the intellectual aspects of faith from the start. This sentiment echoes the seventeenth-century claim of Blaise Pascal: "If we submit everything to reason, our religion will have no mysterious and supernatural element."[59]

Otto warns that if one pushes into the arena of rational theological orthodoxy too quickly or deeply, it can dull the transformational power of the numinous (or, as speaking of it as revival):

> Orthodoxy itself has been the mother of rationalism ... It is not simply that orthodoxy was preoccupied with doctrine and the framing of dogma ... It is rather that orthodoxy found in the construction of dogma and doctrine no way to do justice to the non-rational aspect to its subject. So far from keeping the non-rational element in religion alive in the heart of the religious experience, orthodox Christianity manifestly failed to recognize its value, and by this failure gave to the idea of God a one-sidedly intellectualistic and rationalistic interpretation.[60]

Jonathan Edwards spoke of the qualitative difference between the certainty of natural, rational things versus what is experienced from an encounter with the divine: "The conceptions which the saints have of the loveliness of God and that kind of delight which they experience in it are quite peculiar and entirely different from anything which a natural man can possess or of which he can form any proper notion."[61] This claim asserts that above and beyond our rational nature is something larger, higher, and ultimate, which can find no satisfaction in mere

---

57. Yong, *Spirit-Word Community*, 2.
58. Smith, "Scandalizing Theology," 235.
59. Blaise Pascal, *Pensées*, trans. W. F. Trotter (New York: E. P. Dutton & Co., 1958), 81.
60. Otto, *Idea of the Holy*, 3.
61. Jonathan Edwards, as quoted in James, *Varieties of Religious Experience*, 170.

intellectual impulses and pursuits. The numinous presents the solution to the place of no satisfaction, the ache present in the human soul that knows there must be more than one can feel or experience from the natural world.[62] Is it possible that lingering within the memory of *homo sapiens* is a deep, indescribable longing from Eden's loss; a knowing that we are in a place where there is no water;[63] that we cannot live by bread alone—at least not with the bread that is found here?[64] Ecclesiastes claim that eternity is "set" in us, which may suggest that human beings may never be satisfied with anything less than what issues from the eternal (Eccl. 3:11).

When revivalists use phrases like "seek God and find him" (Jer. 29:13), or when they pray that God will "pour out his Spirit on all flesh" (Acts 2:17), they are talking about a moment that is *not* primarily a rational event. The numinous moment contains what pentecostals speak of as "a move of the Spirit" rooted in a space in the human heart where rational judgment is suspended (or at least not allowed to supervene) while one relies on a more intuitive of rational presuppositions and intellectualizing. This is why the old pentecostal adage asserts that such experiences are "better felt than telt, better walked than talked."[65] Otto claims these kinds of experiences are "the first application of a category of valuation which has no place in the everyday natural world of ordinary experience, and is only possible to a being in whom has been awakened a mental predisposition, unique in kind and different in a definite way from any 'natural' faculty."[66]

The priority of a childlike faith has always been at the core of pentecostals' desire for revival to inspire and transform individuals to be a pietistic and morally upright human beings in union with God, full of the Spirit, and fully committed to impacting the rest of the world with the same renewal. Using Paul's phrase, they wanted to be "fools for Christ" (1 Cor. 4:10)—holy fools who are, in a sense, "in" for God no matter how unreasonable it seems. The holy fool does not need to know *everything* or have the path fully laid out. Holy fools use what Robert Sokolowski calls "a declarative use" of words to express their commitment to being present in and a part of a movement because of an encounter that was pre-theoretical, pre-philosophical, and pre-rational.[67] In his book, *The Phenomenology of the Human Person*, Sokolowski describes the declarative stance of this person:

> To say "I'm still here" in this way is a declarative use of the word *I*. It is neither a cognitional nor an emotive use … This usage is often found in religious language. When using an existential declarative, I do not promise or dedicate myself to any

---

62. Cf. Ps. 73:25.
63. Cf. Ps. 63:1.
64. Cf. Mt. 4:4.
65. Neumann, *Pentecostal Experience*, 101.
66. Otto, *Idea of the Holy*, 15.
67. Robert Sokolowski, *Phenomenology of the Human Person* (Cambridge: Cambridge University Press, 2008), 28.

project in particular; I am just there for whatever may come and whatever needs to be seen or done, but *I am* still there, and I declare myself as such, as a dative, a person engaged in veracity.[68]

Revival's Commitment to Incomprehensibility

This prerational (or pretheoretical) understanding of revival is how pentecostals could commit to rationally define who/what God is while continuing to honor his *incomprehensibility*. Holding discursive theological thinking and God's incomprehensibility together is no small task for Christian theology, and it has struggled to keep this balance from its inception. Christianity is the tale of two cities—Jerusalem and Athens.[69] Jerusalem brings us the metaphysical story of faith; Athens brings the articulation of philosophy, which helped the church Fathers conceptualize and describe that faith.[70] Both were utilized for the construction of what we have come to know as orthodox Christian truth. But problems remain.

One of the early influences from Greek philosophy on orthodox doctrine during the patristic period was the acceptance of the theory of *divine impassibility* caused by *divine aseity* (God is in no way causally dependent.).[71] The Supreme God of the Greeks (viz., the "Prime Mover") was fashioned in the ideal of the wise man who needed no passion or affection because of his perfection.[72] This view of God was eventually assimilated and used to describe the "living God" of scripture. This focus on divine impassibility subjected religious dogma to a strong rationalizing influence (which lingered mostly as an unconscious factor) within Christian orthodoxy, keeping God neatly packaged in the domain of human reason and creating an antithesis between the rational and non-rational, divine, and ineffable aspects of deity. Whenever the conceptual and the doctrinal won the day (the ideal of orthodoxy), it overpowered the genuinely contemplative and devotional aspects of religious life. This could be called *anti*-revival.

Early Christian author, Lactantius (240–320 CE), in his work, *De Ira Dei*, pushed back early from describing the living God of scripture with a conception of God

---

68. Ibid (emphasis original).

69. Cornell West (*The Cornel West Reader* [New York: Basic Civitas Book, 1999], 50) claims that "[T]he legacies of Athens and Jerusalem … [are] the two fundamental pillars of modernity."

70. Robert Louis Wilken, *The Spirit of Early Christian Thought: Seeking the Face of God* (New Haven, CT: Yale University Press, 2003).

71. See George Sauvage, "Aseity," in *The Catholic Encyclopedia*, vol. 1 (New York: Robert Appleton Company, 1907).

72. See Aristotle, *The Metaphysics*. Or, for a short overview, see J. L. Ackrill, "Change and Aristotle's Theological Argument," in *Oxford Studies in Ancient Philosophy*, ed. H. Blumenthal and H. Robinson (Oxford: Clarendon Press, 1991), 57–66.

adopted from the pagan philosophers. He combated the impulse to reduce the Christian God to an idea or to some moral order or principle of being. Lactantius argued for the non-rational and ineffable aspects of God to be celebrated—aspects that can only be appreciated and responded to from the heart, versus apprehended by the mind: "[God] whom the human mind has no power to appraise, nor tongue of mortals to utter. For he is too sublime and too great to be grasped in the thought or the speech of man."[73] He goes on to argue that if God is devoid of feelings, as the pagans assert, he cannot love and would "be *immobilis* and not the 'Deus *vivus*,' the *living* God of scripture."[74]

It would be anathema for the pentecostal to perceive God simply as an aloof, ethereal Being, who lives far beyond the mundane concerns of his created beings, and who lives in the realm of Stoic *apatheia*—with neither feeling, nor being moved by creaturely need. Pentecostalism centers on the revelation that God is a loving, engaging, and personal being.

For pentecostals, the divine Word signifies an intensely living, relational reality. Scripture is not there just to harvest dogma or to learn some bits of knowledge not previously known—it is an event where Almighty God intervenes into the lives of human persons. A "passage" of scripture is literally a place where God is *passing through*. God bursts into our world through sacred text to impress us by his presence, which is tangible and masterful. This is reminiscent of how ancient Jews viewed sacred text, as Roman Catholic thinker, Louis Boyer, points out:

> For the pious Jew, and to the utmost for those Jews who mediated the divine Word at the end of all that we call the Old Testament, the divine Word signified an intensely living reality ... It is not a discourse, but an action: the action whereby God intervenes as the master in our existence, "The lion has roared," says Amos, "Who will not fear? The Lord God has spoken, who can but prophesy?" This means that the Word, once it has made itself heard, takes possession of man to accomplish its plan.[75]

This echoes what the writer of Hebrews states: "For the word of God is living and active and sharper than any two-edged sword, and piercing as far as the division of soul and spirit, of both joints and marrow, and able to judge the thoughts and intentions of the heart" (Heb. 4:12, NASB). If sacred text is properly heard and honored, pentecostals believe there are consequences—consequences that are disruptive, creative, and salvific. God himself comes to us in the Word; in it he descends into our story and fills that story with his presence.

---

73. Lactantius, quoted by Otto, *Idea of the Holy*, 96.
74. Ibid.
75. Louis Bouyer, *Eucharist: Theology and Spirituality of the Eucharistic Prayer*, trans. Charles Underhill Quinn (Notre Dame, IN: University of Notre Dame Press, 2006), 31–2.

Revival Keeps Theological Reflection in Check

Revival for pentecostals is not an *exclusion* of rational thought but a simple management of its priority. As already acknowledged, it remains critical within any theistic conception (and certainly within Christianity) to think of God rationally. Only on such terms can one engage in belief versus nothing more than mere *feeling* or subjective *experience*. The very concept of religion demands deep conceptions about God, but pentecostals prioritize conceptions of God through the process of Christian discipleship. Revival precedes this.

The revivalist contends that the rational should never be allowed to preponderate the spiritual, or to reduce the spiritual way scripture speaks and witnesses to the human heart to a residuum of formulas or propositional truths. A revivalist believes that a sure way to ensure that rationalism does not dominate the culture of faith is to infuse all processes of discursive, theological reflection with a priority on revival that keeps alive the non-rational feeling of absolute dependence upon God. Speaking of the priority of the numinous, Otto writes, "This permeation of the rational with the non-rational is to lead, then, to the deepening of our rational conception of God; it must not be the means of blurring or diminishing of it."[76] This is the way one can deepen one's rational understanding and conception of God without quashing the very person of God in the process. Insofar as this holds true, the goal of a clear-thinking pentecostal theologian should be to permeate the discursive theological enterprise with the Spirit of God and the non-rational elements revivalism affords (e.g., humility, awe, a "creature-consciousness," etc.). Yet importantly, revival also generates theology. Through revival, pentecostals seek to experience (not just mentally assent to) what the Christian tradition has affirmed dogmatically.

Pentecostals, like other Christians, and people in other faiths, believe a person who has encountered the holy can be confident in what they know of God on some level, but on another, the living God is wholly other, and one should stand bewildered. The temptation is to try to overreach using one's human faculty of conception in the name of theology. Though we can know God in some ways, some things about God remain unknowable to us—aspects of God that exclude the possibility of inquiry and questioning and places where we have nothing within the human experience with which to orient our rational discussions. John Chrysostom from the fourth century points this out:

> We call Him the inexpressible, the unthinkable God, the invisible, the inapprehensible; who quells the power of human speech and transcends the grasp of moral thought; inaccessible to the angels, unbeheld of the Seraphim, unimagined of the Cherubim, invisible to principalities and authorities and powers, and, in a word, to all creation.[77]

---

76. Otto, *Idea of the Holy*, 109.

77. John Chrysostom, "On the Inconceivable in God," accessed February 15, 2019, https://www.wilmingtonfavs.com/religious-experience-2/appendix-i.html. Accessed February 15, 2019.

Good pentecostal theology will hold the "inexpressible" and "inapprehensible" in mind. This is why the goal of a pentecostal theologizing is one that remains faithful to a priority on revival, which will contend for the non-rational inconceivability to be retained and intensified as rational revelation proceeds.

Otto theorizes that *all* religious experiences are of the numinous ilk before they become theologized or loaded with ethics—they are first feeling (or a group of feelings like "awe,"[78] "sense of dependence,"[79] something that seems "uncanny,"[80] etc.) as the result of the engagement with the holy *before* they are systematized. For Otto, it remains critical to take note of these non-rational feelings/senses, and then to recognize that they must be accounted for and accommodated to in religious studies precisely because they are antecedent to what becomes rational, ethical, theological, or ecclesiastical in religion. It turns out that there is always tension between the numinous and what becomes a fully explicated religious system (e.g., Christianity) because the numinous is non-rational (viz., mysterious, confusing, unfamiliar), whereas the rational demands the elimination of the mysterious, confusing, and unfamiliar. The numinous does not resist the logical (in fact, in what follows we will see that Otto suggests that the numinous does not function apart from the context of some rational religious system), but insofar as his account is right, it is not rooted in, nor dependent on it.

What is at the heart of what pentecostals would say they are after in revival is the evoking of and awakening to everything that comes of the Spirit. This focus on the Spirit does not diminish the role of Jesus Christ for the pentecostal, either experientially or theologically. Yong insists that "Jesus the Christ is the full revelation of God precisely as borne by the Spirit: conceived, birthed, anointed, and raised from the dead by the power of the Spirit. The Spirit is concretely manifest and revealed as the power of God in the person and work of Jesus Christ."[81] According to Yong, any pneumatological theology "is a robustly trinitarian theology,"[82] and as such "the Spirit is both universal and particular, both the Spirit of God and the Spirit of Jesus the Christ."[83] This becomes a foundational pneumatology for pentecostal theologizing (at the center of what this writing proffers) and reveals how "God is present and active in the world and that such presence and activity is understood through the symbol of the Holy Spirit."[84]

---

78. Otto, *Idea of the Holy*, 14.
79. Ibid., 11.
80. Ibid., 16.
81. Yong, *Beyond the Impasse*, 135.
82. Ibid., 20.
83. Ibid., 21.
84. Ibid., 131.

The Second Essential: Mysticism

Before describing the kind of *mysticism* some suggest is embedded in pentecostalism, it will be helpful to explore mysticism more generally.[85] Again, Otto is helpful. As seen above, he (and others influenced by him) present the numinous as being in the category of "personal religion," considered antecedent and more fundamental than either theology or ecclesiasticism. Otto's thought was inspired by post-Romantic movement concerns, which had shifted the emphasis of religious thought from the realm of theology to that of "religious experience" under the banner of mysticism.[86] The mystics claimed they had experienced profound transcendental experiences that empowered and informed their ideas and actions—ideas and actions typically characterized by paradox; they were personal yet self-transcending, noetic while in some sense ineffable, striven after but also recognized as independent of human effort.[87] In general, mystics felt they had entered a *union* or *oneness* with God/gods/Reality.

Some advocates of this approach (though not true of Otto) believed they had found a path to union with the divine that was devoid of unnecessary specialized religious contexts (including Christianity). This notion framed out what begins to be known as "perennial truth."[88] Perennialism is a perspective within the philosophy of religion that holds that all of the world's religious traditions point to one universal transcendental reality from which all esoteric and exoteric knowledge and doctrine have emerged. David McMahan, a religious studies' academic who writes from a Buddhist perspective, claims that perennialism sees all paths as "different ways to the same mystical experience or ultimate reality" and that "their distinctiveness is less important than their common goal."[89] Hence, perennialism is sometimes called the discovery of "Universal Religion." The conception of the

---

85. For a fuller explication of mysticism in general (not limited by the bounds of Christianity), see Rudolf Otto, *Mysticism East and West: A Comparative Analysis of the Nature of Mysticism* (Wheaton, IL: Theosophical Publishing House, 1987); James, *Varieties of Religious Experience*; Robert C. Zaehner, *Mysticism Sacred and Profane: An Inquiry into Some Varieties of Praeternatural Experience* (Oxford: Oxford University Press, 1961); William T. Stace, *Mysticism and Philosophy* (London: Macmillan, 1960); Joseph Maréchal, *The Psychology of the Mystics* (Mineola, NY: Dover Publications, 2004); James Bissett Pratt, *The Religious Consciousness: A Psychological Study* (New York: Macmillan, 1920); Mircea Eliade, *Patterns in Comparative Religion* (New York: Sheed & Ward, 1958); and Walter Stace, "The Nature of Mysticism," in *Philosophy of Religion: Selected Readings*, ed. William L. Rowe and William J. Wainwright (Oxford: Oxford University Press, 1998).

86. See James, *Varieties of Religious Experience*, 19–37.

87. Louis Dupré Louis, "Mysticism," in *Encyclopedia of Religion*, ed. Lindsay Jones (Detroit, MI: Macmillan Reference USA, 2005), 9:6341–55.

88. See Aldous Huxley, *The Perennial Philosophy* (New York: Harper, 1970).

89. David L. McMahan, *The Making of Buddhist Modernism* (Oxford: Oxford University Press, 2008), 243.

perennial philosophy (*philosophia perennis*) was first suggested in the sixteenth century by Augostino Steuco and developed by Leibniz.[90] It was formulated more entirely by Aldous Huxley, who claimed that the perennial philosophy exists "in every region of the world, and in its fully developed forms it has a place in every one of the higher religions."[91] At the heart of perennial thought is the insistence that the divine is present in every religious tradition, insisting that no tradition has a monopoly on it.

Interestingly, this thrust emerged during the mid-nineteenth century in the academy because of a growing interest in ecumenism, which led to the recapitulation of the term *mysticism* and its extension to comparable phenomena between Christian and non-Christian religions. Perennialism seemed to offer an irenic resolve to the "conflicting claims of various religions and secular philosophies in a purified experiential realm" by offering a "well-intentioned attempt to find common ground" in a world that seems bent on fighting over differences.[92] McMahan says this new approach afforded a "parallel to science," which was attractive to many because it suggested that one can investigate religious experience from an internalized "view from nowhere," separating it from any particular traditional religious hegemony.[93] Dan Merkur claims "[M]ost varieties of what had traditionally been called mysticism were dismissed as merely psychological phenomena and only one variety, which aimed at union with the Absolute, the Infinite, or God, and thereby the perception of its essential unity or oneness was claimed to be genuinely mystical."[94] Hence, the definition of mysticism as it had been used was discharged, and a new, modern one emerged that began to serve the purpose of comparative religious study and theoretical analysis—one which attempted to draw into a single arena beliefs/ideas and practices that had otherwise been isolated from each other within their own local names, categories, and histories.

Perennial mysticism advocates a spirituality that is more an inner process or experience than something situated in a historical tradition or institution. Here, spirituality is dislodged from any traditional religious construct and is considered as something distinct *from* religion—especially any institutional religion. McMahan cites this as "the emergence of a new crosscultural conception of 'spirituality' as the individual's search for, or experience of, this reality."[95] This new cosmopolitan spirituality made all religious traditions moot as they were replaced by the spiritual "universal search for a divine, ineffable reality, transcendent yet

---

90. Ibid., 71. See also Gabriela Pohoata, "Leibniz Universalism," *Cogito: Multidisciplinary Research Journal* 4, no. 1 (2012): 1–13.

91. Huxley, *Perennial Philosophy*, vii.

92. McMahan, *Making of Buddhist Modernism*, 269.

93. Ibid., 269.

94. Dan Merkur, "Mysticism," *Encyclopedia Britannica*, accessed May 22, 2021, https://www.britannica.com/topic/mysticism.

95. McMahan, *Making of Buddhist Modernism*, 71.

pervading everything and to which the individual mind is directly connected or even identical."[96] This position, however, is not without problems as it fosters an ultimate religious pluralism that funds the wildly popular claim (so prevalent in the twenty-first century) that people are spiritual but not religious.

William Parsons warns that perennialism offers "what might at times seem to be a straightforward phenomenon exhibiting an unambiguous commonality," but it "has become, at least within the academic study of religion, opaque and controversial on multiple levels."[97] McMahan also offers a critique of this approach, saying it ultimately "marginalizes and relativizes that which is specific to any [religious] tradition," by avoiding the specifics of any religious texts or practices that do not "conform to the tenets of the perennial philosophy," deeming those specifics as "incidental, parochial, institutionalized, ritualized, corrupted, or simply for the common people."[98]

William Harmless captures the current concern over the kind of mysticism that occurs when the numinous is interpreted as no more than a cosmopolitan spirituality:

> If you wander into your local Barnes & Noble or Border's, you soon discover whole shelves devoted to what booksellers catalog as "mysticism." There you usually find legitimate books on mysticism mixed in with stuff on the occult and witchcraft, fortune-telling, mind reading, and alien abductions. Mysticism, of course, has nothing to do with such matters, but the confusion on the shelves illustrates how in popular parlance "mysticism" can become a catch-all for religious weirdness.[99]

McMahan claims that though perennialism has lost none of its popularity, it has been largely dismissed by scholars[100] in favor of what is known as a "constructivist" approach.[101] This is an approach claiming that *all* religious experiences come to us from within a particular context, and individuals are conditioned by their culture or religious heritage as they encounter such experiences. Robert Forman claims that the constructivist view contends that "mystical experience is significantly shaped and formed by the subject's beliefs,

---

96. Ibid., 70.
97. See William B. Parsons, "Teaching Mysticism: Frame and Content," in *Teaching Mysticism*, ed. William B. Parsons (Oxford: Oxford University Press, 2011), 3.
98. McMahan, *Making of Buddhist Modernism*, 71–2.
99. William Harmless, *Mystics* (Oxford: Oxford University Press, 2008), 3.
100. McMahan, *The Making of Buddhist Modernism*, 269.
101. Notable constructivists include Steven T. Katz, Hans H. Penner, and Robert Gimello. See Steven T. Katz, "The Conservative Character of Mystical Experience"; Hans H. Penner, "The Mystical Illusion"; and Robert Gimello, "Mysticism in Its Contexts," in *Mysticism and Religious Traditions*, ed. Steven T. Katz (Oxford: Oxford University Press, 1983).

concepts, and expectations."[102] Adam Tyson writes, "Put simply, constructivism asserts that the individual constructs the surrounding world through his or her understanding, explaining experience and perception with mental constructs."[103] The claim on this view is that mystical experiences without an interpreted context are not valid—that numinous reality is not an objective reality the mystic can interact with or identify outside of some pre-understanding. The numinous demands mental and cultural constructs.

Hence, the suitability of utilizing the numinous as a kind of pure mysticism—or a neutral, global term—is in question. What is missing if one just describes the numinous as pure mysticism is religion *proper*—with its rituals and corporate worship. William James, for example, limits the numinous to the "experiences of individual men."[104] Religion, however, demands more than the individual solitary experience. Mysticism as naked mysticism (if such a thing is even possible) is not tethered to any particular religious narrative; it is religiously agnostic, which allows it to easily slip into an escapist, disembodied self-delusion or a confusion of thought from mysterious (occult) agencies.[105] The idea of an untethered numinous/mystical experience without a conditioning context may be comforting to the modern mind seeking common ground in a pluralistic, divided world, but it does not appear tenable for many and may simply be a product of post-Enlightenment universalism. This is certainly not the kind of mysticism fostered within the Christian narrative or accepted by pentecostalism.

A Constructivist Mysticism

Though Otto holds to the mystical, non-rational aspect of the numinous, he suggests that this experience of union cannot be separated entirely from rational or theological contexts. Some preconceptions about religion or expectations of the numinous experience are always present. Again, one could argue that there is no such thing as a religiously detached form of the numinous; cultural/religious boundaries always superintend mystical space to some degree.[106] Jesse B. Hollenback avers that the kind of space afforded by the numinous "incorporates two important elements: a distinctive mode of experience ... and the individuals'

---

102. Robert K. Forman, "Introduction: Mysticism, Constructivism, and Forgetting," in *The Problem of Pure Consciousness: Mysticism and Philosophy*, ed. Robert K. Forman (Oxford: Oxford University Press, 1997), 3.

103. Adam Tyson, "The Mystical Debate: Constructivism and the Resurgence of Perennialism," *Intermountain West Journal of Religious Studies* 4, no. 1 (2012): 77–92.

104. James, *The Varieties of Religious Experience*, 34.

105. James K. A. Smith, *Thinking in Tongues: Pentecostal Contributions to Christian Philosophy* (Grand Rapids, MI: William B. Eerdmans Publishing Company, 2010), 98.

106. See Jonathan Garb, "Mystics' Critiques of Mystical Experience," *Revue de l'histoire des religions* 221, no. 3 (2004): 293–325.

responses to that unusual modality of experience."[107] In other words, rational reflection on prerational experiences is a natural, instant reflex informed or evoked by some previous understanding. Otto says that a person immersed in the numinous moment will experience a complicated, experimental process that will eventually enlighten a person to the realm of the holy by bringing other experiences and understandings "already known and familiar to resemble, or again to afford some special contrast to, the particular experience."[108] He goes on to explain this process rather cryptically:

> Then we must add: "This X of ours is not precisely *this* experience, but akin to this one and the opposite of that other. Cannot you now realize for yourself what it is?" In other words our X cannot, strictly speaking, be taught, it can only be evoked, awakened in the mind; as everything that comes "of the spirit" must be awakened.[109]

Certainly, this understanding was true within nascent pentecostalism as pentecostals brought their previous religious experiences and understandings that were "already known and familiar" to them from their deep Wesleyan-Holiness and Keswick theological influences and expectations.[110] From Otto's view one could argue that these previous influences and experiences matter because the numinous is vulnerable—malleable to and reflective of influences that surround it.

Christian/Pentecostal Mysticism

The mystical tradition within Christianity[111] can be traced back to second-century Origen but has roots in earlier New Testament writings (i.e., Paul being caught up to the "third heaven" where he "heard unspeakable words, which it is not lawful for a man to utter" [2 Cor. 12:2-4] and John's vision of heaven as he "was in the spirit" [Rev. 4:1]). Early church Fathers, like Augustine and the Cappadocian Fathers, used the interpretive schema of Platonic and Neoplatonic thought as they tried to make sense of the mystical encounters with the God they experienced. They were

---

107. Jesse Byron Hollenback, *Mysticism: Experience, Response and Empowerment* (Philadelphia, PA: Pennsylvania University Press, 1996), quoted in Garb, "Mystics' Critiques," 294.

108. Otto, *Idea of the Holy*, 7.

109. Ibid.

110. I explore this in the next chapter.

111. For a deeper dive into Christian mysticism, see Evelyn Underhill, *Mysticism: The Development of Humankind's Spiritual Consciousness* (London: Bracken Books, 1995); Denys Turner, *The Darkness of God: Negativity in Christian Mysticism* (Cambridge: Cambridge University Press, 1995); and Bernard McGinn, *The Flowering of Mysticism: Men and Women in the New Mysticism (1200–1350)*, vol. III (New York: Crossroad Publishing, 1998).

looking for language to describe the God who was *with* them and yet transcendent *from* them.¹¹²

The conviction of these Fathers of the church was that mystical encounters with the living God were not reserved for special saints but were available to all believers; they were to be seen as *normative*. Latin Catholic, Marie-Dominique Chenu, writes, "The mystical life, at its source, is nothing other than the Christian life."¹¹³ Nicholas Lash reshows this: "If ... the 'mystical element' in Christianity is a matter of preparing for, becoming conscious of and reacting to, the ever deeper sense and recognition of God's presence, then it is—in vastly varying degrees of actualization—an element in every Christian life."¹¹⁴

This kind of language is not foreign to pentecostalism. Pentecostal scholar, Terry Cross, writes: "Like Christian mystics throughout the ages, we experience God's presence in ways that feel like God is filling us to overflowing."¹¹⁵ Early in the pentecostal narrative, those deeply immersed in the movement claimed they had a sense of being *united* with divinity by becoming "temples of God [who were] fitted for the constant indwelling of the Holy Ghost ... 'O joy sublime, I've Jesus with me all the time.' There is constant communion with God. The experience is no longer fluctuating."¹¹⁶ This is the heart of what pentecostals say they are after in revival—*union* with the presence of God. In his work on pentecostal mysticism, Daniel Castelo writes:

> Much of the language, happenings, and practices of the first Christians and the early church can be understood as inherently and thoroughly mystical. Consider the farewell discourses of the Gospel of John, the Day of Pentecost happenings as recorded in the Book of Acts, the early practice of sacraments such as Eucharist and baptism, and even the formulation of such doctrines as the incarnation and the Trinity—these all can be said to have mystical dimensions and qualities. No

---

112. It was Jesus who introduced the "mystical" language of divine union in making statements like, "The Father is in me, and I in the Father" (John 10:38). Jesus extends this kind of "unity" with his disciples (who, by extension includes us) when he says, "On that day you will realize that I am in my Father, and *you are in me*, and I am in you" (14:20, emphasis added).

113. Marie-Dominique Chenu, "Une theologie de la vie mystique," *La vie spirituelle* 50 (1937): 49, quoted by Kevin L. Hughes, "The Crossing of Hope, or Apophatic Eschatology," in *The Future of Hope: Christian Tradition amid Modernity and Postmodernity*, ed. Miroslav Volf and William Katerberg (Grand Rapids, MI: William B. Eerdmans Publishing Company, 2004), 107.

114. Nicholas Lash, *The Beginning and the End of "Religion"* (Cambridge: Cambridge University Press, 1996), 171.

115. Terry L. Cross, "The Divine-Human Encounter: Towards a Pentecostal Theology of Experience," *Pneuma* 31, no. 1 (January 2009): 3–34, 19.

116. William F. Manly, "A Sanctified Heart," *The Household of God* 2, no. 9 (September 1906): 12.

wonder, then, that mystical impulses repeatedly appear in Christianity whether cultivated in local churches embodied by venerable figures, or manifest within schools, abbeys, and revivals of various sorts.[117]

What is different within the Christian mystical tradition (over against other religious traditions or secular scholarship attempting to locate the anthropological origins of religions) is the focus on the role of the Holy Spirit, and the immutable telos always being salvation in the person of Jesus Christ. Green points out that the directionality of this kind of mysticism is what helps unify pentecostals "even across irreconcilable doctrinal, liturgical, and ministerial differences" because it carries "a shared openness to the Spirit and a shared admiration for Jesus."[118] Walter Hollenweger (both critical of and sympathetic to pentecostalism) claims that pentecostals' love for Jesus was characteristically a "blood and wounds mysticism."[119]

Castelo believes pentecostalism carries a "particular kind of resurgence" of the mystical expression within Christianity that is found in both the West and in global contexts that is not a path to escape but a path to intermediation.[120] He does recognize that there are forms of mysticism that are "too esoteric, self-absorbed, archaic, or—worst of all—pagan."[121] These are mysticisms of withdrawal. But he insists that pentecostal mysticism is not *that*; it is a mysticism of mediation and intermediation. Castelo believes pentecostalism holds an expression of Christian mysticism that is "vitally relevant to the challenges of today";[122] he feels convinced that this trait of global pentecostalism helps to explain why pentecostalism was so easily received in the various cultural contexts around the world.

James Smith also weighs in on the mystical nature of pentecostalism. He speaks of "how pentecostal spirituality implicitly says that the affective and emotional core of [a person's] identity needs to be reformed and redirected" and that real changes in person's life will not take place until the affective core of the disciple is touched. Smith stresses, "It is this, I think, that makes pentecostalism a 'mystical' tradition as expressed, say, in the disciplines of Saint John of the Cross, *Dark Night of the Soul*," and adds, "that is exactly what the tactile, visceral, and emotional nature of pentecostal worship aims to effect."[123]

Cox writes, after perusing the primary documentary evidence of the pentecostal tradition:

---

117. Castelo, *Pentecostalism as a Christian Mystical Tradition*, 38.
118. Green, "Pentecostalism," 6.
119. Hollenweger's phrase, "blood and wounds mysticism" (*Pentecostals*, 387) refers to the Lord's Table where the suffering and death of Jesus along with the eschatological expectation of the Lord's return and the marriage feast of the Lamb are coalesced.
120. Castelo, *Pentecostalism*, xx.
121. Ibid., 37.
122. Ibid., 36.
123. Smith, *Thinking in Tongues*, 77.

I quickly found that my new attitude allowed me to follow the spectacular spread of Pentecostalism better than either credulity or skepticism could. As I poured over these archaic accounts, it became clear to me that for those early converts, the baptism of the Spirit did not just change their religious affiliation or their way of worship. It changed everything. They literally saw the whole world in a new light. Spirit baptism was not just an initiation rite, it was a mystical encounter. That is why they sometimes sounded like Saint Teresa of Avila or Saint John of the Cross although they had probably never heard of either one.[124]

Cox continues to describe pentecostalism as a tradition that carries an "elemental spirituality" that houses "primal speech" (viz., glossolalia), "primal piety" (with its mystical experiences like dreams and visions), and "primal hope" (the expectation of good from God's active hand), which comports well to the category of mysticism (which pentecostals generally feel more comfortable referring to as "spirituality"). Mysticism is a category that is only adequate for pentecostals when mystical experiences are validated by being coupled with theological concerns that include rational explications made liable to Christian orthodoxy.

Clearly, how one defines *mysticism* and its cognates proves critical. Castelo is careful to articulate nuances in those definitions and claims that key to the pentecostal theological task is to distinguish the concept and language of pentecostal mysticism from the general, un-theologized mysticism. He contends that one will bypass any of the pitfalls of general mysticism as long as the category remains a "subtheme within the broader domain of Christian spirituality."[125] He recognizes that the danger of an unqualified mysticism is how it tends to "reflect significant privatization, interiority and subjectivity."[126] Castelo asserts that though pentecostals notice and resist those dangers, they naturally continue "seeking instead a genuine interface" between mysticism and the intellectual enterprise of theologizing.[127] The safety within Christian mysticism is that experience is the adjective contextualized by Christian truth, whereas in general mysticism it is the noun.[128]

Generally speaking, pentecostals are uninterested in mystical experiences that carry no clear theological boundaries and/or praxis. For pentecostals, at least as they are faithful to their tradition, the validity of mystical experience is discerned through the lenses of the full gospel and the presence of God as revealed through Jesus Christ by the power of the Holy Spirit. Pentecostals insist on describing spiritual experiences using theological terms that appeal to scripture, the revival tradition, shared dogma, etc. In this regard, Castelo avers:

---

124. Cox, *Fire from Heaven*, 70–1.
125. Castelo, *Pentecostalism*, xix.
126. Ibid., 5.
127. Ibid., 37.
128. See Harmless, *Mystics*, 15.

> Ultimately, Pentecostals focus their attention, testimonies and passions on *who God is* and *what God is doing,* and they specify "God" as none other than the One proclaimed by and at work in Jesus through the power of the Holy Spirit. This distinction is not incidental or ancillary to the task at hand; quite the contrary, it points to a methodological crossroads.[129]

This is to say that the only way the category of mysticism can be included in a pentecostal setting is by that category being conceived, appropriated, and applied in a way emic to accepted pentecostal theological orthodoxy.

Pentecostal mysticism, then, refers specifically to the divine-human encounter supervened upon by the Holy Spirit, with the addition of careful rational explication within the bounds of Christian orthodoxy. Pentecostals believe that the theology that emerges from such an encounter is largely a reactive enterprise responsive to (and so following) God's initial self-revelation. Marius Nel speaks on how this works: "The element of a direct and unique encounter between God and a human being or a group of believers is essential for the hermeneutical process; otherwise revealed knowledge consists merely as cognitive data, when the experiential dimension is neglected."[130] Terry Cross says it crisply: "How one experiences God influences the way one reflects on God."[131] Returning again to Castelo, "Pentecostalism can be identified as a mystical tradition within the church-catholic, but only if we recognize the mystical features of Christianity that hold the knowledge of God to be both intellectual and relational."[132] We can use the term, *mysticism*—but only when that term is *qualified*.

The Third Essential: The Pneumatological Imagination

I have claimed that the first essential to what makes pentecostalism pentecostal is *revival*. Revival within the pentecostal tradition emerged from a primitive, a priori impulse (viz., the numinous) as it sought an experience with God. The second essential of pentecostalism I suggest entails a constructivist form of Christian/pentecostal mysticism. However, at the center of both revivalism and mysticism—what gives revivalism and mysticism its force—is the Person of the Holy Spirit. Hence, the third essential (the genesis of all the essentials) is that pentecostalism always privileges the pneumatic, which gives rise to a *pneumatological imagination*.

---

129. Castelo, *Pentecostalism,* 47 (emphasis original).

130. Marius Nel, "A Distinctive Pentecostal Hermeneutic: Possible and/or Necessary?" *Acta Theologica* 37, no. 2 (2017): 89.

131. Terry L. Cross, "The Rich Feast of Theology: Can Pentecostals Bring the Main Course or Only the Relish?," *JPT* 8, no. 16 (2000): 34–5. Cross deals with this concept more fully in Terry L. Cross, *Serving the People of God's Presence: A Theology of Ministry* (Grand Rapids, MI: Baker Academic, 2020).

132. Castelo, *Pentecostalism,* 81.

2. Pentecostal Qua Pentecostal

Yong writes extensively about a "pneumatological imagination."[133] He suggests that this "imagination" becomes "an epistemological theory that proceeds from specifically thematized constructs of experiences of the Spirit."[134] This is significant. Yong continues that a pneumatological imagination occurs by "focusing on certain primordial pneumatic experiences" that "enable large-scale coherent visions of the world" as well as enabling a person to consider other "visions" that seem outside that pneumatological framework because of the capacity of such an imagination to absorb and explain the "other" in its own terms.[135]

Yong's argument is situated within a pneumatological framework which he claims derives "from a *pneumatic* intuition."[136] He takes care to say that the "pneumatological and pneumatic are not synonymous."[137] The pneumatological is, as with any concept in theology, a second-order discourse about what experiences Christians claim to have had when encountering the Holy Spirit. Yong explains that this theological reflection is made based upon a series of pneumatic encounters (that may be ongoing). The pneumatic intuition, however, is antecedent to the pneumatological and "proceeds from such pretheoretical encounters with and experiences of the Spirit of God."[138] Yong insists that these "experiences" must then be "thematized for purposes of theological reflection and communication"[139]—the pneumatic intuition gives birth to *pneumatology*. He takes care to *only* use the term *pneumatic* when addressing the pretheoretical experiential (which I see as Yong's version of Otto's numinous), and he uses the term *pneumatological* when addressing the theological aspects of the Spirit. Veli-Matti Kärkkäinen essentially holds this same view using different descriptors:

> It has been the task of the rapidly growing Pentecostal and charismatic movements to remind the church-catholic that in devotion to God's Spirit, it is not theology that is primary but rather a revitalization of the experience of the Spirit. Even though the experience of the Spirit always leads to theological reflection on its meaning, spirituality is the first contact point. This is clearly evident in the biblical record: a powerful, often charismatic experience of the Spirit came first; only afterward, and in a slow tempo, came theological reflection.[140]

---

133. See Yong, *Spirit-Word-Community*, 36.
134. Yong, *Spirit-Word-Community*, 123.
135. Ibid., 133.
136. Ibid., 7 (emphasis original).
137. Ibid.
138. Ibid.
139. Ibid.
140. Veli-Matti Kärkkäinen, "Hermeneutics: From Fundamentalism to Postmodernism," in *Toward a Pneumatological Theology: Pentecostal and Ecumenical Perspectives on Ecclesiology, Soteriology, and Theology of Mission*, ed. Amos Yong (Lanham, MD: University Press of America, 2002), 6, 3–21.

To integrate Kärkkäinen with Yong, one could say a universal, essential concern for pentecostals is to engage in the pneumatic through devotion to God's Spirit, and then to proceed to theological reflection on the meaning of that engagement (viz., pneumatology), in order to move forward with a pneumatological imagination—or an imagination that sees the order of things (ontology) and the order of knowing (epistemology) mediated through the eternal Spirit and the God-breathed Word.

Saying pentecostals are pneumatocentric essentially entails a tautology. The Holy Spirit became central to the lives of the disciples of Jesus as evidenced from the record in the Book of Acts beginning with the Day of Pentecost:

> When the day of Pentecost came, they were all together in one place. Suddenly a sound like the blowing of a violent wind came from heaven and filled the whole house where they were sitting. They saw what seemed to be tongues of fire that separated and came to rest on each of them. All of them were filled with the Holy Spirit and began to speak in other tongues as the Spirit enabled them.
>
> (Acts 2:1-4)

The people in this story were the apostles of Jesus of Nazareth—his inner-circle followers who had gathered to celebrate *Shavuot* (or Pentecost, the celebration of the expression of anticipation and desire for the giving of the Torah). The apostles had been waiting in an upper room in obedience to the conspicuously absent, ascended Christ. After some ten days, there was a sudden arrival of the Holy Spirit as a rushing wind, appearing as "tongues of fire" on their heads, and enabling them "to speak in other tongues" (glossolalia). This operation of the Spirit is interpreted as a sanctifying work that enabled these disciples to stand in the role of their glorified leader and marks the origin of the Christian church.

The shift in language about the ongoing activity of God being initiated by "the Lord" in the Gospels to the activity being compelled by "the Spirit" in the Book of Acts is striking. The post-Pentecost concentration on the Spirit can be seen in this sampling from the Book of Acts: "Then Peter, filled with the Holy Spirit, said" (4:8); "spoke by the Holy Spirit" (v. 25); "they were all filled with the Holy Spirit" (v. 31); "to be full of the Spirit" (6:3); "the wisdom the Spirit" (v. 10); "they received the Holy Spirit" (8:17); "saw that the Spirit" (v. 18); "The Spirit told Philip" (v. 29); "the Spirit of the Lord suddenly took Philip away" (v. 39); "encouraged by the Holy Spirit" (9:31); "the Spirit said to him" (10:19); "the Holy Spirit came on all" (v. 44); "the gift of the Holy Spirit had been poured out" (v. 45); "The Spirit told me" (11:12); "the Holy Spirit came on them" (v. 15); "full of the Holy Spirit and faith" (v. 24); "the Spirit predicted" (v. 28); "giving the Holy Spirit to them" (15:8); "It seemed good to the Holy Spirit and to us" (v. 28); "kept by the Holy Spirit" (16:6); "but the Spirit of Jesus would not allow them to" (v. 7); "the Holy Spirit came on them" (19:6); "compelled by the Spirit" (20:22); "the Holy Spirit warns me" (v. 23); "the Holy Spirit has made you overseers" (v. 28); "Through the Spirit they urged Paul not to go on to Jerusalem" (21:4); "The Holy Spirit says, 'In this way … '" (v. 11); and "The Holy Spirit spoke the truth" (28:25).

As their name suggests, pentecostals of the modern era believe that they share in this ancient Pentecost, which enables them to continue in the same relationship to Jesus as the apostles enjoyed, along with the way they were empowered and directed by the Holy Spirit thousands of years ago. Green writes, "We can perhaps also say that Pentecostals are peculiarly convinced both that the Spirit empowers believers for [being Christian] and that supernatural experiences, therefore, can and should be basic to the normal Christian life. Of course, in some sense all Christians hold these convictions in one form or another. But Pentecostals, it seems, afford them an unusual importance and centrality."[141] This pneumatic connection, which triggers personal and corporate transformation, has become known to pentecostals as the baptism in the Holy Spirit. Emerging from this transformation is often a highly enthusiastic approach to worship and the manifestation of charismatic power (as indicated by enacted gifts of the Holy Spirit listed in 1 Cor. 12).

The pneumatological imagination, as framed by Yong, is the result of a *pneumatological epistemology* I am reflecting on in this writing. A pneumatological epistemology is a knowing roused from encounters with the Spirit.[142] It is inchoate and pretheoretical as it erupts, but, as shown above, reflection advances synchronously as the impulse of the human mind is to make sense of spiritual encounters. But the pretheoretical, non-rational pneumatic intuition is undeniable—the Spirit produces a sense of profound mystery within a person which becomes the genesis of a new epistemic reality. In these moments, the Spirit awakens something within an individual's lived experience. Here is a description given of this epistemic reality from a participant after such a divine-human encounter:

> I remember the night, and almost the very spot on the hill-top, where my soul opened out, as it were, into the infinite, and there was a rushing together of the two worlds, the inner and the outer. It was deep calling unto deep—the deep that my own struggle had opened up within being answered by the unfathomable deep without, reaching beyond the stars. I stood alone with Him who had made me, and all the beauty of the world ... The perfect stillness of the night was thrilled by a more solemn silence. The darkness held a presence that was all the more felt because it was not seen. I could not any more have doubted that *He* was there than that I was. Indeed, I felt myself to be, if possible, the less real of the two.[143]

This new epistemology houses both the divine experience and revealed knowledge—not as two separate things but as two aspects of the *same thing* (like two

---

141. Green, "Pentecostalism," 6.

142. For previous developments of a pneumatological epistemology, see Killian McDonnell, "The Determinative Doctrine of the Holy Spirit," *Theology Today* 39, no. 2 (1982): 142–61; and Killian McDonnell, "A Trinitarian Theology of the Holy Spirit," *Theological Studies* 46, no. 2 (1985): 191–227.

143. James, *Varieties of Religious Experience*, 49 (emphasis original).

sides of a coin), which becomes a lived certainty. This "lived certainty" embraces the reality/experience perceived without attempting to eliminate contradictions or ambiguities that may be found in that perception/experience. This is a very different kind of certitude than one garners while using the rationality of the Enlightenment (explored in Chapter 4).

Epistemology is at the heart of any theological work (or any intellectual work, for that matter). What is our knowledge grounded in? How do we determine its limits or its validity? Howard M. Ervin anticipates Yong's proposal, claiming that the theological work of pentecostals is rooted in a "pneumatic epistemology."[144] Ervin claims, "What is needed is an epistemology firmly rooted in the Biblical faith with a phenomenology that meets the criteria of empirically verifiable sensory experience (healing, miracles, etc.) and does not violate the coherence of rational categories. A pneumatic epistemology meets these criteria."[145] This is one of the unique aspects of the pentecostal voice in the métier of theology.

Unlike the modern rationalist epistemology that sought reasoned, incontestable first principles and indubitable beliefs upon which one could base knowledge-claims, a pneumatological epistemology does not begin with arguments or proofs but with events that seize the human heart. This is the kind of knowledge that ancient Christians called the "fire of love,"[146] which began in the moment of encounter with—and conversion by—the Spirit. It was seen as a "love" that "wounds" (according to the Greek version of the Sg 2:5[147]). This is not knowledge from a distance but what patristic scholar Robert Louis Wilken calls "the knowledge of sensuous intelligence."[148] Without this kind of knowledge, Wilken claims, we "remain voyeurs and spectators, curiosity seekers" who rely on knowledge limited to human reasoning, which never can "enter the mystery of God's life and penetrate the truth of things."[149]

One of the earliest apologists, Justin Martyr (also considered the most sophisticated), was born in Palestine at the beginning of the second century and practiced as a philosopher before his conversion to Christianity. Even after his conversion, he continued to practice philosophy while wearing the philosopher's distinctive garb. Justin Martyr's conversion came after an encounter with an aged saint who explained the way of God to him. He felt surprised that the old man did not attempt to persuade him with arguments or proofs but simply prayed for God

---

144. H. M. Ervin, "Hermeneutics: A Pentecostal Option," *Pneuma* 3, no. 1 (1981): 12.

145. Ibid., 12.

146. Augustine, *City of God*, trans. Marcus Dods (New York, NY: Random House, Inc., 1993), 306.

147. "For I Am wounded with love," Sg 2:5, BST. This "wounding" language is the metaphor used by many Christian mystics. Also, see St. John of the Cross, *Dark Night of the Soul*, trans. E. Allison Peers (Mineola, NY: Dover Publications, 2003).

148. Wilken, *Spirit of Early Christian Thought*, 291.

149. Ibid., 293.

to bring him to the "gates of light."[150] Justin Martyr speaks of that moment, saying, "A flame was kindled in my soul and I was seized by love of the prophets and of the friends of Christ. While I was pondering his words in my mind, I came to see that this way of life alone is sure and fulfilling."[151] Though his experience was infused with intellection, there was something *more*. In speaking of the mechanics of this event in Justin Martyr's life, Wilken writes:

> When speaking of how God is known, the Bible seldom speaks of insight or illumination or demonstration; rather, it says that God appeared, did something, showed himself, or spoke to someone, as in the beginning of the book of Hosea: "The word of God came to Hosea" (Hos. 1:1). Accordingly, the way to God begins not with arguments or proofs but with discernment and faith, the ability to see what is disclosed in events and the readiness to trust the words of those who testify to them.[152]

Wilken claims that these kind of experiences with the living God formed a new epistemic knowing protected by the Christian faith from its beginning. The gospel was not just a package of lucid, absolute, propositional, and logical truths which made God known—it demanded Spirit encounters that transformed lives. Wilken explains how the church carefully distanced herself from the pagan conceptualization of knowing God (or the gods) because it was blunted through naked intellection. He asserts: "Among ancient philosophers it was axiomatic that all knowledge of God came through the activity of the mind … In this view the knowledge of God was achieved by very few, and even the seer divined but little of God."[153] For example, the pagan philosopher Celsus (*c.* 175 CE) urged that the way to God was through the "ascent of the mind."[154] His claim was that one must turn from any encounter of affection because the knowledge of God could not be accessed except through mental steps or philosophic analysis. However, the church father, Origen, pushed hard against Celsus's claim. Origen argued that any knowledge of God acquired solely by the activity of the mind was "partial and defective" and that such knowledge effected no real change.[155] Wilken summarizes how true "knowledge of God" becomes a new epistemic reality in the life of one who experiences it: "The knowledge of God has to do with how one lives, with acting on convictions that are not mere premises but realities learned from other persons and tested by experience."[156]

---

150. Justin Martyr, *Dialogue with Tropho*, accessed July 3, 2023 http://www.earlychristianwritings.com/text/justinmartyr-dialoguetrypho.html, 8, Wilken, *Spirit of Christian Thought*, 6.
151. Ibid.
152. Ibid., 7.
153. Ibid., 8.
154. Ibid., 8.
155. Ibid., 12.
156. Ibid., 7.

The pneumatological epistemology within pentecostalism ensures that this ancient tradition of "true knowledge" is preserved within the church. This pneumatic pretheoretical knowing highlighted within pentecostalism resolves a problem within Western theology that began to dominate after the Enlightenment. There continues to be an unresolved false dichotomy between faith and reason that limited theology to an either/or commitment to historical-critical exegetical methods or to non-rational mysticism. According to Ervin, the pneumatological epistemology of pentecostals provides a way out of this conundrum and "provides a resolution of (a) the dichotomy between faith and reason that existentialism consciously seeks to bridge, though at the expense of the pneumatic; (b) the antidote to a destructive rationalism that often accompanies a critical-historical exegesis; and (c) a rational accountability for the mysticism by a piety ground in *sola fidei*."[157] In other words, the pneumatological epistemology brings a resolution to the beetling dualism found in theology and philosophy between faith and the oft-destructive rationalism that emerges as one approaches the supernatural message of God, mystical experiences, and the interpretation and application of such things in the human experience.

Nel agrees that the pneumatological epistemology secures true knowledge: "The boundary between Creator and creature is not erased but the Spirit creates the conditions where humans may hear and understand the Word that he makes present or reveals."[158] Nel goes on to say that apart from the presence of a pneumatological epistemology, theologizing is futile. "For this reason," he writes, "one has not heard the Word when one understands it only in cognitive terms. Bible study *per se* cannot reveal the Word of God, apart from the revelation by the Spirit to the contemporary reader."[159]

The pneumatic impulse that gives rise to a pneumatological epistemology that facilitates a pneumatological imagination is something on which all pentecostals can agree—pentecostals find commonality in a shared openness to the Spirit. I contend that pentecostalism's pneumatological imagination is a gift that pentecostals need to be recapitulate, prioritize, and offer to the church-catholic. Pentecostals instinctively felt from their origins that this way of doing theology should be the "standard operating procedure of a New Testament/indigenous church."[160] Kärkkäinen speaks of a "pneumatological renaissance"[161] fostered by the pentecostal movement: "The dramatic spread of Pentecostal and charismatic movements throughout the world has made other Christians wake up to the significance of the Holy Spirit in the everyday lives of all Christians. The rise of

---

157. Ervin, "Hermeneutics," 12.
158. Nel, "A Distinctive Pentecostal Hermeneutic," 2.
159. Ibid.
160. Nel, "A Distinctive Pentecostal Hermeneutic," 3.
161. Kärkkäinen, *Pneumatology*, 2.

the charismatic movement within virtually every mainstream church has ensured that the Holy Spirit figures prominently on the theological agenda."[162]

Interestingly, toward the end of his life, Karl Barth began to affirm that pneumatocentricity was the lens through which all theology should be done: "Everything that one believes, reflects and says about God the Father and God the Son ... would be demonstrated and clarified basically through God the Holy Spirit, the *vinculum pacis* between Father and Son. The work of God on behalf of creatures for, in, and with humanity would be made clear in a teleology which excludes all chance."[163] Barth believed that pneumatology was to become a major focus of the theology of the future.

Though, in one sense, there are many pentecostalisms, I assert that these three elements (viz., revivalism, mysticism, and a pneumatological imagination) are unique and essential to *all* pentecostals *everywhere,* irrespective of differences in doctrinal formulation, theological methods, interpretation of scripture, institutional structure, devotional practices, ethical commitments, etc. I find it fascinating that the reports and descriptions of the various scholars concerning the pentecostal experience are remarkably similar. From anthropological religious scholars to pentecostal academicians; the insiders and the outsiders; and the participants and observers, all seem to point to the same things. There may be terminological differences, but there is a shared reality. I think this shows that it is possible to name essences to pentecostalism—to highlight its beauty and life without pinning the butterfly to its death. As Jürgen Moltmann writes, "Theologically, the Pentecostal movement has come of age! It is designed to serve theological clarification in the Pentecostal movement itself and to bring about a common, universal thrust."[164] It is precisely this "theological clarification" that I believe can give rise to new pneumatological theological methodologies, one of which I offer in the constructive chapter of this project (Chapter 7).

Evidences of Genuine Pentecostalism

I have claimed that pentecostalism *qua* pentecostalism must inhere a triad of essential traits: revivalism, mysticism, and a pneumatological imagination. Though pentecostalism is expressed globally with a plethora of evidences (too many and too variegated to fully address here), there are four that I believe show up universally that could therefore be used to discern whether pentecostal *qua* pentecostal is truly present: (1) affection; (2) a priority of love; (3) theological openness; and (4) being Jesus-centered and missional.

---

162. Ibid.

163. *Schleiermacher-Auswahl mit einem Nachwort von Karl Barth*, ed. Heinz Bolli (Munich: Siebenstern-Taschenbuch, 1968), 311, Quoted In Kilian Mcdonnell, "A Trinitarian Theology of the Holy Spirit?," *Theological Studies* 46, no. 2 (1985): 193.

164. Jürgen Moltmann, "Introduction," *The Spirit in the World*, viii.

Evidence 1: Affection

An ongoing criticism of pentecostal revivalism (and revivalism in general) has been on how emotional experiences are valued in the revivalist context and how those experiences are seen by onlookers as nothing more than effusive emotionalism filled with odd, "psycho-motor manifestations."[165] Grant Wacker says this of early revivalist groups who became pentecostals:

> In the fire-baptized holiness services of the late 1890s, one leader remembered, the "people screamed until you could hear them for three miles on a clear night, and until the blood vessels stood out like whip cords." A newspaper reporter visiting Maria Woodworth-Etter's divine healing rallies in Oakland in 1889 wrote that her services produced "mental debauchery" and that those who attended did so "at their own risk." Another said that her prayer meetings sounded like the "female ward of an insane asylum."[166]

There is some merit to this criticism, but overall, it is not valid. Using the clarifying term, *affections*, serves as a useful apologetic. One must move back before the German and Scottish Enlightenments of the late eighteenth century to comprehend the role of affection in the Christian tradition. Dale Coulter writes, "The language of affections was paramount in eighteenth-century revivalist literature and continued to serve as the primary conduit of older traditions in the subterranean channels of nineteenth-century holiness movements."[167] Affections are not the same as emotions, though being *affected* can produce deep and even demonstrative emotion. Affective movement therefore more accurately expresses how revivalists like John Wesley, Jonathan Edwards, and the scores of pentecostal revivalists who followed would have described what was happening in their midst. These revivalists had a sense that the emotions they were witnessing at the revival altars were not the result of *emotionalism* but evidences of deep "sets of internal movements (physiological and psychological) that work together to produce action."[168]

Methodist theologian, Theodore Runyon, sees these emotional expressions as the result of "right affection," which he coins as "orthopathy"—a term that serves as a critical complement to orthodoxy and orthopraxy.[169] He claims

---

165. See Steven Jack Land, *Pentecostal Spirituality: A Passion for the Kingdom* (Cleveland, TN: CPT Press, 2010), 34.

166. Wacker, *Heaven Below*, 23.

167. Dale Coulter, "Introduction: The Language of Affectivity and the Christian Life," in *The Spirit, the Affections, and the Christian Tradition*, 8.

168. Ibid., 9.

169. In the 1970s, Theodore Runyon coined the term *orthopathy* to capture the Wesleyan and Pentecostal revivalist expectation that in a divine encounter, "right affections fuse with right beliefs (orthodoxy) and right practices (orthopraxis)" culminating in a changed life. See Coulter, "Introduction," in *The Spirit, the Affections*, 5.

that orthopathy is "religious experience as an event of knowing between the Divine Source and human participant."[170] For Coulter, the goal of the revivalist setting was the emergence of right affections in the believer in order to accomplish what he calls, "the connection between divine encounters and the process of Christian development."[171] This echoes the conviction of Augustine: "The soul can be changed, not indeed spatially, but nonetheless in time by its affections."[172] The concept that "The soul can be changed" is one of the central goals of genuine pentecostalism.

The early centuries of Christianity viewed any uncontrolled emotion (along with the bodily impulses or sexuality in general) with a great degree of pessimism and as forces in opposition to matters of the spirit.[173] Only in the past few decades have academics begun to speak of the emotional dimension as "an acknowledged and accepted dimension of human existence and study" and that one can "now express and discuss emotion openly without embarrassment."[174] Coulter affirms, "Over the past several decades there has been a virtual renaissance in the study of emotion and desire occurring in different disciplines and for diverse purposes."[175]

However, by the time of the emergence of Wesleyan and Holiness revivals (from which the pentecostal renewal emerged[176]), emotions had been relegated to the domain of the "sentimental."[177] The broader cultural milieu of the day made it difficult *not* to be jaded about emotion, much less to look for the ways in which emotion could disclose the beauty and dignity of the work of the Spirit. The relegation of emotion to the sentimental is why so many misread the emotional force of the revivals that arose in the eighteenth through twentieth centuries. Skeptics believed the meetings were filled with mawkish, purposeless emotionalism that left the average, cultured person embarrassed and offended.

In William Lecky's exhaustive work of eight volumes, *History of England in the Eighteenth Century*, Lecky poignantly expresses the disdain of the intellectuals of his day against the emotionalism expressed in revivalism. He writes of highbrow

---

170. Theodore Runyon as quoted in Land, *Pentecostal Spirituality*, 32.

171. Coulter, "Introduction," in *The Spirit, the Affections*, 5.

172. Augustine, *De vera religione*, 10.18, quoted in Coulter, "Introduction," in *The Spirit, the Affections*, 7.

173. Historically, emotional expression was often viewed with suspicion and mistrust, causing it to be "marginalized and suppressed." See Elizabeth A. Dreyer, "The Transformative Role of Emotion in the Middle Ages: Deliverance from Lukewarm Affections," in *The Spirit, the Affections, and the Christian Tradition*, ed. Dale M. Coulter and Amos Yong (Notre Dame, IN: University of Notre Dame Press, 2016), 115.

174. Dreyer, "The Transformative Role of Emotion," 115.

175. Coulter, "Introduction," in *The Spirit, the Affections*, 1.

176. I examine this more carefully in Chapter 2.

177. Coulter, "Introduction," in *The Spirit, the Affections*, 3.

Englishmen criticizing Wesleyan revivalists as a ragged legion of preaching barbers, cobblers, tinkers, scavengers, draymen, and chimney sweepers:

> It was essentially a popular movement, exercising its deepest influence over the lower and middle classes. Some of its leaders were men of real genius, but in general the Methodist teacher had little sympathy with the more educated of his fellow-countrymen. To an ordinarily cultivated mind there was something extremely repulsive in his tears and groans and amorous ejaculations, in the coarse anthropomorphic familiarity and the unwavering dogmatism with which he dealt with the most sacred subjects, in the narrowness of his theory of life and his utter insensibility to many of the influences that expand and embellish it, in the mingled credulity and self-confidence with which he imagined that the whole course of nature was altered for his convenience.[178]

But the preponderance of research shows that the true impulse of revival did not have the experience of emotion as its ambition.[179] Its goal was (and *is*) to create an "interior disposition of compunction, contrition, or holy sorrow" for the ways in which we break faith with Almighty God.[180] This is where the affections of human beings come under the influence of God, which often elicits a reaction on an emotional level. Having deep, expressive emotions is *not* emotionalism. Emotions can be "constituting judgments that shape human identity and supply meaning to life."[181]

Those who experience revival consistently speak of a strength of assurance that comes from the existential experience of the divine that feels real and is ultimately significant for them. It is this deep sense of connection with the divine that transcends pure intellect (and may even contradict it) and transforms the human life, causing one to be willing to give one's life in total commitment to God and to God's will. Returning to Lecky's disparaging commentary from the elites about Methodist revivalism above, he ultimately points out the amazing transformation that could not be denied by those participating in the revivals others were criticizing. This quote is contiguous with the one above with no transitional words or new paragraph:

---

178. William Edward Hartpole Lecky, *History of England in the Eighteenth Century*, Vol. III (London: Longmans, Green, and Co., 1913), 99–100.

179. Wacker (*Heaven Below*, 112–20) highlights evidence that there *were* revivalists who were guilty of encouraging emotionalism as the point, and they would at times use such tactics to manipulate the crowds who followed them. However, this was an aberration from the theological outcome sought in true revival concern.

180. Michael J. McClymond, "Holy Tears: A Neglected Aspect of Early Christian Spirituality in Contemporary Context," in *The Spirit, the Affections, and the Christian Tradition*, edited by Dale M. Coulter and Amos Yong (Notre Dame, IN: University of Notre Dame Press, 2016), 90, 87–111.

181. Coulter, "Introduction," in *The Spirit, the Affections*, 4.

But the very qualities that impaired his influence in one sphere enhanced it in another. His impassioned prayers and exhortations stirred the hearts of multitudes whom a more decorous teaching had left absolutely callous. The supernatural atmosphere of miracles, judgments, and inspirations, in which he moved, invested the most prosaic life with a halo of romance. The doctrines he taught, the theory of life he enforced, proved themselves capable of arousing in great masses of men an enthusiasm of piety which was hardly surpassed in the first days of Christianity, of eradicating inveterate vice, of fixing and directing impulsive and tempestuous natures that were rapidly hastening towards the abyss. Out of the profligate slave-dealer, John Newton, Methodism formed one of the purest and most unselfish of saints. It taught criminals in Newgate to mount the gallows in an ecstasy of rapturous devotion. It planted a fervid and enduring religious sentiment in the midst of the most brutal and most neglected portions of the population, and whatever may have been its vices or its defects, it undoubtedly emancipated great numbers from the fear of death, and imparted a warmer tone to the devotion and a greater energy to the philanthropy of every denomination both in England and the colonies.[182]

Lecky's commentary provides an excellent example of the tension always present in the pentecostal milieu. There is always a longing for the immediate transformative presence of the Spirit even at the expense of being judged as being less intellectually astute, rational, or clear-minded.

Affection as Motivation "Affections" is also a helpful catch-all word for the motivation a Christian must possess in order to pursue all-things-spiritual, such as cultivating a general hunger for God and the things of God; a commitment to prayer; growth in knowledge and discipleship; Christian service/volunteerism; a desire for the manifestation of spiritual gifts; a pursuit of faith, hope, and love; a yearning to love things/people rightly and to live rightly; a longing for Christ's appearing; following the impulse to care spiritually and practically for those in need; being quick to confess sin/failure and to shift toward a godly, sober, and righteous life; and sustaining one's first love for Christ (cf. Rev. 2:4).

Persons with deep affections feel alive spiritually and feel the wind of God in their sails as they move toward all things holy and good. This is a treasure that pentecostals guard. The presence of affections is crucial evidence to them of what is pentecostal because it is evidence of the Spirit's presence and power and conforms to the promise of scripture and the example of Jesus' own life and the lives of his first followers, the church.

---

182. Lecky, *History of England*, 100–1.

The Difficulty with Affection The manifestation of right affection, however, is notoriously difficult to sustain—strong orthopathic feelings are not perpetually sustainable. They simply do not last. Here is Wesley's practical thoughts on this point:

> I do not see how it is possible in the nature of things for any revival of religion to continue long ... How then is it possible that Methodism, that is, a religion of the heart, though it flourishes now as a green bay tree, should continue in this state? ... [People] increase in pride, in anger, in the desire of the flesh, the desire of the eyes and the pride of life. So, although the form of religion remains, the spirit is swiftly vanishing away. Is there no way to prevent this—this continual decay of pure religion?[183]

There are several important impairments to affections one could consider, but I briefly look here at two. First, the back and forth of human nature (like that reflected in the narratives of the Book of Judges) shows that there is a serpentine openness—and then resistance—to God when human beings are simply being human. Our hearts are "prone to wander."[184] Wesley says it is much easier to hold on to the "form of religion" (practices and knowledge) than to its "spirit" (affections). This means that not all time continues as "revival" time.

Second, a sense of vibrant spirituality historically comes and goes in seasons. There are, according to sacred text, "seasons of refreshing" (Acts 3:19)—not just one constant, unending one. Spiritual winters—where there is no evidence of affection—are evidently part of God's plan for our spiritual development. As winter prepares the earth for spring, believers need spiritual winters (revival absence) to prepare their souls for growth (cf. John 15:1-2). Revival moments that foster affection should be sought after and can be experienced again and again, but they cannot serve as the sole characteristic of one's faith experience. Faith cannot be lived in constant wonderment and ecstasy. Just as a lifelong, loving, and enduring friendship or marriage does not sustain constant wonderment and ecstasy, neither does a life of faith.

Many revivalists of the past (along with some Christian leaders in churches today) believed they could stir up revivals vis-à-vis seasons of prayer and repentance, but it is a mistake to believe revivals can be forced; they cannot. Revival is initiated by the *nod* of the Lord (viz., the numinous) and is only entered into with innocence. Acts 3:19 claims that the "times of refreshing" come only "from the Lord," not from the intention of human beings (though the response to the *nod* via human volition plays a critical role). To try to force

---

183. Wesley, quoted in Richard H. Niebuhr, *Social Sources of Denominationalism* (New York: World Publishing, 1972), 70-1.

184. A lyric from the Christian hymn, "Come Thou Fount of Every Blessing," written by the pastor and hymnodist, Robert Robinson in 1758, accessed January 3, 2022, https://en.wikipedia.org/wiki/Come_Thou_Fount_of_Every_Blessing.

a revival does not guarantee a restored affection and may even cause people to become simple posers—making them victims of their past revival experiences, which can quickly become a bondage that fosters inappropriate and false imitation.

This does not mean revivals cannot carry an ongoing influence, they can. However, they only can as they are *remembered*. The poet A. R. Ammons speaks of the inability of human beings to produce metaphysical experiences (viz., revival), except to access those that have happened in the past via *memory*. He writes, "I am a mystic—but by memory only. For an instant, about ten years ago, I felt the perspective from space to earth … I was there. By the use of the intelligence, of course, you can work up such perspectives at will, but it's a very different thing from being there."[185] Christian Wiman brushes up against this idea as well.

The great Jewish theologian Abraham Joshua Heschel once defined faith as primarily faithfulness to a time when we had faith. We remember these moments of heightened awareness in our lives, these clearings within consciousness in which faith is self-evident and God too obvious and omnipresent to need that name, and we try to remain true to them. It is a tenuous, tenacious discipline of memory and hope.[186]

In truth, pentecostals can only put up "Ebenezers"[187] and "piled stones"[188] to remind themselves of the "times of refreshing" that may not be present. Just as the celebration of Eucharist (the Great Thanksgiving) is rooted in a "remembrance" tradition,[189] remembrance is how an experienced revival can carry an ongoing impact into one's spiritual vitality.

The important claim being made here is that the evidences discussed in this section—like affection—prove germane to what it means to be a pentecostal. This suggests that a person who is not actively seeking and prioritizing these evidences is not being truly pentecostal.

Evidence 2: A Priority of Love

The second evidence of pentecostalism is the prioritizing of Christian love. In the first edition of *The Apostolic Faith*, a witness to the Azusa Street Revival tried to explain what happened to him in the experience of the baptism with the Spirit: "It was a baptism of love. Such abounding love! Such compassion seemed to almost

---

185. From a 1955 letter to the poet, Josephine Miles, from A. R. Ammons, quoted in Christian Wiman, *He Held Radical Light: The Art of Faith, The Faith of Art* (New York: Farrar, Straus and Giroux, 2018), 33-4.
186. Ibid., 33.
187. Cf. 1 Sam. 7:12.
188. Cf. Gen. 31:46; Josh. 4:6.
189. "Then He took the bread, and when He had given thanks, He broke it and gave it to them, saying, 'This is My body which is given for you. Do this in remembrance of Me'" (Lk. 22:19).

kill me with its sweetness! People do not know what they are doing when they stand out against it. The devil never gave me a sweet thing, he was always trying to get me to censure people. This baptism fills us with divine love."[190]

The immediate appearance of love for God and others is a nod to the nonrational aspect of the divine-human interaction. The great theologian of the Christian East, Gregory Palamas (1296–1359) asserts, "Not through rational thought, but through the Holy Spirit within us do we achieve the experience of love and the gifts it bestows."[191] William Joseph Seymour (1870–1922), one of the pentecostal movement's founders, recognizes the strong presence of love at the dawn of pentecostalism in America. Seymour writes:

> The Pentecostal power, when you sum it all up, is just more of God's love. If it does not bring more love, it is simply a counterfeit. Pentecost means to live right in the 13th chapter of First Corinthians, which is the standard ... Pentecost makes us love Jesus more and love our brothers more. It brings us all into one common family.[192]

There were several reports in *The Apostolic Faith* (which Seymour oversaw) that show the priority of loving neighbor: "The feast of Pentecost came at the time of the wheat harvest and ripening of the summer fruits. They were commanded to leave some of the wheat and fruits in the fields, not to glean it. So when we get the baptism with the Holy Ghost, we have overflowing love, we have rivers of salvation."[193] Another sample follows below:

> The Portland campmeeting opened at Twelfth and Division streets with 1000 people in attendance, sometimes hundreds could not get in. They had all things common at the camp, and such love and unity exists [sic]. The poor saint could have a ten[t], as well as the rich one and all were free to eat at the tables ... O I wish you could hear these Holy Ghost people testify. "No straps on anyone. The Holy Ghost works here" ... Such humble people, such love and unity I never saw.[194]

For most of church history there existed (at least as an ideal) an inclination toward *unity* and *catholicity*. The Apostle Paul claims in Ephesians 1 that "the

---

190. Anonymous, "The Old-Time Pentecost," *The Apostolic Faith* 1, no. 1 (June–September 1907): 2.

191. Gregory Palamas, *Defense of the Hesychasts 2.1.28*, quoted in Veli-Matti Kärkkäinen, *One with God: Salvation as Deification and Justification* (Collegeville, MN: Liturgical Press, 2004), 29.

192. William Joseph Seymour, *The Apostolic Faith* 2, no. 13 (May 1908): 3.

193. Anonymous, "Old Testament Feasts Fulfilled in Our Souls Today," *The Apostolic Faith* 1, no. 9 (June–September 1907): 2.

194. Anonymous, "In the Last Days," *The Apostolic Faith* 1, no. 9 (June–September 1907): 1.

mystery of God's will" was "to bring all things in heaven and on earth together under one head, even Christ" (vv. 9–10). There was to be no division: "Here there is no Gentile or Jew, circumcised or uncircumcised, barbarian, Scythian, slave or free, but Christ is all, and is in all" (Col. 3:11). Christ not only throws down the old walls of social and national division, but he also becomes the cornerstone of a new building; it is this one building where Christ is to be worshipped. As Paul asserts:

> So then you are no longer strangers and foreigners, but you are fellow citizens with the saints, and of the household of God, being built on the foundation of the apostles and prophets, Christ Jesus himself being the chief cornerstone; in whom the whole building, fitted together, grows into a holy temple in the Lord; in whom you also are built together for a habitation of God in the Spirit (Eph. 2:19-21).

In the early centuries of the church, St. Maximus wrote, "The devil, man's tempter from the beginning, had separated him in his will from God, and had separated men from each other."[195] In contrast to the devil's aim, French Jesuit priest, Henri De Lubac, whose writings played a key role in shaping the Second Vatican Council, wrote:

> God is working continually in the world to the effect that all should come together into unity, by this sin which is the work of man, "the one nature was shattered into a thousand pieces" and humanity which ought to constitute a harmonious whole, in which "mine" and "thine" would be no contradiction, is turned into a multitude of individuals, as numerous as the sands of the seashore, all of whom show violently discordant inclinations.[196]

Because unity is the fruit of the love of God and of neighbor—the summation of all the commandments (see Mt. 22:36-40)—the New Testament seems obsessed with the idea. Unity is also stressed over and over by the church Fathers. Augustine writes, "You unite together the inhabitants of the cities, the different peoples, nay the whole human race, by belief in our common origin, so that men are not satisfied in being joined together, but become in some sort brothers."[197]

However, this commitment to love and unity became threatened at the beginning of the pentecostal movement in America when Charles Fox Parham (1873–1929) expressed an aggressive racism and contempt for Seymour.[198] This caused Seymour to double down on his conviction about the baptism with the Spirit being a baptism of love for the purpose of building human community. Seymour writes, "Many may start in this salvation, and yet if they do not watch

---

195. Maximus the Confessor, quoted by Henri De Lubac, *Catholicism, Christ and the Common Destiny of Man* (San Francisco, CA: Ignatius Press, 1988), 35.
196. Ibid., 34.
197. As quoted in de Lubac, *Catholicism*, 55.
198. See Green, "Spirit That Makes Us," 1–24.

... they will lose the Spirit of Jesus which is divine love."[199] Cecil Robeck, Senior Professor of Church History and Ecumenics at Fuller, adds, "For Seymour unity was manifested in the interracial and transcultural experience of worship in the Spirit, with the gift of tongues playing an important (but not exclusive) role as a biblical sign of the fullness of the human community."[200]

Because pentecostalism is the fruit of an encounter with God through the Holy Spirit, the scriptures anticipate the presence of love—from John's claim that "love" is the first evidence of moving from "death to life," and that anyone "who does not love remains in death" (1 John 3:14) to Jesus' claim that "all men will know that you are my disciples, if you love one another" (John 13:35). The appearance of love is pneumatologically loaded in Romans 5:5 as Paul claims that there is a flow of love into the faithful because the work of the Holy Spirit is within them. The Christian love that celebrates the *other* unconditionally is one evidence of true pentecostalism.

To talk of a love like this is to make sense of why Plato calls love "holy madness."[201] This kind of love is not based on the merit of the one being loved or on what they do for us. It is love that has no cause beyond itself and needs no justification outside of itself. The presence of the Spirit in our lives (Rom. 5:5) brings out this divine love as our deepest identity and what we are created in and for. It is a love sufficient unto itself. It carries its own end, merit, and satisfaction. The pentecostal conviction is that only a transformed consciousness filled with the Spirit can see another person as another self—one also loved by Christ and not as an object separate from ourselves with whom we must compete. Only when love gets filtered by our biased humanity can we see other people as tasks, commitments, or threats, instead of as extensions of the Person of God.

In the divine-human encounter, the Christian becomes a work of Christ and, as a participator in the love (nature) of God, becomes Christ to his or her neighbor. In effect they become *in ipsa fide Christus adest* (the "ever present Christ" to the world). The importance of love as the key trait of Christ's presence in the believer is caught in Luther's assertion, "No virtue can be compared to [love], neither is it possible to describe or name any specific work for it as with regard to other virtues, which are actually partial virtues, such as purity, charity, patience, and goodwill, etc. Love does everything."[202]

---

199. William Seymour, "To the Baptized Saints," *The Apostolic Faith* 1, no. 9 (September 1906): 2.

200. Cecil M. Robeck Jr., "William J. Seymour and 'The Bible Evidence,'" in *Initial Evidence: Historical and Biblical Perspectives on the Pentecostal Doctrine of Spirit Baptism*, ed. Gary B. McGee (Grand Rapids, MI: Zondervan, 1988), 72–95, quoted by L. William Oliverio, Jr., *Theological Hermeneutics in the Classical Pentecostal Tradition: A Typological Account* (Boston: Brill, 2012), 65.

201. Michael A. Screech, *The Anatomy of Madness: Essays in the History of Psychiatry*, ed. William F. Bynum et al. (London, UK: Routledge, 2004), 27–30.

202. Martin Luther, *Weimarer Ausgabe* 17 II, 10026–101, 4, (*Lent Postil, 1525*), trans. Kärkkäinen, quoted in Kärkkäinen, *One with God*, 60–1.

Sadly, the love and unity that were immediately present within nascent pentecostalism dissipated swiftly. Wacker reports how quickly divisiveness appeared among early pentecostal leaders who were charismatic in their style but often obstreperous in their perspectives on dogma:

> The evidence for pentecostals' determination to exact goose-step conformity in matters of doctrine is so voluminous it is hard to understand how the contrary notion ever arose ... The large number of schisms between 1915 and 1935, which typically began as disputes over seemingly minor points of belief, suggested that pentecostal groups held little interest in compromise and none at all in theological pluralism. The proper form of church government, the timing of sanctification, the proof of Holy Spirit baptism, the morality of seeking a physician, the possibility of universal salvation—all issues that most evangelicals considered more or less open for discussion—triggered lockouts, personal denunciations, and an iron-fisted determination always to speak one's mind, regardless of the human cost. The evidence bulges with examples.[203]

This devolution was not intended. Early in the movement, Seymour averred, "We are not fighting men or churches, but seeking to displace dead forms and creeds and wild fanaticism with living, practical Christianity."[204] It seems that the love of God and neighbor turned out to be more difficult to maintain than the orthopathic affections cited above, which begs the question: *How can love—which is the first evidence that we have passed from death to life (1 John 3:14)—be so quickly abandoned in the name of being right?*[205]

If love is one of the key pieces of evidence of genuine pentecostalism, a person claiming to be a pentecostal must function as a loving person. A person may speak in tongues; believe Christ to be savior, healer, sanctifier, baptizer and soon coming king; participate in free and spontaneous worship (raising hands, testimonies, dancing, etc.); and practice gifts of the Spirit, but if they are *not* a loving person who moves toward unity with others in Christ's church, the claim of being a pentecostal must fall into question. Paul speaks of this explicitly in 1 Corinthians:

> If I speak in the tongues of men or of angels, but do not have love, I am only a resounding gong or a clanging cymbal. If I have the gift of prophecy and can fathom all mysteries and all knowledge, and if I have a faith that can move mountains, but do not have love, I am nothing. If I give all I possess to the poor

---

203. Wacker, *Heaven Below*, 77–8.
204. William J. Seymour, "The Apostolic Faith Movement," *The Apostolic Faith* 1, no. 1 (September 1906): 2, Quoted In Kenneth J. Archer, *A Pentecostal Hermeneutic: Spirit, Scripture and Community* (Cleveland, TN: CPT Press, 2009), 100.
205. I return to this question in Chapter 6.

and give over my body to hardship that I may boast, but do not have love, I gain nothing.

(1 Cor. 13:1-3)

This text alone affirms the critical nature of love in the Spirit filled life. Love constitutes pentecostal *qua* pentecostal more than right thinking, right practice, speaking in tongues, etc. ever could.

Evidence 3: Theological Openness

What one may not have expected is how the non-rational aspect of revival leaves one open to various theological reflections. The historical record shows that once the movement germinated, pentecostals immediately began to visit, revisit, and even recalibrate key Christian doctrines (such as the baptism in the Holy Spirit and its relationship to glossolalia—see Chapter 2). This was modeled in Wesley a century earlier as he carried an openness to a wide range of Christian thought, even though that meant navigating through inherent contradictory spaces. Kärkkäinen notes that:

> What makes Wesley and his contribution so fascinating is that he was really a product of so many Christian traditions: Puritanism, Anglicanism, Lutheranism by way of Moravian Pietism, Roman Catholicism, and Eastern Orthodoxy by way of the Eastern fathers. What marks his approach, however, is not only a creative adaptation of various influences but also critique and honest wrestling with seemingly conflicting tendencies.[206]

Provocative early in the pentecostal story is that this openness led to the surprising willingness of some to consider what the church had historically considered heterodoxy—even the historical theological doctrine of the Trinity was reevaluated. A group of these early pentecostals developed what is known as Evangelical Unitarianism, which held that the Second Person of the Trinity was really the fullness of the Godhead. Thus, they called themselves the Oneness or "Jesus Only" group.[207]

How could this be? What had been considered as the orthodox position of the Christian church for centuries was challenged by these pentecostals as the result of an emerging subjective hermeneutic that arose from their revival experience. Kenneth Archer calls the hermeneutical approach of early pentecostals, the "Bible Reading Method."[208] Archer explains how this methodology created a theological openness for the Oneness doctrine to arise within pentecostalism:

---

206. Kärkkäinen, *One with God*, 75.

207. Douglas Jacobsen, *Thinking in the Spirit: Theologies of the Early Pentecostal Movement* (Bloomington, IN: University of Indiana Press, 2001), 195.

208. Archer, *A Pentecostal Hermeneutic*, 99–127.

The Bible Reading Method used from a Pentecostal point of view enabled Oneness Pentecostalism to come into existence. Oneness Pentecostalism came out of Trinitarian Pentecostalism; thus, this began as an in-house theological discussion or worse, a major crisis. This crisis could not be resolved by appealing to the correct or incorrect use of interpretive method. The Bible Reading Method lent itself to create new theological mosaics.[209]

By the very fact that this doctrinal position was considered anathema by the general Christian theological milieu of the day shows how prerational, pretheological revivalism positions its participants to consider fresh theological reflection. Early pentecostalism carried the tendency of open, neutral reflection as it embraced a hermeneutic that welcomed innovative doctrines. Archer continues:

> The Bible Reading Method encouraged a synchronic interpretive strategy that would extrapolate a verse from its larger context in its concern to string all the verses that relate to that word or topic together and lump it into one paragraph. However, the early Pentecostals (like the Holiness folk) were concerned in a limited sense about the historical cultural context from which the New Testament emerged as they attempted to understand a passage ... They were also concerned about properly interpreting a passage according to the syntactical relationships of words and sentences ... From a modernistically critical perspective (both liberal and conservative), the Pentecostals were blurring the boundaries of the past and present as they exegeted Scripture ... It allowed the Pentecostals to push theological boundaries and make interpretive connections within the Scriptures that had not been previously noticed.[210]

Parham is an example of and influencer on the emergence of this hermeneutic in early pentecostalism. Douglas Jacobsen writes that, "Parham was very much a believer in the Bible, but he bluntly rejected the notion that Christian orthodoxy should set any limits on his own interpretation of that book."[211] Jacobsen further states, "the clearest central conviction of the movement seems to be that 'God is doing a new thing,'"[212] which suggests that one of the prevailing hermeneutics within early pentecostalism was that God was using the pentecostals to bring "new revelation" and a more complete reformation

---

209. Ibid., 112.
210. Ibid., 125–6.
211. Douglas Jacobson, *A Reader in Pentecostal Theology: Voices from the First Generation* (Bloomington, IN: Indiana University Press, 2006), 31.
212. Idem., "Pentecostal Hermeneutics in Comparative Perspective," (Paper presented at the Annual Meeting of the Society for Pentecostal Studies, Patten College, Oakland, CA, March 13–15, 1997), 21, quoted in Oliverio, *Theological Hermeneutics*, 50.

to the church.[213] Smith affirms that one of the key elements of a pentecostal worldview is the "positioning of radical openness to God, and in particular, God doing something *differently* or *new*."[214]

Oliverio supports the appearance of the "new" in saying, "The ability to see theological things anew was what was so special about the original Classical Pentecostal hermeneutic. As a result, a new Christian tradition was born."[215] This fostered theological innovation that included a move toward the restoration of lost biblical doctrines (i.e., the "full gospel"). Early on, there was a guilelessness and a delightful naïve theological openness that preponderated the pentecostal narrative, and much good emerged from this openness (though it had its problems).

Abraham Joshua Heschel claims that sacred text is not just given to "vicariously" replace our thoughts and thereby "seal" our minds from "new thoughts," but that we are to be open to the "unveiling" of new meaning as part of our "worship" of God:

> The Bible is not an intellectual sinecure, and its acceptance should not be like setting up a talismanic lock that seals both the mind and the conscience against the intrusion of new thoughts. Revelation is not vicarious thinking. Its purpose is not to substitute for but to extend our understanding … The full meaning of the Biblical words was not disclosed once and for all. Every hour another aspect is unveiled. The word was given one; the effort to understand it must go on for ever [sic]. It is not enough to accept or even to carry out the commandments. To study, to examine, to explore the Torah is a form of worship, a supreme duty. For the Torah is an invitation to perceptivity, a call for continuous understanding. Taken as vicarious thinking, the Bible becomes a stumbling block.[216]

Although Heschel was not a Christian, this approach to scripture fosters the kind of theological openness I claim as native to that which is pentecostal. Pentecostal theology did not begin with a rigidity about orthodoxy but emerged unapologetically embracing a methodology that interpreted the primary revelation of God as shown in scripture while reflecting on those texts as they considered how the Spirit was impacting their human experience. The pentecostal

---

213. It is fascinating to compare pentecostals to the late second-century Montanists who welcomed New Prophecy and ecstatic visions from the Holy Spirit, believing the Spirit was giving them revelation for the present age not necessarily tethered to the customs/traditions handed down by the historic Christian church. See Christine Trevett, *Montanism: Gender, Authority and the New Prophecy* (Cambridge: Cambridge University Press, 1996).

214. James K. A. Smith, "What Hath Cambridge to Do with Azusa Street? Radical Orthodoxy and Pentecostal Theology in Conversation," *Pneuma* 25, no. 1 (Spring 2003): 97–114 (109) (emphasis original).

215. Oliverio, *Theological Hermeneutics*, 51.

216. Abraham Joshua Heschel, *God in Search of Man* (New York: Farrar, Straus, and Giroux, 1955), 273.

invitation to those interested in studying the Bible was an invitation to *experience* God. The Bible in the world of pentecostals was literally God *speaking*. It was not regarded merely as a collection of books by various authors communicating objective propositional truths; it was considered a continuous communication from God himself to all people in all places at all times. Pentecostals approached scripture to hear and experience God through it. They communicated this hermeneutic through their preaching, periodicals, and testimonies. The Bible was authoritative when it became a *lived experience* (viz., a pneumatic epistemological event).

The early pentecostal hermeneutic fought to keep scripture and experience in dialogue. As Oliverio claims, "The first, and foremost, interpretive assumption is that the Protestant Christian scriptures were the sole ultimate authority for Christian belief and living which functioned dialogically with the religious and general experiences of early pentecostals to form a theological understanding of their world."[217] This established a clear relationship between the authority of scripture (orthodoxy) and the primacy of experience, though Oliverio asserts that "the Scriptures were certainly considered the authority over experience, a dynamic of interdependence between the authority of Scripture and the experience of Pentecostal Christian living emerged."[218] Jacobsen insists that early "Pentecostal theology was born out of that need to bring words and experience together—to connect thought with the experiences of the Spirit in ways that fostered God's work in the world."[219] This is because pentecostals instinctively wanted more than the *sola scriptura* focus of the old Protestant prolegomena and added a unique nuance to their hermeneutical lens: they factored in general and religious experience into their interpretive methodology.

The expectation on parade in the pentecostal movement of experiencing God while encountering sacred text was also present in the early centuries of the Christian church. As texts were being negotiated as to whether to consider them as part of the canon, experiencing the *now* voice of God was part of their discernment process. The establishment of the biblical canon was a rather desultory path historically.[220] The claim made by the Reformers that sacred text naturally ended up in the Bible because of its perspicuity without the involvement of the church is simply a myth. As Canadian Baptist and professor of New Testament studies Lee McDonald asserts:

> It is generally acknowledged that the church used several criteria in order to determine the contents of its NT. No surviving evidence, however, suggests that all churches used the same criteria in selecting their sacred collections. Likewise,

---

217. Oliverio, *Theological Hermeneutics*, 31.

218. Ibid., 33.

219. Jacobsen, *Thinking in the Spirit*, 2, quoted in Oliverio, *Theological Hermeneutics*, 49.

220. See Lee Martin McDonald, *The Biblical Canon: Its Origin, Transmission, and Authority* (Grand Rapids, MI: Baker Academic, 2007).

no evidence suggests that each separate criterion weighed equally with others in deliberations about canon. In fact, the variety of Scripture canons from the fourth to the sixth centuries suggests otherwise. The most common criteria employed in the canonical process include apostolicity, orthodoxy, antiquity, and use.[221]

Various texts were used by the early church and, depending on their adaptability, were eventually integrated into the canon. McDonald states that, "The writings eventually incorporated into the NT apparently met the worship and instructional needs of the churches, while the others did not. The writings that did not remain in the church's sacred collections were those that did not meet the needs of the greater church and had more difficulty being adapted to the churches' changing needs."[222] This approach is deeply congruent with pentecostalism in terms of the functionality of sacred text—it is a continuous communication from God himself to all people in all places at all times. They were on the hunt for the *now* voice of God in the text. This is the idea that is anticipated within the early church as they looked for, recognized, and embraced what came to be seen as the NT canon.

McDonald continues, "Scriptures were adaptable to the changing circumstances of the church's life. Some of the writings that functioned as Scripture earlier in the church's history, such as *Barnabas, 1 Clement,* the letter of Ignatius, *Shepherd of Hermas,* and *Eldad and Modad,* did not survive the criterion of adaptability. They fell into disuse and dropped from the Scripture collections."[223] This commitment to the ability of sacred text to speak affirms the pentecostal's theological openness to the speaking voice of scripture.

It is important to remember that the essences of pentecostalism (viz., revival, mysticism, and a pneumatological imagination) demand a commitment to the ongoing process of submitting to God's voice and participating in God's activity as individuals and as members of Christ's church "until we all reach unity in the faith and in the knowledge of the Son of God and become mature, attaining to the whole measure of the fullness of Christ" (Eph. 4:13). These essences always transcend a one-time "event." Maintaining a theological openness requires that a deep humility inheres the theological enterprise—where there is a welcoming of criticism and recalibration, thereby allowing for fresh articulations of dogmas and theological positions (while avoiding pride and dogmatism). But, as my research has indicated, the pentecostal essences, like revivalism and mysticism, are hard to maintain, so is pentecostal theological openness, and it quickly evaporated. Oliverio reports that:

> The words of Scripture (almost always in the King James Version of the Bible) were identified in relation to the common sense supernatural experience of early

221. Ibid., 495.
222. Ibid., 414–15.
223. Ibid.

Pentecostal readers. Because of this tacit naïve realism, the understanding of direct correspondence between early Pentecostals' theological views and the realities to which these articulations pointed, in many cases, led to an absolutism which engendered the significant splintering of Pentecostalism in the decades following the Azusa Street Revival.[224]

However, if pentecostals wish to carry a voice that is prophetic and transformational, there must be a commitment to reappropriate and maintain a theological openness. I am suggesting that this is pivotal in ensuring a theologue's pentecostalism is actually pentecostal. Barth warned of the danger of abandoning this pneumatological focus in theology: "Theology becomes unspiritual when it lets itself be enticed or evicted from the freshly flowing air of the Spirit of the Lord, in which it alone can prosper. The Spirit departs when theology enters rooms whose stagnant air automatically prevents it from being and doing what it can, may, and must be and do."[225]

Evidence 4: Jesus-Centered and Missional

The last evidence I want to address that I believe certifies that which is pentecostal *qua* pentecostal is that pentecostals everywhere aspire to center their lives on Jesus Christ—their soteriology has always been Christocentric, both experientially and theologically. The pentecostal movement was open to and pursued direct experiences with the Spirit—experiences that they felt were central to what they called the baptism in the Spirit, but in Moltmann's words, "In this spiritual baptism a personal relationship to Jesus was born: Jesus lives—Jesus heals—Jesus comes ... it is that which distinguishes Pentecostalism from spiritism."[226] Wacker observes about the emergence of the pentecostals:

> God the Father came first, of course, but only technically. The omniscient, omnipotent, omnipresent God of the Protestant Reformers took a curtain bow now and then, in official theological texts and printed Sunday School lessons, but in actual practice, in the daily devotional life of ordinary believers, Jesus Christ the Son readily upstaged God the Father. One historian's assertion that early pentecostalism, like all modern revival movements, was a Jesus cult, may have been too strong, yet Jesus' predominance in grass-roots piety is hard to deny. One study of 700 early pentecostal hymns revealed, for example, that Jesus the Son was mentioned three times more often than God the Father.[227]

---

224. Oliverio, *Theological Hermeneutics*, 32.
225. Karl Barth, *Evangelical Theology: An Introduction*, trans. Grover Foley (Grand Rapids, MI: Eerdmans, 1963), 56.
226. Moltmann, *The Spirit in the World*, ix.
227. Wacker, *Heaven Below*, 87–8.

References to the "blood of Jesus," the "power of Jesus' name," and "Jesus the only reality" continue to ring through the ranks of pentecostals. For many, Jesus is in everything—"Jesus in justification, Jesus in sanctification and Jesus in the baptism of the Holy Ghost."[228] Pentecostals everywhere find commonality in a shared admiration for Jesus. Whatever is to be said about the way in which God is universally present and active in the Spirit in all creation, that investigation presupposes that Jesus will not be relegated to some irrelevant place.

Directly connected to this commitment for pentecostals is the impulse to spread the news about Jesus across the globe. A personal commitment to Jesus Christ, Savior of the world, anticipates a corresponding launch into *mission*—the mission being the commitment to reach those who have not been saved in the name of Jesus. Any theological reflection in pentecostalism that favored speculation over action—especially the action to reach out to those without hope (viz., the "lost")— was viewed with suspicion by the earliest pentecostals. This passion always trumps any concern for philosophical or theological speculation. The mission to reach others always feels urgent to the pentecostal. From the beginning of the movement, pentecostals spoke of a therapeutic salvation (as healing from the disease of sin), ushered in the beauty of living like Jesus would—simply, promoting moral and family values, inspiring people to care for the poor, bringing healing to the sick, and launching evangelism and missionary projects around the globe. These are the tasks powered by the great pietistic energy of early pentecostals and continue to be the focus of most pentecostals today.

Conclusion

In this chapter, I presented what I believe to be pentecostal—that which centers around what pentecostals hold to be the sum and substance of their narrative: the deep work of God within the human heart. I explicated what I believe to be the three essentials of pentecostalism: revivalism, mysticism, and a pneumatological imagination. These, I suggest, can be found not only in the pentecostalism of the West but in pentecostalisms found in any cultural context around the world and throughout the movement's history.

I do understand that many believe the essence of pentecostalism as more explicit than what I suggest here. They would argue that pentecostalism requires the presence of the initial evidence of glossolalia, miracles, prophecy, gifts of the Spirit, personal internal confirmation for guidance, a shared set of idiosyncratic dogmas, priorities, and hermeneutics, instead. The problem is that many of those descriptors are not universally present among those who consider themselves pentecostal. Furthermore, those idiosyncratic descriptors do not seem to get to the heart of what is pentecostal. I believe something more primal is needed.

228. Ibid., 88.

I acknowledge that pentecostalism is globally diverse, which makes the task of determining pentecostal identity cumbrous. Cultures have disparate theoretical expressions, concepts, and priorities, and the pentecostals who live in those varied contexts may not reflect the same spiritual contours as another particular group (e.g., the classical Pentecostals of North America)—though some think it should.[229] Anderson contends in response to this: "The debate about the meaning of 'Pentecostal' and 'Pentecostalism' must conclude that it is a definition that cannot be prescribed."[230] However, the evidence suggests that the global pentecostal movement *does* carry identifiable shared essentials one can broadly use to define it.

I was careful to suggest that the road to identifying what makes pentecostalism pentecostal demanded a shift from searching for a simple taxonomic list of similarities to a more complex process of understanding. What it is to be pentecostal cannot be found by articulating additions and subtractions or by displacing and rearranging characteristics presented in mere aggregation. Something more profound than the sum of mere traces and impressions is going on in the story of pentecostalism; it is (in point of fact), a *story*, and as such there is the existence of a quale—something that carries a potential all its own that is capable of *becoming*. Pentecostals are a people who have a history and whose course has come equipped with divine endowments and tendencies that afford them to *be something* while they are continuing to *become something*. Unearthing this is not possible by listing items as they appear moment by moment (as though appearing on the *tabula rasa* of a mind), but as a biographical sketch, where the interplay of the predisposition and endowment of the divine mixes with how human beings experience and respond to that. This is where the unique religious expression known as pentecostalism emerges.

Broadly speaking, I have approached this biographical sketch of pentecostalism in four ways. First, I showed how Otto's concept of the numinous; the way mysticism functions; and the rise of the pneumatic impulse all lead to the predisposition of the human heart to be open to divine encounter. God is calling us. Second, I discussed the recognition that must erupt from the human heart (a kind of "groping," to use Otto's term[231]) in response to that predisposition—an inclination that leads to specific moments in a person's history where they encounter the holy and its

---

229. As one might expect, this sentiment is held by many pentecostals who live in the United States. Some feel this is evidence of a conflation of religious concerns with the "manifest destiny" that influences American pentecostals to think in expansionist terms. When this is coupled with the belief that the superior forms of Christianity are "made-in-America" (which dominates much of what Americans call "foreign missions"), it becomes a kind of neo-imperialism that often alienates US missionaries from indigenous, local leaders around the world. This hegemony is only strengthened by the US economic and military strength that dominate the world. See Anderson, *An Introduction to Pentecostalism*, loc. 299, Kindle.

230. Ibid., 231.

231. Otto, *Idea of the Holy*, 115.

consequent religious experience. Third, on the basis of these other two, there is achieved an attitude/imagination specifically qualified to engage in a religious expression (i.e., pentecostalism). Fourth, the previous three ways to approach this sketch cannot function apart from the context of some rational religious system—in this case, pentecostal Christianity. From this framework we can arbitrate labels for the essentials we find in pentecostalism: revivalism, mysticism, and a pneumatological imagination, which gives us language to account for the many pentecostalisms that have emerged globally, and, yet this labeling is sufficient enough to show how they are all parts of a one coherent whole.

I also highlighted a sampling of four evidences that emerge from pentecostalism's triad of essentials: *affection*, the *priority of love, theological openness*, and *being Jesus-centered* and *missional*.[232] Additionally, I claimed that both the essential elements of pentecostalism and their evidences are notoriously difficult to maintain. It turns out that pentecostalism is deeply vulnerable. The impress of revivalism, mysticism, and the pneumatological imagination fade; they are not static. Sometimes the moment is as 1 Samuel 3:1 describes: "In those days the word of the Lord was rare; there were not many visions." Just as food quickly loses its freshness, so too does pentecostalism can lose its spirituality.

Perhaps this is true because true pentecostalism, true revival, and genuine mystical experience is not under human control—one cannot make it happen. To be sure, pentecostalism needs human cooperation, but that is not to say that human creatures control it. Revivalism, mysticism, and a pneumatological imagination are engagements/interactions with the holy—not the solo performance of human persons. However, when it comes to universal evidences of revivalism (viz., affection, a priority of love, etc.), there seems to be a bit more responsibility to cooperate that rests on human beings in order to see them in full blossom.

When one considers the essences and evidences of pentecostalism, its vulnerability should cause great concern. Truth be told, one should not feel surprised at the loss of those essences and evidences but instead remain honest about seasons when revivals (viz., mystic sensibilities and pneumatic impulses) seem dull. Just as the feelings and intimacy of relationships ebb and flow, so with one's relationship with God. The dull times are described by St. John of the Cross as "the dark night of the soul."[233] The believer's response should entail the cultivation of humility, surrender, quiet, mistrust of one's own righteousness, and a deep remembrance of past encounters with God (one's Ebenezers), coupled

---

232. Though I assume that this list is not exhaustive, I *am* making the claim that these must be present for pentecostalism to be pentecostalism—suggesting they are *sine qua non* to the pentecostal movement.

233. See St. John of the Cross, *The Dark Night of the Soul*. "The Dark Night of the Soul" is a poem written by the sixteenth-century Spanish Latin Catholic mystic and poet St. John of the Cross to spiritually describe the spiritual crises that faithful Christians experience in their journey with God.

with patience and perseverance.[234] God will come.[235] They were all waiting for days in prayer at that first Pentecost—until "suddenly."[236]

In my next chapter I examine the rational influences that began to preponderate upon the pentecostal tradition—particularly in the West. Historically, pentecostals were influenced by a swirl of intellectual shifts raging around them as they were trying to articulate their views in coherent ways. These forces—religious and philosophical in nature—strengthened pentecostals in some ways but served to weaken them as well.

---

234. In Isa. 43:22, the prophet cries out God's call: "Yet you have not called on me, Jacob, you have not wearied yourselves for me, Israel." The pentecostal spirit is one that perseveres even through weariness until a refreshing of the Spirit comes.

235. Hos. 6:3 promises, "Let us acknowledge the Lord; let us press on to acknowledge him. As surely as the sun rises, he will appear; he will come to us like the winter rains, like the spring rains that water the earth."

236. Cf. Acts 2:2.

Chapter 3

THE RELIGIOUS RATIONAL INFLUENCE WITHIN EARLY AMERICAN PENTECOSTALISM

Introduction

In this chapter I trace the theological path of the pentecostal movement as it dawned in North America. In the first chapter, I described how the experience of God, though initially prerational and pretheological, cannot be separated entirely from rational/philosophical or theological contexts. When a person has a religious experience, some preconceptions about religion and philosophy are *always* present. In agreement with Rudolf Otto, I argued that no such thing exists as a religiously detached form of the numinous—that cultural/religious boundaries always superintend rationally on the divine/human encounter. In other words, rational reflection on prerational experiences is a natural, concomitant reflex informed or evoked by previous theological and philosophical understandings.

As I will show in this chapter, American pentecostals reflected on their revival experiences through the prism of their cultural values as Americans and with their previous religious understandings already known and familiar to them from their deep Wesleyan-Holiness and Keswick theological influences and expectations. This is to suggest one's cultural framework and religious history matter because once the moment a religious experience occurs, theologizing and philosophizing (of varied sorts) begin to refract the light of that experience through the lens of one's intellectual/cultural context.

The theological constructs human beings come up with to describe what a divine/human encounter is—as it happens or after it happens—are at best external to it. The descriptions themselves are like pieces of colored glass distinct from the light that refracts through them. The actual experience is less like the colored glass and more like the light refracting through it. The light of the experience has no color and no preference to what it shines *through*. It is just light. In this example, one could say that the classical Pentecostals are represented by red glass and pentecostals interpret their revival experience using the red-hued structure of the Wesleyan, Holiness, and Keswick theological traditions (explicated below). Whereas the Roman Catholics, represented by, say, blue glass would describe pentecostal revivalism from within their religious context with the bluish-hue of Latin Catholic language and imagery. Another group, like the Lutherans, represented perhaps by a yellow glass, would describe their pentecostal experience using the yellowish-hue of Lutheran religious language and imagery familiar to them.

This idea would hold true for the various ways or varied colored-glasses through which different cultures perceive, prioritize, and apply truth. A pentecostal influenced by the American philosophy of pragmatism would emphasize effectiveness, professionalism, and triumphalism. Biblical texts that value discipline, prosperity, physical healing, overcoming obstacles, and victory would jump off the page. But what if this individual was an African pentecostal deeply formed by the *Ubuntu* philosophy that emphasizes "a unifying vision or worldview enshrined in the Zulu maxim *umuntu ngumuntu ngabantu*, i.e., 'a person is a person through other persons'?"[1] In that case, biblical texts like Mt. 18:19-20[2] that welcome the "us-ness" of faith come alive to them as they encounter them.[3]

Ubuntu is an African word that captures the human experience as "universal" rather than as an "individual" concept. Clifton Clarke and Marcia Clarke write, "It is a Zulu word that captures the spirit of the philosophical foundation of African societies as a collective whole."[4] They continue,

> As *Ubuntu* holds up the value of ultimate human good through our inescapable interrelatedness, so too, African Pentecostalism presents a vision of human wholeness available to all by the resurrection of Christ through the power of the Holy Spirit to heal and deliver. There is therefore a sense that the healing and deliverance of our neighbor is inherently tied up with our own. In other words, "I am because we are; because we are, I am." The logical negation of this is, "I am not because we are not"; or, "I am ill because we are ill."[5]

---

1. Clifton Clarke and Marcia Clarke, "Church Unity and the Spirit of Ubuntu: Insights from the Global South," in *Pentecostal Theology and Ecumenical Theology* (Leiden, The Netherlands: Brill, 2019), 335, 333–58.

2. "Again, truly I tell you that if two of you on earth agree about anything they ask for, it will be done for them by my Father in heaven. For where two or three gather in my name, there am I with them."

3. Archbishop Desmond Tutu is a great example of how Christians in the African context carry the influence of the *Ubuntu* philosophy. He writes, "A person with *Ubuntu* is open and available to others, affirming of others, does not feel threatened that others are able and good, for he or she has a proper self-assurance that comes from knowing that he or she belongs in a greater whole and is diminished when others are humiliated or diminished, when others are tortured or oppressed." Desmond Tutu, *No Future without Forgiveness* (New York: Doubleday, 1999), 9.

4. Clarke, "Church Unity," 335.

5. Ibid., 336.

Clarke and Clarke contend that this is why "Africa, and by extension the African diaspora, has been the vanguard of church unity almost since the inception of the Church."[6]

As a consequence of the *Ubuntu* philosophy, the pentecostals of the Global South[7] tend to shun the individualistic mindset of the West that favors an individualized focus on success and victory. Pentecostals of the Global South have a unique commitment to unity and "us-ness" that is often absent in pentecostals in the West. Clarke and Clarke point out that there is an "African Pentecostal reimaging of *Ubuntu* [that opens] up new avenues for African Pentecostal pneumatology, in which the Spirit is not only engaging in personal deliverance but also national and even cosmic deliverance."[8] Though the pentecostals of the Global South carry different expectations rooted in different philosophical traditions and views, they are just as pentecostal as the pentecostals of the West.

This would also hold true for those of various theological, demographic, or psychographic come-froms: white male theologians from Europe and North America will have a different take from theologues of color from Latin America, Africa, or Asia. Female theologians who represent feminists (white women, Asian women, Latina women, African American women, etc.) have convictions influenced by their various needs and challenges that influence their theologizing of the divine-human encounter. Additionally, there are cultural *zeitgeists,* political and economic sensitivities, green concerns, and liberation concerns—all of which influence the pneumatologists who do theology within the pentecostal world. All these groups would have different theoretical descriptions and proposed structures describing the *same* divine/human experience. This remains possible precisely because experiences with God start out as pretheorectical and prestructural, and those experiences are vulnerable to the contexts in which they occur.

In this brief chapter I examine the religious rational influences that began to preponderate upon the pentecostal tradition in North America. I limit my focus to pentecostalism in the American context primarily because that is where I am situated. I contend, however, that one could examine any pentecostalism emerging in any context around the globe and be able to trace how its primal essences (revivalism, mysticism, and a pneumatological imagination) were or are impacted by each culture's theoretical expressions, concepts, rationales, and priorities. People who carry a foundational pneumatology may have the same numinous experiences, primal essences, and initial evidences but will not report identical theological reflections.

---

6. Ibid., 333.

7. Clarke and Clarke (ibid.) write, "The concept of 'South,' however, is an enormous generalization that includes a vast range of diversities with distinctions not only between countries as distinct as Nigeria and Indonesia but also regional distinctions between rural and urban dwellers in countries such as China and Brazil."

8. Ibid., 337.

Religiously, early American Pentecostalism reflected the theological hermeneutics of faith communities antecedent to them that impacted their orthodoxy, orthopraxy, and orthopathic expectations. When speaking of the pentecostal ethos of early pentecostalism, we cannot speak in blanket terms.[9] Theirs was a montage of traditions and tendencies that shared a number of similarities.[10] Donald Dayton in his work, *Theological Roots of Pentecostalism*, shows that most early pentecostals were Christians who already occupied a place of belief in some branch of the church-catholic.[11] Hence, as we will see, they carried a number of theological views with them into their culture of belief—views not generated solely by reflecting on their own idiosyncratic pentecostal experience.

The theological distinctives that appear within early pentecostalism in the United States were simply new approaches to their own previous theological predispositions. After their revivalist experiences, pentecostals did take a fresh look at the theological knowledge they had ferried from previous religious associations, which resulted in the new construct of the full-gospel, a reprioritization of focus on the charismata of 1 Corinthians 12–14, and a shift from solely Christological concerns to the power and immediate presence of the Holy Spirit. Though novel in some ways, their theologizing really did not distance them from being recognizably orthodox as Christians.[12] This gives us a clear snapshot of how pentecostal theologizing was molded by the religious convictions that were present antecedent to its emergence.

It turns out that early pentecostals carried a fierce commitment to a classical set of beliefs, such as trinitarian thought (generally held but admittedly with exceptions[13]), a high Christology, God as "holy love," the primacy of scripture, salvation as the restoration of God's image in the human race being therapeutic in nature (healing from the disease of sin), the gospel for the poor, the wisdom of God in creation, the renewal of the church, the restoration of all creation, a commitment to missiology, and the practices of water baptism and the Lord's Table—all of which showed their pledge to what the church-catholic had historically held to be *esse* within the Christian faith. Again, previous religious perspectives—already known and familiar to them—influenced their theological reflection about their pretheoretical and pretheological religious experience. This constituted a theological *gestalt* within American Pentecostalism that framed the

---

9. Oliverio (*Theological Hermeneutics*, 2) gives a helpful typological account of variations in hermeneutics in the pentecostal historical record.

10. Oliverio (*Theological Hermeneutics*, 78) points to these.

11. See Donald W. Dayton, *Theological Roots of Pentecostalism* (Grand Rapids, MI: Baker Academic, 1987).

12. See Chris Green, *Toward a Pentecostal Theology of the Lord's Supper: Foretasting the Kingdom* (Cleveland, TN: CPT Press, 2012), 2.

13. Some early pentecostals adopted a heterodox "Evangelical Unitarianism," which held that the Second Person of the Trinity was really the "fullness" of the Godhead—ergo, they called themselves the "Oneness" or "Jesus Only" group. See Dayton, *Theological Roots*, 18.

pentecostal hermeneutics through which they theologized and which (I contend) diminished the essences of pentecostal *qua* pentecostal.

The Rational Theological Gestalt in Pentecostalism

The pentecostal movement that emerged at the beginning of the twentieth century in the United States was not born independently *de novo* in a Bible School near Topeka, Kansas; it had a number of former influences that were hegemonic on its hermeneutics. As Dayton states, "The 'new' in Pentecostalism, especially over against its immediate predecessors, cannot be denied, but ... various Pentecostal themes may be traced back until they become less and less distinctively Pentecostal and begin to take the shape of similar themes in the more classical Christian tradition."[14]

We find, for example, that early pentecostals were using a shared religious language or "semiotic cathedral"[15] adopted from preceding groups (e.g., "Bible salvation," "old-time Pentecost," "Apostolic faith," "Holy Ghost fire," "Latter Rain," "Jesus-is-coming").[16] This means that many of the early theological views within pentecostalism were not endemic.[17] As Land attests, "The streams of Pietism, Puritanism, Wesleyanism, African-American Christianity, and nineteenth-century Holiness-Revivalism form a confluence which has today become a sea of Pentecostal believers,"[18] and the literature substantiates this. For example, the Puritanism of the sixteenth century emphasized a "latter-day glory," which foreshadowed the deep influence of the latter rain theme of classical Pentecostals.[19] Kärkkäinen avers that, "Revivalist movements inherited from Anabaptists and Spiritualists an intensive eschatological awareness coupled with the emphasis on the Holy Spirit's transforming power."[20] Seventeenth-century Pietism emphasized the way grace would help one overcome sin and the world (*posse non peccare*), which anticipated the way sanctification was articulated

---

14. See ibid., 36.

15. A term coined by Gerd Theissen in his work on primitive Christianity. See Gerd Theissen, *A Theory of Primitive Christian Religion*, trans. John Bowden (London: SCM Press, 1999), 287.

16. These *meaning-making* phrases were already present in the first publications of early pentecostalism. See for example, *The Apostolic Faith* 1, no. 1 (September 1906).

17. This is not to say that the theological positions held by early pentecostals were void of distinctions. To this point, Pinnock demonstrates that the pentecostal hermeneutic carries a unique and helpful, value-adding approach to all theological discourse. See Clark H. Pinnock, "Divine Relationality: A Pentecostal Contribution to the Doctrine of God," *JPT* 8, no. 16 (2000): 2–26.

18. Land, *Pentecostal Spirituality*, 37.

19. Dayton, *Theological Roots*, 37.

20. Kärkkäinen, *One with God*, 68.

by the early pentecostals.[21] The emphasis on the "heartfelt salvation through faith in Jesus Christ" dated back to at least as early as the Great Awakening of the eighteenth century.[22] The point is the thoughts, practices, doctrines, and theological and cultural habits of eighteenth-century Methodist revivalism impacted the thoughts, practices, doctrines, and theological and cultural habits of nineteenth-century Holiness movements, which impacted the thoughts, practices, doctrines, and theological and cultural habits of twentieth-century American Pentecostalism.

Overall, the general theological positions held by early pentecostals (e.g., the nature of God, soteriology, anthropology, hamartiology, etc.) reflected what was already present in orthodox Christianity.[23] Furthermore, many embedded doctrines within classic Pentecostalism were rooted in the more ancient historical, general orthodoxy of the Christian church. Though the connection to former Christian groups is obvious in pentecostalism, clearly "there was little to no awareness of how the [previous traditions] had formed their interpretive habits or how they were drawing on them."[24] Accordingly, pentecostal beliefs and practices were most often un-criticized reiterations of the ideas of their revivalist ancestors and/or what they believed to be the positions of the ancient church.[25] If a dogma from previous religious ancestors seemed to ring true to early pentecostals, there was no need for further investigation. This is how many of the doctrines and hermeneutical views maintained their force without being reexamined or reconsidered.

Though pentecostalism had been influenced by the Christian theological tradition generally, clearly from the historical record pentecostalism was directly influenced by Methodism and later Holiness movements. John Wesley's emphasis on sanctification as a deeper experience beyond justification and on the agency of the Holy Spirit in the Christian life not only resulted in the founding of Methodism but also contributed to the Holiness Movement, which later "became a major factor in the rise of Pentecostalism."[26] Methodist revivalism had spread in North America with such force that some historians refer to the nineteenth-century as "The Methodist Age in America."[27] Donald Dayton avers that we can "demonstrate

---

21. Dayton, *Theological Roots*, 37.

22. Wacker, *Heaven Below*, 2.

23. T. Jacobsen, J. E. Jacobsen, and L. Ahonen ("Denmark," in *NIDPCM*, ed. Stanley M. Burgess and Eduard M. Van Der Maas (Grand Rapids, MI: Zondervan, 2002), 80) hold that early pentecostals relied on past theological positions because they never imagined themselves starting new denominations—they believed they were a revival movement that would impact and renew the entire church-catholic.

24. Oliverio, *Theological Hermeneutics*, 63.

25. See Jacobsen, *Thinking in the Spirit*, 10–11.

26. Howard A. Snyder, "Wesleyanism, Wesleyan Theology," in *Global Dictionary of Theology*, ed. William A. Dryness, Veli-Matti Kärkkäinen, et al. (Downers Grove, IL: IVP Academic, 2008).

27. Dayton, *Theological Roots*, 64.

actual historical links and developments that will climax in Pentecostalism,"[28] especially in America.[29] Tony Richie claims that "the significance of this historical trajectory is nearly universally acknowledged."[30]

Because the Wesleyan doctrinal tradition is panoramic and variegated, it is not possible to collapse Methodism into early pentecostalism as one narrative, but clear connections are there. Furthermore, there is strong evidence that Wesleyan thought was a sort of vessel that carried many theological constructs for pentecostals, who then portaged them from the Methodist stream over to their pentecostal one, evidencing again that what made the movement pentecostal was *not* its initial theological hermeneutics.

I look here at two common principles or themes found in these revivalist streams that became insuperable within the original classical Pentecostal hermeneutic as it dawned in America: (1) the *role of scripture* as the sole ultimate authority for belief, and (2) *apostolicity*.

The Role of Scripture

French Arrington avers that the "hermeneutical tendencies of eighteenth-century theologian John Wesley bear tremendous implications for the study of Pentecostal hermeneutics."[31] Wayne McCown recognized that Wesley, who represents the revivalist ethos, emphasized the primacy of scripture and believed the Bible should be read in longer (chapter-length) segments in order for "its language and thoughts" to be "spontaneously interwoven into his mode of self-expression."[32] Arrington claims that Wesley was not just interested in "Scripture quoting or proof texting" but in "an integration of the biblical text into the fabric of his own thought," which would allow him to become a "living Bible."[33] Wesley saw the Bible as the primary and ultimate authority for Christian belief and practice and believed the purpose of its study was "to discover the will of God and then to act on that discovery."[34] To accomplish this goal, Wesley thought it important *not* to approach sacred text merely as "an academic exercise but as a devotional experience tempered by heartfelt prayer."[35]

---

28. Ibid., 38.
29. Ibid., 54.
30. Tony Richie, "Pentecostalism's Wesleyan Roots and Fruit," *Seedbed*, Asbury University, March 2014, accessed May 11, 2022, http://www.seedbed.com/pentecostalisms-wesleyan-roots-fruit/.
31. French Arrington, "Hermeneutics," in *DPCM,* ed. Stanley M. Burgess, Gary B. McGee, and Patrick H. Alexander (Grand Rapids, MI: Zondervan Publishing House, 1988), 378, 376–89.
32. Quoted in Arrington, "Hermeneutics," 378.
33. Ibid.
34. Ibid.
35. Ibid.

The highest authority for American classical Pentecostals rested principally in the Bible, then in the historically orthodox doctrines contained in the Bible in tandem with the Holy Spirit's role of illuminating those biblical texts and doctrinal truths. The unrefuted assumption was that the Bible contained all the information one needed for faith and practice. Daniel Warren Kerr (1856–1927), an influential figure among early pentecostals, writes:

> Scriptures are our only rule of faith and practice, superior to conscience and reason, though not contrary to reason … we are not at liberty to avail ourselves of any material outside of the Bible in order either to establish or to overthrow some cherished opinion … Our declaration excludes all outside evidence pro or con which is derived from mere observation.[36]

For the pentecostal, the Bible was central to how one was to navigate through any problems encountered in life. Pentecostals believed that "Scripture thus embodied God's thoughts, pure and simple."[37] Wacker adds, "In scores of ways, then, the early [Pentecostal] literature revealed the breadth and depth of the conviction that the Bible offered a compendium of answers for all significant questions. It needed only to be read, believed, and obeyed."[38] Wacker calls this pervading biblical hermeneutic among pentecostals the "principle of plenary relevance."[39] Their reasoning was that the Bible "had dropped from heaven as a sacred meteor,"[40] promoting the assumption that the Bible was errorless in addressing matters of faith, history, and science. Consequently, for at least the first decade of their existence, pentecostals used nothing but the Bible for *all* their educational programs. The reasoning went: *if the Bible was the only text free from error, why invite error by reading other books?* It was believed that no matter what one faced in life, one could "open the Book" and listen to the voice of God on the matter.[41]

In our last chapter I introduced Archer's "Bible Reading Method" where he claims pentecostals utilized that method as their hermeneutic in their Bible study. Archer states how this method evolved into "proof-texting":

> The Bible Reading Method was a commonsensical method that relied upon inductive and deductive interpretive reasoning skills. Once the biblical data was analyzed, it was then synthesized into a biblical doctrine. Harmonization

---

36. Daniel Warren Kerr, "The Practice of the Presence of God," *The Pentecostal Evangel*, February 14, 1925, 3, quoted in Oliverio, *Theological Hermeneutics*, 95.
37. Wacker, *Heaven Below*, 72.
38. Ibid., 71.
39. Ibid., 70.
40. Ibid., 73.
41. Wacker (ibid., 71) referring to pentecostal Quaker, Levi Lupton, who, when asked about whether Christians should wear jewelry, quipped that there was "but one way" to make the discovery and that was to check the "Christian Dictionary," the Bible.

was the acceptable and necessary way to synthesis [sic] all the biblical data on a particular subject.

In traditional scholastic Protestant Christianity, one developed a logically biblical doctrine with the preferred interpretive method, which was later dubbed the "proof-texting system." The Bible Reading Method was a modified form of the proof-text system. It involved looking up a specific word in an English Bible concordance, compiling and exhaustive list of its occurrences, and deducing a biblical truth based on the reading of the texts. This interpretive method employed by Pentecostals was the Bible Reading Method, which they had inherited from their Wesleyan/Keswickian ancestors.[42]

The Bible Reading Method is key to understanding the early pentecostal hermeneutic in scripture study. It was a commitment (though perhaps unwittingly) to utilizing Baconian methodology and Scottish Common Sense realism as interpretive hermeneutics (explicated in Chapter 3)—though in a much lighter version.[43] The Baconian methodology in biblical study fostered a tenacity for linking text after text based on key words or phrases (or connecting similar experiences described in sacred text) "where individual verses or passages of Scripture are interpreted in light of one another in support of a harmonizing interpretation, using each as a proof text to support the doctrine as a whole."[44] This was done in connection with Common Sense realism that asserted one could confidently distinguish identifiable and knowable truths, as long as one was a rational person.

Though higher criticism of the Bible and modern theories of inspiration were all the rage by the 1900s, evidence shows that the first-generation of leaders within pentecostalism knew little about those claims. However, as they heard of these criticisms and theories, they rejected them out of hand. Their apologetic was simply a commitment to *literalism*, which seemed reasonable if one believed the meteoric hypothesis of the Bible's origin: "If God's word tumbled from His hand without taint of error, then it should be read as literally as reasonably possible."[45] The practical hermeneutical result of this kind of biblical approach was a commitment to listen for the immediacy of the text as it was preached or read. This was central to the early pentecostal hermeneutic as it embraced the belief that God was speaking at the very moment the texts were encountered, lifting the texts from their historical settings and preserving them from the errors that theological, scientific, or historical criticism could deliver. Consequently, "little or no significance was placed upon the historical context, and the Bible was understood at face value."[46] Doing theology was about reflecting on primary texts

---

42. Archer, *A Pentecostal Hermeneutic*, 101–2.

43. Oliverio (*Theological Hermeneutics*, 81) reports that early pentecostals "employed a folksy version of common sense realism."

44. Ibid., 56.

45. Wacker, *Heaven Below*, 73.

46. Kärkkäinen, "Hermeneutics," 5–6, quoted by Oliverio, *Theological Hermeneutics*, 35.

after taking into consideration how the Spirit was impacting human experience in the moment of *hearing*.

Arrington agrees with this claim and asserts that for pentecostals, "at every point, experience informs the process of interpretation, and the fruit of interpretation informs experience."[47] Kärkkäinen concurs: "Experience came first; theology followed: 'In the beginning there was an experience and a testimony, then came an explanation in the form of a theological construct.'"[48] Arrington considers this hermeneutical position as evidence of an intense interest on the part of early pentecostals for engaging in an existential continuity with the apostolic church.[49]

This hermeneutic assumed that scripture did *not* need to be interpreted—it simply needed to be *heard*, surrendered to, and accepted at face value.[50] Oliverio reports that the consequence of this hermeneutic is that "a consensus emerges in which early Pentecostal hermeneutics is characterized—in general—as oral, charismatic, largely ahistorical and minimally contextual, 'literal' in its interpretations, morally and spiritually absolutizing, pragmatic and pastoral."[51] This is why Kärkkäinen refers to this hermeneutical stage in American Pentecostalism as the "oral, charismatic spirituality in early Pentecostal Bible reading."[52] He suggests that the sermon "was an occasion for the listener to immediately experience the biblical message rather than being characterized by a hermeneutics that spent its time exegeting a text in historical-critical manner," claiming "the preacher focused on the immediate meaning of a text." Terry Cross adds that in a faithfully expressed pentecostal theology, "the Spirit confronts a person with the reality of God in the story and in one's present situation, thereby affecting one's cognitive response to the event."[53] All this points to the pentecostal putative conviction that the narrative nature of scripture must be served by theology, not the other way around.

In the American pentecostal context, the belief that God was present in the text and that God could be easily comprehended by any rational person through a literal reading of sacred text shifted the pentecostal expectations from the raw pretheoretical and pretheological mystical encounters jammed with awe, mystery, and imagination (an essential of pentecostal *qua* pentecostal) to a

---

47. Arrington, "Hermeneutics," 384.

48. Kärkkäinen, "Hermeneutics," 6.

49. Particularly unique to the pentecostal hermeneutic was the privileging of the Book of Acts. They seemed to consciously imitate the experiences they found in Luke's account as they sought to validate their own beliefs and experience. See Vondey, *Pentecostalism*, 30.

50. The hermeneutic of literalism was not without problems. An unyielding literalism arose that was harsh and unyielding over issues like divorce and remarriage, and odd practices like snake handling and drinking poison emerged that seemed to be supported from a plain reading of texts like Mk 16:18.

51. Oliverio, *Theological Hermeneutics*, 51.

52. Kärkkäinen, "Hermeneutics," 6.

53. Cross, "The Rich Feast of Theology," 10.

pentecostalism expressed through a rational naïve realism. Psychologically, this made pentecostalism more manageable for those leading the movement. Though pentecostal leaders did not all take advantage of this, humanly speaking, religious control to religious leaders is like pure gold—a Siren song to people in power.

Apostolicity

John Wesley's commitment to return to the authority of the beginning of the Christian narrative and to the texts that emerged there was also embraced by early pentecostals. From the inception of the movement, pentecostals believed that they were in the time of the "latter rain," an underlying historical hermeneutic that placed their movement in a "new dispensation" where God's supernatural power was especially on display.[54] This Latter Rain Covenant motif held that "God's sovereign acts at the close of the age duplicated the pattern demonstrated at the opening of the age."[55] In other words, what God did at the first Pentecost, he was doing at the emergence of the modern pentecostal movement. On the first page of the first edition of the *Apostolic Faith* periodical in September 1906 was, "Pentecost has surely come and with it the Bible evidences are following, many being converted and sanctified and filled with the Holy Ghost, speaking in tongues as they did on the day of Pentecost."[56] This emphasis was carried over from revivalist concerns and was a strong part of Wesley's ministry as he advocated for a focus on "old religion" and the expression of a "primitive, apostolic faith." To this point he writes, "As the Christian Religion is not an Invention of Men, but the Work of God, it received its full Perfection at the Beginning of it. For who can imagine, the Apostles were ignorant of any Truth necessary or useful to Salvation."[57]

The commitment to return to the ethos of the apostolic church spilled into early pentecostalism (indeed it continues to be sacrosanct to the pentecostal movement today). As Land writes, "Pentecostals referred to themselves as an apostolic faith movement due to their desire to recover for the present age the faith and the power of the apostolic church."[58] The early pentecostals tenaciously held to the belief that God had providentially restored the apostolic faith found in the pages of the New Testament.

Azusa Street adherents believed in a restorationism that, according to Cecil ("Mel") Robeck, "viewed the church as returning to its New Testament glory ... Appeal was also made to the 'apostolic faith,' 'once delivered to the saints' (Jude 3)

---

54. D. William Faupel, "The Function of 'Models' in the Interpretation of Pentecostal Thought," *Pneuma* 2, no. 1 (1980): 54–5.

55. Ibid., 55.

56. Anonymous, "Pentecost Has Come," *The Apostolic Faith* 1, no. 1 (September 1906), 1.

57. John Wesley, *The Manners of the Ancient Christians Extracted from a French Author*, 2nd ed. (Bristol: Felix Farley, 1749), as quoted in Dayton, *Theological Roots*, 41.

58. Land, *Pentecostal Spirituality*, 50.

to demonstrate the relationship between the contemporary faith and that of the first apostles."[59] Here is Land at length on this point:

> When men and women came into Pentecostal services and experienced this eschatological power, this restoration of the apostolic age, they saw the Scriptures, themselves, and the world differently: the resurrection of Jesus as their own resurrection, the first Pentecost as their own "Pentecost," the crucifixion of Jesus as their own crucifixion. All these events were telescoped, fused, and illumined by the expectation that became the message of the entire Pentecostal movement: "Jesus is coming soon!" And how did they know that this outpouring of the Spirit was the Latter Rain, the sign of the imminent arrival of the king? Because they, like those with Peter in Cornelius's household, heard them speak with other tongues. Signs and wonders, even outbreaks of tongues, had occurred throughout history but never as part of such a large-scale restoration of apostolic faith and power.[60]

Oliverio contends that "the Latter Rain motif gave Pentecostals the narrative which provided the overarching story from which they identified themselves and their relation to the biblical text."[61] There were those who claimed that the real aim of the pentecostal ethos was to see the "book of Acts re-enacted."[62] This adamant commitment to restorationism is what precipitated the importance of scripture as the first and final authority in early pentecostal hermeneutics and elevated texts like the Book of Acts to being the blueprint for the church—though Wacker makes the important claim that the restorationism of pentecostals:

> represented more than a merely rational effort to mine the Good Book for blueprints. They yearned physically to enter the apostolic world, to breath its air, feel its life, see its signs and wonders with their own eyes. So they gave biblical names to their meeting houses and to the streets in their retreat grounds.[63]

Oliverio adds, "The original Classical Pentecostal hermeneutic was thus a theological hermeneutic seeking to interpret the Scriptures and the world by reforming Christian beliefs in order to return to the 'apostolic faith.' But the goal of this theological hermeneutic was living out and experiencing this 'apostolic faith,' not just forming true beliefs about it."[64] There was a deep longing within the

---

59. Cecil ("Mel") Robeck Jr., "Azusa Street Revival," in *The New International Dictionary of Pentecostal and Charismatic Movements (NIDPCM)*, ed. Stanley M. Burgess and Eduard M. Van Der Maas (Grand Rapids, MI: Zondervan, 2002), 344–5.
60. Land, *Pentecostal Spirituality*, 52.
61. Oliverio, *Theological Hermeneutics*, 47.
62. Wacker, *Heaven Below*, 71.
63. Ibid., 72.
64. Oliverio, *Theological Hermeneutics*, 31–2.

movement to honor the scriptures but to experience them as well, as the church of the Book of Acts had experienced them.

To assert being an existential continuity with the apostolic church was a Herculean claim that was ubiquitous within early pentecostalism. Of significance here is the problem of history. Historians must always be suspect of the impulse to say, "We" are the "Them" from the past. In his work, *The Past Is a Foreign Country*, David Lowenthal argues that as new generations arrive on the planet, they quite naturally find an affinity with the past because it seems to be a thing that is "fixed, unalterable, and indelibly recorded."[65] It is especially attractive because the future has a hazy uncertainty about it. Even the present fails to offer solace since it "lacks the felt density and completeness of what time has filtered and ordered."[66] In other words, we humans are drawn to the past. When the past is articulated in richly elaborated filtered and ordered words through story, it becomes more familiar to us than the nearby present. Additionally, the past carries the safety of no surprises or ambiguity and feels very homey when we think about it.

Then there is the issue of *nostalgia*, basically what occurs when we look back, but it is looking back in a fanaticized, daydream-ish kind of way that filters out all the mistakes and challenges of life. The past is utopia. This creates such a natural pull for people that Lowenthal quips, "If the past is a foreign country, nostalgia has made it a 'foreign country with the healthiest tourist trade of all.'"[67] In a way, nostalgia shores up a person's (or group's) sense of self-esteem.

It is just not credible to claim that the human proclivity for idealizing the past, along with nostalgia's fantasizing influence had *no* impact on the pentecostal longing to make the apostolic age its own history. Making this move naturally feeds a dream of recapitulating a bygone, idyllic, Christian era, and doing so serves to validate the beliefs, actions, and points of focus within pentecostalism. This impulse has always been present in human culture, and it tends to influence groups, especially religious ones who are pietistic and eschatologically energized. This is not to say that I believe the perspectives and theological priorities within early pentecostalism were just the result of human idealization or misplaced longings and not of God. I simply suggest that God may not have been the *only* influence, and that those influences were not necessarily pentecostal.

All of this shows that Methodism and the subsequent revivalist movements were the bulb from which the tulip of American pentecostalism emerged. Land confirms this understanding: "Had there been no eighteenth-century Wesleyan and nineteenth-century Holiness movements there would have been no twentieth-century Pentecostalism; and Pentecostalism is at any rate inexplicable without this theological heritage."[68]

---

65. David Lowenthal, *The Past Is a Foreign Country* (Cambridge: Cambridge University Press, 1985), 4.
66. Ibid., 3–4.
67. Ibid., 4.
68. Land, *Pentecostal Spirituality*, 39.

Conclusion

The noetic qualities within pentecostal hermeneutics did not arise in a vacuum. The religious influences can be traced back to several groups and/or emphases. Arguably, the early pentecostal theological view did not arise indigenously (other than some of their distinctive pneumatocentric idiosyncrasies). Many of their beliefs and practices were carried over from and native to the influences articulated here. Mark Noll asserts that, "Pentecostalism emerged fully [as] a culmination of emphases, many of them emerging from the Holiness movement and some more generally from the concerns of sectarian Protestants."[69]

Beyond the direct influences from these religious movements of the eighteenth and nineteenth centuries, we find that many embedded doctrines within early pentecostalism are less and less distinctive to movements immediately surrounding it and that they arise more from the historical, general orthodoxy of the Christian church. It turns out that what is generally expressed theologically by pentecostals in North America is not exclusively pentecostal, nor does it necessarily represent that which is pentecostal. What *is* important to note for the purpose of this research is that Wesleyanism and the Holiness movement cast a long shadow into the biblical hermeneutics of pentecostalism. Accordingly, pentecostal beliefs and practices were most often un-criticized reiterations of the ideas of their revivalist ancestors and/or what they believed to be the positions of the ancient church.[70]

Dogma that seemed to ring true—based upon catechesis from previous religious affiliations—remained. Overall, general systematic theology was not a priority within the early pentecostal theological narrative. The unique theological views written and spoken about by pentecostal thinkers did not stretch beyond the small constellation of theological concerns rooted in their full-gospel schema. They expressed little concern of the wider world of theology and, as a general rule, did not revisit historical categories of theological inquiry using their unique pentecostal hermeneutics. They also tended to ignore areas of theology more rooted in academic or philosophic ideas. Metaphorically, they had moved into an existing historical, "theological" house, though they updated it with biblicist fixtures, pneumatocentric paint, and retro apostolic-era furniture. However, it was the same theological house lived in by preceding generations of saints. Hence, the foundations and walls of the house (e.g., Christology, hamartiology, soteriology) were simply parts of the house they inhabited—largely, if not entirely—without inquiry.

---

69. Mark A. Noll, *The Scandal of the Evangelical Mind* (Grand Rapids, MI: William B. Eerdmans Publishing Company, 1994), 116.

70. See Jacobsen, *Thinking in the Spirit*, 10–11. Here Jacobsen asserts that much of the orthodoxy and orthopraxy of early pentecostals were vestiges from previous religious backgrounds/experiences.

I turn next to other influences beyond the religious ones and point to evidence that shows how those who participated in the pentecostal movement were also touched by the cultural and philosophical forces surrounding them. These forces were not native to pentecostalism yet were absorbed into the pentecostal theological ethos. Here, we must remember the vulnerability of pentecostal experiences (Chapter 1). Again, pentecostal experiences are malleable to and reflective of the influences that surround them. They never simply stand alone. Divine-human encounters may be the direct work of the Spirit, but when those moments are reflected upon (which, as beings of reason, automatically occurs), that reflection is invariably influenced by rational thought that is *not* only of the Spirit.

Next, I look at how pentecostals were influenced by secular forces as they articulated their faith. Though, as I have shown, a beautiful theological openness dominated the pentecostal narrative at its origin, there were unconscious, constraining forces already at work, diminishing the freedoms their early pneumatological priorities had afforded. These forces—philosophical in nature— strengthened them in some ways but also weakened them. These philosophical leanings limited the open and generous impulse within pentecostalism over time, which, upon reflection, gives credence to the Pauline warning: "See to it that no one takes you captive through hollow and deceptive philosophy" (Col. 2:8). As the evidence will suggest, the American pentecostals (along with many theological conservatives) were unwittingly taken captive by the philosophical demands of modern thought.

Chapter 4

THE RATIONAL PHILOSOPHICAL INFLUENCES WITHIN EARLY PENTECOSTALISM

Introduction

Besides the religious influences discussed in Chapter 2, there were also secular rational influences to pentecostalism that were philosophical, political, cultural, and sociological in nature. In this chapter, I look at how these forces impacted (and continue to impact) the American pentecostal ethos. Pentecostalism has proven itself to be a great translating and transforming tradition. From the start it has worked within the patterns of thought and conceptions rooted in whatever culture it found itself in and then transformed it so profoundly that in the end something new appeared. This is much like what was done by the early church as described by Patristic scholar, Robert Wilken: "Christian thinking, while working within patterns of thought and conceptions rooted in Greco-Roman Roman culture, transformed them so profoundly that in the end something quite new came into being."[1] This is one of the marks of authentic pentecostalism and helps to explain how it rapidly expanded around the globe.

Pentecostal *qua* pentecostal always emerges with the primal essences of revivalism, mysticism, and pneumatological imagination, along with a theological process that is always vulnerable to the influence of the cultures in which it emerges. What becomes problematic is that when the secondary theological reflections start, they offer analyses and conclusions that pentecostal groups fixate on. Once that happens, those analyses and conclusions tend to replace the passionate, pursuit of the pentecostal *qua* pentecostal. The result is a dulling of that which is truly pentecostal. The record shows that this happened in early American pentecostalism and is one of the central reasons that pentecostals' second-level theological reflections became reductionist as they tried to articulate their identity, which (I maintain) incorrectly redefined what is pentecostal. Returning to the metaphor of the butterfly, this reductionist work "pins" the butterfly to the display board and the theologue stops having to chase butterflies while they are flying free, alive, and full of surprises. When one's particular kind of theologizing kills what is being studied, it should be abandoned. The theologizing rooted in a foundational

---

1. Wilken, *The Spirit of Early Christian Thought*, xvii.

pneumatology makes theology a pneumatology of quest as it embraces the tension of having the nonrational with the rational; the pretheological with the theological; the apophatic with the cataphatic—it welcomes the conflict that enjoys the chase, catch, and release of what it is we are trying to understand and describe. This process (which is certainly not easy to maintain) will be explicated more fully as a pneumatological theological methodology in Chapters 6 and 7.

Just as we saw that there were strong religious influences on early pentecostalism in North America, the philosophical thought surrounding influenced them as well. By the time pentecostalism rose to the level of an organized movement (which happened relatively quickly) many pentecostal thinkers (in concert with other everyday American conservatives) reacted to what they perceived as threats to the culture and to the Christian faith. There were reactions against the liberal theological academy (who were using historical and textural criticism); to the scientific community (who were using the theory of evolution to eradicate the necessity of a belief in God to explain origins, along with quashing any system of ethics or morality rooted in metaphysics); and to the social and political turmoil that was rampant all around them. This influenced the way pentecostals thought about their faith and read their Bibles, which suggests again that much of the way pentecostals thought and lived was not *just* in response to the Spirit and the Word; they were also mirroring the concerns of the times in which they lived.

But antecedent to pentecostalism itself and what ended up supervening the trajectory of pentecostal theological hermeneutics was the earlier shifting of philosophical thought that led up to the twentieth century. We now turn to the arc of intellectual history that influenced the theological work leading up to and including pentecostalism. The historical record strongly suggests that *all* theological development after the dawn of the Enlightenment was done through one of two particular and restrictive philosophical lenses or intellectual positions[2] (which is why a discussion of philosophical progression leading up to the twentieth century is so relevant to this project). This will include an examination of the emergence of *foundationalism* and the prevailing theological methodologies and hermeneutics that sprung from it.[3] The research shows that the debates about epistemology and metaphysics that led up to the twentieth century left little intellectual freedom for theologians to do their work. It turns out that philosophical assumptions (visible and invisible) always limit the imaginations of those who do theology.

Though pentecostal theologians had a litany of religious convictions preponderating their theological work, they were also modern Americans; and as such, they *thought* like other modern Americans. Their philosophical and cultural

---

2. See Nancey Murphy, *Beyond Liberalism & Fundamentalism: How Modern and Postmodern Philosophy Set the Theological Agenda* (Harrisburg, PA: Trinity Press International, 1996).

3. The term *foundationalism* to represent this theory of knowledge as such is a fairly recent move in philosophy. See Murphy, *Beyond Liberalism*, 13.

"come-from's" colored their epistemological and hermeneutical lenses through which they interpreted the Bible and did theology. All theological views are dependent upon reason, and reason flows from a network of beliefs, theological doctrinal positions, epistemological grounding, and one's understanding of divine action in the world, along with other anthropological concerns. These distinct epistemic principles, which serve as guiding assumptions and authoritative foundations of interpretation, functioned interdependently to help constitute the unique pentecostal theological paradigm through which pentecostals understood the scope, context, and circumstances of their lives.

Philosophical views frame the arc of intellectual history. Philosophy is the process of evaluating the information and beliefs we have about the universe at large and the world of human affairs. There are several philosophical questions that all human beings seek to answer: *What is truth? When should I be convinced that something being claimed to be true, is true? What should I find persuasive, and why? When must I say, "Yes, I must believe that?"* What we think of as knowledge seeks to address these questions. It tries to answer: *What is the nature of the world around us* (metaphysics); *What makes change occur* (causality); and *How can one be assured that one's knowledge has veracity* (epistemology). Though a person may not notice its influence explicitly, philosophy matters. Speaking of the relation of philosophy to the culture at large, Huston Smith writes:

> The dominant assumptions of an age color the thoughts, beliefs, expectations, and images of the men and women who live within it. Being always with us, these assumptions usually pass unnoticed—like a pair of glasses which, because they are so often on the wearer's nose, simply stop being observed. But this doesn't mean they have no effect. Ultimately, assumptions which underlie our outlooks on life refract the world in ways that condition our art and our institutions: the kinds of homes we live in, our sense of right and wrong, our criteria of success, what we conceive our duty to be, what we think it means to be a man or a woman, how we worship our God or whether, indeed, we have a God to worship.[4]

The shifting views of philosophy always carry significant influence on theological development. The central reason one should uncover these often-invisible philosophical assumptions present in the minds of theologians is to create enough margin to suggest possible improvements (or replacements) when philosophical assumptions are proven to be less tenable, or when new ones seem more tenable. Though the content of theology has its own unique sources (i.e., revelation, sacred text, tradition, etc.), the way theology is categorized, conceptualized, and argued as theologians discuss and defend their content is the provenance of philosophy. We will see that the debates about epistemology and metaphysics at the dawn of modernity rationed limited options from which theologians did their work.

---

4. Huston Smith, *Beyond the Postmodern Mind: The Place of Meaning in a Global Civilization*, 3rd ed. (Wheaton, IL: Quest Books, 2003), 3.

The secular influences of philosophical, political, cultural, and sociological development deeply impacted the early theological work within pentecostalism. True, pentecostals historically resisted referencing or being open to influences outside of the Bible proper; however, that does not mean that pentecostals did not philosophize or live under the influence of various philosophies unwittingly.

A quick epitome of Western intellectual history is doomed from the start to be an oversimplification, articulated all too neatly. Even a brief sketch, however, of the cognitive path that leads up to the emergence of the pentecostal revival of the 1900s will help us see how and why pentecostals approach theology the way they do and may offer us room to recalibrate that discussion where and when appropriate.

Intellectual History

It is challenging for many modern people, including people of faith, to accept that *how we think* in our culture is the result of an intellectual history. In other words, we tend not to consider the fact that we do not think the way we think because it is natural to think that way. Not every person at all times and in all places has thought about the world in the same way we think about the world in our era and geographical location. How we think and see the world in the West has a unique intellectual history that can be charted, and it has changed over time. We think the way we do because we have been influenced by notional currents, winds, and gravitational pulls from the generations of thinkers who have come before us. Their work has shaped us. We are the inheritors of several intellectual and conceptual revolutions.

If you asked an educated man from the thirteenth century (and only the men were educated then) why a rock fell to the earth when he let go of it, he would reply that it is because the rock must move toward its predetermined perfection in God's great *chain of being*. The fall of the rock away from the heavens to the earth would be the rock's "final cause"; its teleology (Aristotelian).[5] If you

---

5. This line of argument is rooted in Aristotelian scholasticism. To be sure, a monolithic description of "premodernity" is not possible, but to get a sense of the thinking processes of the world from pre-history to late antiquity (from the theistic Christian West dating from the first century to the fifteenth century), see Georg W. Oesterdiekhoff, "The Nature of 'Premodern' Mind: Tylor, Frazer, Lévy-Bruhl, Evans-Pritchard, Piaget, and Beyond," *Anthropos: International Review of Anthropology and Linguistics* 110 (January 2015): 15–25; Peter Brown, *The World of Late Antiquity: AD 150–750* (New York: W. W. Norton & Company, 1989); Euan Cameron, *Interpreting Christian History: The Challenge of the Churches' Past* (Malden, MA: Blackwell Publishing, 2005); Beatrice Caseau, "Sacred Landscapes," in *Late Antiquity: A Guide to the Postclassical World*, ed. G. W. Bowersock, Peter Brown, and Oleg Grabar (Cambridge: Belknap Press of Harvard University Press, 1999); Josef Lossl, *The Early Church: History and Memory* (New York: T&T Clark, 2010); Lowenthal, *The Past Is a Foreign Country*; and Rowan Williams, *Why Study the Past? The Quest for the Historical Church* (Grand Rapids, MI: William B. EerdmansPublishing Company, 2005).

mentioned gravity, the same educated person would not understand and would think you are speaking about some strange occult force, not taking you seriously. Further, if you asked a person from this same period about what efforts were being made to improve the economic or social conditions of the times, he would not understand the question. The whole idea of progress and of changing one's environment for the common good was not imagined.

We turn to Yuval Harari to get a quick snapshot of the world as-it-was before modernity changed everything:

> Until the Scientific Revolution, most human cultures did not believe in progress. They thought the golden age was in the past, and that the world was stagnant, if not deteriorating. Strict adherence to the wisdom of the ages might perhaps bring back the good old times, and human ingenuity might conceivably improve this or that facet of daily life. However, it was considered impossible for human know-how to overcome the world's fundamental problems. If even Muhamad, Jesus, Buddha and Confucius—who knew everything there is to know—were unable to abolish famine, disease, poverty and war from the world, how could we expect to do so?[6]

For the most part, premoderns thought things were as they were by God's providence and one's duty was simply and uncritically to accept that. Beliefs, like the earth being motionless and at the center of the universe with the sun and stars moving above, were believed unquestioningly because those beliefs had been handed down from the presumed authorities of the past, not because those truth-claims had passed the proof of scientific experiment. The *authority* behind what was considered true was rooted in the *authors* who made those truth-claims—they were authors who were considered sages (or saints) and their opinions had endured the test of time.

We think differently today because something enormous happened in the West that shifted us from the conclusions held by the ancients. A history of thought has left a trail of breadcrumbs which mark from the *there-and-then* straight to the *here-and-now*. If we attend to this trail, we discover that humans think philosophically whether they are aware of it or not. We have inherited theories of being, causality, and knowledge that account for the uniqueness of the moment of intellectual history in which we find ourselves and with which we use to navigate toward what we believe to be the truth.

By the thirteenth century, Western culture was above all else *theistic*—all of life and nature was presumed to be under the loving care and surveillance of a personal God who had nothing but the good in mind for humanity, and whose power to implement that *good* was limitless. In *this* world resided transparent meaning. The European populace understood the divine purpose of their lives more than they

---

6. Yuval Noah Harari, *Sapiens: A Brief History of Humankind* (New York: Harper Perennial, 2015), 264.

actually understood the world around them. Their comprehension of the universe was simple: at every point it was the direct result of the divine will. The world was *enchanted*. Knowledge of the workings of nature was not a concern. In reference to this era, Huston Smith writes, "Christian man lived in the world as a child lives in his parents' house, accepting its doings unprobed."[7]

The culture of the day was a traditionalist one intellectually. Only a small fraction of the population was literate and educated, and for the most part those educated individuals were men training to be clergy. Whether because of the short human lifespan[8] or the lack of leisure from the demanding, relentless labor of a subsistence economy, people did not take interest in what was true or untrue about the nature of things. They simply defaulted to the long-standing habit of trusting the authorities of the past in such matters.

Though there were a number of ancient thinkers who had articulated various paradigms about reality and *the way things really are,* the early fathers and Doctors of the Christian church (particularly in the West) most often adopted Greek philosophical luminaries (e.g., Plato, Aristotle) as they attempted to explain the universe and the fineries of Christian dogma. After the recovery of his writings in the Middle Ages, many report that Aristotle was at the top of the heap in this regard and carried a privileged status up through most of the seventeenth century. The teaching of Aristotle was the center for discourse in the medieval universities and schools of the day and was known as *Aristotelian scholasticism*. By using Aristotle's schemata, it was believed that one could contemplate the true purpose of things and comprehend the reason for change and the operation of the universe. It was believed that through Aristotle's eye one could see the coherence of the universe, knowing *how* and *why* things happen around us. The chief intellectual assumptions that pervaded this explicitly Christian period in the West were (1) that reality was the result of and rested in a personal God; (2) that the way the world worked (the mechanics of it) was beyond human comprehension; and (3) that help for humanity (salvation) was found in following God's commands, not in an attempt to understand and master nature for the common good (which became the central drive for later scientific development).[9]

The second of these assumptions—that the mechanics of the universe exceed human capacity for understanding—began to unravel in the sixteenth and seventeenth centuries. During the high Middle Ages, thinkers began to explicate a cosmology that led to a transition from the premodern world to modern thought

---

7. Smith, *Beyond the Postmodern Mind*, 4.

8. Records indicate that the mortality rate ranged from 12–13 percent of children in Europe dying in their first year of life during the 1600s, with another 30 percent dying before age fifteen. The life expectancy for the general public that survived beyond fifteen was thirty-five years, though some poorer areas of Europe had a life expectancy of only twenty-one years. See Lisa M. Bitel, *Women in Early Medieval Europe, 400–1100* (New York: Cambridge University Press, 2002).

9. See Smith, *Beyond the Postmodern Mind*, 3–16.

and scientific analysis. As eyes began to fix on the heavens, unexpected discoveries were made. Interest in the creation itself began to rise as people began to look intently *at* creation instead of beyond it to God—or to some purpose or will of God (which was the pattern used in Aristotelian scholasticism). It was here that the work of Copernicus arrived on the scene (*c*.1543) and seeded an intellectual and conceptual revolution never seen before in human history. His claim of a heliocentric solar system over and against the Ptolemaic astronomy (the conventional thought within Aristotelian scholasticism) rocked the intellectual world. The Copernican revolution changed the conversation from the theistic *knowing-the-God-of-the-universe* to the humanistic *knowing-the-universe*. Thinkers began combing through nature's details, peering into them as the potential messengers of meaning. Soon, "the rage to know God's handiwork was rivaling the rage to know God himself."[10] The consequence of all of this was the dawning of modern science and what came to be seen as the awakened modern mind.

As the implications of Copernicus's work expanded, it was met with great resistance.[11] Challenging ancient presuppositions and presumed authorities from the past caused the whole intellectual project of the West to begin to crumble, and the academic, political, and social landscapes began to erode. Questions like *Is it possible that everyone who came before us had been wrong? Can presumed authority ever be wrong?* began to haunt the thinkers of the day. Ideas about truth and the nature of things, such as *What is knowable? What is possible or impossible? What causes the changes we see?* and *What things can be mastered by us or must master us?*, all began to be recalibrated. As this epistemological crisis arrived, it began to redress the thought, behavior, and the expectations of the Western world.

Modernity dawns in the discovery that the old methodology rooted in the truth-claims of presumed authorities and the use of deductive reasoning from those claims had led humanity into falsehood. *Even our senses had deceived us about the motion of the earth and the motion of heavenly objects!* How could human beings be sure of anything? As a result skepticism began to rage. The world wanted a new methodology that would lead to "certain" knowledge—a foundation for truth that could assure humanity that it was not getting it wrong again. This was the quest for incontestable first principles and indubitable beliefs upon which one could base knowledge-claims. Humanity did not want to look with faith to special voices or special revelation—that project had failed—they wanted to use their own independent reasoning faculties to arrive at truth.[12] The *vox populi* wanted universal, objective justifications for true knowledge which would be able to be perceived by any rational person. Knowledge—true knowledge—they believed

---

10. Smith, *Beyond the Postmodern Mind*, 6.

11. See Owen Gingerich, "From Copernicus to Kepler: Heliocentrism as Model and as Reality," *Proceedings of the American Philosophical Society* 117, no. 6 (December 31, 1973): 513–22.

12. See S. Paul Schilling, "Revelation and Reason," *Journal of Bible and Religion* 16, no. 1 (1948): 13–72.

could only advance when a new basis for its veracity could be located—a new, modern epistemology was required.

This ubiquitous effort resulted in the appearance of *foundationalism*, the theory of knowledge that uses the metaphor of a *building* to justify truth-claims. On this view, any system of knowledge is like a building whose stability and soundness are dependent on its foundation. Epistemic foundationalism claims that we can know some truths without basing them on any other truths, and that we can use *that* foundational knowledge to identify further truths. The central agenda for foundationalism was to overcome the human penchant for error by means of grounding the whole edifice of human knowledge on indubitable facts or ideas. Stanley Grenz and John Franke explain it thus:

> According to foundationalists, the acquisition of knowledge ought to proceed in a manner somewhat similar to the construction of a building. Like a physical edifice, knowledge must be built on a sure foundation. This epistemological foundation consists of either a set of unquestioned beliefs or certain first principles on the basis of which the pursuit of knowledge can proceed. These basic beliefs or first principles are supposedly universal, context-free, and available—at least theoretically—to any rational person. The foundationalist's initial task, then, becomes that of establishing an epistemological foundation for the construction of the human knowing project by determining, and perhaps even demonstrating, the foundational beliefs or principles on which knowledge rests. Viewed under the foundationalist rubric, therefore, reasoning moves in only one direction—from the bottom up, that is, from basic beliefs or first principles to resultant conclusions.[13]

The methodology of foundationalism basically overtook the epistemological and metaphysical projects of the modern period. Murphy writes of foundationalism: "If readers who are not philosophers believe they have not been affected by this view, I suggest they consider how we talk about knowledge. Scientific knowledge is *based on* the facts; suspicions are *unfounded* or *groundless* or *baseless*; good arguments are *well-constructed* and *solid*."[14]

Two systems (or paradigms) of knowledge emerged from the new methodology of foundationalism that promised to give rational human beings an absolute, uncontestable certainty about truth-claims: *empiricism* and *realism*. This new method of looking at the world allowed thinkers to completely reimagine the possibilities for human life. For those who believed in progress, there was a palpable sense of excitement in the air. What people had believed for millennia had been swept away. Human beings could know in a way never understood before (and in a way that did not require fideism). Certain knowledge could be theorized rightly

---

13. Stanley J. Grenz and John R. Franke, *Beyond Foundationalism: Shaping Theology in a Postmodern Context* (Louisville: Westminster John Knox Press, 2001), 30.

14. Murphy, *Beyond Liberalism*, 12 (emphasis original).

and proven concretely through experimentation. These new methods created a new world of knowledge where thousands of questions previously asked could be reexamined, and new discoveries could be had that would enrich humanity. This conceptual and cultural revolution was a historical phenomenon that gave birth to what is now known as modern thought.

It is impossible to ignore the revolutionary force and effect of the foundationalist methodology, especially in the arena of science: Kepler on planetary motion; Galileo on mechanics and motion; Harvey on the circulation of the blood; Fauchard as the father of modern dentistry; Boerhaave in physiology; Agricola in metallurgy; Hooke on elasticity; Torricelli on air pressure and the vacuum; Snell in reflection and refraction; Huygens on pendulum and telescopes; Newton on motion and optics and universal gravitation; Gilbert on magnetism and electrification; Pascal on the first mechanical calculator; Papin on the origins of the steam engine; Darby on the blast furnace (which played a critical role in the Industrial Revolution); Boyle on pneumatics; and the list goes on.[15] Progress and knowledge were married, and there was no turning back. The world had become *enlightened*.

However, the two philosophical positions that emerged from foundationalism—empiricism and realism—instigated a deep displacement of theology by the eighteenth century (from what had been done by previous generations). Murphy argues that in this era, "Science and religion stood for two paths to knowledge: pure reason versus traditional authority,"[16] which left theologians standing out in the cold. The problem was that the Enlightenment made man "the measure of all things" and made religion "a mere function of the soul, hence something belonging to this world and purely subjective."[17] Murphy suggests that this dulled the role of theology (at least until it made significant adjustments in its methodology) in public discourse. In order for theologians to speak in a way that made sense to the modern world, they needed to reframe the discussion. Murphy avers that theologians were left with no other choice "given the constraints of the modern philosophical worldview" than to develop "two sets of theological moves" that would be considered "rational and consistent" within a modern world.[18] These "two sets of theological moves" were grounded in the foundationalist tradition and ended up compelling a reshaping of modern theological structures. The first theological move was rooted in the *realist* methodology, which triggered

---

15. See John R. Gribben, *The Scientists: A History of Science Told Through the Lives of Its Greatest Inventors* (New York: Random House, 2002).

16. Murphy, *Beyond Liberalism*, 13.

17. Gustav Krüger, "Theology of Crisis: Remarks on a Recent Movement in German Theology," in *Harvard Theological Review*, 19, no. 3 (July 1926), 233, as quoted in William R. Hutchison, *The Modernist Impulse in American Protestantism* (Cambridge: Harvard Press, 1976), 332.

18. Murphy, *Beyond Liberalism*, 6.

theological liberalism.[19] The second theological move was grounded in the *empiricist* methodology, which precipitated *theological conservatism*.[20] For our limited purpose here, I focus primarily on impact of empiricism within early pentecostal thought.

The Philosophy Influencing Early Pentecostalism (c. 1900–25)

From the beginning of the pentecostal movement, empiricism had a foothold in pentecostal thought. Empiricism is an "outside-in" approach where human knowledge is garnered from external sense experience data that is then reflected upon as conclusions are *induced*. Francis Bacon (1561–1626) is often referred to as the father of empiricism; his work shifted scientific methodology from deductive reasoning to inductive reasoning. Bacon's central tenet was that inductive reasoning was the methodology that would lead to true knowledge. Bacon's methodology (cohered into the biblical studies of the pentecostals and other conservatives) is the simple process of reduction through description and taxonomy. This was the beginning of what is later called the *scientific method*. Bacon's methodology, referred to as the *Baconion method*, fostered the first wave of scientific revolution.

Empirical data is believed to be referential to *things-as-they-are*. When empirical language is used in science, it refers to *real* things perceivable through the senses. When this language was appropriated by early pentecostals, it referred directly to immaterial realities, understood as realities nonetheless (e.g., God; God's relation to the world and humankind, angels, and devils; the narrative of creation; the narrative of redemption). To claim that pentecostals were empiricists is to assert that they believed eternal truth was *directly* accessible to humankind—that rational human beings can *know* spiritual things as much as we can *know* natural things. The way one accessed theological knowledge that was *certain* was through the experience of reading (or hearing) the Bible, along with the confirming work of the Spirit within.

The pentecostal confidence in the world of facts came by using Baconian logic (the earlier version of the methodology of empiricism), along with Scottish Common Sense Realism.[21] Scottish Common Sense Realism contended that every human has a capacity to acquire undeniable truths through careful, objective observation not skewed by corrupted, sinful thinking (which Bacon claimed could

---

19. Ibid.

20. Ibid., 6.

21. Scottish Common Sense Realism was rooted in the thoughts of Scottish philosophers like Thomas Reid, Adam Ferguson, James Beattie, and Dugald Stewart from the eighteenth-century Scottish Enlightenment. It held that all persons of common sense could know the truth from a single unified order (via God's design). See S. A. Grave, *The Scottish Philosophy of Common Sense* (Oxford: Oxford Clarendon Press, 1960).

not be overcome) as they utilized their divinely given a priori faculty of naïve common sense. Oliverio affirms this point:

> But when it came to expressing their theological understanding, these early Pentecostal theologians still employed a folksy version of common sense realism. They seemingly did so because it was the default form of rationality among the American populace, especially among conservative Protestants. Common sense realism had been engrained into the American mind during the nineteenth century, and its epistemological, metaphysical and ontological assumptions were found to be conducive with Arminian Protestantism. It denied, or greatly minimized, the mediatory role of ideas, categories and contexts for human thought to relate to reality ... The original Classical Pentecostal hermeneutic combined this common sense realism with a strong affirmation of the supernatural. It employed this kind of rationality in regard to the supernatural as well as the natural so that Pentecostal rationality served as an alternative to a more complex and naturalistic modern scientific rationality. In doing so, Pentecostals rejected the mind of the disenchanted modern world, implicitly claiming that that mind failed to see spiritual realities and God's actions that are present in the world.[22]

The Scottish Common Sense brand of realism was not the standard inside-out epistemological realism that claims knowledge begins with mental ideas that only *resemble* reality. Thomas Reid, founder of this philosophical school, in a manner more consistent with empiricism held that what people experience with their senses is what is *actually* there. So, when a person grasps a ball, that individual is not grasping the idea of "roundness" but grasping a ball that *is* round. Roundness is not an a priori sensation in our minds from which we deduce the ball (consistent with Cartesian realism); it is the actual property of the ball that produces the sensation:

> [A]n "outside-in" epistemology. Reid took the position that God had constituted human beings to naturally believe the sensations we experience from the objects that surround us. The reason Scottish Common Sense philosophy is classified as realism versus empiricism is because of its claim that there is innate, a priori knowledge elemental to rational people—that God has implanted in all human beings certain beliefs, such as the existence of the external world, and other minds, the uniformity of nature, and the existence of God.[23]

This was its inside-out epistemological trait. Common Sense Realism (or *neo-realism*) held that human beings could know reality directly, that there were certain things that do not need to be proven before they are accepted, and that to

---

22. Oliverio, *Theological Hermeneutics*, 81–2.
23. Murphy, *Beyond Liberalism*, 32.

doubt those sort of things (self-evident things) would be a sign of madness, not intelligence.

By utilizing a synthesis of these two foundationalist paths—empiricism and realism—groups like the pentecostals believed they had found a guarantee that rational human beings could have absolute, incontestable certainty about their truth-claims. Princeton theologian Charles Hodge (1797–1878), a deeply respected thinker in early pentecostal circles, emphasized this "blend" of empiricism and realism:

> The Bible is to the theologian what nature is to the man of science. It is his storehouse of facts; and his method of ascertaining what the Bible teaches, is the same as that which the natural philosopher adopts to ascertain what nature teaches [empiricism]. In the first place he comes to his task with all the assumptions mentioned. He must assume the validity of those laws of belief which God has impressed upon our nature [Common Sense realism] … In the second place, the duty of the Christian theologian is to ascertain, collect, and combine all the facts [empiricism] which God has revealed concerning himself and our relation to Him [Common Sense realism]. These facts are all in the Bible … everything that can be legitimately learned … will be found recognized and authenticated in the Scriptures [empiricism].[24]

As a practical example of how this process works, consider how a person experiences a masterful work of art. The interchange between the art and the observer has been called an "event of understanding."[25] First, one experiences the art's materiality, shape, color, design, etc. (the outside-in view), but then there is an array of possible internal reactions: recognition, surprise, awe, shock, disgust, etc. (the inside-out view). This combo of the outside-in process (that presents the piece of art *as it is*), along with the internal inside-out process (that harnesses interpretations based on innate ideas that are *self-evident*, like beauty or disorder), can elicit a valid opinion about the piece of art. If this kind of process was effective when assessing areas of thought that are subjective (like art), it was thought that it could afford certitude when applied in the pursuit of the unchanging, absolute truth. It was believed that God had built this capacity into human reasoning precisely so human beings could be confident about matters of truth. This was a powerful and accessible process to the average person and became the chief methodology for discerning truth in pentecostal theological camps.

Soon after the beginning of the pentecostal movement, this methodology of neo-realism in pentecostal theologizing began to predominate. And as it did, it dulled some of the allure and charm of pentecostalism's distinctive epistemology and theological hermeneutic. Though pentecostals continued advancing

---

24. Charles Hodge, *Systematic Theology*, vol. 1 (New York: Scribner, Armstrong, and Co., 1877), 9–15.

25. David Tracey, *The Analogical Imagination: Christian Theology and the Culture of Pluralism* (New York: Crossroad, 1981), 102.

concerns of their revivalist, pietist, and holiness traditions, the philosophy of foundationalism, which was part of the basecoat of the culture in which they lived, began to bleed through. As pentecostals succumbed to this philosophical framework and its unique priorities, it served to construe the faith primarily into a message, or constellation of beliefs and propositions to which believers must give assent. Pentecostals thus began to deemphasize their unique Spirit-centeredness (causing a major shift in how pentecostals read sacred text). This began to blunt the beautiful innocence present in the inchoate pentecostal context—an innocence that did not prioritize exact characteristics or demand precise theological forms.

Early pentecostals had held that faith *qua* faith carried an inherent openness as faith was explicated with an appropriate dose of *mystery*—which needed to be conserved in all theological discourse. When the pentecostal movement began to mature, though, it unconsciously embraced foundationalism (in specific— empiricism conflated with Common Sense Realism) as its central heuristic tool (as did the other religious conservatives). The rigorous rational restrictions of empiricism became the lens through which they did their theologizing. This necessitated that they prioritize reason over the encounter with the divine (the primary concern of revivalism, mysticism, and the pneumatological imagination). Though it is arguable that all philosophical concerns (conscious or unconscious) served as a substructure to the now active voice of God through scripture in the early pentecostal experience, this changed quickly—particularly as pentecostals cooperated more and more with conservative-fundamentalist tendencies that radicalized *reason* over *revelation*. As argued earlier, pentecostals had always valued reason, but not at the expense of the charismatic dimension of the faith.

This exaltation of the role of reason ended up subverting the priority of the early pentecostal hermeneutic, which had held that theological work should only be done as a derivative of faith versus the result of objective standards of reason. The original pentecostal invitation to those interested in studying the Bible had been an invitation to *experience* God; now the leaning was more toward doing science on the text. This loss began to close the door for pentecostal thinkers to revisit and recalibrate doctrinal positions, as they had previously done. The prevailing hermeneutic within early pentecostalism claimed God was using pentecostals to bring new revelation and a more complete reformation to the church. This conviction gave way to doing erudite, scientific Baconian taxonomy of texts using rational Common Sense arguments. Though it may have helped pentecostals fit in with other conservatives (which carried some social implications of more open acceptance among them), I suggest it sated a key ingredient of that which makes pentecostal *qua* pentecostal.

The Challenge of Theological Liberalism

To put the theological reaction of pentecostals to the culture around them in context, we must take a short journey into *theological liberalism*. What may be surprising to modern-day pentecostals (including conservative theologians of all stripes) is that early liberal theologians responded the way they did and embraced the theological positions they embraced with *gospel intent*[26]—they were fighting against the impulse of the general culture to dispose of the claim that God is actively present in the world.[27] The new rationalism of the eighteenth and nineteenth centuries was boldly and defiantly fostering a sense of war between science and faith, and liberal thinkers fought back claiming that religion and science did not have to be adversaries.[28] The liberals, generally, did *not* think fideism was a necessary aspect of Christianity (as did the conservatives/revivalists); however, they still contended that the laws being uncovered by the scientists were not to be used in opposition to faith but should be used to put God's wisdom and power on display in a way that should engender worship.

In response to the modern epistemological shift to foundationalism, liberals believed that religion was in need of reformation—not with old, conservative thought (which held to the presumptive authorities of the past or to empiricism) but with wider and bolder appeals to the spirit of the age. Liberal theologian, William Ellery Channing, claimed in 1902 that "Religion must be dispensed by men who at least keep pace with the intellect of the age in which they live."

This New Theology imagined by liberals was nuanced, but three points remain particularly germane to our discussion: (1) the liberal saw truth as an accumulating and evolving reality and not as just something preserved from the past (which implies we know more today than those who preceded us, and we know less today than we will tomorrow); (2) the Bible gave us only partial, though, necessary truth; and (3) humanism ends up being the hope of the world because "God is immanent in human cultural development and revealed through it" (which is basic humanistic optimism).[29]

The positions of theological liberalism constituted a crisis for theological conservatives because they saw that liberalism was leading to modifications of the cardinal doctrines concerning God's sovereignty, human wickedness, and the exclusiveness of Christian revelation. It was obvious that what the Bible *was* in the minds of the religious was being renegotiated.

---

26. The initial liberal agenda was not the full, sometimes atheistic "modernist liberalism" that evolved later, and it carried an evangelical impulse. In 1925, Shailer Matthews (*The Faith of Modernism* [New York: The Macmillan Co., 1924], 34–5, quoted in Hutchison, *The Modernist Impulse*, 21) of the University of Chicago wrote, "modernists as a class are evangelical Christians … They accept Jesus Christ as the revelation of God … [Their] religious staring point is the inherited orthodoxy."

27. Hutchison, *The Modernist Impulse*, 20.

28. The conflict between religion and science that seems to appear almost daily in the parlance of the modern press and conversations over coffee has not been around long— no serious historian affirms that it has. See David C. Lindberg and Ronald L. Numbers, eds., *God and Nature: Historical Essays on the Encounter between Christianity and Science* (Berkeley: University of California Press, 1986), 1–14.

29. Ibid., 102.

Marsden claims that by the end of the Civil War, theological liberalism had abandoned supernatural explanations of causation of events (God and demons) for things that could be explained from the ordinary course of things: "The kingdom was not future or otherworldly, but 'here and now.' It was not external, but an internal ethical and religious force based on the ideals of Jesus."[30]

Matters became more complex as liberal preachers and theologians of this era began to wrestle within their own ranks about the relative weight to be given to scripture in assessing particular points of doctrine. A basic split emerged in the late 1800s within the liberal camp between those referred to as the "evangelical liberals" and those referred to as the "modernist liberals." Kenneth Cauthen defined "modernist liberals" as those "who stood squarely within the Christian tradition and accepted as normative for their thinking what they understood to be the essence of historical Christianity, [yet] had no real sense of continuing in the line of historic faith."[31] By the 1920s, many liberals believed humankind was outgrowing theism.[32] It was the "modernist liberal" group that generated the greatest reaction from conservative groups, like the pentecostals.

Ultimately, humanism began to overshadow any orthodox meaning of the incarnation, to which Hutchinson says, "The symbolic function of Jesus, the God-Man, is to teach mankind to find Divinity in Humanity, and Humanity in Divinity. By presenting us God and Man united in one person, shows us that both are holy."[33] The pentecostals (along with the other conservatives of the day) believed that the New Theology of liberals was diluting and secularizing orthodox Christianity and that it constituted a crisis in their minds.

I now turn to the conservative backlash—fierce and passionate—that ultimately erupted into *fundamentalism*. Pentecostal theologizing was certainly influenced deeply by both conservative theology (rooted in empiricism) and its more radicalized version, fundamentalism. But, as we shall see, it was not ultimately restrained by them (which I take to be evidence of the enduring presence of that which is pentecostal).

Pentecostalism's Overreaction

The conservative theological response to liberalism was that of defense—sometimes with firm apologetics that aimed to demonstrate that the Bible was a trustworthy record of the workings of God in the human race and other times

---

30. George M. Marsden, *Fundamentalism and American Culture*, 2nd ed. (New York: Oxford University Press, 2006), 50.

31. Kenneth Cauthen, *The Impact of American Religious Liberalism* (New York: Harper & Row Publishers, 1962), 27, quoted in Hutchison, *The Modernist Impulse*, 26.

32. Hutchison, *The Modernist Impulse*, 219.

33. Hutchison, *The Modernist Impulse*, 27.

with a strong denunciation of the controversialists themselves (at times using *ad hominem* attacks against any who abandoned what was understood to be the traditional faith). By the middle of the nineteenth century, many conservative church leaders began to double-down on their commitment to the veracity of the Bible and felt "that criticism of the Bible should be treated as the equivalent of blasphemy and infidelity."[34] This reaction grew in intensity as liberalism gained strength within the culture.

Though some within conservative camps wanted to simply give witness to the plain truth of scripture and salvation while quietly ignoring the error of liberals (pentecostals were often in this group), a growing majority felt it was their duty to attack all error openly and decisively. The hegemony within what was to become fundamentalism fell on the side of the hardliners who took an opprobrious tone— not exhibited by previous conservatives—as they critiqued the whole liberal enterprise with its attempt to discredit the cardinal doctrines of the Christian faith. These hardliners claimed liberalism as nothing more than the work and attack of Satan.

This reaction was only exacerbated by the disorienting swirl of social change that had been occurring in America during the nineteenth and twentieth centuries and that appeared to be increasing. During this time, the culture saw a rise in professionalism and specialization in career paths, along with a tremendous expansion of industry. It was an era of exceptionally gross materialism and corrupt politics. A great burst of industrial activity and corporate growth gave rise to a group of energetic entrepreneurs who became known as the captains of industry. Men like Andrew Carnegie, Cornelius Vanderbilt, J. P. Morgan, and John D. Rockefeller created monopolies that pushed the cultural, familial, and political landscape into chaos by uprooting the citizenry out of rural towns and villages and into urban cities with the chief goal being that of more efficiency and production versus living accountably within a community where one is known.[35] The result was a laxity in principled standards, which many perceived as a threat to the moral foundations of America. All of this created deep ethical, social, labor, and political crises whose solutions had not yet been worked out. A rise in paranoia over new global threats emerged (caused in great part by the advent of the First World War). Difficult American labor disputes erupted. Strikes were rampant. Terrorist bombs were set off in America, which fueled the rumor of foreign influence (i.e., Red Scare),[36] and the rise in the acceptance of Darwinism continued to challenge

---

34. Ernest R. Sandeen, *Roots of Fundamentalism: British & American Millenarianism 1800-1930* (Chicago: The University of Chicago Press, 1970), 106.

35. Marsden (*Fundamentalism and American Culture*, 21) writes of this period, "Change was rapid and doubtless often disconcerting. The social changes were the most dramatic. America was changing rapidly from a culture of small towns and country sides to one shaped by cities and suburbs."

36. Marsden (*Fundamentalism and American Culture*, 149) states, "German barbarism could be explained as the result of an evolutionary 'might is right' superman philosophy. The argument was clear—the same thing could happen in America."

4. The Rational Philosophical Influences

popular assumptions uncritically presumed to be orthodox. This gave pentecostals a great sense of urgency, which began to reverse an earlier disengagement with politics and society. They began to believe that the radical conservatives (viz., the fundamentalists) were right, and that the Christian's responsibility needed to reach beyond merely heralding and defending the truth—one needed to defend democracy and the whole of Christian civilization.

A Dangerous Detour

The rise of *fundamentalism* was basically theological conservatism on steroids, and it emerged primarily as a reaction to and as a polemic against radical liberalism and the disorienting moral, political, and social change. Conservatives saw these changes as a peril to Christianity, along with the whole of Western civilization, and reacted like forest creatures suddenly on the alert, bursting into a run, and giving rise to fundamentalism.

Historically, the conservative Evangelical camp of the eighteenth and nineteenth centuries became the fundamentalist camp of the twentieth century. However, not until the 1920s was the label "fundamentalism" popularized, and most Protestants were shocked at the cutting sharpness of the polemic it represented (as well as being disheartened by the level of alienation it caused among American Protestants). Fundamentalism came to represent an increase of intensity and a greater insistence on points of disagreement by conservatives over against liberal theology and scientism. It is clear from the research that fundamentalism was not something new; it was simply a more intense reaction to what was new in the culture.

Exiting Fundamentalism

The central theological project of fundamentalism (echoed in pentecostalism) was the defense of "old-time religion" and the truth of God's Word. This response and apologetic became a successful way to calm souls by promising to choke off the destructive trends playing out in the culture. The emphasis of the fundamentalists grew beyond preserving essential biblical truths to include the preservation of civilization that seemed to be drifting naturally into human depravity (a view in antithesis to the liberal view of culture). As a result, these fundamentalist/pentecostal leaders began to see themselves as more than religious leaders—they became moral reformers and protectors of Christianity—and they did so with rising fervor.

The weight of this new focus is reflected in the words of David S. Kennedy, editor of *The Presbyterian* in 1920:

> It must be remembered that America was born of moral progenitors and founded on an eternally moral foundation. Her ancestors were Christian of a high order,

purified by fire, and washed in blood. Her foundation is the Bible the infallible Word of God. The decalogue written by the finger of God is her perfect guide in her religious and social life. There has been some weakening of this moral standard in the thought and life of America. This is the result of an age of luxury within and freedom from conflict from without. There is but one remedy: the nation must return to her standard of the Word of God. She must believe, love and live her Bible. This will require the counteraction of that German destructive criticism which has found its way into the religious and moral thought of our people as the conception and propaganda of the *Reds* have found their way with poisoning and overthrowing influence into their civil and industrial life. The Bible and the God of the Bible is our only hope. America is narrowed to a choice. She must restore the Bible to its historic place in the family, the day school, the college and university, the church and Sabbath-school, and thus through daily life and thought revive and build up her moral life and faith, or else she might collapse and fail the world in this crucial age.[37]

The paradox for the fundamentalists was that they were fighting vehemently for people to stand up for the truths they felt could save the culture, which, ironically, was the very culture they believed could not be saved! Their eschatological stance was that of premillennialism, which framed for them to weight a message of salvation that was marked by escapism. D. L. Moody, who carried a central place in the heritage of the twentieth-century fundamentalism, claimed, "I look upon the world as a wrecked vessel. God has given me a lifeboat and said to me, 'Moody, save all you can.'"[38] Again, it was salvation that promised deliverance *from* a hopeless world.

This fundamentalist stance supported a view of history that was the juxtaposition of the forces of good versus evil—God and angels versus Satan and demons. This constituted a very nonhumanist-centered and anti-developmental view of history. What was going on naturally in human history and culture was essentially inconsequential in light of this predetermined apocalyptic battle—"humans participate in a larger cosmic struggle, the details of which have been planned and often revealed in advance."[39] They believed the unfolding of history was God's domain as he conducted new tests for humanity. It was providence that preponderated the shape of history—not God's mediated presence through humanity and culture (the stance of liberal theologians). In a sense, fundamentalism did not deal with history at all.

According to Marsden, the fundamentalist movement evolved into three principle forms: (1) those who "identified themselves with the fundamentalist

---

37. David S. Kennedy, "Christianity and the Social Order," *The Presbyterian* XC (January 8, 1920): 3, quoted in Marsden, *Fundamentalism and American Culture*, 159.

38. D. L. Moody et al., *The Second Coming of Christ* (Lawton, OK: Trumpet Press, 2019), 22.

39. Marsden, *Fundamentalism and American Culture*, 63.

tradition" but realized that modernism was here to stay and fighting it was little more than a futile jeremiad; (2) various groups within denominations that were *not* "purely fundamentalist" (i.e., Holiness and Pentecostal groups who had been "reshaped by fundamentalist example and influence"); and (3) the most extreme fundamentalists, who splintered into a large number of denominations and independent churches that "were mainly dispensationalists for whom strict separation was an article of faith" (this group was the only one of the three that proudly continue wearing the badge of "fundamentalist" to this day).[40]

At least by some measurements, the influence of fundamentalism turned out to be rather short-lived within the pentecostal theological ethos (though there were several common fundamentalistic traits that lingered within pentecostalism). By the late 1920s, pentecostals began distancing themselves from the internecine arguments of the fundamentalists over both theological and societal issues. To trace the path of the departure of pentecostals and other conservatives from the fundamentalists, one must begin with how fundamentalist groups felt the call to action because of what they perceived to be the deleterious Darwinian version of evolution invading the public schools (especially poignant with the formation of public high schools on the rise). Through biology textbooks that favored teaching Darwin's version, evolutionary ideas were spilling into the general population and into the church, alarming and inflaming fundamentalists. Fundamentalist preachers, parents, and even politicians had already come to believe that Darwinian evolutionary thought was eroding Western civilization, claiming that it enhanced criminal behavior and helped to incite the First World War. William Jennings Bryan, the Democratic politician and revered church leader, claimed in 1925, "The same science that manufactured poisonous gasses to suffocate soldiers is preaching that man has a brute ancestry and eliminating the miraculous and the supernatural from the Bible."[41]

Early on, many of the arguments offered by the fundamentalists were cogent, and their criticisms of modern culture were representative of the popular concerns of a majority of Americans. However, it was the *way* they approached those issues that caused other groups to reject their voice (though they may have been sympathetic to their concerns). In 1929, Walter Lippman argued that though fundamentalists actually *did* have something to say that was worth listening to, "In actual practice [fundamentalism] has become entangled with all sorts of bizarre and barbarous agitations with the Ku Klux Klan, with fanatical prohibition, with the 'anti-evolution laws' and with much persecution and intolerance."[42] He went on to claim that the bumptious practices of the fundamentalists showed "that the

---

40. Ibid., 195.
41. A comment made by Bryan to a reporter covering the famous Scopes trial, quoted by Numbers, *The Creationists*, 56.
42. Walter Lippman, *A Preface to Morals* (New York: Macmillan, 1929), 31–2, Quoted in Marsden, *Fundamentalism and American Culture*, 191.

central truth which fundamentalists have grasped, no longer appeals to the best brains and the good sense of the modern community, and that the movement is recruited largely from the isolated, the inexperienced, and the uneducated."[43] Marsden reports that "These bizarre developments in fundamentalist activities meant that in the years after 1925 it became increasingly difficult to take fundamentalism seriously."[44]

Though pentecostal and Holiness groups had shared a number of fundamentalist tendencies with the fundamentalists, disagreements prevailed. I will mention three. First, pentecostals believed that the Darwinian version of evolution was dangerous; however, they were swift to deem the issue of evolution as far less important than salvation. In 1926, the bombastic pentecostal preacher Andrew Johnson (1875–1959) claimed in the *Pentecostal Herald*, "There is nothing like an old-fashioned, soul-saving revival of Holy Ghost religion. So, let it be distinctly understood that the lectures on Evolution are absolutely secondary to the main line work of intense, soul-saving evangelism to which we have been called and in which we expect to remain."[45]

Second, fundamentalists held to a fixed view of revealed truth found solely in scripture that they considered true for all people at all times, whereas pentecostals embraced a more dynamic, anti-creedal truth and saw God working new things into the world that had not yet been revealed. According to K. A. Smith: "[Pentecostalism] contests the 'cognitive fundamentalism' that seems to characterize philosophical understandings of Christian faith, construing Christianity as primarily a 'message,' a constellation of beliefs and propositions to which believers give assent."

The result is a reductionism: religion, which is primarily a "form of life" and lived experience, is slimmed down to the more abstract phenomena of beliefs and doctrines. The rich, dynamic, and lived experience of worshiping communities is reduced to propositions that can be culled from artifacts produced by these communities (e.g., documents, creeds, scriptures).[46]

Third, many fundamentalists had by and large relegated the supernatural move of God (through miracles and gifts of the Spirit) to a past dispensation, which was a key distinction of the pentecostal ethos that pentecostals were unwilling to abandon. Veli-Matti Kärkkäinen claims:

> Charismatic, eschatalogically flavored spirituality lies at the heart of the Pentecostal phenomenon … The starting point is the essence of Pentecostalism with "its persistent emphasis upon the supernatural within the community," and the supernaturalistic horizon of pentecostalism "marked by living in and

---

43. Ibid.
44. Marsden, *Fundamentalism and American Culture*, 191.
45. Andrew Johnson, "The Evolution Articles," *Pentecostal Herald* 38 (September 29, 1926): 6. See Numbers, *Creationists*, 336.
46. Smith, *Thinking in Tongues*, 111.

from the eschatological presence of God." ... Pentecostalism's manifestations of charismatic gifts "offered invincible certitude that the supernatural claims of the gospel were really true."[47]

Archer adds:

> The supernaturalistic environment of Pentecostal culture was in direct opposition to the dominant modernistic, naturalistic worldview that was pervading the culture in the nineteenth—and twentieth centuries, *plus*, the existential nature of the supernaturalistic environment also became the greatest point of contention among [pentecostals] closest sisters—the Holiness folk and their cousins—the Fundamentalists. This meant that the Pentecostals were on a direct collision course with modernity and cessationist Christianity.[48]

Additionally, and of particular consequence, pentecostals found the often bizarre and combative style of the fundamentalists increasingly untenable and began looking for an alliance with the more moderate groups—groups who went by the moniker, *Evangelical*. Oliverio agrees: "While Pentecostals found much to affirm in Fundamentalism, they were only able to partially integrate the hermeneutics of Fundamentalism into their own. The broader Evangelical tradition which was about to reemerge in a more moderate coalition was more amenable."[49] Marsden adds, "Most of the other groups that had been touched by the fundamentalist experience of the 1920s re-emerged in the new post-fundamentalist coalition. Their basic attitude toward culture is suggested by their successful appropriation of the more culturally respectable term 'evangelical.'"

The Longing to Belong

We must consider (at least tangentially) that prior to their alignment with the fundamentalists, pentecostals had been labeled as the "disinherited" and relegated by the intellectual elite as those of a "low social status" with "poor or no education."[50] Archer alleges that "Sociologists, psychologists, and many historians have predominately explained the origin, attraction and expansion of the Pentecostal movement through the utilization of some form of Social Deprivation theory, which includes social disorganization and/or psychologically defective individuals."[51] Archer asserts that this is a misrepresentation of the data

---

47. Veli-Matti Kärkkäinen, *Toward a Pneumatological Theology: Pentecostal and Ecumenical Perspectives on Ecclesiology, Soteriology, and Theology of Mission*, ed. Amos Yong (Lanham, MD: University Press of America, 2002), 4.
    48. Archer, *A Pentecostal Hermeneutic*, 43 (emphasis original).
    49. Oliverio, *Theological Hermeneutics*, 113.
    50. Archer, *A Pentecostal Hermeneutic*, 31.
    51. Ibid., 24.

and the neglect of evidence that contradicts that conclusion, but it does point to the validity that pentecostals have often been pushed out of the cultural center and have felt as if they have been the butt of some social joke.

This labeling, however, did not begin with the embarrassing association with the fundamentalists iterated above, nor had it begun with the pentecostals themselves. Revivalists in general had been receiving a black eye from the culture's elite since emerging in the late eighteenth century.[52] Though most scholars believe the observation that pentecostals were from the wrong side of the tracks has been overstated, there is a seed of truth to the claim. Archer admits the point: "The Pentecostal movement was formed from the margins of mainstream society and was birthed as an 'oppressed people.'"[53]

After the 1925 Scopes Trial, the ridicule of fundamentalist groups in popular American culture rose to a pitch that was both unfair and embarrassing for all the revivalist groups. However, unlike the fundamentalists who came to celebrate and to define their faithfulness to God through separation, pentecostals as a group seem to have had a deeper commitment to unity and community, which may be the real motivation behind why pentecostals want to belong—an ecumenical impulse (at least as it emerged). Perhaps that is why Oliverio claims pentecostals began to shift toward the evangelicals,[54] or perhaps it was a little of this and a little of that. Archer insists that the switch in hermeneutics to a more evangelical one happened because pentecostals "were attempting to prove themselves and adapt to the theological and hermeneutical standards of their conservative siblings."[55] Kärkkäinen also affirms this view, pointing out that pentecostals joined the National Association of Evangelicals "motivated by the desire to receive acceptance from the larger Evangelical movement."[56] He explains the importance of this: "When Pentecostalism was birthed it existed on the fringes of the society and ecclesial spectrum. Pentecostals were both rejected and eschewed by those who had power. In order to improve their status, Pentecostals sought for more respected colleagues in society."[57]

Conclusion

In this chapter I have presented some of the rational philosophical influences that impacted the early theological work within the pentecostal ethos. We have seen that, though pentecostals were avid revivalists, their thinking and lives were also influenced by the cross-pressures and concerns of forces outside their religious

---

52. See Niebuhr, *Social Sources*, 30–1.
53. Archer, *A Pentecostal Hermeneutic*, 24.
54. Oliverio, *Theological Hermeneutics*, 83–184.
55. Ibid., 108.
56. Kärkkäinen, *Toward a Pneumatological Theology*, 7–8.
57. Ibid., 6–7.

sensibilities (e.g., philosophical, social, cultural). Just like Smith's "pair of glasses" metaphor above, pentecostals and other conservatives may not have noticed that they were being influenced by the undercurrents of empiricism and Common Sense Realism as they read sacred text, but they were.

This influence only became more radicalized as pentecostals became influenced by the fundamentalists and the seductive hope and longing for certitude. Fundamentalism asserts a clear description and analysis of what it considers factual. It is a view that demands absolute certainty within a fixed, infallible system of beliefs. It is a view that carries a deep exclusivism and the dichotomizing of issues—there can only be black and white, even if that can only be accomplished by exerting a Promethean certitude.

As pentecostals navigated away from fundamentalism, they intentionally moved toward Evangelicalism. It would be a mistake to assume that evangelicals and pentecostals were homogeneous in their approach to theological knowledge— there were a number of nuanced differences—but Oliverio claims that the dominance of Evangelical thought "has emerged as the major theoretical and academic hermeneutic of contemporary American Classical Pentecostalism."[58]

As pointed out in Chapter 2, pentecostalism was a movement whose members had been grounded theologically in antecedent groups and had not done much of its own theological work to support their beliefs and experiences. As pentecostals began theologizing, they reinterpreted scripture around new categories under the banner of the "full gospel." This process was in step with the general Protestant view of scripture being authoritative, but pentecostals saw their experience as authoritative too. In the early classical Pentecostal hermeneutic, scripture and experience were used dialogically to interpret each other, and they utilized both Common Sense Realism and a supernaturalistic orientation to identify what they believed to be normative Christianity. Oliverio asserts that this nascent pentecostal hermeneutic "ended up beginning a new Christian tradition, opening up new theological readings of both the biblical texts and all of life. It provided a new imagination for new forms of Christian experience."[59] Oliverio is pointing to one of the essentials (viz., pneumatological imagination [see Chapter 1]) of pentecostal *qua* pentecostal—which must be carefully protected.

What should be recognized and appreciated is that pentecostals could not remain categorized as "modernist conservatives" with the accompanying epistemological restrictions articulated above. The modernist philosophical siege was not native to pentecostals. Early on, they did not want to fight the challenges posed by liberalism as their central focus—they were simply responding to the world swirling around them with counter-cultural practices of a people who seemed to be experiencing heavenly things.

It should be noted that there were many other influences (beyond the scope of a full investigation in this chapter) at play in the development of the pentecostal

---

58. Oliverio, *Theological Hermeneutics*, 182.
59. Ibid., 83.

hermeneutical construct—the emergence of pragmatism, radical American individualism, or the milieu of dispensationalism. We must be willing to admit, at least for the sake of argument, that the motivations within pentecostalism in the American context arose partly from religious conviction and the work of the Spirit, and partly from an unwitting submission to modern philosophical hegemony and the cultural and social contingencies of the day. To claim that pentecostalism has been influenced by philosophy and culture along with its religious influences, as this writing claims to be true, is not an attack on its divine origins or influences. Christianity has always been in dynamic communication with the contexts in which it is found.

The point is that the way pentecostals thought and believed involved more than their choice to simply "follow the Lord." Theological conservatism within foundationalism (along with its correlative Baconian method and Irish Common Sense Realism) is not a position that is inherently pentecostal. It is just what pentecostals used—like wearing britches with buttons instead of zippers. Foundationalism just happened to be there when pentecostalism emerged. This commends the case that Spirit-filled people are really just regular people too, influenced by philosophical, social, and cultural forces that surround them—maybe more deeply than they care to admit.

Pentecostals may be the Lord's people, but that does not mean that *everything* they think and believe is "from the Lord." And if pentecostals want to carry a prophetic voice in an uncertain world rife with epistemological shifts and metaphysical reimagining, they must be critical about how they are thinking about things and be willing to recalibrate their thinking in ways that are fresh, yet faithful. However, one should also heed the warning of Paul: "Examine yourselves to see whether you are in the faith; test yourselves" (2 Cor. 13:5). It is entirely possible that pentecostals (as all Christian groups) theologically and philosophically wander in and out of what is true faith.

To be sure, beautiful flashes of sheer innocence and intellectual humility dance in the early record of the pentecostal movement. In the words of Pinnock, these early impulses produced a "dynamic not rationalistic" ethos where "openness to the Spirit" was "integrated in the method, so that there would be fresh contexualizations in the service of missions."[60] But, as we have seen, there were other forces afoot—forces that, in my opinion, have proven deleterious to the pentecostal theological process and to what is being proffered here as pentecostal.

Next, I examine how foundationalism and the certitude it engendered began to give way to new ways of looking at the world—ways that carried iconoclastic hermeneutical shifts regarding knowledge, which, surprisingly, recapitulated some of the arguments of the premodern world as well as providing a return to the priority and thought of what is truly pentecostal.

---

60. Pinnock, "Divine Relationality," 4.

Chapter 5

A RETURN TO PENTECOSTAL *QUA* PENTECOSTAL

Introduction

One of the central goals of this writing is to show how pentecostal *qua* pentecostal (described in Chapter 1 from its essences of revivalism, mysticism, and a pnuematological imagination) has been deeply influenced (at least in the North American context) by rational religious (Chapter 2) and philosophical (Chapter 3) forces. Ultimately, these rational forces affected the way pentecostals interpreted their experiences and the way they superintended their theologizing. I contend that these kinds of influences (though they may differ from place to place) are unceasingly present wherever a form of pentecostalism emerges. The pentecostal movement is like a ship at sea influenced—not only by the steering of its pilots (viz., theologues), but by the winds and currents external to it (viz., rational impressions). Therefore, pentecostals and pentecostal theologians should commit to identifying forces that are coming to bear upon them and to discern if those forces are causing the movement to drift away from that which is pentecostal *qua* pentecostal—adjusting as needed. This is the church's historical commitment to *semper reformanda*.

In the last chapter I described how two philosophical positions (empiricism and realism) reshaped the theological structures of the Christian West into what became known as theological liberalism and theological conservatism. In this chapter I consider another intellectual revolution—one as dramatic as the one precipitated by Copernicus. Like the Copernican Revolution, this one transfigured everything from science to theology. This revolution began to dismantle and deconstruct modernity along with its certitude. This move, which extends into our present historical moment, unfolds as a complex and desultory process and it lands the Western intellectual tradition in a philosophical space often referred to as *postmodernism*. Though the term "postmodernism" suggests that we are at the end of a historical period marking the end of modernity, some feel that is an overstatement.[1] That said, a dramatic philosophical shift has occurred that

---

1. There is no universal confidence that "postmodernism" is an actual "era," as some contend it is only another development within modernism. Nancey Murphy and James

cannot be ignored. James K. A. Smith states, "Nobody thinks [postmodernism] is a definitive 'school of thought' or even a unified phenomenon. But it seems to remain a useful heuristic term, a loose moniker that names a certain Zeitgeist (or Angst) and functions as a big tent that gathers together a constellation of conversations and concerns that articulate a number of different critiques of modernity."[2]

I hesitate to use the term postmodern because within many conservative theological circles (including pentecostal ones) it has become a pejorative designation that is merely a codeword for relativism and, thereby, rejected out-of-hand. Some pentecostal thinkers have expressed strong reactions against the "postmodern bandwagon" within pentecostal academic ranks because they contend that postmodernism is filled with "fallacious arguments and flawed premises."[3] Though the secular philosophical postmodern project can lead to relativism, there are constructive criticisms to be found therein. Even Robert Menzies, who is decidedly anti-postmodernist, admits that "aspects of postmodern hermeneutics help in the growth of knowledge."[4] Smith writes, "While the term postmodern has of late been justly questioned and even discarded as overused and abused, it nevertheless remains helpful as a heuristic term for describing important shifts in Western culture and society."[5]

Whatever term ends up describing the transformation of thought from foundationalism to what we now see, the change in thinking (which we will call "postmodernism" for this writing) has proven to be as radical a revolution as the shift from premodernism to modernism. Postmodernism offers new solutions—with new theories of knowledge, language, and causation to be considered. And, as I will suggest, it offers a philosophical way *back* to what I have defined herein as pentecostal.

Wm. McClendon ("Distinguishing Modern and Postmodern Theologies," *Modern Theology* 5, no. 3 [April 1989]: 191-214) write, "Will the term 'postmodern' have any lasting application in philosophy and theology? From a historian's viewpoint it is too soon to say."

2. James K. A. Smith, "The Logic of Incarnation: Towards a Catholic Postmodernism," in *The Logic of Incarnation: James K. A. Smith's Critique of Postmodern Religion* (With Contribution and Response by James K. A. Smith), ed. Neal DeRoo and Brian Lightbody (Eugene, OR: Pickwick Publications, 2009), 3-4.

3. Oliverio, *Theological Hermeneutics*, 200. Two examples of the kind of rejoinder encountered within the academy are: Robert Menzies, "Jumping off the Postmodern Bandwagon," *Pneuma* 16, no. 1 (Spring 1994): 115-20; and John C. Poirier and B. Scott Lewis, "Pentecostal and Postmodernist Hermeneutics: A Critique of Three Conceits," *JPT* 15, no. 2 (October 2006): 3-21.

4. Quoted in Oliverio, *Theological Hermeneutics*, 199.

5. James K. A. Smith, *The Fall of Interpretation: Philosophical Foundations for a Creationist Hermeneutic* (Grand Rapids, MI: Baker Academic, 2012), 176.

A Second Copernican Revolution

As explicated in Chapter 3, the aftermath of the Copernican Revolution sent intellectuals on a quest to find a methodology that would yield epistemological certitude—a guarantee that one had identified unchanging, absolute truth. It is important to remember that foundationalism is the theory of knowledge that uses the metaphor of a building to justify truth-claims. This system of knowledge claims that the stability and soundness of a truth-claim depends on its foundation. Epistemic foundationalism claims that we can know some truths without basing them on any other truths, and that we can use *that* foundational knowledge to infer further truths. The central agenda for foundationalism was to overcome the human penchant for error by means of grounding the whole edifice of human knowledge on indubitable facts or ideas.

In this milieu, some began to assert that humanity was near the end of gaining any more knowledge, and that progress—not discovery—was going to be the new historical narrative of humankind. Several famous "end-of-science" predictions appeared in this period. In 1894, during the speech given by the soon-to-be Nobel laureate, Albert A. Michelson, on the dedication of the University of Chicago's Ryerson Physics Lab, Michelson claimed: "The more important fundamental laws and facts of physical science have all been discovered, and these are now so firmly established that the possibility of their ever being supplanted in consequence of new discoveries is exceedingly remote … Future discoveries must be looked for in the sixth place of decimals."[6] But the storm clouds of radical change were gathering.

Problems began to emerge as thinkers questioned whether their theories of knowledge (realism and empiricism) had adequately accounted for the source, basis, and certainty of their claims. For example, in empiricism, it became painfully obvious that sense experience had yielded far less information about the world than what the empiricists had hoped. By the dawn of the twentieth century, philosophers from both foundationalist camps began to scramble for a more accurate account for the certainty of their truth-claims. But the task proved too difficult. Even the most believable, common sensical theories of knowledge began to be called into question as the critiques of them showed grave inconsistencies.[7]

Concurrently, scientific knowledge expanded that revealed new data demanding recalibrations to various scientific and mathematical theories and revolutions in thought. The dialectic between what was believed over against what was discovered began to make thinkers reluctant to claim *anything* as certain or permanently true. For example, new theories in physics were offered because of the observation that speed seemed to affect an object's relationship to space and

---

6. Albert A. Michelson, Quoted By John D. Barrow, *The World within the World* (Oxford: Clarendon Press, 1988), 173.

7. See Murphy, *Beyond Liberalism*, 85–109.

time. Albert Einstein observed that normative physical laws became *relative* as an object approached the speed of light. The world was confused and stunned by the new, weird picture of the universe Einstein offered.[8] Certainly, it was nothing like the universally accepted, ordered, and conventional Newtonian view.

In the emerging field of quantum mechanics, scientists like Werner Heisenberg discovered that the smallest units of matter do not behave like regular macroscopic material objects do. The subatomic particles being measured were seen to carry no predictable trajectories at all—which meant that they are indeterministic. Like a scene from Lewis Carroll's *Alice in Wonderland*, Heisenberg's *uncertainty principle* demonstrated that the more precisely one determines the position of some quantum particle, the less precisely its momentum can be predicted from initial conditions, and vice versa. In common parlance, this meant one cannot even picture what is happening at the quantum level—the level that reveals the fundamental framework of the universe.[9] Huston Smith avers, "From Aristotle to Dante, the world was pictured as a series of concentric spheres. Newton replaced that with his clockwork universe, but quantum mechanics gives us, not a new picture of the world, but no picture at all. And philosophy has followed suit."[10]

As a result, scientists became more tentative. New discoveries in physics argued for a dynamic and interrelated world over against a fixed and rational one. This meant that science could no longer be framed out with propositions of fact. Instead, every fact considered or philosophized about needed to be contextualized (or interpreted) with reference to a particular context. Returning to Huston Smith, "The message that reaches us from frontier physics seems to be that the further we track matter toward its causal origins, the more it sheds the attributes it wears ... until at some vanishing point on the horizon it seems to drop these attributes altogether to becoming something we can scarcely guess."[11]

Even the field of mathematics, which historically has had little diversity of opinion compared to any other branch of human inquiry, began to experience disputes and revisions.[12] It was as if the First Book of God (nature) was teaching

---

8. For a clearer view of the impact of Einstein's impact on philosophy, see Don A. Howard and Marco Giovanelli, "Einstein's Philosophy of Science," in *The Stanford Encyclopedia of Philosophy*, ed. Edward N. Zalta (Fall 2019), https://plato.stanford.edu/entries/einstein-philscience/ Accessed July 8, 2023.

9. For more insight on this shift, see David Lindley, *Uncertainty: Einstein, Heisenberg, Bohr, and the Struggle for the Soul of Science* (New York, NY: Anchor Books, 2007).

10. Huston Smith, *Beyond the Postmodern Mind: The Place of Meaning in a Global Civilization* (Weaton, Illinois: Quest Books, 2003), x.

11. Ibid., 178.

12. Bernhard Riemann's "non-Euclidean geometries" (formulated in the nineteenth century) contain theorems that do not hold true under the rules of Euclidean geometry (theorized in the fourth century BC) but are geometries that are logical and consistent nonetheless. To call one type of geometry absolutely true and the other that contradicts it,

humanity that certitude was not possible and that the certitude embraced in modernity was actually less about acquiring accurate and certain knowledge than it was about having beliefs that had been taken too seriously by those who held them. In other words, the kind of certitude that was the goal of the modern foundationalism turned out to be indefensible.

Murphy and McClendon write of the failure of empiricism to guarantee certitude even in the philosophy of science (much less the world of metaphysics): "In philosophy of science the first crack in the positivists' foundations came in Karl Popper's *Logik der Forschung* where he stated explicitly that the facts upon which science is based are not indubitable; they may themselves be called into question when they fail to square with accepted theory."[13] Popper writes:

> The empirical basis of objective science has thus nothing "absolute" about it. Science does not rest upon solid bedrock. The bold structure of its theories rises, as it were, above a swamp, but not down to any natural or "given" base; and if we stop driving the piles deeper, it is not because we have reached firm ground. We simply stop when we are satisfied that the piles are firm enough to carry the structure, at least for the time being.[14]

Howard Ervin carries this same view:

> [The] scientific world view [sic] is neither self-evident nor self-authenticating today. True, the world view [sic] forged from the postulates of Newtonian physics, Copernican celestial mechanics, and Lyellian uniformitarianism may have provided a congenial frame of reference for such speculations. But does the modern scientific mind think in these categories any longer? With the advent of nuclear physics, science has made a quantum leap forward and the older scientific materialism is obsolete.[15]

Both relativity and quantum mechanics had inflamed the notion that science cannot discover the underlying causes that determine physical phenomena. There was no foundation for science, only a "swamp." Foundationalism seemed dead. The best that science could do was to create mathematical formulae to try to predict

---

false, appears both arbitrary and indefensible. There seemed to be no satisfactory answer as to why this is true. Developments like this began to cast doubt on the notion that there are *any* absolutely certain truths about the universe. See Jeremy Gray, *Ideas of Space: Euclidean, Non-Euclidean, and Relativistic*, 2nd ed. (Oxford: Clarendon Press, 1989).

13. Murphy and McClendon, "Distinguishing Modern and Postmodern Theologies," 200.

14. Karl Popper, *The Logic of Scientific Discovery* (New York: Harper, 1965), quoted in Murphy, *Beyond Liberalism*, 88.

15. Howard M. Ervin, "Hermeneutics: A Pentecostal Option," *Pneuma: The Journal of the Society for Pentecostal Studies* 3 (Fall 1981): 19.

the *probability* of phenomena. Probability, not certainty, began to emerge as the only possible goal of scientific inquiry. Robert Webber agrees that:

> The world now appears to be complex and mysterious. While some scientists remain optimistic about the ability of the human mind to comprehend all of reality, a new scientific posture of humility before the vastness and complexity of the universe has taken shape. In the postmodern world scientists will continue to research, to explore, and to offer interpretations of creation and life, but with much more tentativeness than before.[16]

Here, the metaphor of knowledge as a building gave way to a picture that was more ambiguous and relationally dependent. The new metaphor was that of a *web* or *net* where truth values are interconnected and in need of evaluation and reevaluation in the light of other truth values. W. V. O. Quine employs this imagery in his "Two Dogmas of Empiricism" first published in 1951:

> The totality of our so-called knowledge or beliefs, from the most casual matters of geography and history to the profoundest laws of atomic physics or even of pure mathematics and logic, is a man-made fabric which impinges on experience only along the edges. Or, to change the figure, total science is like a field of force whose boundary conditions are experience. A conflict with experience at the periphery occasions readjustments in the interior of the field. Truth values have to be redistributed over some statements. Re-evaluation of some statements entails re-evaluation of others, because of their logical interconnections—the logical laws being in turn simply certain further elements of the field ... But the total field is so underdetermined by its boundary conditions, experience, that there is much latitude of choice as to what statements to reevaluate in the light of any single contrary experience. No particular experiences are linked with any particular statements in the interior of the field, except indirectly through considerations of equilibrium affecting the field as a whole.[17]

Here, Quine is saying that *all* ordinary knowledge (or at least "ordinary knowledge" as it had been defined by scholars in the United States and the UK)—cosmological, scientific, and even mathematical—were now subject to challenge.

Again, knowledge, on this view, became more probable than certain. By the twentieth century the weakness in the claim of certitude began to disorient many (that disorientation continues to the present day). The certitude offered by foundationalism had promised a guarantee of *knowing-things-as-they-are-in-themselves*, but now it began to be seen as more of a blusterous argument than real

---

16. Robert E. Webber, *Ancient-Future Faith: Rethinking Evangelicalism for a Postmodern World* (Grand Rapids, MI: Baker Academic, 1999), 21.

17. W. V. O. Quine, "Two Dogmas of Empiricism," in *From a Logical Point of View* (Cambridge: Harvard University Press, 1953), 42–3.

substance. Intellectuals began to think of certitude—not as clear and dependable affirmative—but as illusion, dissipation, and even (pejoratively speaking) an evasion that weakens. As absolute assertions of modernism were put into question, the idealized principle of certitude began to be seen by many as a dubious, if not simply disproven, principle.

Though there was much good garnered from the modern project (who would want to return to an antibiotic-free world or premodern dentistry?), modernity was not all roses. The force of the modern paradigm entered everyday life through the products of a consumer society, new technologies, the pragmatic view of looking for what could help the most people, and new modes of transportation and communication. This whole project of progression, described as "modernization," valued and strengthened individualization, secularization, urbanization, and commodification. Steven Best and Douglas Kellner acknowledge that although there are many positive aspects of modernity, it also

> produced untold suffering and misery for its victims, ranging from the peasantry, proletariat, and artisans oppressed by capitalist industrialization to the exclusion of women from the public sphere, to the genocide of imperialist colonialization. Modernity also produced a set of disciplinary institutions, practices, and discourses which legitimate its modes of domination and control … whereby reason turned into its opposite and modernity's promises of liberation masked forms of oppression and domination.[18]

There were also political and sociological shifts that ripped through the modern world in both the nineteenth and twentieth centuries. Jürgen Moltmann offers this about the previous two centuries before our current moment:

> The future in the twenty-first century will be determined by these two eras, for they are by no means past and gone, and they confront us with tremendous contradictions. On the one hand we have the nineteenth century (with its twentieth-century extensions), an age of fantastic progress in all of life's different sectors: from the steam engine to the airplane, from the telephone to the Internet, from classical physics to the theory of relativity. It was an age of discoveries and conquests. And on the other hand we have the twentieth century (as distinct from the nineteenth), an age of incomparable catastrophes: Verdun and Stalingrad, Auschwitz and the Gulag Archipelago, Hiroshima and Chernobyl. These names stand for the unimaginable crimes against humanity committed by the progressive West and the modern world. Both of these eras are still present today—their progress and their abysses. What once became possible will never again disappear from reality, but will always remain part of it. Today we are globalizing the nineteenth century's world of progress, and at the same time

---

18. Steven Best and Douglas Kellner, *Postmodern Theory: Critical Interrogations* (New York, NY: The Guilford Press, 1991), 3.

all the weapons of mass destruction developed and employed in the twentieth century are still kept in readiness for mass extermination, which would provide the "final solution" of the question about the human race.[19]

These events challenged the hope that had been offered in modernism. Miroslav Volf and William Katerberg claim modernity had emerged from a premodern "culture of endurance" then established a "resolute optimism"—but that optimism turned out to be more of a "manufactured certainty" than a real one.[20] Stephen Toulmin echoes the failure of modern thought as the intellectual world moves toward an "unease and sense of historical *dis*continuity which people in many fields claim to be experiencing today."[21] He explains:

> Today, the program of Modernity—even the very *concept*—no longer carries anything like the same conviction. If an historical era is ending, it is the era of Modernity itself. Rather than our being free to assume that the tide of Modernity still flows strongly, and that its momentum will carry us into a new and better world, our present position is less comfortable. What looked in the 19th century like an irresistible river has disappeared in the sand, and we seem to have run aground. Far from extrapolating confidently into the social and cultural future, we are now stranded and uncertain of our location. The very project of Modernity thus seems to have lost momentum, and we need to fashion a successor program.[22]

Toulmin's "successor program" is what some refer to as postmodernism.[23] Returning to Volf and Katerberg, they further assert that modernity's "culture of optimism" has, in postmodernism, become a "culture of ambiguity,"[24] and write of the resulting vacuousness within the postmodern construct: "Optimism has given way to a sense of ambiguity, messianic and utopian modes of thought have capitulated before the drawing of apocalyptic scenarios."[25] They conclude that postmodern theories of reality do not promote certainty, but "the extension of an ambiguous present."[26]

---

19. Jürgen Moltmann, "Progress and Abyss: Remembrances of the Future of the Modern World," in *The Future of Hope*, 4.

20. Ibid.

21. Stephen Toulmin, *Cosmopolis: The Hidden Agenda of Modernity* (New York: The Free Press, 1990), 2 (emphasis original).

22. Stephen Toulmin, *Cosmopolis*, 3.

23. It is important to remember that though postmodernism has had a traceable trajectory, it is a philosophical position still in intellectual negotiation.

24. Mirslav Volf and William Katerberg, "Introduction: Retrieving Hope," in *The Future of Hope: Christian Tradition amid Modernity and Postmodernity*, ed. Miroslav Volf and William Katerberg (Cambridge, UK: William B. Eerdmans Publishing Company, 2004), x.

25. Ibid., ix.

26. Ibid.

Postmodernism

We know that philosophy—which always seeks to make sense of the world around us—does not arise out of a vacuum. This is certainly true of the philosophy of postmodernism which arose in response a number of philosophical and cultural changes discussed above. Arguably, the most prominent influence to this sea change of intellectual thought was the scientific breakthroughs involving quantum physics. The shift from a Newtonian mechanistic view of the world to an open and dynamic understanding of the universe (which quantum physics demonstrated) raised new philosophical questions concerning epistemology and ontology, as well as reanimating the field of metaphysics (which had basically died under the reign of empiricism). These developments caused many to question the superiority of reason in general.

It turns out that when left unchecked, postmodern theories aggressively, mischievously, and irreverently undermine reason, leaving nothing in its place. There is no metanarrative left, just individualized narratives/stories whose meanings are entirely provisional. There are no universal or timeless truths—truth is basically the subjective experience of one group's power over another.[27] Arguments are reduced to issues of identity; whose winners are simply the oppressors. The very concept of objective truth is abandoned.

English Anglican theologian John Milbank avers, "Above all, postmodernity means the obliteration of boundaries, the confusion of categories ... Everything is made to run into everything else; everything gets blended, undone, and then re-blended. There are no longer any clear centers of control, and this means that new weight is given to plurality and the proliferation of difference."[28] This is the description of the dark underbelly of postmodernism—though there are many thinkers (including notable theologians) who claim this can be a positive and that one can, proverbially, turn this "lemon" into "lemonade." James K. A. Smith suggests:

> The notion of postmodernism is invoked as both poison and cure within the contemporary church. To some, postmodernity is the bane of Christian faith, the new enemy taking over the role of secular humanism as object of fear and primary target of demonization. Others see postmodernism as a fresh wind of the Spirit sent to revitalize the dry bones of the church.[29]

---

27. See Elizabeth Clark, *History, Theory, Text: Historians and the Linguistic Turn* (Cambridge, MA: Harvard University Press, 2004).

28. John Milbank, "The Gospel of Affinity," in *The Future of Hope: Christian Tradition amid Modernity and Postmodernity*, ed. Miroslav Volf and William Katerberg (Cambridge, UK: William B. Eerdmans Publishing Company, 2004), 149–50.

29. James K. A. Smith, *Who's Afraid of Postmodernism? Taking Derrida, Lyotard, and Foucault to Church* (Grand Rapids, MI: Baker Academic, 2006), 17–18.

Though the failure of foundationalism leaves a sense of pessimism in the air for many, Murphy offers:

> If all the possible moves have been tried within the limits set by modernity, this should be a cause for dismay only if we believe modern thinkers have had the final word on the topics of knowledge, language, and the ultimate nature of reality. It is becoming more and more widely accepted that modern thinkers have *not* had the last word. We must now ask about the new plays that might be possible under the "rules" of the next major philosophical era.[30]

As in any intellectual position, postmodernity does not house a homogenous set of philosophical views. Thinkers offer striking differences as they articulate their positions and insights—differences that carry obvious contradictions and limitations. What *is* shared is that the advocates for a postmodern view work aggressively to quash the presuppositions and values of modernism, along with an attempt to resource some of the lost values of premodernity.

A Return to Mystery

As modernity dawned, it was marked by a "turn to the subject."[31] In philosophy, the subject is the one who is consciousness of (or has a unique experience with) an entity *outside* of itself—the object. Here the subject—the human soul—is *active* while the object is *passive*.[32] Modernity asserted that a human subject could stand back apart from an object being examined and arrive at an objective knowledge about it as it is in reality. The modern investigator's sense of *objectivity*—where humans feel an objective, almost "God-view" of the world—is where the "I" can see the "It" clearly, and the "I" can experience the "It." This is the striking way Martin Buber constructs his famous "I-It" schema as he describes the ways human beings interact with things in the universe.[33] But the postmodern philosophical position is an "I-Thou" orientation to things around us,[34] which is to claim that we cannot

---

30. Murphy, *Beyond Liberalism*, 85 (emphasis original).
31. Murphy and McClendon, Jr., "Distinguishing," 192.
32. Immanuel Kant (*Critique of Pure Reason,* trans. and ed. Paul Guyer and Allen W. Wood [New York: Cambridge University Press, 1998], 29) held that it was the activity of the cognitive mind that made our perception of experience possible. This made the human mind the "active" originator of experience rather than just a "passive" recipient in the world of experience. This was a revolutionary idea because throughout the intellectual history of the West, the soul had always been considered *passive*—as simply receiving information from the world around us (this was the prevailing view all the way back to Plato). Kant referred to this novel observation as his own "Copernican Revolution," ibid.
33. See Martin Buber, *I and Thou*, trans. Walter Kaufmann (New York: Touchstone, 1970).
34. Also a construct of Buber. Ibid.

know things apart from our relationship to them. Hence, our understanding is always colored by our relationship to things around us. This suggests that we are, in Robert Webber's words, "beings in the world enmeshed in social networks, not individual autonomous selves."[35] Hence, the closest we can come to understanding our universe is through a kind of symbiosis of data via the interrelationships we have with things. This aspect of postmodernity is not a return to premodernity, but it recapitulates it by envisioning the world as interconnected and interrelated (though *not* because of Divine Providence).

The I-Thou orientation moves us from thinking of the universe as composed of a vast grouping of individualized particles that were essentially independent of each other to the argument that all things are interrelated and connected dynamically. Everything affects everything else in both space and time—putting everything in flux, not in stasis. In this kind of world, one cannot be certain of rational and scientific facts—there are too many variables. Facts, then, are only *interpreted* facts, not facts in the "modern" understanding. The interconnectedness of the universe (holism versus dualism) opened the door to mystery (a premodern trait) and the idea that facts can only be interpreted facts and not universal or propositional facts that are true-at-all-times-in-all-places. The postmodern view insists that since human experience is always communicated to us through symbiotic relationships, the notion of absolutes must be abandoned. We can no longer say with confidence that the world is constituted by linear absolutes of A, B, and C—all of our existential experience is relative to everything else. We move from a single unifying set of facts to a web of relationships that give us a sense of probability rather than certainty.

Postmodern philosophers argued that because we are immersed in the universe with an interrelationship indelibly filled with interpretations, human persons are always biased in some way by our lived experience, values, and understanding, which contribute to a whole web of data to consider. In postmodernity, the need for a clear picture of reality is not necessary—instead, Murphy claims, each belief needs to be "supported by its ties to its neighboring beliefs and, ultimately, to the whole."[36] James K. A. Smith adds in this regard, "The world is the environment in which we swim, not a picture that we look at as distanced observers."[37] Murphy holds that the goal here is to find a "coherence of the web," and "when inconsistencies appear—conflicts within the web or with 'recalcitrant experience'—there are always a number of ways to revise in order to restore consistency."[38] Certainly this opens the door to *relativity*, but relativity does not have to mean that all views are equally valid. Relativity here means that things are relative to a context. This is the web that replaces foundationalism. It is referred to as *epistemological holism*.[39] This

---

35. Webber, *Ancient-Future*, 23.
36. Murphy, *Beyond Liberalism*, 94.
37. Smith, *Thinking in Tongues*, 114.
38. Murphy, *Beyond Liberalism*, 94.
39. Ibid., 85.

new epistemological holism emerged through the criticisms of modern theories of knowledge, language, and causation, which opened intellectual space for new philosophical and theological methodologies and hermeneutics.

It would be a mistake not to recognize the dangers of this postmodern kind of thinking. In the postmodern worldview, dialectical interaction and questions displace any notion of propositional truth; relativity wins over absolutes; pluralism supervenes any single unifying factor in the universe; symbolism and the primacy of experience masters conceptual knowledge; etc. The postmodern shift has proven catastrophic for established values, institutions, and forms of life honored during modernity and has dramatically affected contemporary science, philosophy, theology, and the arts. Postmodern criticism in all areas of inquiry abandons formalism, realism, and highbrow pretentiousness in favor of attending to the subjective experience of the reader (the one reporting or interpreting the experience). Truth under this influence is no longer considered static or fixed—the psychological, social, and particular historical vantage points determine one's take on truth and are what matter the most. Context is priviledged over truth-claims, which means truth is no longer timeless and universal. Truth-claims need to be considered in terms of their relationship to context; and in this sense, are considered *relative*.

Against the modernist values of seriousness, appropriateness, and purity, postmodernism—in revolt against the Western self—opted for a new anti-literature (or a literature of silence), insouciance, coloring outside the lines, and a new eclecticism. This is why postmodernism has been described by Ihab Hassan as a "decisive historical mutation."[40] The belief here is that multiple ideas/themes/styles must always be drawn upon in order to gain complementary insights into a subject without it being filtered by philosophical, theological, or antiquated social rules. Postmodernism resists any effort to identifying a single paradigm or standard set of assumptions. This obviously poses a direct threat to the foundational assumptions and values of Western society, as well as to Christian theism, in general.

There is a case to be made that the postmodernism leads to the dismantling; not only the traditional standards of modernism (e.g., foundationalism, structuralism, and the notion of a clear and universal metanarrative), but of Christianity as well. Yet, despite the potential problems inherent within postmodern philosophical methodology, many contend that its epistemology affords a unique opportunity for Christian thought to be heralded (even though it does present some strong challenges *against* the historic faith). The upside of postmodern thought is that it opens the way for many ideas to be heard without the need for conflict to demand a winner (this opens the hope of a return to the kind of openness that was present in nascent pentecostalism as one of the evidences of what is pentecostal [Chapter 2]). Here, Christianity is not seen as a particular doctrine but as an ongoing dialectic conversation of thesis and antithesis, which gives rise

---

40. Isab Hassan, *The Postmodern Turn: Essays in Postmodern Theory and Culture* (Columbus, Ohio: Ohio State University Press, 1987), quoted in Best, *Postmodern Theory*, 11.

to the synthesis of new meaning.⁴¹ Some find the postmodern approach a way to foster a welcome tolerance affording a richer understanding of the Christian faith and an appreciation for the many ways the church-catholic has found expressions that have value, though they are different from our own individual theological tradition. Leonard Sweet captures the essence of this:

> In postmodern culture, fluidity wins out over fixity. Instead of "structuring" and "ordering" and "solidifying" reality, [postmodernity] "bends" and "blends" and "melts." Life is a fluid realm. But fluid does not mean "anything goes," as any captain of a boat can tell you; fluid is a different kind of going. Stability is the capacity of a system to return to equilibrium after it has been disturbed.⁴²

Though there was no named philosophy attached to early pentecostal tradition, it is precisely this kind of lens that historically afforded pentecostals a safe space to carefully relook at and potentially reform accepted theologoumena or authoritative doctrines. This was also a move toward romanticism over the cold rationalistic in philosophy, theology, and religion—which is reminiscent of the orthopathic leanings inherent in pentecostalism. It appears that these moves in philosophy can help to create pathways for pentecostal scholars to find their way back to that which is truly pentecostal *qua* pentecostal in their theologizing.

We have seen in this project that the philosophy and general hermeneutics surrounding theologians in any given era have had an impact on the way they theologized. That was true in the premodern world, the modern world, and now, it is holding true in the postmodern world. This suggests that theologians should always examine their theological work to account for presuppositions that may be coloring their thinking unawares. Though pentecostal theology has been influenced by all three of these philosophical worlds, the pneumatic impulse inherent to pentecostalism has kept them from being completely dominated by any of them for long. Just as the earth is influenced by the gravitational pull of the sun without being pulled into it, on the whole, pentecostalism—though under the strong gravitational pulls of the philosophies of premodernism, modernism, and postmodernism—has not been completely pulled out of its own unique spiritual orbit. Though I believe modernity has had too great of a stranglehold on American pentecostalism, the way pentecostals process their faith—with a value placed on the supernatural and a fresh openness to the Spirit— there is growing evidence that they are avoiding modernity's general inflexibility in the way they are doing theology. The theologizing within pentecostalism and its discipline of hermeneutics share the trait that both have been able to function on the edges of the *zeitgeist* of the age without being completely subsumed by it.

---

41. I return to this "Hegelian" arc within a pneumatological theological methodology in Chapter 5.

42. Leonard Sweet, *Soul Tsunami: Sink or Swim in New Millennium Culture* (Grand Rapids, MI: Zondervan, 1999), 81.

Before sketching out the rationale for a theological methodology that would remain tethered to the pre-theological, non-rational essentials of pentecostalism (which I do in Chapter 5), let me say that the three worlds of premodernity, modernity, and postmodernity have influenced pentecostalism without completely dominating it. While carrying some of the historic, rich aspects of premodernism in their orientation, pentecostals were also influenced by the benefits of the rationalism of modernity. And, as postmodernism began to emerge around them, they have been able to draw in its positive, hopeful emphases without being limited by its claims that are contrary to the Christian faith. In this sense, pentecostals have been able to live *out of time*, as it were.

Pentecostals as Metamoderns

We have seen that pentecostalism has not submitted rigidly to any particular *zeitgeist*—premodern, modern, or postmodern. Archer avers that "Pentecostals were not full-fledged citizens of modernity. They were like the traveling circus sideshows, living on the margins of society and presenting to those who ventured into their tents and electrifying vision of Pentecost revisited."[43] Consequently, pentecostals have been notoriously hard to classify philosophically. They were not *just* premodern, modern, or postmodern—they have always carried a bit of each. Archer suggests that:

> Pentecostalism should not be viewed as "pre-modern" because it was born in the modernistic age. It shared characteristics of the so-called pre-modern era, but it relied upon the adaptation of modernistic language and belief to discover and articulate its practices and beliefs (thus it insisted on tangible, visible signs of the Holy Spirit's presence) even though it was in opposition to modernity … Pentecostalism emerged within modernity (a historically definitive time period), yet existed on the fringes of modernity (both in a sociological and economical sense and by its emphasis on physical evidence for the Spirit's presence—a modernistic slant on scientific experimentation language). Pentecostalism could never accept modernity's worldview completely, but it did utilize aspects of modernity (like technology, language, inductive reasoning) to advance the Pentecostal cause. Pentecostalism was (and is) a protest to the central features of modernity.[44]

To try to pin down exactly what pentecostalism is philosophically would endanger it. In truth, pentecostalism is an alternative version of all modernities and seeks a kind of *via media* between them. This could be called, as Wolfgang Vondey asserts, "religion as play."[45] Pentecostals have not played by the strict rules

---

43. Archer, *A Pentecostal Hermeneutic*, 97.
44. Ibid., 44–5.
45. Wolfgang Vondey, "Religion as Play: Pentecostalism as a Theological Type," *Religions* 9, no. 80 (2018): 1–16.

of any particular modernity. They have not been contained. A better classification is that pentecostals are *metamodern* as defined by Jason Storm:

> What is metamodernism? It aspires to be a theoretical revolution. It charts a number of things: a process social ontology, a new multispecies semiotics, a revaluation of the place of values in the human sciences, and an alternative to the sterile opposition between realisms and anti-realisms. It seeks to establish a new model for producing humble knowledge that is capable of tracing the unfolding of de-essentialized master categories in their full complexity.[46]

Being metamodern, according to Storm, is not to describe a new zeitgeist or periodization, but to put forward a way of looking at philosophical and cultural movements in a way inspired by Hegel's dialectic where the dialectic struggle/conflict between premodernism, modernism, and postmodernism are synthesized to find what is of most value in each so that a higher order of understanding emerges. One could argue that this is why pentecostals often acted (and continue to act) in counter cultural ways. As Cheryl Bridges Johns reports:

> A radical counterculture identity characterized the early Pentecostal movement. In the era of the war to end all wars, Pentecostals were pacifists. In an era when women were excluded from public voice, Pentecostals were ordaining women as ministers. In an era of the KKK, Pentecostal Blacks and whites were worshipping together. This subversive and revolutionary movement, not based upon philosophic ideology nor totally upon critical reflection (although it did exist), had a dual prophetic role: denouncing the dominant patterns of the status quo and announcing the patterns of God's order.[47]

It is in the hope of supporting this kind of countercultural activity that the aim of this project is to present a theological methodology rooted in the pentecostalism. I am convinced this methodology could help pentecostals offer clear, Spirit-directed ways of speaking faithfully for God in this historical moment, launching their prophetic voice into the global church and into her future. As Pinnock claims, "It is time for Pentecostals to realize that they have a distinctive doctrine of God implicit in their faith and that they need to make it explicit—not just for purely academic purposes but for revival too, because Christianity is only as dynamic as its understanding of God."[48]

The twenty-first century will continue to offer new scientific discoveries and deep social and political change—the need for the prophetic voice continues. Pentecostalism has proven itself to be a great translating and reforming tradition. Pentecostals carry on the great tradition of the early church, as described by

---

46. Jason Storm and Ananda Josephson, *Metamodernism* (Chicago: University of Chicago Press, 2021), ix.
47. Johns, "Adolescence of Pentecostalism," 4–5.
48. Pinnock, "Divine Relationality," 5.

Wilken: "Christian thinking, while working within patterns of thought and conceptions rooted in Greco-Roman Roman culture, transformed them so profoundly that in the end something quite new came into being."[49]

Harvey Cox, one of the foremost observers of modern religions, speaks of pentecostalism as "the reshaping of religion in the twenty-first century."[50] He believes pentecostalism carries a "primal spirituality" that:

> [T]ells us a lot about who we human beings are as we approach the twenty-first century, and that its meaning transcends all merely social or psychological explanations. In an age that has found exclusively secular explanations of life wanting, but is also wary of dogmas and institutions, the unforeseen eruption of this spiritual lava reminds us that somewhere deep within us we all carry a *homo religiosus*. Pentecostalism is not an aberration. It is a part of the larger and longer history of human religiousness. [It is] devoted to primal speech, primal piety, and primal hope ... after a mere ninety years, what began as a despised and ridiculed sect is quickly becoming both the preferred religion of the urban poor and the powerful bearer of a radically alternative vision of what the human world might one day become.[51]

Cheryl Bridges Johns concurs with the view that pentecostals hold a prophetic role for all of humanity. She begins by quoting the late president of Princeton Theological Seminary, John McKay, who said, "America's future will abide in a reformed Catholicism and a mature Pentecostalism," to which Johns adds, "I believe that the statement may be broadened to include the future of the world."[52]

Conclusion

I have examined the evidence showing that pentecostals engaged with and were influenced by the various zeitgeists: premodernism, modernism, and postmodernism. I have also showed how the rise of postmodernism opened a philosophical path for pentecostals to reappropriate their rich premodern orientation and quash some of the deleterious aspects of modern philosophical thought that had held them captive. What is hopeful is that pentecostalism has proven to be a movement that is born out of time, and though there were times when pentecostals as a group were taken hostage, no philosophical construct could dominate them for long.

---

49. Wilken, *Spirit of Early Christian Thought*, xvii.
50. This is the subtitle of his book.
51. Cox, *Fire from Heaven*, 83.
52. Johns, "The Adolescence of Pentecostalism," 3.

All these considerations support the idea that pentecostalism is a movement that ultimately transcends philosophical considerations, where we can aptly call pentecostals *metamoderns*. As one watches their narrative unfold, particularly in the pentecostal academy, pentecostalism does not end up being *philosophized* as much as philosophy ends up being *pentecostalized* and pentecostals end up careening back to the primal essences of pentecostalism (revivalism, mysticism, and a pneumatological imagination). I contend that these essences should *always* be kept in focus as pentecostals reflect on their religious experiences (viz., do theology). This is how they can theologize from their foundational pneumatology, which, Yong suggests, "is a thought experiment in hermeneutics and method from a pneumatological perspective. As such, it might be called a 'pneumatology of quest.'"[53]

In the next chapter, I give the rationale behind why pentecostal theologians should construct a pneumatological theological methodology that emerges from that which is pentecostal. I am convinced that such a uniquely pentecostal methodology would help theologues of all stripes remain faithful to Christ as they maneuver through new scientific discoveries, the vicissitudes of philosophical development, and the helter-skelter changes that preponderate the global evolving social milieu.

53. Yong, *Beyond the Impasse*, 22.

Chapter 6

IN SEARCH OF THE BUTTERFLY

Introduction

This project began with the identification of the triadic morphology of pentecostal essences (viz., *revival, mysticism,* and the *pneumatological imagination*). Though the evidence shows that there are always constellations of supernatural effects (i.e., the presence of glossolalia, miracles, prophecy, gifts of the Spirit, answered prayer, etc.), along with shared sets of idiosyncratic dogmas, priorities and hermeneutics, etc., from pentecostal group to pentecostal group that can be identified and explicated, they are not ubiquitous. The essences iterated herein are universally present and therefore I contend constitutes the *sine qua non* of the global pentecostal movement.

Though these essences were prevalent in the pentecostal narrative at its beginning (at least on one reading of the evidence), there were unconscious, constraining, religious, and secular forces that began to diminish them (Chapters 2–4). I briefly surveyed how the religious (e.g., streams of Pietism, Puritanism, Wesleyanism, African American Christianity, and nineteenth-century Holiness-Revivalism) and philosophical historical (viz., premodernism, modernism, and postmodernism) narratives impacted the theological enterprise generally, and pentecostalism specifically. As I have said, pentecostals were deeply influenced by these narratives/*zeitgeists* and pointed to how those forces limited their theological work. However, the critical note that sounded from this review is how pentecostalism has proven to move past these religious/philosophical limitations, proving it to be a movement on a pneumatological quest, where no rational construct could dominate it long.

In this chapter, I outline the rationale for a theological methodology that would remain tethered to the foundational pnuematological essentials of pentecostalism while launching into second-level intellectual theologizing that is distinctively pentecostal.[1] At its fount, pentecostalism appears with an admixture of thought—pretheological and theological, non-rational and rational—at the same time! This is why pentecostals can and should construct theological methodologies that privilege the pretheological and non-rational over the theological and

---

1. My work here is embryonic at best because any true theological methodology would require erudite work and voluminous space(s) far beyond the boundaries of this project.

rational—precisely because it is pentecostal to do so.² Pentecostals need to keep the pretheological and non-rational in view as the "mother" of the movement, like a young toddler wandering from its mother to explore the world while looking back again and again to ensure the mother is *right there*—as a warrant for the child's safety. Pentecostal theologizing should refuse to wander far from its mother (viz., revivalism, mysticism, and the pneumatological imagination) and should frequently look back because theologizing without her in view would no longer be pentecostal.

In my effort to sketch a methodology of this ilk, I continue to resource Yong's schema of the *pneumatological imagination*.³ In his project, he argues for a "foundational pneumatology" as the basis of ontology and metaphysics.⁴ Simo Frestadius affirms that "Since Yong follows the common epistemic principle of allowing the order of things (ontology) to determine how things are known (epistemology), it naturally follows that for him God can only be known truly in the Spirit, and hence Yong's epistemology is logically pneumatically orientated."⁵

The use of the term "imagination" within Yong's pneumatological imagination is the human belief-forming faculty in relation to God and the world—for Yong a kind of *worldmaking* capacity.⁶ Yong uses *imagination* not as a reference to a priori concepts but as real images that have formed in the mind through experiencing the world.⁷ Yong carefully follows a number of philosophers like Charles Sanders Peirce and Stephen Pepper in his argument, but this is beyond the scope of my usage of his phrase. What *is* critical to my work is how his pneumatological imagination frames the theologue's understanding of God and the world *after* divine encounters have been experienced. Yong writes:

> I am interested in how pneumatology informs and relates to the "object" of theological knowledge, broadly considered, i.e., God-self-world. Correlatively, the pneumatological inquiry to be conducted includes not only theological, but also epistemological (related to the self) and metaphysical (related to the world) trajectories. I wish to explore how pneumatology structures and relates to the world, to the knowing process, and, ultimately, to theological hermeneutics and method. [This] may be better understood as a thought experiment in hermeneutics and method from a pneumatological perspective. As such, it

---

2. Kärkkäinen, *Pneumatology*, 6.
3. See Yong, *Spirit-Word-Community*.
4. Ibid., 215.
5. Simo Frestadius, *Pentecostal Rationality: Epistemology and Theological Hermeneutics in the Foursquare Tradition* (New York: T&T Clark, 2021), 11.
6. Yong, *Spirit-Word-Community*, 151.
7. In a sense, all knowledge accessed via Yong's pneumatological imagination is experientially based and can be perceived as a form of empiricism (in the Wesleyan sense of "experimental") mediated by the Holy Spirit.

might be called a "pneumatology of quest." Certainly, the pneumatological imagination arises from specific encounters with the divine, specifically the Holy Spirit.[8]

Here, I propose a theological methodology that emerges from this "pneumatological imagination" (which I articulate explicitly in Chapter 6). For simplification, I will refer to this methodology as a *pneumatological theological methodology* (PTM).

Why New Theological Methodologies?

Paul Allen claims that "Christian theology is presently undergoing a time of attention to particulars" and further asserts that theological method is too important "to disappear as an urgent matter of attention."[9] Why is this the case? Allen points to prevailing complications within theology resulting from theology's "relationship to philosophy, the balance afforded to sources, the nature of the theological task and criteria of judgement in theological claims."[10] He further claims that there needs to be a "fusing of theological styles" which will lead to "new directions in theological method."[11] Allen is nodding to the challenge for the modern theologian to make room for modern developments in methodology to be considered for an integration into the methodologies of the past.

The theologue should always work to blend new methods in ways that enrich or expand the inherited Christian tradition. The risk of new theological methodologies is to forget that—though they enable us to express the received tradition in new ways—they do not change that tradition. Theologians must refuse a novelty in method that would lead one to making the faith unrecognizable to those who have gone before. Reformed church historian Euan Cameron gives an example of this:

> In the Eastern Orthodox tradition there is a dedicated and often intellectually refined discourse about tradition or *paradosis*. This pattern of thought defines faithfulness to traditional witness in terms of being true to the Spirit, rather than merely following formal or creedal standards inherited from the past. It speaks of a "living tradition" that is expressed anew but is always the same. The rhetoric emphasizes tradition even as it acknowledges change.[12]

---

8. Yong, *Spirit-Word-Community*, 8.
9. Allen, *Theological Method*, 228.
10. Ibid.
11. Ibid., 228.
12. Cameron, *Interpreting Christian History*, 165.

Expressing the faith "anew" while guarding it, so that it is "always the same," is the standard by which new methodologies should be considered.

Another reason new theological methodologies need to be considered is the *speed of change*—the radical, revolutionary change that is happening all around us. Rapid change continues in all disciplines, from science to philosophy, sociology, and economics. These changes must influence the way theology is done, or theologizing will become irrelevant. Acknowledging this reality, The Second Vatican Council (1962–5) reports:

> Today, the human race is involved in a new stage of history. Profound and rapid changes are spreading by degrees around the whole world. Triggered by the intelligence and creative energies of man, these changes recoil upon him, upon his decisions and desires both individual and collective, and upon his manner of thinking and acting with respect to things and to people. So we can already speak of a true cultural and social transformation, one which has repercussions on man's religious life as well.[13]

The church has historically adjusted its theological methodology. A survey past theological methodologies clearly shows that though similar in many ways, methodologies needed to evolve. This is in part because no methodology can square faith claims with the shifts in knowledge and philosophy in a way that can make sense of things at all times and in all places. The methodologies from the Patristic era did not work for the Antiochene fathers, and those had to be reimagined in the medieval era and again for the Reformers. Methodologies must continue to develop in order to acclimatize twenty-first century minds to an understanding of Christian spirituality and gospel claims.

Theologians in all eras need to work to incorporate what they can from the past while remaining open to new approaches. What worked in the past (or is working today) will not necessarily work tomorrow. This is an especially critical perspective in a milieu where abrupt and unexpected changes constantly play out—changes that no one in the past had ever imagined, and which, at first blush, can look more like an enemy of the gospel than a friend to it. If we pause to think about this, all of us recognize the pace of profound upheaval unfolding in the modern world and the disorientation it can cause to those of us tethered to the ancient world with its sacred stories. A good theological methodology can prevent us from defaulting immediately to a reactive and polemical stance against change, giving us space for the process of discernment so we can respond appropriately to unexpected discoveries.

There is not enough room in this project to adequately explore the many ways the world has changed in just the past 500 years. This landscape of change has directly or indirectly influenced everything—including the world of theology. I contend that imagining a theological methodology informed by a pneumatological

---

13. *Guadium et Spes* (Vatican Council II), no. 4. Quoted by Coda, *From the Trinity*, 43.

imagination can afford theologues an effective heuristic process for faithfully addressing the theological/spiritual implications of these changes and the possible ways they may or may not speak to us about God and/or God's purposes.

Before explicitly articulating the PTM I have in mind, I address three things a bit more sharply: (1) theology, (2) theological methodology, and (3) the pneumatological. Aspects of what I articulate in these three areas will become essential constituents of the PTM imagined here, which I contend will ensure the presence of the essences and evidences of that which is truly pentecostal (articulated in Chapter 1).

Theology

Amid the rapidly shifting world of science and philosophy, theology has become very conscious of itself and feels the need to explain the concept of theologizing in the hope that someone/anyone will comprehend what theological understanding is pursuing.[14] *Why theology?* is a legitimate question in the twenty-first century. This has not always been the case. In the medieval period, Thomas Aquinas described theology as the "queen of the sciences," which, based upon the Aristotelian notion of science, meant it was concerned with certain knowledge of the necessary, universal, and immutable.[15] Of course, that has changed. As we have seen (Chapter 4), even science is no longer considered to be "certain knowledge." Today, science claims nothing more than probability. How the mighty are fallen![16] This would suggest that theology must learn the language of "probability" rather than holding to a language of "certainty" if it is going to be understood in the modern world.

Not only does it hold that theology must learn to use new idioms and descriptors, there is the extra challenge for the pentecostal theologian to do theology from a uniquely pentecostal perspective. As Cross points out:

> While Pentecostals share many theological tenets in common with other Christians, we have experienced God in ways others do not confess. Rather than viewing theology as a description of our distinctives, we need to understand the all-encompassing difference which our experience of God makes in every area of our lives—especially those that are theological. For Pentecostals, the beginning

---

14. See O'Collins, *Rethinking Fundamental Theology*; Allen Diogenes and Eric O. Springsted, *Philosophy for Understanding Theology*, 2nd ed. (Louisville, KY: Westminster John Knox Press, 2007), Kindle; Robert W. Jenson, *A Theology in Outline: Can These Bones Live* (New York: Oxford University Press, 2016); and Allen, *Theological Method*.

15. Thomas Aquinas, *Summa Theologica* 1:1, 5. Technically, Aquinas does not use the phrase "queen of the sciences" regarding theology, though that simile is often attributed to him.

16. This common expression was derived from 2 Sam. 1:25.

and end of theological reflection will be infused with our experience of God through his Spirit. We may be evangelical in that we hold to the common truths of the faith handed down for generations, but we are not just evangelicals who speak in tongues! We are a people invaded by the Spirit, knocked off our horses as was Saul (Acts 9); therefore, we cannot think, live or write as if this experience of the living God were peripheral.[17]

This is the pentecostal insistence that, though theology is the discipline that speaks about God, it is first rooted in God's active self-revelation.

Pentecostals believe that God's self-revelation is recorded in God's Word, the Bible, but that God is *still present* in that revelation. Theology for pentecostals is a discipline that not only talks about God discursively but seeks for the *activity* of God that remains present *in the text*. The writer of Hebrews affirms that "the word of God is alive and active" (Heb. 4:12), and that in this sense the writer says, "See to it that you do not refuse him who speaks" (12:25). Because God is still speaking, theologizing for the pentecostal is not the result of mere human investigation; it carries the possibility for divine encounter (though one comes at that possibility through prayerful second-order discourse and rational thought). Though theology is a second-level intellectual activity that speaks *about* God, it is still rooted in the Person of God—a Being beyond being. This insistence serves as a correction to what is often problematic in the theological academy. Allen reports:

> One thorny issue which confronts the student of theology is to what extent theological method needs to be articulated in "purely" rational terms. The most profound difficulty with regards to a systematic theology and method is the tendency to over-abstraction. The concern over the relationship between the demands of rationality and the distinctive spiritual basis for theological reflection is a constant methodological worry. Spiritual or religious experience is often cited by theologians to differentiate theological reflection from other forms of reflection or knowledge. The acts of praying, worship or contemplation are the kinds of acts that put into question a strictly epistemological approach to theological methodology.[18]

The theologian emphasizes the importance of incorporating "spiritual or religious experience" into theological activities. They insist that pentecostals must personally encounter God while engaging in theology, allowing for moments of adoration and pneumatic experiences through prayerful theologizing. This means that theology is not to be an attempted objective "I-It" experience of human-to-God. God can never qualify for such an approach because God is distinctly *otherly*—one who is *in* but not *part* of the known universe. God is the Creator, not a subset of the created. In that sense, God does not *exist;* God is the source of

---

17. Cross, "The Rich Feast," 33–4.
18. Allen, *Theological Method*, 3–5.

existence. This means that God is ontologically different from the rest of creation and not really observable, except as he "passes by" (cf. Exod. 33:19-20). This means that theologians cannot really study God as an "It"—like a pinned down butterfly. Critical to theologizing are discernment and faith—which are living approaches that anticipate encounters with the holy. These are the approaches that are embedded within pentecostals and their pneumatological imagination.

Certainly, it is the task of theology to apprehend, understand, and speak of God in rational terms. And it is critical within any theistic conception to think of God rationally. Only on such terms can one engage in belief versus nothing more than mere *feeling*. Pentecostals have always understood that they must bring conceivable and comprehensible concepts to bear in order to explicate their experience, but they knew this was only one side of religion—and in comparison to an encounter with the Living God, the less significant side.

Pentecostals (as a community, a tribe) are not (and never were) against rational thought. They have understood that the very concept of faith in God, whose characteristics include purpose, good will, supreme power, and selfhood, are definite concepts which necessitate the use of reason. However, rational descriptions are not, properly speaking, the essence of the Christian faith; rather these are the things that are derived from it (viz., *fides qua/fides quae*). Pentecostals consider faith to be the miracle that emerges when one has an encounter with the divine or infinite—rational thoughts (like dogmas) are the reflections we make on that miracle.

The pentecostal contends that the rational should never be allowed to preponderate the spiritual. This is important because the notion of privileging the spiritual is not always prioritized in modern theologizing. Diogenes Allen and Eric Springsted claim:

> Christian spirituality is not usually considered doctrinal theology or theological inquiry. But for all theologians of the ancient church and for many in the medieval period, the practice of spirituality was considered necessary for theological inquiry, as can easily be seen in Augustine's inquiry on the Trinity or Anselm's prayers in his inquiry into the existence of God. In addition, in the past four decades there has been an immense increase of interest in Christian spirituality.[19]

Because spirituality in theologizing is native to the pentecostal ethos, pentecostal theologues can serve as exemplars in this regard. Privileging spirituality within the theological enterprise has always been central for and innate to pentecostalism.

Pentecostals believe a sure way to guarantee that rationalism does not dominate the culture of faith is to infuse the process of discursive, theological reflection with a priority on an orthopathy that keeps alive the non-rational feeling of absolute dependence upon God without blurring or diminishing the need for clear, rational

---

19. Diogenes and Springsted, *Philosophy for Understanding Theology*, loc. 59–61, Kindle.

theological conceptions of God. The goal of a clear-thinking pentecostal theologian should be to permeate the discursive theological enterprise with the Spirit of God and the non-rational elements encountered with God afford (e.g., humility, awe, a creature-consciousness, etc.), as described in Chapter 1.

Experiences with God may carry the non-rational, but the indescribable, non-rational work of the Spirit in divine encounter (viz., revival) becomes a fully religious, rational sentiment as the non-rational and rational elements of religious consciousness are woven together, like (in Otto's metaphor) "the interweaving of warp and woof in a fabric."[20] The prerational experience of the divine encounter necessarily proceeds to the rational theological construction of belief. Hence, orthopathy is critical to the pentecostal theological enterprise—one must foster spiritual "affection" while pursuing truth. This is why pentecostalism emphasizes prayer when approaching the Bible. Pentecostals feel theological study should only be done within the context of prayer while looking for the leading of the Spirit, which is a Wesleyan impulse (Chapter 2). Theological study for pentecostals has historically emerged from their spirituality, as Land affirms: "Theology begins in the prayerful response of persons to God."[21]

Theological Methodology

The specific PTM I posit in Chapter 6 is done in the hope of advancing a heuristic methodology deeply influenced by pentecostalism and tuned ecumenically to help theologians of all stripes contribute meaningfully and distinctly to the global theological enterprise of the twenty-first century. Though space limitations here prevent defending all the reasons for doing so, this PTM does share much common ground with the methodologies and sources used by the pentecostal and evangelical camps. But it also welcomes voices from the broader church-catholic. The differences between these various methodologies and the PTM are largely a matter of emphasis and priority. The dance between various methodological choices is not a decision to be all things to all people, nor is it a loophole for personal preference and bias. The intent is that the theological *dance* must be governed by the goal of the theologue—whether trying to interpret a particular passage of scripture or to determine a hermeneutical approach to a subject/person or to formulate a doctrinal position on an issue or to discern an appropriate ethical position, and so on. I believe it is appropriate for any methodology to resource other methodologies native to Christian theologizing based on *what* the theologian is attempting to do.

To offer a new theological methodology to the academy is nothing short of hubris—unless one realizes that such an endeavor is not really new at all (nor is it being offered as a comprehensive theological methodology). This work is

---

20. Otto, *Idea of the Holy*, 46.
21. Land, *Pentecostal Spirituality*, 24.

an attempt to add nuance to the theological work already done throughout the history of the Christian church—rather like a scarf as an accessory to a clothing ensemble. In a very real sense, this writing is one sentence in a long, vigorous conversation that has been taking place for thousands of years, and yet I argue it is a valid sentence that makes a helpful contribution to the conversation.

Generally speaking (which dangerously oversimplifies this deeply variegated and complex subject), a theological method is a particular way that one participates in discourse that investigates God, God's works, and God's ways. Each methodology carries certain attitudes, dispositions, and orientations. For example, all theological methodologies have come-froms (e.g., they may be conservative, liberal, postliberal, postconservative, canonical-linguistic, and/or participate in radical orthodoxy). Different methodologies choose to prioritize (or utilize) different resources, sources, or tools. Every methodology also embodies unique theological mechanics, set of procedures, and techniques.[22] That being said, the central objective of *any* theological methodology in the Christian tradition is to survey and analyze reflections regarding how we speak of God and the life of the world in relation to God.

The methodology a theologian chooses will ultimately impact her or his theological outcomes or conclusions in the various branches of theology from systematics to moral theology to matters of scripture and doctrine.[23] One must approach a methodology carefully, and should endeavor to protect the theological enterprise against the tendency of oversimplification or to be too dominated by a particular opinion or *zeitgeist* (i.e., like the foundationalist presupposition that a human being is just a *tabula rasa* who comes to perspicuous, inerrant, sacred text to be "written upon" resulting in "right belief" explicated in Chapter 3); or against the postmodern infinite number of possible interpretations (addressed in Chapter 4). To attain any level of objectivity in the methodological process, the theologian must be honest about her or his own biases, and these must be recognized, acknowledged, and accounted for in the theologizing. A fruitful and compelling methodology will always make room to hold one's own particular read (after identifying and honestly accounting for one's own biases) while hearing other "reads" that readdress or even contradict theirs—and do this with openness and humble consideration.

One should not be surprised that reasonable and faithful people make very different theological claims. Marilynne Robinson speaks of how theology is

---

22. See Allen, *Theological Method*.

23. Bernard Lonergan (*Method in Theology* [New York: Seabury Press, 1972], 7–54) suggests that theological methodology is the "science" of theology and, as such, must be approached carefully and patiently. He uses the analogy of the growth of a child and how a child can only mature as he or she reflects on and grasps the process of maturing itself. Methodology is the process by which theologians can come to understand theology's own process of development.

jammed with paradoxes that house confusion, inconsistency, change, and anomaly:

> Theology, because it is anchored in pre-modern thought, not only accommodates anomaly but is devoted to its exploration. Why should irreconcilable things be equally true? How can we be precious and yet so appallingly mortal? Why our predisposition to evil when we feel so strongly predisposed to good? Why were the lives of the patriarchs, those bearers of God's intention for the world, so bitter and sad? Why the suffering of the chosen people? These anomalies, or paradoxes, prepare for the one that crowns them all. Why the God Man?[24]

Attending to one's theological methodology is important but is often neglected in favor of the interest in the contents of theology itself: God, soteriology, biblical interpretation, natural theology, the Person of Jesus, and so forth. Sometimes the sheer fact that a formidable introduction to philosophy is a necessary aid in theological methodology can be off-putting, which may explain the negative reason behind the neglect of theological method. Allen quips, "Clarifying one's theological methodology instead of doing theology is like sharpening a knife without cutting into anything," but, he adds, "The sharpness of one's knife determines how well one is able to cut. If one's theological method is consciously chosen, then the scope and precision of the theological claims being made are bound to be clearer."[25]

Allen asserts that since the middle of the twentieth century, discussions of method within the Christian theological academy have become increasingly urgent.[26] In spite of this, the ongoing conversation does not appear to be resolving in any demonstrably clear way in terms of whether one method is better than another. Many believe this has been exacerbated in the overall discipline of theology for two major reasons. First, the practical effects that have come to the fore from the rise in agnosticism and atheism that precipitate a stout skepticism concerning the very plausibility of God. This tempts theologians to base their work on empiricism or realism (see Chapter 3). Second, the diversity of theological methods continues to expand in large part by the many theological sources that can be reasonably considered, along with the different interpretations and prioritization of those sources (I return to the issue of sources below).

To move forward with a description of the particular PTM I propose, we must name *where* it is to start. According to Michael Jinkins, "The single greatest challenge

---

24. Marilynne Robinson, "Happiness" (a paper presented at the Yale Center for Faith and Culture Consultation on Happiness and Human Flourishing, sponsored by the McDonald Agape Foundation, accessed June 7, 2018, https://faith.yale.edu/sites/default/files/robinson_1.pdf.

25. Allen, *Theological Method*, 1.

26. Ibid.

in theology is finding the right place to start."[27] If Jinkins is right, one's starting point is fundamental to and perhaps the most important aspect of a theological methodology. Our starting point is caught in the very phrase pneumatological imagination. I begin with the pneumatological.

The Pneumatological

Pentecostalism is more correctly seen in a broader context as a movement concerned primarily with the experience of the working of the Holy Spirit. Much has already been said about the pneumatological commitment within the pentecostal ethos in Chapter 1 with an articulation of the morphology which I claim is pentecostal *qua* pentecostal. We do not need to revisit that here in any significant detail. However, we *do* want to explore what might be prioritized in a theological system that privileges the role of the Spirit.

In his important work, *Pneumatology: The Holy Spirit in Ecumenical, International, and Contextual Perspective,* Kärkkäinen writes, "A renaissance concerning the doctrine and spirituality of the Holy Spirit has stirred much interest and even enthusiasm from all theological corners. The reverberations can be felt everywhere from new theological studies in the academy to the publication of popular books to the emergence of new spiritual orientations and movements."[28] Kärkkäinen cites Roman Catholic theologian Elizabeth Dreyer as she speaks of the "hunger" for the pneumatological:

> Renewed interest in the Holy Spirit is visible in at least three contexts: individual Christians who hunger for a deeper connection with God that is inclusive of all of life as well as the needs of the world; the church that seeks to renew itself through life-giving disciplines and a return to sources; and the formal inquiry of academic philosophy and theology. In effect, one can hear the petition, "Come Creator Spirit" on many lips these days.[29]

This author has just returned from Rome where I participated in an ecumenical meeting with Pope Francis and a small group of other Christian leaders. Both Francis and the new Secretary General of the International Theological Commission in the Roman Catholic Church, Piero Coda, repeatedly affirmed

---

27. Michael Jinkins, *Invitation to Theology* (Downers, Grove, IL: InterVarsity Press, 2001), 43 (emphasis original).

28. Kärkkäinen, *Pneumatology*, 1.

29. Elizabeth A. Dreyer, "An Advent of the Spirit: Medieval Mystics and Saints," in *Advents of the Spirit: An Introduction to the Current Study of Pneumatology*, ed. Bradford E. Hinze and D. Lyle Dabney (Milwaukee: Marquette University Press, 2001), 123, quoted by Kärkkäinen, *Pneumatology*, 1.

that this century is the "century of the Holy Spirit" and that the Roman Church is attending to all things Spirit in fresh and very intentional ways.[30]

Kärkkäinen points out that there have been a number of treatises on the Holy Spirit offered in church history (e.g., those of Athanasius and the Cappadocians, particularly Basil the Great), but that in the past two decades or so, pneumatological studies have exploded on the theological scene.[31] Anglican Alister McGrath asserts, "The rise of the charismatic movement within virtually every mainstream church has ensured that the Holy Spirit figures prominently on the theological agenda. A new experience of the reality and power of the Spirit has had a major impact upon the theological discussion of the person and work of the Holy Spirit."[32]

Kärkkäinen notes that the interest in pneumatology has not always been keen. "Historically," he writes, "there were centuries where a minor role was assigned to the role of the Spirit."[33] He references that before the Great Schism of the church between East and West in 1054, the theologians of the East accused their Western counterparts of a "forgetfulness of the Spirit."[34] Kärkkäinen cites a few reasons for this—one being ecclesial. As early as the second and third century, the charismatic-prophetic movement known as Montanism was rejected by church leadership because it was believed that the movement was causing chaos and the loss of order. Instead of being open, investigative, and welcoming, the church reacted negatively to the pneumatological spirituality that was prioritized in Montanism, failing to integrate it into the church's life.[35] Another reason for a "forgetfulness of the Spirit" that Kärkkäinen points to is that traditional pneumatology was not addressed separately as its own locus within Christian systematic theologies. Kärkkäinen writes, "Unlike the doctrine of the Trinity or the church, the discussion of the Spirit has not stood on its own feet, so to speak. Most often pneumatological topics have been incorporated into the doctrine of salvation (soteriology) and inspiration of Scripture."[36] But the winds have changed. A question posed by the Catholic

---

30. This meeting that happened on October 27, 2022, was casual and "off the books" with approximately forty leaders at The Domus Sanctae Marthae where Pope Francis resides. We met with Pope Francis and other Roman Catholic and Protestant leaders for over two hours discussing ecumenism and Francis's most recent book: *Let Us Dream: The Path to a Better Future* (New York, NY: Simon & Schuster, 2020).

31. Kärkkäinen, *Pneumatology*, 10.

32. Alister McGrath, *Christian Theology: An Introduction*, 5th ed. (Oxford: John Wiley & Sons, 2011), 227, quoted in Kärkkäinen, *Pneumatology*, 2–3.

33. Kärkkäinen, *Pneumatology*, 8.

34. Ibid.

35. Ibid., 8.

36. Ibid., 9. Kärkkäinen also shows how it was the late Canadian Baptist Clark Pinnock's work, *Flame of Love*, where Pinnock takes a "turn to the Spirit." There Pinnock endeavored to construct a full-scale systematic theology from a pneumatological perspective.

theologian, John Sachs, regarding the surprising fresh interest in the Spirit today signals this: "What is it that invites us, perhaps compels us, to think and to speak about the Spirit today?"[37]

Pneumatological Theology

Remember that all theology speaks of God, so a pneumatological theology speaks of the Holy Spirit. Jürgen Moltmann remarks:

> From the very beginning, the personhood of the Holy Spirit was an unsolved problem, and the problem is as difficult as it is fascinating. To start from the experience of the Spirit meant finding largely nonpersonal personal words and phrases to describe it: the Spirit is a divine energy, it is wind and fire, light and a wide space, inward assurance and mutual love. Because of what the Spirit effects, its nature was often described through analogies of this kind, drawn from other experiences.[38]

Augustine reflected on the difficulty one encounters when speaking about the Spirit—the problem being that the Spirit "withdraws from us into mystery even more than Christ."[39] Kärkkäinen reports that for Augustine, there were three conditions one must hold in view when speaking of the Spirit. First, one must not rely on "pure theory," but must have experience of having been touched by the Spirit. Second, experience alone is not to be trusted—it must be honestly and assiduously examined so that "one's own spirit" does not supplant the Holy Spirit. Discerning this is central to the task of all theologizing. Third, whatever the theologue deduces must be compared to the discernment of the whole church—living and past—to ensure that the illumination of the theological process has come from the same Spirit and does not contradict what has been made known to the church-catholic.[40]

Doing pneumatological theology can be challenging. On one hand there is the danger of trying to put too fine a point on *who* the Holy Spirit is and *how* the Spirit acts in and outside of creation. On the other hand, the descriptions can be too broad and free for some theologians to embrace. Moltmann warns that some

---

37. John R. Sachs, "'Do Not Stifle the Spirit': Karl Rahner, the Legacy of Vatican II, and Its Urgency for Theology Today," *Catholic Theological Society of America Proceedings* 51 (1996): 15, quoted in Kärkkäinen, *Pneumatology*, 4.

38. Jürgen Moltmann, *The Spirit of Life: A Universal Affirmation* (Minneapolis, MN: Fortress Press, 2001), loc. 264–67, Kindle.

39. Augustine, as interpreted by Joseph Ratzinger, "The Holy Spirit as *Communio*: Concerning the Relationship of Pneumatology and Spirituality in Augustine," *Communio* 25 (Summer 1998): 324; accessed May 17, 2022, http://www.communio-icr.com/files/ratzinger25-2.pdf, quoted in Kärkkäinen, *Pneumatology*, 5.

40. See Kärkkäinen, *Pneumatology*, 5.

theologians who are part of more hierarchical, traditional churches resist what he calls "a holistic pneumatology"[41] because they fear too much liberty is taken by the

> "[F]ree thinking" of the modern world which led to more and more reserve in the doctrine of the Holy Spirit. In reaction against the spirit of the new liberty—freedom of belief, freedom of religion, freedom of conscience and free churches—the only Spirit that was declared holy was the Spirit that is bound to the ecclesiastical institution for mediating grace, and to the preaching of the official "spiritual pastors and teachers." The Spirit which people experience personally in their own decision of faith, in believers' baptism, in the inner experience of faith in which "they feel their hearts strangely warmed" (as John Wesley put it), and in their own charismatic endowment, was declared "unholy" and "enthusiastic." Even today, in ecclesiastical discussions about the Holy Spirit, people like to turn first and foremost to "the criterion for discerning the spirits"—even when there do not seem to be any spirits to hand.[42]

Kärkkäinen also speaks of the concerns one should have when articulating a theology of the Spirit. He starts with a warning he garnered from Sachs: "Theologians from who[m] I have learned the most, both ancient and modern, all warn against trying to comprehend the Spirit in a systematic way."[43] Sachs recommends what he calls an "attitude of honorable silence," which cautions against useless speculations about the Spirit.[44] The concern here is that a theologue may become overly speculative when studying claims about the Spirit, which could actually draw one *away* from being more open to and sensitive to the Spirit.

It is not a simple matter to strike a balance between an orthodoxic approach to the pneumatological and one that privileges an orthopathic seeking of the Spirit. Kärkkäinen claims that "a healthy pneumatology requires balance between these two seemingly contradictory orientations."[45] He believes that the role of pentecostal and charismatic movements should be to help the church-catholic see that pneumatological work demands—and to model, first—a devotion to God's Spirit before launching into intellectual theological reflection. Kärkkäinen asserts, "[Pneumatology] is not theology that is primary but rather a revitalization of the experience of the Spirit. Even though the experience of the Spirit always leads to theological reflection on its meaning, spirituality is the first contact point."[46] He adds: "The Spirit is not an 'object' of human study in the same way that, for

---

41. Moltmann, *Spirit of Life*, loc. 112, Kindle.
42. Moltmann, *Spirit of Life*, loc. 147–51, Kindle.
43. Sachs, "Do Not Stifle the Spirit," 15, quoted by Kärkkäinen, *Pneumatology*, 4.
44. Ibid.
45. Kärkkäinen, *Pneumatology*, 5.
46. Ibid.

instance, the objects of the physical sciences are. In fact, as mentioned, the Spirit, rather than being an object of our scrutiny, is the One who searches us (1 Cor. 2:10-11). The Spirit and spirituality belong together."[47]

That being said, Robert Jenson offers a reflection on the Holy Spirit existing within the context of God's triune nature that is more formal, yet, important and helpful as we proceed:

> In God, personal identity is indeed prior to essence. God the Father is first of all Father of that other personal identity the Son and he has that nature we call divine nature only in and by and on account of that relationship. The relationship and the personal identity given in the relationship—Father to the Son—that is the first fact about God. And that he is God—and then we will start laying out predicates: omnipotent, omnipresent, and so on—that is the second thing. So also then the Son: Jesus of Nazareth is first of all the Son of the Father and only thereby does he have the "divine nature." So also then the Spirit: the Spirit is first of all the mutual Spirit of the Father and the Son together and only by and in that relationship can he be construed as divine. In God the personal identities are constituted in each one's relationship to the other two.[48]

To do pneumatological theology we must stay tethered to that formal place, but to bring us back one step to the beauty of the living Spirit outside any theological construct and back to a living experience, we return to Dreyer:

> Christians desire to encounter a Holy Spirit who brings new life to their spirits in the concrete circumstances of their lives and who renews the face of the earth as we enter the third millennium. Not unlike earlier times of perceived crisis, Christians today attempt to reconnect with the wellsprings of the faith, hoping these roots will bring stability, order and meaning to a postmodern world that is often felt to be hopelessly fragmented. In particular, many seek to retrieve a three-personed God who is related to the human community and to the entire universe in love, challenge, and care—a personal God who identifies with human joys and sorrows.[49]

Both the formal and the informal ways of addressing the Spirit are necessary to a faithful pneumatological theology. There are so many ways to speak about the Spirit, and the well of pneumatological theology is vast and deep, but I will highlight four particular ways the Spirit is identified as being "of"—"Spirit of's" that deeply inform a constructed PTM: (1) the *Spirit of Life*, (2) the *Spirit of Truth*, (3) the *Spirit of Love*, and (4) the *Spirit of the Wind*. Here, we shift away from historical theology into biblical studies and constructive theology.

---

47. Ibid.
48. Jenson, *A Theology in Outline*, 70-1.
49. Dreyer, "Advent of the Spirit," 123, quoted by Kärkkäinen, *Pneumatology*, 4.

The Spirit of Life

Romans 8:2 explicitly calls the Holy Spirit "the Spirit of life" (NKJV). In creation, the life-giving Spirit is first mentioned as "hovering over the waters" (Gen. 1:2). The result? The earth that was "formless and empty" with "darkness [that] was over the surface of the deep" is awakened with light and organized to be a place of order and life (Gen. 1). Kärkkäinen points out that Luther, echoing the metaphor of the "hovering Spirit" in Genesis, calls the Holy Spirit "the hen who broods her eggs and keeps them warm to have them hatch," which is another way of saying, "the office of the Holy Spirit is to make alive."[50]

Nimi Wariboko writes that:

> In Genesis 1, the breath of God is the bridge between "nothingness" and "somethingness." This Spirit (*ruach*, the breath of God) and the pronouncement of "let there be light" (controlled breath as sound; latent potentiality lighted, set on "fire") are the set of primal thrust that set potential and possibility surging forward toward greater and greater actuality.[51]

In the creation account, the Holy Spirit seems to be *both* the breath of God and the Word that calls life into being. Moltmann is helpful here:

> If the *ruach* is associated with God, and God with the *ruach*, then Yahweh's *ruach* and Yahweh's *dabar*—his word—are very close to one another. *Ruach* is thought of as the breath of God's voice ... If this unity of breath and voice is carried over to God's creativity, then all things are called to life through God's Spirit and Word.[52]

The biblical imagery of the Spirit may seem ambiguous—from "breath" to "fire" to "dove" to "Paraclete," but what is *not* ambiguous is that wherever the Spirit is, *life* emerges. When God spoke the universe into being, he used "breath"—*ruach* in the First Testament and *pneuma* in the New. It was *then* that the world (and perhaps other worlds in the universe that we know not of) filled with order and life. First, there was nonhuman life, and then, God calls humanity into life by *breathing* into Adam's nostrils,[53] and he became a living being (Gen. 2:7). God does the same for the nation of Israel as God calls them into "life" when Israel seemed dead (Ezek. 37). Here, God's *ruach* comes upon the "dry bones" (representing a spiritually dead Israel), and they "come to life," as Ezekiel proclaims:

---

50. Kärkkäinen, *Pneumatology*, 71.

51. Nimi Wariboko, *The Pentecostal Principle: Ethical Methodology in New Spirit* (Grand Rapids, MI: William B. Eerdmans Publishing Company, 2012), loc. 427–8, Kindle.

52. Moltmann, *Spirit of Life*, 41, quoted in Wariboko, *Pentecostal Principle*, loc. 407–9, Kindle.

53. The Hebrew word used for "breath" in Gen. 2:7 is *neshamah*, which could be translated "spirit" or "soul."

> This is what the Sovereign Lord says to these bones: I will make breath enter you, and you will come to life. I will attach tendons to you and make flesh come upon you and cover you with skin; I will put breath in you, and you will come to life. Then you will know that I am the Lord.
>
> (Ezek. 37:4-6)

The same way God called humanity into life and Israel into life—he calls the church into life. The act of God's *ruach* into human beings at creation and upon the dry bones of lost Israel is the archetype of the *pneuma*—when Jesus breathes on his disciples in John 20:22 saying, "Receive the Holy Spirit." The point is, the Holy Spirit carries life itself as a gift of God. Pinnock writes that, "Most fundamentally the Spirit is associated with the gift of life and with every new beginning."[54] The Holy Spirit is the source of human (and animal) life. The psalmist declares, "When you send your Spirit, they are created, and you renew the face of the ground" (Ps. 104:30), but he is careful to add that "breath" (viz., life) belongs to God, who can recall it at his pleasure: "when you take away their breath, they die and return to the dust" (Ps. 104:29). "Spirit," "breath," and "life" are not exactly the same, but they are not too distinct from each other either. The work of the Holy Spirit in the human experience (that we refer to as "spirituality")—to return to our metaphor of the butterfly—is *less* about a taxidermized construct to be analyzed and studied and *more* about a discovery of the One from whom all life emerges—including our own.

Certainly, a pneumatological theologizing will house seemingly static and schematized dogma and doctrine, but the theology must be made *alive* or becomes *visible* as a lived or incarnated pneumatology in order for it to be truly of the Spirit. As Wariboko avers:

> In Acts 2, we can identify and retrieve the pentecostal principle. Here we see that the spiritual content and its material bearers are combined or networked as the infinite restlessness of existence (life). The creative spirit becomes comes "incarnate" in 120 material bodies, just as spiritual form can become come visible as it was in the Doric column Martin Buber admires in his *I and Thou*. In Buber's reporting, the material column is occluded by the spiritual form it "incarnates," but on that fateful day of Pentecost in first-century century Jerusalem we find the materialization of spiritual content. It was a moving-together of spirit and matter toward actualized goodness.[55]

When considering that the Holy Spirit is the Spirit of life, it carries a wider, more cosmic influence. In relation to the encounters we humans have with the Holy Spirit, Moltmann gives us a juxtaposition:

> [If one asks,] when did you last feel the workings of the Holy Spirit? [It] embarrasses us. The Spirit's "holiness" fills us with religious awe. We are

---

54. Pinnock, *Flame of Love*, 50.
55. Wariboko, *Pentecostal Principle*, loc. 591–5, Kindle.

conscious that the Spirit is something apart from secular life, and sense our own remoteness from God. Religious experiences, as we all know, are not everyone's line of country.

It is a different matter if we are asked: when were you last conscious of "the spirit of life?" Then we can answer out of our own everyday experiences and can talk about our consolations and encouragements. Then "spirit" is the love of life which delights us, and the energies of the spirit are the living energies which this love of life awakens in us.[56]

Moltmann's focus is on the way the Spirit is engaged cosmically with all life throughout the universe: "We have got used to death, at least to the death of other creatures and other people. And to get used to death is the beginning of freezing into lifelessness oneself. So the essential thing is to affirm life—the life of other creatures—the life of other people—our own lives."[57]

I believe that Moltmann's "holistic approach" broadens, instead of compromises, the aspects of the Spirit's work in our lives that brings holiness, awe, sanctification, and the miraculous. Moltmann explicates, "The operations of God's life-giving and life-affirming Spirit are universal and can be recognized in everything which ministers to life and resists its destruction. This efficacy of the Spirit does not replace Christ's efficacy, but makes it universally relevant."[58]

What is important here is that Moltmann is making a case against limiting the working of the Spirit to *just* religious activity (viz., highly enthusiastic worship; speaking in tongues; inspired to believe Christ to be savior, healer, sanctifier, baptizer, and soon coming king; practicing the gifts of the Spirit; etc.). The Spirit is present in *all things*—sustaining *all things* in *all people*. This is not to say that all people are "saved" in the Christian soteriological sense, but it certainly does mean that "all flesh" (including the animal and inanimate creation) are under the care of God via the Spirit of life. Moltmann continues about how "the possibility of perceiving God in all things, and all things in God, is grounded theologically on an understanding of the Spirit of God as the power of creation and the wellspring of life."[59]

Moltmann may seem like he is setting up the grounds for a soteriological pluralism in his claim that:

> Every experience of a creation of the Spirit is hence also an experience of the Spirit itself. Every true experience of the self becomes also an experience of the divine spirit of life in the human being. Every lived moment can be lived in the inconceivable closeness of God in the Spirit: *Interior intimo meo*, said Augustine—God is closer to me than I am to myself.[60]

---

56. Moltmann, *Spirit of Life*, 64–8 loc., Kindle.
57. Ibid., loc. 100–1, Kindle.
58. Ibid., loc. 81–2, Kindle.
59. Ibid., loc. 573–9, Kindle.
60. Ibid.

But, again, the claim he is making is *not* that all people everywhere have a clear revelation of God in Christ but that all people are being cared for by the Spirit by the very fact that they are *alive*. This means that all of creation is under the careful watch and care of God even though creation may be unaware. This, it turns out, is actually evidence of the work of prevenient grace setting up the work of salvation in Christ and helps make sense of ideas like the famous one espoused by Augustine: "Late have I loved Thee, O Beauty so ancient and so new; late have I loved Thee! For behold Thou wert within me, and I outside; and I sought Thee outside and in my unloveliness fell upon those lovely things that Thou hast made. *Thou wert with me and I was not with Thee.*"[61]

Augustine's "You were with me, and I was not with you" captures in large part the beauty of a theological methodology centered in pneumatology (PTM). It is the recognition that the Spirit is "hovering" over all of creation—drawing, caring for, sustaining all. Again, this is not scandalous to the unique exclusive work of salvation in Jesus Christ—the Spirit is not in competition against the Christ and only *always* acts to glorify Jesus. However, the Spirit should be seen to be the One who falls upon "all flesh" to bring newness and vitality for the actualization of new possibilities to all people everywhere.

Systematic theologian, Michael Welker, writes of the Spirit (echoing Isa. 55): "The Spirit of God acts in the same way as the rain which, coming down from heaven, enables an entire landscape with the most varied living beings to burst into new life together, full of freshness and vitality."[62] Paul Tillich argues in *The Shaking of the Foundations* that the Spirit's creative impulse always gestures toward the particularity and universality of the Spirit's presence upon all existence:

> In the story of the Pentecost, the Spirit of Christ shows its creativity in both directions, the individual and universal. Each discipline receives the fiery tongue that is the new creative Spirit. Members of all nations, separated by their different tongues, understand each other in this New Spirit, which creates a new peace, beyond the cleavages of Babel.[63]

This means that the gospel is not a story for those who are beyond God's care, *all* are right in the midst of God's care. Many are simply unaware of it because, in Paul's words, they are living "in the futility of their thinking" because "they are darkened in their understanding," which separates them "from the life of God" that is *right there* with and in them—the "separation" exists "because of the ignorance that is in them due to the hardening of their hearts" (Eph. 4:17-18). The tragedy is that God is with people who are not aware enough or open enough to be *with* God.

61. Augustine, *Confessions*, 210, emphasis added.
62. Michael Welker, *God the Spirit*, trans. John Hoffmeyer (Minneapolis: Fortress, 1994), 126, quoted in Wariboko, *Pentecostal Principle*, loc. 3036, Kindle.
63. Paul Tillich, *Shaking of the Foundations* (Eugene, OR: Wipf & Stock, 1948), 138, quoted by Wariboko, *Pentecostal Principle*, loc. 392-4, Kindle.

The Spirit of Truth

When Jesus addressed the privilege of worship, he said, "God is spirit, and his worshipers must worship in the Spirit and in truth" (John 4:24). Jesus is saying that *truth* is central to our worship of God. As Jesus continues in this vein of pneumatology, he calls Spirit "the Spirit of truth" and claims that the Spirit "will guide you into all the truth" (16:13). Spirit, then, is not only the One who holds and embodies truth; Spirit is our promised *guide* into the oft-complicated world of truth discovery. The complication of truth is not found in its straightforwardness, but in the wide-open spaces that Moltmann's "holistic pneumatology" points toward. Moltmann states that we should expect that the breath of God is not just the place of experiencing God's force of life, but where one can experience spatiality in the pursuit of truth:

> [We] may call *ruach* the confronting event of the personal presence of God, and the life force immanent in all the living, this is still not enough to exhaust the full meaning of the word. The term is probably related to *rewah* = breadth. *Ruach* creates space. It sets in motion. It leads out of narrow places into wide vistas, thus conferring life. To experience the *ruach* is to experience what is divine not only as a person, and not merely as a force, but also as space—as the space of freedom in which the living being can unfold. That is the experience of the Spirit: "Thou has set my feet in a broad place" (Ps. 31:8). "You also he allured out of distress into a broad place where there is no cramping" (Job. 36:16).[64]

Incorporating such a concept into one's theological methodology is to push past the tendency to be too confined or overly precise in one's pursuit of truth, and it suggests that Spirit is not limited to how truth is revealed to humanity, and that *all* truth—irrespective of source—is important to consider. Therefore, the way truth negotiated within a PTM should not be restrictive or cramping but should be a joyful/playful process. A process not evidenced by nervousness or scrupulosity, but by a kind of dance with the Spirit of truth.

Before going further, we should nod to what we explored in Chapter 2 concerning how early pentecostals in America reinterpreted the Christian faith in a way that "was understood as an imitation of the early church."[65] But once those reinterpretations were expressed, there was a general heavy-handedness expressed by leaders for their followers to accept those reinterpretations as the voice of God. Arrington reports, "Because the interpreter has claimed divine guidance, the resulting interpretation is assumed to be above questioning and thus implicitly demands an authority on par with Scripture itself."[66] Many pentecostals came to

---

64. Moltmann, *Spirit of Life*, loc. 668–75, Kindle.
65. Oliverio, *Theological Hermeneutics*, 78.
66. Arrington, "Hermeneutics," 383.

believe that "there was one truth and therefore one interpretation of Scripture."[67] In a fashion informed by the demands of modernity for certitude (see Chapters 3 and 4), the emphasis was placed on doctrinal accuracy. "The goal then was precision—first, last, and always precision. Authors rarely acknowledged, let alone took pleasure in, the possibility that language might bear multiple meanings."[68] A PTM resists this kind of restrictive view within theological work.

Welcoming open spaces theologically causes the PTM I am imagining to be inclusive of (but not be limited to) a number of commitments. Two of them being, (a) exploring truth in an *interdisciplinary way*, and (b) carrying a *doxastic logic* as a kind of warrant for truth.

Interdisciplinary To surrender to the Spirit of truth, one must be open to truth irrespective of its provenance. To be sure, not all truth is the same kind of truth—revealed truth about the nature of Jesus Christ is not the same kind of truth as the molecular structure of water. But even natural truths can have an impact on theological discussions. On January 1, 1925, scientists discovered the universe as we now know it. It was the birthday of a new cosmology that has transformed our myopic and blinkered view of reality and carried significant implications for theological thought. Think of it: the God who created and cares for the vast, seemingly limitless universe is the same God who "so loved" this single world (that lies off-center on the mapped vast universe) that he was incarnated into it. The notion is nothing short of scandalous! Or consider the claim that the creation is not thousands of years old, but billions? What might this say about God, or about our understanding of eschatology? If the scale is "billions" instead of "thousands," then the least we must say is that this God we know "in part" is more patient and in less of an eschatological hurry than most of faithful pentecostals have considered. My point is that information from other disciplines must be accounted for when we theologize.

This is why I believe that a theological methodology that is rooted in pneumatology should be done using an *interdisciplinary approach* to theology, which seeks to analyze, synthesize, and harmonize the shared themes and ideas found in theology with other outside disciplines (e.g., sociology, anthropology, psychology, philosophy, anthropology, economics, political science, etc.).

One may ask: *Shouldn't theology—the "queen of the sciences"—stand alone and not be mixed or intermingled with other disciplines? And shouldn't theology draw all its understanding and insight from the Bible, the word of God?* Certainly, the Bible warns us to avoid "the opposing ideas of what is falsely called knowledge" (1 Tim. 6:20, ESV). Instead, we are asked to strive to "correctly handle the word of truth" (2 Tim. 2:15). It is this understanding that is to be the starting point for learning: "The fear of the LORD is the beginning of knowledge" (Prov. 1:7). It is noteworthy that often through history the *vox populi* considered any facts outside

---

67. Ibid., 382.
68. Oliverio, *Theological Hermeneutics*, 40.

of eternal truths articulated by priests or scripture as unimportant.[69] Often in the ancient world, people assumed that whatever God (or the gods) and the prophets and sages did *not* tell them was deemed unnecessary to discuss. Philosophers and theologians simply focused on their texts and traditions to answer *everything*—from theology to science to social, political, and economic issues.

Early Christian theologians, however, knew that blending the ideas and constructs of one discipline with another would aid the rational enterprise, adding context, nuance, and fresh insight. They did this cautiously because they knew doing so could lead to an untenable syncretism that violated critical faith positions or could foster unnecessary cognitive dissonance. But the risk was taken because faithful Christian theologians found that resourcing their own religious texts, prophets, and tradition was not always enough to address complex questions—like the development of new doctrines that were only present in embryonic form in sacred text (i.e., the Trinity, or later when issues arose that had not been present or imagined when sacred text was penned [viz., defining orthodoxy over against heterodoxy]). Christian theology was not formed by Christian thinkers being solely in dialogue with scripture—much of the detailed work happened as those thinkers engaged the criticisms and insights afforded from non-Christian philosophers and pagan intellectuals who surrounded them. Wilken reveals:

> [Early apologists] did not draw the conclusion that Christian thinkers should ignore the arguments of the philosophers or dismiss questions that arose from logic, history, or experience. "It is far better," wrote Origen, "to accept teachings with reason and wisdom than with mere faith" ... Some critics, notably Galen, had tried to brand the Christians as fideists because their teachings seemed to be based solely on faith. But these cultured despisers soon learned that Christian thinkers were as conversant with the philosophical tradition as they were and respected arguments from reason. In their works in defense of Christianity the apologists met Greek and Roman thinkers argument for argument, a dialogue that was carried on without interruption for three centuries and resumed in the high Middle Ages. Even the Bible was a book to be argued from, not simply an authority to brandish when arguments failed. Origen's assertion that the gospel had a "proof proper to itself" was not a confession of faith, but the beginning of an argument.[70]

Another reason early Christian apologists took an interdisciplinary approach to their theologizing was because of their commitment to translating the Christian faith to outsiders. Wilken goes on to say that these apologists faced the "daunting task of presenting Christianity for the first time to a society that knew nothing of the Christian religion."[71] (This task still haunts the twenty-first century theologian!)

---

69. Harari, *Sapiens*, 251.
70. Wilken, *The Spirit of Early Christian Thought*, 14.
71. Ibid., 4.

Wilken asserts it took Christianity at least a hundred years for people across the empire to have any real knowledge of its claims, and that using arguments from their intellectual milieu helped them to have a context for those claims.[72]

It turns out that hearing from multiple disciplines is particularly helpful when trying to elucidate a concept that lies beyond the language of the particular discipline one is working in (e.g., the use of philosophy in explaining the "economic Trinity"). Or consider how theologians might address the motivations, dispositions, and affections of one who is *doing* the theologizing versus the one who is *hearing* it. Such an analysis would require some implicit knowledge of psychology. Or, what of the anthropological or ethical commitments one brings to the theological enterprise? The knowledge and wisdom afforded by other disciplines can make a significant impact in the theological enterprise.

That said, disciplines outside of theology should not be given too great a role. The words of Allen are helpful here:

> The "how" and "for whom" God reveals God's-self to is a significant question to address. Theology within Christianity makes claims about God and about how God acts in the world in ways that other disciplines could not imagine nor accept. The church claims knowledge of what God has revealed, but that it is a knowledge that is imperfect and a kind that we only see "through a glass darkly." This implies it is a knowledge that is subject to an analysis according to how it was received—through historical acts of God, word of the prophets, traditions of God's people, etc. From the "revelation" of God's-self theologians draw inferences, deductions, inductions and retrodictive claims on the basis of these forms of "revelation," which become, in some analogous sense, a theological epistemology. Theology does involve human cognition and analysis, but it also points beyond the world of inference and language in ways that other disciplines could not and would not imagine.[73]

Approaching theology in an interdisciplinary way brings up the very important issue of *sources*. What are the sources of theology? From whence does the *Spirit of truth* speak? Theologians do not all agree on which sources are valid when approaching the question of "how God reveals God's-self" to humanity. But the question of sources is an important one in any theological methodology. Generally speaking, the most important sources recognized within Christian theology include scripture, reason, tradition, experience, and creation. But the priority and weight of the sources relied upon by theologians throughout history have varied. Pre-sixteenth century, the primary sources for theologians were scripture and tradition (including the tradition of philosophical reason). The Reformation introduced a new distance between Christian thought and philosophical reason

---

72. Ibid.
73. Allen, *Theological Method*, 12.

(viz., scholasticism). Enlightenment reason was reacted to with Romanticism, which brought on an explicit attention to human experience as an additional source for theology.[74]

Conservative groups, like pentecostals and evangelicals, have traditionally claimed to source the Bible almost exclusively (though, as we are shown throughout this project, experience and the leading of the Spirit has consistently weighed heavily in pentecostal theologizing). We have already seen how conservative theological camps ended up being criticized for carrying the uncritical assumptions of Enlightenment foundationalism, including its corresponding naive belief that one can read ancient texts objectively (Chapter 3). In response to this postconservatives have arisen, who continue to hold to the notion that the Bible is the "norming norm" (viz., *kanon*) of Christian theology, but they are more aware of hermeneutical problems. Plus, postconservatives tend to be more open to other sources (outside the Bible) informing the interpretive process. Millard Erickson, a leading proponent of the propositional approach to theology, affirms that the Christian tradition and the many nonbiblical disciplines (e.g., psychology and sociology) should play a role in theology.[75]

A number of thinkers in recent years have been making extrabiblical data and analysis more fundamental to their theological methodology.[76] Though I think it right for some sources to carry more weight in the theological enterprise than others, the welcoming of any truth-bearing source acknowledges that sources give us approximations more than totalizing explanations. In speaking of the philosophy of science, Ian Hacking provides a helpful perspective about sources:

> God did not write a Book of Nature of the sort that the old Europeans imagined. He wrote a Borgesian library, each book of which is as brief as possible, yet each book of which is inconsistent with every other. No book is redundant. For every book, there is some humanly accessible bit of Nature such that that book, and no other, makes possible the comprehension, prediction and influencing of what is going on. Far from being untidy, this is New World Leibnizianism. Leibniz

---

74. See Friedrich D. E. Schleiermacher, *Brief Outline of the Study of Theology*, trans. Terrence N. Tice (Richmond, VA: John Knox Press, 1966).

75. See Millard J. Erickson, *Christian Theology*, 2nd ed. (Grand Rapids, MI: Baker Academic, 1998). Other examples of sourcing an interdisciplinary approach are found in F. LeRon Shults and Steven J. Sandage, *The Faces of Forgiveness: Searching for Wholeness and Salvation* (Grand Rapids, MI: Baker Academic, 2003); and Jack O. Balswick, Pamela Ebstyne King, and Kevin S. Reimer, *The Reciprocating Self: Human Development in Theological Perspective* (Downers Grove, IL: InterVarsity Press, 2005).

76. There are several examples. Stanley Grenz and John Franke hold tradition and culture, along with scripture, as the three sources for doing theology. See Stanley J. Grenz and John R. Franke, *Beyond Foundationalism*. Also see Gordon R. Lewis and Bruce A. Demarest, *Integrative Theology* (Grand Rapids, MI: Zondervan, 1996). Thomas Oden's three-volume presentation of "paleo-orthodoxy," sources the wider historical

said that God chose a world which maximized the variety of phenomena while choosing the simplest laws. Exactly so: but the best way to maximize phenomena and have simplest laws is to have the laws inconsistent with each other, each applying to this or that but none applying to all.[77]

Whatever sources one chooses to draw from in one's theologizing, the inclusion of outside disciplines gives the theologue fresh ways to describe reality—the language of law, science, anthropology, sociology, or literary approaches all help to generate new understandings that can be coordinated into a coherent whole. Hence, the interdisciplinary approach affords new conceptual, theoretical, methodological, and translational innovations that can broaden theological study and its relationship to the real world.

Doxastic Logic When the Spirit of truth is guiding the church, the result is transcendent knowledge (or *knowing*) that we called a *pneumatological*

---

tradition of Christian theology as foundational to methodology; see Thomas C. Oden, *The Living God* (San Francisco, CA: HarperSanFrancisco, 1987); Thomas C. Oden, *The Living Word* (San Francisco, CA: HarperSanFrancisco, 1989); and Thomas C. Oden, *Life in the Spirit* (San Francisco, CA: HarperSanFrancisco, 1992). Oden's work has become widespread even among the most theologians toward the conservative end of the spectrum. See Roger E. Olson, *The Mosaic of Christian Belief: Twenty Centuries of Tradition and Reform* (Downers Grove, IL: InterVarsity Press, 1999); Webber, *Ancient-Future Faith*; D. H. Williams, *Retrieving the Tradition and Renewing Evangelicalism: A Primer for Suspicious Protestants* (Grand Rapids, MI: Baker, 1999); and InterVarsity Press's three-volume series, Angelo Di Berardino, ed., *Encyclopedia of Ancient Christianity: Ancient Christian Doctrine, Ancient Christian Commentary,* and *Ancient Christian Texts*, 3 vols (Downers Grove, IL: IVP Academic, 2014). Of course, there are the more mainstream theological figures who have also vied for the use of multiple sources—including natural sciences, salvation history, biblical texts, personal experience, existentialist and liberation concerns, etc. to be at the locus of concern. These include thinkers like Tillich, Bultmann, Gadamer, Barth, and Rahner. See Paul Tillich, "Theology and Symbolism," in *Religious Symbols*, ed. F. Ernest Johnson (New York: Harper and Row, 1955); Rudolf Bultmann, *Essays Philosophical and Theological* (London: SCM Press, 1955); Ted Peters, "Truth in History: Gadamer's Hermeneutics and Pannenberg's Apologetic Method," *The Journal of Religion* 55, no. 1 (1975): 36–56; Karl Barth, *Church Dogmatics*, vols I–V, trans. G. W. Bromiley (Edinburgh: T&T Clark, 1936); and Karl Rahner, *Theological Investigations XI* (New York: Crossroad, 1960). Still others (Lonergan, Pannenberg, McGrath, and J. Wentzel van Huyssteen) call for theological engagement with scientific, historical, and hermeneutical thinking in a comparable way in their approaches. See Lonergan, *Method in Theology*; Peters, "Truth in History," 36–56; McGrath, *Christian Theology*; J. Wentzel van Huyssteen, *Alone in the World? Human Uniqueness in Science and Theology* (Grand Rapids, MI: William B. Eerdmans Publishing Company, 2006).

77. Hacking, *Representing and Intervening*, 219.

epistemology (Chapter 1). A pneumatological epistemology is a knowing roused from encounters with the Spirit. This creates what could be seen as a new foundation for truth (or what some would call a "weak" or "minimalist" foundationalism),[78] rooted in a doxastic logic (to which I return below). The claim is that this new foundationalism—animated by the Spirit—replaces the "classical" foundationalism, which traces back to the Cartesian and Baconian quests for certainty. Remember, the hope of those who built on Descartes's or Bacon's foundations was to ensure that knowledge had a universal rationality that yielded indubitable, uncontestable truth.

We saw in Chapter 5 how this position began to be deconstructed by postmodern thinkers, to which Yong responds, "The problem is that the death of foundationalism appears to have relativized all truth claims, resulting in a debilitation if not paralysis of theological thinking."[79] However, Yong argues, "the demise of foundationalism does not entail the rejection of truth"; "On the contrary," he insists, "I hope to show that the evangelical insistence on truth in its strongest form can be reframed even if knowledge is admitted to be foundationless."[80] Yong proceeds by asserting that the "minimal" or "weak" foundationalism

> has a variety of formulations, including that proposed more recently by Reformed thinkers such as William Alston and Alvin Plantinga. They have insisted on a different sort of "foundation," one that is "properly basic" and non-justifiable on evidentialist grounds but which emerges out of doxastic (belief forming) practices and is therefore warranted and not irrational.[81]

Doxastic practices emerge from using doxastic logic, which is different from Western deductive or inductive logic. All epistemic logics are logics that allow one to reason about knowledge in some way. Doxastic logics are similar to deductive and inductive logics, but a doxastic logic allows one to reason about *belief* rather than about *knowledge*. In a sense a doxastic logic seeks an "epistemic justification," rather than knowledge.[82] So, for example, there is no attempt to try to find evidence to *prove* some piece of knowledge. The focus is on belief. Doxastic logic reasons, "It is believed that *x* is the case" and then seeks to organize a formal system of statements (viz., *modal logic*) that represent belief, necessity, and/or possibility.

The question *What is required for knowledge?* is not the question doxastic logic is asking or trying to answer. It seeks to answer the question *What is required*

---

78. "Minimal Foundationalism" is a term from William Alston (*Epistemic Justification: Essays in the Theory of Knowledge* [Ithaca: Cornell University Press, 1989], 39–56).

79. Amos Yong, "The Demise of Foundationalism and the Retention of Truth: What Evangelicals Can Learn from C.S. Peirce," *Christian Scholar's Review* 29, no. 3 (Spring 2000): 563.

80. Ibid., 564.

81. Ibid.

82. Alston, *Perceiving God*, 2.

for belief? Doxastic logic seeks to give warrant to a person's belief. It will claim, for example, that "a person can become justified in holding certain kinds of beliefs about God by virtue of perceiving God as being or doing so-and-so."[83] Here is a snapshot of Alston's view on doxastic logic:

> A person can become justified [using what] I shall call "M-beliefs" ("M" for manifestation). M-beliefs are beliefs to the effect that God is doing something currently vis-à-vis the subject—comforting, strengthening, guiding, communicating a message, sustaining the subject in being—or to the effect that God has some (allegedly) perceivable property—goodness, power, lovingness. The intuitive idea is that by virtue of my being aware of God as sustaining me in being I can justifiably believe that God is sustaining me in being.[84]

It is easy to see how doxastic logic would be native to pneumatological theology and a central part of any constructed PTM.

Obviously, using doxastic logic in the context of Christian theology presupposes that God exists (and, in truth, if any theologue refuses to antecedently accept such presuppositions, this logic will not be desirable). Doxastic logic welcomes axiomatic truths embedded in a faith tradition. Ronald Thiemann calls axiomatic truth "background beliefs" that are "beyond controversy"[85] (viz., existence of God, prevenient grace, etc.). By using doxastic logic, one can claim knowledge of a loving God because one has experienced love that they attribute as coming from God. This experience *itself* implies that God exists—though that is NOT what doxastic reasoning argues for—it simply argues that such beliefs about God are justified, based on what one perceives God as having done.

Hence, doxastic logic is a category of logic that seeks to ground existing theories into a finite, complete set of axioms by providing proofs that these axioms are *consistent*. The kind of persuasion used in doxastic logic is different than trying to persuade through universalizing reason. This logic persuades by drawing the thinker into an understanding of *holism*—where there is the recognition of the consistent interconnectedness of the universe (holism versus dualism) that insists that facts can only be "interpreted" facts, not universal or propositional facts that are *true-at-all-times-in-all-places*. For example, in speaking of the axiomatic doctrine of divine provenience, Thiemann writes of how holism becomes the justification for belief (viz., doxastic logic): "We convince someone of something by appealing to beliefs he already holds and by combining these to induce further beliefs in him, step by step, until the belief we wanted finally to inculcate in him is inculcated."[86] In response to this, Murphy writes, "Thiemann

---

83. Ibid., 2.
84. Ibid., i.
85. Ronald F. Thiemann, *Revelation and Theology: The Gospel as Narrated Promise* (Eugene, OR: Wipf & Stock Publishers, 2005), 11.
86. Ibid., 75–6.

claims that belief in God's provenience is logically tied both to beliefs and to practices that are not in dispute among Christians and, further, that these beliefs and practices are so central to Christian identity that to give them up would constitute a drastic change in Christian identity."[87]

A doxastic belief is not irrational but a warranted truth one can insist upon in the strongest way even though it is "foundationless" (in the classic sense of the word) knowledge. In *Perceiving God*, Alston is clear that though "the wise of this world, believers and unbelievers alike" are convinced that "religious experience is a purely subjective phenomenon" and that "its cognitive value can be safely dismissed without a hearing,"[88] he is intentionally tenacious in challenging that assumption and marshals the resources needed to support its rejection.

Knowledge through Story We now return to the new epistemic reality (viz., pneumatological epistemology) described above. This epistemology emerges from encounters with the Holy Spirit (from which doxastic practices can emerge to provide a warrant for faith) and is not justified on evidentialist grounds, but in an epistemology grounded in the transcendent realm that is beyond the conventional ways of knowing. This is a claim that God should not be crowded out of the world of human reasoning. In describing the shift between the standard modern epistemology and the kind that emerges from encounters with God, Richard Lints avers:

> The dream of finding self-evident, or even plainly empirical truths which could serve as an epistemic foundation has been revealed as simply that—a dream. Certainty is no longer a virtue but a vice, a mere chimera of earlier conceptual systems. Every belief is potentially (and ought practically to be) revisable. The epistemological enterprise is less like building a house than it is like engaging in *telling a story*.[89]

Lints continues: "The justification of beliefs is not a process of mapping beliefs onto the world but rather of finding warrant within the confines of a particular [tradition]."[90]

A hermeneutics framed in story has given the Christian church the ability to evolve and change as it reached for the formation of dogma over its history. Simon Chan reveals that "The progress of dogma has the character of plot, the

---

87. Murphy, *Beyond Liberalism*, 97.
88. William P. Alston, *Perceiving God: The Epistemology of Religious Experience* (Ithaca, NY: Cornell University Press, 2014), 4.
89. Richard Lints, "The Postpositivist Choice Tracy or Lindbeck?" *Journal of the American Academy of Religion* 61, no. 4 (1993): 664, emphasis added.
90. Lints, "The Postpositivist Choice," 665. Lints makes this claim based on the work of George Lindbeck, who borrowed the concept from the social sciences.

ongoing story of God's action in the world, and the story of the church is part of that development."[91] He continues by speaking of the pneumatocentricity of this story:

> But what is the church's story? It is the story centering on the Third Person of the Trinity: the sending of the Spirit. The coming of the Spirit, as noted earlier, constitutes the church by uniting the body to the Head. In this very act, as Jenson puts it, the "Spirit frees an actual human community from merely historical determinisms, to be apt to be united with the Son and thus to be the gateway of creation's translation into God." The story of the church, therefore, could be said to be the story of the Spirit in the church ... This is why Pentecost is so vital to the continuing growth of the Christian story. Without telling the story of the church, which is the story of the Spirit in the church, we have an incomplete gospel.[92]

Because most moderns (at least those raised in the North America) have been shaped by Enlightenment logic, there is a tremendous upside to seeking for solutions to theological problems through the lens of story[93] and not by a reliance on Enlightenment proofs. The focus of story (or narrative) is not an objective, comprehensive analysis of *what* is true, but on *how* a truth emerges in time and what its effects are as it is worked out in the lives of people. English historian, Lawrence Stone, writes that "Narrative is taken to mean the organization of material in a chronologically sequential order and the focusing of the content into a single coherent story, albeit with sub-plots" and that "its arrangement is descriptive rather than analytical"; therefore, "its central focus is on man not circumstances."[94] Stone affirms that story brings an analysis of truth via a narrative path but that the analysis privileges "the particular and the specific rather than the collective and the statistical."[95] This means that truth can be particularized and interpreted through the lens of an individual person's life, not by focusing on the

---

91. Simon Chan, *Liturgical Theology: The Church as Worshipping Community* (Downers Grove, IL: IVP Academic, 2006), 32.

92. Ibid.

93. Lawrence Stone ("The Revival of Narrative: Reflections on a New Old History," *Past & Present* 85, no. 4 [November 1979]: 3) makes the claim that there has been a "revival of narrative" afoot since the 1970s, and that this is good because "historians have always told stories, from Thucydides and Tacitus to Gibbon and Macaulay" and that "the composition of narrative" was always considered the historians "highest ambition" until the turn of the twentieth century.

94. Stone, "Revival of Narrative," 3–4. For the history of narrative, see Lionel Gossman, "Augustin Thierry and Liberal Historiography," *History and Theory* 15, no. 4 (December 1976): 3–6; and Haydon White, *Metahistory: The Historical Imagination in the Nineteenth Century* (Baltimore: Johns Hopkins University Press, 1973).

95. Stone, "Revival of Narrative," 3–4.

discovery of propositional truths that can be applied to all people at all times in all places. In *this* sense, truth is made relative to persons. At times this may open the Pandora's Box of borderless relativism that oft appears in postmodernism, which is a fair criticism of the narrative advance.[96]

However, as thorny as that sounds, it is not as thorny as rational absolutism has turned out to be. Allen claims that one of the "thorniest issues" that confronts the theologian is to what extent theology "needs to be articulated in purely 'rational' terms"; the "tendency to over-abstraction" is tempting because it helps to lay claim to universal "Truth."[97] Though the Christian story *does* claim to carry a capital "T" truth for all (viz., axiomatic truths), truth must always be "made flesh" in order for it to have any real impact on the human experience. Story affords such a transformation. Story/narrative makes everything connected and whole—it does not present truth as abstraction or something separate. Truth and life become one in story, and yet like the Trinity, are also different. Truth is not communicated simply by understanding things at an abstract level, but its deepest meaning is found in the experiencing of it—as the word made flesh. This validates the brilliance of the pentecostal default of including experiences of God into the exegetical-theological methodology of pentecostal theologizing.[98]

Christopher Stephenson warns that theology is not fruitful if it tries to simply systematize itself into "an entirely coherent account of all theological loci around a single integrating theme or principle."[99] Theology worked out using a pneumatological lens makes the theology *relational* (versus being solely theological reflection). Stephenson adds that we should "resist the notion that there could be a single system of timeless doctrines that does not constantly need to be reevaluated and reformulated in new times and places."[100] The PTM steers from this kind of error because of how it takes up doxastic logic in its nonfoundationalist pneumatological epistemology communicated through story.

However, those who think theological truth is only true when one can apply it universally and timelessly (a key foundationalist value) will find narrative approaches off-putting. It may be helpful for the story-diffident among us to be aware that particularizing truth through story does *not* necessitate a borderless

---

96. Demurrers include George Aichele, *The Limits of Story* (Philadelphia, PA: Fortress Press, 1986); Paul Lauritzen, "Is 'Narrative' Really a Panacea? The Use of 'Narrative' in the Work of Metz and Hauerwas," *Journal of Religion* 67, no. 3 (July 1987): 332–9; Wesley J. Robbins, "Narrative, Morality and Religion," *The Journal of Religious Ethics* 8, no. 1 (Spring 1980): 161–76; Ronald L. Grimes, "Of Words the Speaker, of Deeds the Doer," *Journal of Religion* 66, no. 1 (January 1986): 1–17.

97. Allen, *Theological Method*, 3.

98. Kenneth J. Archer, "Pentecostal Story: The Hermeneutical Filter for the Making of Meaning," *Pneuma* 26, no. 1 (Spring 2004): 37–8.

99. Christopher A. Stephenson, *Types of Pentecostal Theology: Method, System, Spirit* (Oxford: Oxford University Press, 2016), 6.

100. Ibid.

relativism. There is a good kind of narrative theology that carries a kind of "pregnant principle" where themes and arguments can be applicable to others[101]—just not magisterially.[102]

Of course, there are still modern conservatives who are drawn to the details of theological systems that speak in exclusive either/or terms and who enjoy debating over theological points and want to maintain the theological status quo. Those being formed by postmodernity, however, want generalities rather than specifics and want to speak inclusively rather than exclusively—more concerned with unity than diversity (Chapter 4). This is what *story* affords—a more open dynamic approach than a static-fixed one, which allows a high level of tolerance and ambiguity. A postmodern sensibility tends to call attention to chaos because there are neither objects (in the premodern sense of a natural order) nor subjects (in the modern sense of "transcendental subjects"), but only *relationships* that never give a full-bodied view of the way things *really* are. Truth, then, can only be discussed in story form, with narratives that agree, overlap, clash, and repeat with suspicious familiarity over and over again with nothing really becoming truly "known."[103]

Narrative theology began to burst onto the religious scene in the 1970s.[104] Religious philosopher Gary Comstock points to the plethora of books and articles that continue to be written in support of the use of the narrative in the Bible, its use in theology, narrative and morality, narrative practice and tradition, and even narrative truth. He claims, "Narrative theology, reflection on religious claims embedded stories, is one of the most significant currents of late twentieth century thought."[105]

This tradition is carried forward in pentecostalism, which Archer refers to as a "storied theological tradition [that provides] the hermeneutical lens through which reality is interpreted and by which an individual in community goes about organizing and making sense out of life."[106] Story, in the context of that which

---

101. Stone, "Revival of Narrative," 4.

102. Gary L. Comstock, "Two Types of Narrative Theology," *Journal of the American Academy of Religion* 55, no. 4 (1987): 687–717.

103. See Cameron, *Interpreting Christian History*, 220.

104. Mostly through the works of John S. Dunne, *The City of the Gods* (New York: Macmillan, 1965); *A Search for God in Time and Memory* (New York: Macmillan, 1970); *The Way of All the Earth* (New York: Macmillan, 1972); and *Time and Myth: A Meditation on Story Telling as an Exploration of Life and Death* (Notre Dame, ID: University of Notre Dame Press, 1973). See also, Stephen Crites, "The Narrative Quality of Experience," *Journal of the American Academy of Religion* 39, no. 3 (September 1971): 291–311; and Michael Novak, *Ascent of the Mountain, Flight of the Dove: An Invitation to Religious Studies* (New York: Harper and Row, 1971).

105. Comstock, "Two Types of Narrative Theology," 687.

106. Kenneth J. Archer, "A Global Pentecostal Theological Methodology: Worship, Witness, and Work" (a paper presented to the III International Seminar on Pentecostals, Theology and the Sciences of Religion at the Methodist University of Sao Paulo (UMESP), Sao Paulo, Brazil, August 17–19, 2016, 3.

is pentecostal *qua* pentecostal, is a methodology that communicates truth that is organically connected to pentecostal communities via the interrelated roles of the Holy Spirit, the community, and the scripture.[107] This creates a hermeneutical dialogue that can be used by pentecostal thinkers to negotiate toward clear and uniquely pneumatological theological meanings. Archer refers to this as "a narrative approach to theology" and believes "that the practice of orthodoxy (right worship) and orthomartus (right witness to the world) should serve as our primary context for doing theology with orthopathos as the interlocutor between praxis and beliefs."[108]

Putting the biblical story into a narrative understanding of God's action is what yielded a practice that was integral to pentecostal worship: *testimony*. Testimony has been described as "the poetry of Pentecostal experience."[109] K. A. Smith holds that "Testimony is central to pentecostal spirituality because it captures the dynamic sense that God is active and present in our world and in our personal experience while also emphasizing the *narrativity* of pentecostal spirituality."[110] Wacker observes that, "Like countless Christians before them, early pentecostals assumed that their personal faith stories bore normative implications for others. Consequently, they devoted much of the time in their worship services—maybe a third of the total—to public testimonies about their spiritual journeys."[111] In testimony, pentecostals could write themselves into the larger story of God's redemption.[112] Smith adds, "'I know that I know that I know' is a common refrain in pentecostal worship services that makes room for testimony and witness. And making room for testimony is central to pentecostal spirituality precisely because narrative is central to pentecostal identity."[113] Smith also claims it as normative for pentecostals to "embrace the centrality of testimony in their pentecostal theorizing, seeing such narratives as central to the theological task."[114]

Wacker summarizes that, "The testimony forcefully asserted that the believer's passage on this earth formed part of a magnificent drama in which cosmic good

---

107. See Yong, *Spirit-Word-Community*; Archer, *Pentecostal Hermeneutic*.

108. Archer, "Global Pentecostal Theological Methodology," 11.

109. Steven J. Land, Rick D. Moore, and John Christopher Thomas, "Editorial," *JPT* 1, no. 1 (1992): 5.

110. Smith, *Thinking in Tongues*, xxii (emphasis original).

111. Wacker, *Heaven Below*, 58.

112. Land (*Pentecostal Spirituality*, 72) writes, "Crucifixion, resurrection, Pentecost, parousia, all formed one great redemption, one story in which they were participants with assigned roles to play." He further asserts that narrative theologizing provided a framework that could make sense of their own struggles and victories: "by interpreting their daily life and worship in terms of the significant events of biblical history, their own lives and actions were given significance."

113. Smith, *Thinking in Tongues*, 50.

114. Ibid., 9.

vanquished evil ... Each person's private struggles somehow soared above the merely private and reappeared in a framework that spanned the millennia."[115] Returning to Smith:

> Because of an emphasis on the role of experience, and in contrast to rationalistic evangelical theology (which reduces worship to a didactic sermon and conceives of our relation to God as primarily intellectual, yielding only "talking head" Christianity), pentecostal spirituality is rooted in affective, narrative epistemic practice. According to this model, knowledge is rooted in the heart and traffics in the stuff of story. It's not that propositional truths can be "packaged" in narrative format for "the simple"; rather, the conviction is that story comes before propositions—imagination precedes intellection. We know in stories. Implicit in pentecostal spirituality is the epistemological intuition that we are narrative animals.[116]

It seems that all forms of story carry an embedded doxastic logic. Remember, doxastic logic does *not* ask *What is required for knowledge?* Instead, it asks *What is required for belief?* It seeks to give warrant to the idea that "a person can become justified in holding certain kinds of beliefs about God by virtue of perceiving [or experiencing] God as being or doing so-and-so."[117] Again to Comstock:

> For [narrative theologians], an adequate description of Christianity should come not in terms of imported categories but in terms of the Bible's own narratives and Christians' own autobiographies. An appropriate explanation of Christianity should come not in terms of external philosophical theories or social-scientific laws but in terms of the internal rules and procedures of its own language game. Finally, the justification of Christianity should come not in the form of a logical proof that God exists, or [that] Jesus arose, or that the Church serves ends all rational persons ought to desire. Rather, it should come in the form of a pragmatic demonstration that this tradition entails a liberating, authentic, and non-self-deceived form of life, an appropriate response to God's actions toward us.[118]

In Acts 1:8, when Jesus prepares the disciples to begin the journey of taking the claims of the gospel to the "ends of the earth," he reveals, "You will receive power when the Holy Spirit comes on you; and you will be my witnesses." To be a "witness" is to share the story of an experience. Witnesses don't always share the same aspects of an event they are a part of—sometimes they even contradict each other. What we *do* know when we hear the testimonies of various witnesses is

---

115. Wacker, *Heaven Below*, 69.
116. Smith, *Thinking in Tongues*, 43–4.
117. Alston, *Perceiving God*, 2.
118. Comstock, "Two Types of Narrative Theology," 690.

that *something happened*. We generally try to weave together all the reports (even holding to their inconsistencies and contradictions) to get the fullest picture. What if that is exactly what the nature of theologizing should be? Biblical materials, historical traditions, and theological reflections—perhaps all these provide the fodder of story. And what if story serves as the best way one can navigate through the seeming contradictions, incompletenesses, paradoxes, and complexities of sacred text and the Christian tradition?

I suggest that what we see in Jesus' command to those first disciples was a call to a doxological approach to theology, which gave space to personal and communal testimony to be the primary mediators of the message about God. The Book of Acts is a story of persons-in-community testifying to the redemptive work of God. They were the people of Pentecost—the Church of God.

Rowan Williams makes the claim that story helps us to accept and make sense of the "complicated and muddled bundle of experiences" we all bear. He claims that at "the heart of 'meaning' is a human story, a story of growth, conflict and death, every human story, with all its oddity and ambivalence, becomes open to interpretation in terms of God's saving work."[119] On this view, "the goal of a Christian life becomes not enlightenment but wholeness—an acceptance of this complicated and muddled bundle of experiences as a possible theatre for God's creative work."[120]

Swedish Professor of Practical Theology R. Ruard Ganzevoort writes of the value of story in Christian thought:

> We live our lives from day to day, but we understand our life as if it were a story. Our collective identity, history, and religious tradition are likewise structured as stories. Even non-narrative forms (like creeds, commandments, buildings, garments, hierarchies) can be interpreted in this narrative perspective. The central notion here is that meanings are not fixed or defined by something intrinsic to the facts or texts. Instead meaning is attributed in the act of reading the text or approaching an external reality. This places the reader center stage. The main question becomes how individuals and communities construct their stories in conversation with other "readers," incorporating that which presents itself as "real" and aiming at the construction of a consistent and meaningful story of the self. The reader thus creates his or her own story vis-à-vis self, others, and "reality." This process of narrative construction of a story can thus be seen as a negotiation of possible meanings.[121]

Those who like to speak of truth in universal ways using foundationalist schemas see narrative as a potential compromise. In one sense, identifying absolutes makes

---

119. Rowan Williams, *The Wound of Knowledge* (Cambridge, MA: Cowley Publications, 1990), 11.

120. Ibid.

121. R. Ruard Ganzevoort, Maaike de Haardt, and Michael Scherer-Rath, eds., *Religious Stories We Live By* (Leiden, The Netherlands: Brill, 2013), 3.

truth simpler, cleaner, and actually feeds a hubris that wants to believe human beings can hold a modicum of control/predictability vis-à-vis knowledge.[122] But narrative theology has arrived in the modern theological enterprise, and it has had staying power (perhaps due to advocates of the use of narrative in theology from notables like: Paul Ricoeur, George Lindbeck, Hans Frei, David Tracy, Stanley Hauerwas, Julian Hartt, Sallie McFague, and Johann Baptist Metz).

It is not that story abandons any sense of universal truth. By utilizing story, one can take what is personal and consider how it would expand to the universal. Walter Brueggemann calls this "the scandal of particularity."[123] A narrative affords an examination of what is present in the ordinary, concrete moment of experience, which can then be wrestled with using scripture, tradition, and reason, and put forward as truth writ large. It is a potentially scandalous methodology precisely because it is so ordinary. Stories are easily domesticated; we know them *by heart*. Using narrative in this way simply shows how suspicious we are that what is true in one place may end up, in some way, being true everywhere—but not dogmatically. Here, we simply hold the truth lightly in our stories of pursuing the love of God and neighbor, and that sort of thing applies to everyone.

Approaching truth as narrative is, in the words of Ganzevoort, "not necessarily reductionistic towards religion, but may in fact help us to appreciate religion's truth claims in relative rather than ultimate terms."[124] When considering truth claims in stories, Ganzevoort says that people "are more pre-occupied with the consequences of casting one's life in a particular imaginative frame or set of practices than with the content of specific beliefs, affirmations, and doctrines."[125] This fosters a religious openness to truth as readers process truth claims vicariously through the characters and circumstances of story (which I see as a reappropriation of one of the initial evidences of pentecostalism: *theological openness* [Chapter 1]). True, it is a less direct way to be exposed to truth, but it is less hegemonic. The narrative approach invites "readers to connect the stories of the divine with stories of their own existence, neither allows for the absolute truth claims as may have been harbored by the most confessional of theologians, nor for the distantiated objectivism of the most armored of religious studies scholars."[126]

The PTM I propose commits to using a narrative approach to truth. Two powerful take-aways exist for the PTM's use of story. First, when we see and/or

---

122. John Poirier ("Narrative Theology and Pentecostal Commitments," *JPT* 16, no. 2 [2008]: 70), takes the opposite view claiming that narrative theology carries a deep hubris in that it dares to obviate the intent of the authors of sacred text adverting instead to "both the centrality of a readerly (or ecclesial-readerly) hermeneutic *and* the centrality of the narrativity of one's life for one's identity." He claims it is really a program of human "conceits."

123. Walter Brueggemann, *The Message of the Psalms: A Theological Commentary* (Minneapolis, MN: Augsburg Publishing House, 1984), 162.

124. Ganzevoort, *Religious Stories*, 5.

125. Ibid.

126. Ganzevoort, *Religious Stories*, 13.

hear truth in a storied way from lived events, those stories carry deep meaning for us and show us how we can build a somewhat coherent (but at least meaningful) story involving ourselves from the elements presented therein. Story has the dimension of emplotment and, as such, immediately implies issues of ontology and truth correspondence (though not by using a forced dogmatism). Second, story immediately relates us to others who also find themselves in the same story (relationality)—we automatically find ourselves placed within a community of faith. We become peopled.

The gift of the foundationless foundation afforded by the pneumatological epistemology cannot be overstated. It is an epistemology that welcomes axioms of Christian faith with confidence rooted in more than fideism but less than rational certitude. It carries a doxastic logic that fosters doxastic practices communicated in narrative form. This means that theology can easily take place in the space of prayer, reflection, study, and conversations where theologians can engage with other theologues (past and present), along with the perspectives of everyday, common sense practitioners (pastors) and parishioners. Here the theologue invites the engagement of all parties, along with all sources, disciplines, and cultural zeitgeists into dialogue as they develop ideas, overcome misunderstandings, and address new theological questions and challenges.

Here is Pinnock on the value of this storied, PTM that feels like home to the pentecostal:

> Much theology, in contrast, reads the Bible as a book of concepts and disregards the historical and experiential dimensions, a practice that allows theology to be influenced more by speculative concepts of God. Pentecostals are in the happy position of being able to avoid categories that have long burdened classical theism, because they stick closer to biblical metaphors and biblical narrative. They experience God in dynamic and relational ways because they are oriented to the biblical narrative and are much less impressed by non-relational philosophical notions. In their world, as in the world of the Bible, there is real drama, real interaction and real spiritual conflicts. They experience the dynamic presence of God in a manner evident to insiders and outsiders … They are a people caught up in the story of God and in the momentum of the Spirit of the last days and are engaged in a mission which is itself a sign of the last days. They deal with a God who is free and personal and who responds to them in surprising and unpredictable ways … To them, God is not a metaphysical iceberg but a living person.[127]

The Spirit of Love

The Holy Spirit is the Spirit of love. In Chapter 1 love was shown to be one of the first evidences of that which is pentecostal *qua* pentecostal. Any theological

---

127. Pinnock, "Divine Relationality," 10.

methodology that is pneumatological (a PTM) needs to demonstrate love at every level. "God is love" is the daring way the Apostle John put it (1 John 4:8). He further claims that we only "know that we have passed from death to life" when we are loving persons. John also claims that anything we do that is *not* loving is an indication of spiritual death (3:14).

Chapter 1 also showed how the love that flourished within nascent pentecostalism dissipated quickly. The problem was that when disagreements appeared, schismatic factions were close at hand and unitive love was less prioritized. Schism in the church is certainly not novel. It is a repeating problem that has haunted the church all through her history—sometimes threatening her very existence. So, how does a people filled with the Spirit of love, who are supposed to be *known* by their love and unity devolve into being cold, hostile, and schismatic? More often than not, the problem seems to be a human lust for *being right*.

Theological Pluralism As Wacker reports above, "[P]entecostal groups held little interest in compromise and none at all in theological pluralism."[128] Why? Because often within the religious world, when people think about truth, they think about it dualistically: black or white, evil or righteous, orthodox or heterodox, etc. Then, it is presumed that someone must be right, which means someone must be wrong. When groups of people become rigid about what is true or false, they feel like it would be compromising "the truth" to not press the matter. Hence, allowing two opposing views to remain in tension in the same room carries a deep cognitive dissonance that is not easily dismissed. When one hoists the need to be right as a critical aspect for unity to remain intact, unity becomes univocal and cannot bear disagreement. Additionally, some believe that when one is not "right" about a theological point, it makes that believer unholy or unclean in some way. Perhaps this is the fear that motivates many to believe there is always a way to identify the *actual* truth of any matter and that theology should never house plurality. But what if that position is untenable?

St. Paul tells us that we only "see through a glass, darkly"; we only "know in part"; and it will only be "then" that we shall really "know even as" we are known—when we see him "face to face" (1 Cor. 13:12, KJV) in the *eschaton*. *That* is not *now*. Yong insists that until *then*, "All knowledge is provisional, relative to the questions posed by the community of inquirers and subject to the ongoing process of conversation and discovery."[129] Having partial knowledge does not make us unholy or unclean; it makes us human. Of course, all Christians (including foundationalists) affirm what Paul declares—that none of us knows all things perfectly. But some hold that we can and should carry intellectual certainty about some things—particularly those that matter for our salvation. I am arguing, however, that all knowledge is

---

128. Wacker, *Heaven Below*, 77–8.
129. Yong, *Beyond the Impasse*, 58–9.

partial, and because it is, then it (and we) must always remain open to at least nuanced adjustments in our views.

This openness was how the first Christians, filled with the Spirit, faced and appropriated the new ideas that were not orthodox at the time. A careful study of the early church shows they needed to worth through and identify the values and motifs that were very different from their native Judaism.[130] In order for them to make that shift, they needed to work through a host of theological problems that would have caused a deep cognitive dissonance for them. Many aspects of truth had to be negotiated and adjudicated as Christians came to a self-understanding. Hearing many sides and framing a way forward was present in the church from its inception.[131]

Milbank insists that prioritizing many voices (viz., harmony) over a single voice (viz., dogmatism) can bring Christians together in a way that has not been possible since before the Reformation. This commitment could "subsume rather than merely abolish difference: Christians could remain in their many different cities, languages and cultures, yet still belong to one eternal city ruled by Christ, in whom all 'humanity' was fulfilled."[132] He is suggesting that celebrating the many voices with a generous orthodoxy offers the best hope of reversing the fragmentation that pervades the Christian church. With Augustine's *De Musica* in mind, Milbank offers this reflection on the side of building unity within the Christian community:

> For Christianity, true community means the freedom of people and groups to be different, not just to be functions of a fixed consensus, yet at the same time it totally refuses indifference; a peaceful, united secure community implies absolute consensus, and yet, where difference is acknowledged, this is no agreement in an idea, or something once and for all achieved, but a consensus that is only in and through the interrelations of community itself, and a consensus that moves and "changes": a *concentus musicus*.[133]

The musical analogy is a brilliant one as we think about how radically different the instruments within an orchestra are from one another—the oboe from the trumpet, the piccolo from the cymbal—and, yet, how all the instruments in the inter-relations of an orchestral community can be ordered together to make the varied sounds and movements in a consensus that is truly beautiful and inspiring. However, if the tuba player believed that all music should sound like and be played through the tuba, or a xylophone player was convinced her instrument was the only "orthodox" instrument authorized to play "true" music, then the world of music would be strangely limited. *This* is the danger of too much demand for exactness in

---

130. See Theissen, *A Theory of Primitive Christian Religion*.
131. The Acts 15 Jerusalem Council is an excellent example of this.
132. John Milbank, "'Postmodern Critical Augustinianism': A Short Summa in Forty-Two Responses to Unasked Questions," *Modern Theology* 7, no. 3 (1991): 225–37, 227.
133. Ibid., 228.

the modern church. I find Milbank's contention both provocative and promising. Milbank alleges that this vision of unity—which is open to difference—is built into the fabric of Christianity. Earlier we heard Milbank say, "Christianity is peculiar, because while it is open to difference—to a series of infinity new additions, insights, progressions towards God, it also strives to make of all these differential additions a harmony."[134]

Even Jesus does not communicate in only noncontradictory, simple, and perspicuous truth—he harmonizes seemingly disharmonious truth as he speaks in different ways about creation, money, power, the demonic, sex, miracles, love, etc. Truth is not always simple or easy. Spirit also comes to us in various ways that may seem contradictory. This implies that a Spirit-centered theologizing is one that can handle varied interpretation, contradiction, confusion, inconsistency, paradox, and anomaly. What if a pneumatological methodology can bear lots of *what ifs*? That would mean a PTM is *not* nervous about pinning down exact truth or against participating in pluralistic theological discussions. We have already seen that no one is totally right anyway. No theology exists without having some amount of alloy from our sinful nature mixed into it. And we know that all knowledge this side of eternity is fallible. As precious as the Bible is to Spirit-filled people, it is not without fallible epistemological issues that need to be addressed. Murphy avers:

> When conservative theologians were forced to admit that the biblical texts contained contradictions, a common move was to argue that only the original autographs were inerrant. This claim is incorrigible (since all of these are lost) but the incorrigibility comes at the cost of needing to ground theology on something inaccessible to contemporary theologians; the lost autographs that are inerrant but useless.[135]

This is not an attempt to cast doubt on the veracity of sacred text, nor am I hinting that the Bible is not authoritative. It is authoritative. Kärkkäinen reports that there are many deeply pietistic and orthodox pentecostal theologians today who "claim that it is possible to question and even cast serious doubts on traditional understandings of and proofs for infallibility and inerrancy among pentecostals without seriously challenging their understanding of the Bible as the authoritative word of God."[136] Even those who contend that the scripture is inerrant and infallible recognize that any human *read* of it is deeply flawed. Precisely because we adhere to a robust understanding of sin and the Fall, the pneumatocentric theologue should be one of the first to embrace her or his own fallibilism while dispensing with any kind of demand for certainty (by which I mean a certainty beyond correction or adjustment).

This holds that within the Christian faith, certitude (of the Enlightenment ilk) is not necessary. We should strive at being right *enough*—where we steer clear of

---

134. Milbank, "Postmodern Critical Augustinianism," 227–8.
135. Murphy, *Beyond Liberalism*, 92.
136. Kärkkäinen, *Toward a Pneumatological Theology*, 8.

heterodoxy and can have a sense that we are safe in an orthodoxy that is generous. But we don't have to be fearful about being right. Our quest should be to interpret the scriptures and to do the best theology we can *as life actually unfolds* within the context of communities (historic and present), recognizing that the Spirit will show us what we need to know when we need to know it. We can trust that this kind of knowledge will grow as we are "directed toward the eschaton."[137] Until then, we cannot know fully—there will continue to be a mystery; unknowing. There continues to be a hiddenness in God.[138]

All said, the problem of fear concerning theological pluralism continues to rage among many, and people of the Spirit—who are to carry a theological openness and who are to be known by their love and unity (which we saw in Chapter 1 were "essentials" of what is pentecostal)—often became cold, hostile, and schismatic. But this problem is not unique to Spirit-filled people; it seems endemic to the human race. From the arena of theology to politics, science, and family life, many seem to have a lust for *being right*. There is evidence for this going all the way back to the first recorded human family in the Bible where a brother's blood spilled on the ground over who was right.[139]

The Spirit of the Wind

As I said above, there are many ways to speak about the Spirit from which we draw pneumatological theology. I highlighted three of the four "Spirit of's" that deeply inform the PTM I am constructing: (1) the *Spirit of Life*, (2) the *Spirit of Truth*, and, (3) the *Spirit of Love*. The final one I will point to is the *Spirit of the Wind*. The basic biblical terms for the Holy Spirit are *ruach* in the First Testament and *pneuma* in the New Testament. Both are actually ambiguous images of the Spirit and his work as they are translated: "breath," "air," and "wind."[140] Kärkkäinen says that St. John, in "speaking of the mysterious nature of wind and the Spirit's role in a believer's new birth, more explicitly connects the image of wind with God's Spirit."[141]

The Spirit of the wind enters the human situation in both subtle and demonstrative ways—but always for our good. As St. Paul's writes, "Now to each one the manifestation of the Spirit is given for the common good" (1 Cor. 12:7). Etymologically, the word "manifestation" comes from the compound Latin word, *manus* (hand)—*festus* (to strike or to be in motion). It gives the image of the Spirit being the hand of God in motion as God reveals God's self to us; or as individuals being overpowered by (or *caught* by) the hand; or as the gentleness of

---

137. Yong. *Spirit, Word, Community*, 43.

138. Isaiah 45:15 says, "Truly you are a God who has been hiding himself, the God and Savior of Israel."

139. Cf. Gen. 4:10.

140. Kärkkäinen, *Pneumatology*, 13.

141. Ibid.

being *touched* by the hand; or (my favorite) being witness to the *dancing* hand; etc.—all rich imagery of the Spirit of the wind who is moving in this world with life and purpose. Jenson says of the Spirit of the wind:

> The Old Testament is full of references to and appearances of the *ruah* of God, the breath of God by which he blows things around and so keeps Israel's history moving. Whenever things seem to come to a halt—if the Philistines, say, have once again got Israel stymied—the same thing happens again and again. The *ruah* of the Lord falls upon so and so, and thus takes over and rescues Israel. That is to say, it is the wind of God's own life blowing on history that keeps it moving.[142]

Returning to Moltmann:

> I am calling these metaphors movement metaphors (wind, breath, fire, etc.) because they express the feeling of being seized and possessed by something overwhelmingly powerful, and the beginning of a new movement in ourselves. They describe a movement that sweeps people off their feet, which possesses and excites not only the conscious levels but the unconscious depths too, and sets the men and women affected themselves on the move toward unsuspected new things.[143]

Wariboko adds that Moltmann's *movement metaphors* all

> point to the creativity of the Spirit, the restlessness of becoming. The Spirit (the breath of God, Yahweh's *ruach, pneuma*) comes upon the disciples as fire (creativity), after a gale of tempest (wind, breath, *ruach*) and they spoke (words are controlled breath). This dramatic display, interplay, and interpenetration of word and breath point to the principle of creativity, the initiation of the new in a very moving way.[144]

Yong gives voice to the vastness and mystery of this: "The Spirit is that elusive revelation of God, whose comings and goings are like the wind, and beyond our ability to define with precision (cf., Jn 3:8)."[145] That being said, there are two specific aspects of the movement metaphors ascribed to the Spirit of the wind that I want to highlight: (1) the *surprising* and (2) the *making-all-things-new creative*.

The Surprising There is an unpredictable nature of *all-things-Spirit*. Jesus described the Spirit as being like the wind that "blows wherever it pleases. You hear its sound, but you cannot tell where it comes from or where it is going" (John 3:8). Divine touch is always unexpected and usually unconventional—*surprising*.

---

142. Jenson, *A Theology in Outline*, 50.
143. Moltmann, *The Spirit of Life,* loc. 3853–5, Kindle.
144. Wariboko, *The Pentecostal Principle,* loc. 403–7, Kindle.
145. Yong, "The Demise of Foundationalism," 579–80.

Looking at the early church and the testimonies of the saints throughout history, there are often places where nothing prepared them for what they ended up witnessing. They were unprepared for what happened. If one selects almost any vignette from Jesus' life, they find it jammed with surprise. For example, Yale scholar Wille James Jennings writes of the surprising nature of the post-Passion reality:

> The unbelievable has happened: Jesus was killed and rose from the dead. Death has been overcome in and through him. Yet this was no singular miracle but rather the great announcement of the new order—Jesus is the judge of the lifting and the dead. He is the Lord of all. All living creatures are now bound to him. In him and through him, there will be forgiveness of sins. In him and through him, prophetic word finds its final and definitive home.[146]

The prophets hinted at these things, but not with much clarity. People were unprepared for Jesus being the key currency of a whole new world order—a whole "new creation" (2 Cor. 5:17). This is the way of the Spirit, which always carries notes of the unexpected.

When humans work, we generally have goals in mind, and we execute particular ends. To the extent that our work has a final product, an endpoint, and a final cause outside itself—it is *predictable*. But predictability is not an essential value for the Spirit of the wind. When the Day of Pentecost came, unexpected things happened. This surprising event was an interruption in an ongoing situation. This rupture was signified by tongues of fire and a wind that blew "suddenly," creating new space for the Twelve and the other disciples to begin anew. Those hundred-and-twenty or so had gathered in that Upper Room and by divine action ended up expressing a diversity and universalism that was inescapably captured by the multiple languages they spoke on the Day of Pentecost under the power of Spirit. This diversity of the tongues points to the irreducibly pluralistic nature of the new that the Spirit was doing. No one human being can incarnate creativity like this; only the Spirit does.[147]

As Acts continues, we see the Spirit leading and directing at every turn. And, as I discussed in Chapter 1, the pneumatocentric focus following the Day of Pentecost is apodictic. The language about the ongoing activity of God shifting from being initiated by "the Lord" in the Gospels to being compelled by "the Spirit" in the Book of Acts is striking. (No Gospel, other than Luke, speaks of the Spirit more than twenty times, whereas Acts alone speaks of the Spirit some sixty times.)

---

146. Willie James Jennings, *Acts* (Louisville, KY: Westminster John Knox Press, 2017), 110.

147. Wariboko (*Pentecostal Principle*, loc. 638–9, Kindle) writes, "The spirit universalizes love that particularizes caring: lifts up our intention, care, or commitment and extends it to the social whole. It wills for one as well as for all others the same thing in relevantly similar situations. A corollary of the Spirit's freedom and inclusiveness is its creativity."

Jennings's commentary on the Book of Acts is a theological tour of the Spirit's daring formation of a new people in surprising and disruptive ways. In one section, where Jennings is concerned with the story of Cornelius and the welcoming of Gentiles into the church (Acts 10-11), he claims that the Spirit came with intention to "explode across space and time reaching to us and beyond us into a future we cannot see. Luke at this point in the story inscribes the door through which we, Gentiles, enter in and, in so doing, performs what Karl Barth called the strange new world within the Bible."[148] As Jennings presses into the story of Cornelius, he is interested in how the Spirit goes about the work of instituting the "new creation"—God's Kingdom coming to earth, as in heaven. Jennings asks, "How do you change the world? How do you turn it right side up if not by turning it upside down?"[149] He claims, "God, Peter, and Cornelius—this is the unexpected. God brings Peter to Cornelius—this will be the new thing."[150] This, for Jennings could not have been imagined. It was a complete surprise to *everyone*. He continues: "This moment schools us in divine transgression. God brings Peter to one outside of the covenant, transgressing God's own established boundary and border. We must not weaken the radical implications of this epic meeting."[151]

Divine *transgression*? Yes. Jennings insists that the whole story of Jesus and the church is replete with "the unexpected and the usually unconventional" precisely because it is the fruit of the "divine touch"—not just of the touch from those in this world.[152] Jennings asserts:

> Jesus was God transgressing, and now in the Spirit and in a private room made public, that transgression will take its full form. Jesus will draw Jew and Gentile together, not moving past the one to get to the other, not choosing one and rejecting the other, but precisely bringing together, drawing close what was far apart. The meeting is the new order—Jew and Gentile will share in one Spirit. This is the will of God, made known in the Son and realized in the Spirit, and this new order requires new listening.[153]

This kind of new was the destruction of boundaries and borders that had been sacrosanct to the members of the early church who were all Jewish. They would need space and time to wrestle with what was going on—to how "God has transgressed, and that transgression was real."[154]

There are times when the surprise of the Spirit reduces the church to silence. We do not know what to say or what to do with what has confronted us. These

---

148. Jennings, *Acts*, 102.
149. Ibid., 109.
150. Ibid.
151. Ibid., 110.
152. Ibid., 111.
153. Ibid.
154. Ibid., 114.

are usually the times when, in Jennings's words, "God yet speaks and the word of God always presses against word of God. What God has said in the past is pressed against by what God is saying now."[155] These are the very difficult places when God is remaking or bringing God's new into the world. Jennings calls it the "in-between position" because it is a place between the comfort of the old and hope of the new that is not quite clear. He says, "The struggle of the church has been twofold: we struggle to hear the new word that God is constantly speaking, and we struggle to see the link between the new word and the word previously spoken."[156]

Obviously, the past is extremely important for the Christian—this is a faith we have *received*. If we were to live without a sense of our history, we would be adrift, and there would be no recognizable "we." The church was designed to be a distinctive kind of community, one formed by reverence for those who had gone before, by veneration of exemplary men and women (the martyrs and saints), by fixed forms of worship and a common calendar, by an organized ministry and ecclesiastical structure, and by commitment to a shared belief. Christianity is a historical religion which has a historicity. Understanding our past proves critical and integral for any person or group to have a sense of identity. Knowing who we are is only possible when we know who we were. One of the great fears of those with brain diseases like Alzheimer's is that one loses one's memory. We all intuitively know that if we lose our memory, we lose our identity. Remembering who *we are* and who *we were* gives us a sense of futurity. This means that all roads to a significant future must go through one's past.

Jennings agrees: "The church exists only because God has spoken in the past, and without a sense of that history we lack clarity about our current path and journey."[157] But he is clear that this penchant for looking to the past to govern the now has sometimes caused the church to collaborate with and even help create the "shaping of the world and the formation of its most devastating operations and regimes."[158] So, Jennings continues:

> The past, though important, is never the point for the life of faith. The point is the present moment with the living God who is with us, beckoning us to communion. The God who speaks to us now calls us into the risk of hearing a new word, a word that orients us toward the unanticipated and the unprecedented where the reconciling God is active.[159]

This, I would suggest, is the prophetic nature of a pneumatological people. The prophet sees what has happened but also sees that we are going somewhere

---

155. Ibid., 119.
156. Ibid.
157. Ibid.
158. Ibid., 119–20.
159. Ibid., 120.

else—that the new is coming. In this sense, the prophetic is in a move toward *deconstruction*.[160] Deconstruction is always the first stage toward *reconstruction*. If one thinks a belief or practice is beyond the scope of deconstruction, that belief or practice can easily become idolatrous. On one level, the prophets have always been religious deconstructionists. The biblical prophets would have thought of it as the toppling of idols. It isn't that prophets are always clear on *where* God is leading—they just know God *is* leading and that the ways of the past are sometimes that—the past. They get glimpses of what is to come, but not with full understanding (cf. 1 Pet. 1:10-11). Additionally, prophets do not see clearly enough to become crusaders—those who fight, claw, and kill for what they see. Prophets are not that. Prophets enter the tension of "hearing God's new words pressed against the old ones,"[161] so they are the ones who usually get persecuted or killed by the true crusaders—those who see the past as unchanging and in need of protection, no matter the cost.

Being prophetic is not easy, and it is more like *art* than science. When the prophets speak in the church, there is a need for calm, order, and space for "the others to weigh carefully what is said" (1 Cor. 14:29)—they must be *peer reviewed*. The prophetic is often surprising, somewhat confusing, and a sometimes-dangerous charism. Wariboko offers in this regard, "A commitment to an emergentist worldview obliges us to embrace the *prophetic-pentecostal spirit*. It calls forth a citizenry that can sense the unprecedented, identify opportunities and threats, and craft the appropriate responses rooted in their creative and prophetic power."[162]

A note of hope: Jennings says a new word may come "in places strange and alien to us, among peoples not our own," but he insists that "these words should never be understood to live antagonistically. They are bound together in the life of a speaking God who wills to bind us together through space and time, through borders and boundaries, from life through death and to the life anew and eternal found in Jesus Christ."[163] Hopeful indeed.

The Wild Goose In his chapter entitled "The Wild Goose," Robert Kruschwitz explains the etymology of that phrase: "The wild goose, in addition to the dove, is a Celtic Christian symbol for the Holy Spirit. Sometimes God's Spirit hovers comfortingly like a dove. But the Spirit also surprises us and disturbs our plans.

---

160. This "deconstruction" is not to be conflated with the Derridian "deconstruction" that argues that ideal concepts such as truth or justice, are so irreducibly complex or unstable that truth is impossible to determine. Rather, this is a recognition that as fallible human beings, we always have space to be corrected, which is at the heart of the *semper reformanda* within the Christian tradition. This is a commitment to the "openness" described in Chapter 1 as one of the universal "evidences" of pentecostal *qua* pentecostal.

161. Jennings, *Acts*, 121.

162. Wariboko, *The Pentecostal Principle*, loc. 552-3, Kindle (emphasis in original).

163. Jennings, *Acts*, 120-1.

Like a wild and unpredictable goose, the Holy Spirit sweeps in unexpected, astonishing directions."[164] Kruschwitz then describes a moment in a church meeting that shows the confusion and the need for discernment when dealing with the Spirit of the wind:

> In one business meeting, however, the Spirit was like a wild goose, or a whole flock of them! We were debating a committee's proposal to build a new sanctuary. One member stood up in the back and announced: "The Holy Spirit has told me this week that we should not build this sanctuary, for if we do, the church will grow and we will lose touch with one another. Our fellowship is too precious a gift to risk in this way." There was silence for half a minute. Then a member right in front rose to speak: "I've been praying about this decision too," she reported, "and the Holy Spirit has spoken clearly to me. We must build this sanctuary in order to extend our ministries to our growing town." Now everybody was talking at once. Several tried to speak to the entire group, while others seized this opportunity to convince a person sitting in the next chair. A few stood to be heard, and only managed to block others' view of the commotion. Visions of the dueling prophets and prophecies in the Corinthian church flashed across my mind.[165]

Reading this report is reminiscent of Acts 15, where the apostles and the elders came together to look into the requirements that should be placed on the Gentiles who had newly come into the Christian church. There was no small debate about it. Some were absolutely convinced that the will of God demanded that the "Gentiles must be circumcised and required to keep the law of Moses" (v. 9). Paul and others strongly disagreed. Everyone had a chance to be heard (when discerning the voice of God or what the Spirit is saying, every person within community is a critical component to discernment). Then, James, who appears to be the leader of the church in Jerusalem, stands and gives his "judgment" or discernment on the matter (v. 19). A letter was sent to all the churches afterward that made the claim, "It seemed good to the Holy Spirit and to us" (v. 28), which then iterated the decision.

Historically, the church did not always start with every belief or practice exactly right. They had to discern what was *right enough* and did the best theology they could as life unfolded within the context of their community. They believed that the Spirit was showing them what they needed to know when they needed to know it. I think this is the assumption rooted in the Spirit-led life—one must be *led*. Which begs some questions: *How do we know when an idea/doctrine should be imagined or revisited? And, what does a new word from the Spirit look like and how does one navigate into the new word in ways that are faithful to the old or previous word?* I think the central way we know when

---

164. Robert B. Kruschwitz, "The Wild Goose," in *Prophetic Ethics*, vol. 6 of *Christian Reflection, A Series in Faith and Ethics*, ed. Robert B. Kruschwitz (Waco, TX: Baylor University Press, 2003), 40.

165. Kruschwitz, "The Wild Goose," 42.

it is time to imagine or reimagine is when what we know and practice does *not* satisfy the intellectual craving or settle the presenting problems of our historical situation. Here, we begin to experience the dawn of *epistemological crises*. Then we must seek what the Spirit is saying (new word), and how to navigate into that new word.

Epistemological Crises There are times within any tradition (religious or otherwise) when debates arise over areas where there was former agreement. Sometimes these get triggered by external things (i.e., new discoveries, significant cultural/philosophical shifts, etc.), or it may arise from internal reconsiderations over inadequacies that have been identified. When tensions like this persist, they give rise to epistemological crises. When a group or tradition experiences an "epistemological crisis," it is time to stop and examine what exactly is in crisis, name it, and seek ways to resolve it using as much of the logic, beliefs, and values of the tradition as one can in order to remain as faithful as possible to that tradition. At these moments we anticipate the Spirit of the Wind to carry us into safe, though sometimes surprising, spaces. Discovering the need for new approaches and communicating that "new word" for a community's acceptance is no small task. Alister MacIntyre's rationality in addressing epistemological crises is helpful here.[166] MacIntyre, a Roman Catholic philosopher, offers an approach to incorporating new thought by using a dialectical justification for the progressive quest of faithful knowledge—while staying historically informed.[167] And it is a methodology that does not dead-end in relativism or simple fideism.

Broadly speaking, MacIntyre's methodology is in tandem with Enlightenment thinkers by starting with the basic laws of logic (e.g., the law of non-contradiction). These are principles that, in MacIntyre's own words, "are evident to all rational persons [which] indeed provide standards and direction from the outset."[168] Simo Frestadius, who utilizes MacIntyre to address crises

---

166. See Nancey Murphy, "MacIntyre, Tradition-Dependent Rationality and the End of Philosophy of Religion," in *Contemporary Practice and Method in the Philosophy of Religion: New Essays*, ed. David Cheetham and Rolfe King (New York: Bloomsbury Academic, 2008), 32–44.

167. For an overview of MacIntyre and his work, see Kelvin Knight, "Introduction," in *The MacIntyre Reader*, ed. Kelvin Knight (Cambridge: Polity Press, 1998), 1–27; Christopher Stephen Lutz, *Tradition in the Ethics of Alasdair MacIntyre: Relativism, Thomism, and Philosophy* (New York: Lexington Books, 2009), 7–32; David Trenery, *Alasdair MacIntyre, George Lindbeck, and the Nature of Tradition* (Eugene, OR: Pickwick Publications, 2014), 4–139.

168. Alasdair MacIntyre, "First Principles, Final Ends, and Contemporary Philosophical Issues," in *The Tasks of Philosophy: Selected Essays, Volume 1*, ed. Alasdair MacIntyre (Cambridge: Cambridge University Press, 2007), 160, quoted in Frestadius, *Pentecostal Rationality*, 45.

within the theological context of the Elim tradition of the Foursquare Gospel denomination, asserts that MacIntyre may begin with the "'formal rationality' of Enlightenment thought and the 'necessary' conditions of rationality," but "he does not believe that they are 'sufficient' conditions."[169] In other words, formal rationality may be needed to ground the reasoning of human beings, but that kind of rationality is not a guarantee that what one has reasoned is decidedly true or false. "What is needed for making genuine epistemic judgments," Frestadius insists, "is not just formal rationality but 'substantive rationality,'" which MacIntyre claims "includes all those determinations and judgments about good reasons and acceptable evidence, that arise through tradition and convention."[170]

Frestadius finds that MacIntyre's approach is more convincing than other ways of approaching the problem of epistemological warrant (specifically referring to Enlightenment foundationalism; Yong's critical realism and pragmatic and coherence theories of epistemic justification;[171] Smith's affective, embodied, and narrative knowing;[172] and Oliverio's hermeneutical realism[173]). Frestadius finds that MacIntyre's approach provides the most effective criterion one should use for judging "truth and falsity"[174] while also safeguarding arguments by grounding them in a "peopled" faith tradition. The *relationality* of theologizing is critical for Frestadius, which he thinks MacIntyre protects:

> [N]ot just an argument by individuals, but by a community of people interested in and committed to the common object of enquiry. And since the argument is carried out by a group of people over time, it inevitably becomes "socially embodied" and "historically extended." Moreover, for the argument to be successful and sustained, it needs to be supported by appropriate institutions created by the community.[175]

Frestadius holds that traditions can only be understood when one listens for "the community of 'arguers'" within the tradition. Only through those collective voices can one understand "their history, social embodiment and institutions,"[176] opening a path for bringing change while remaining faithful to the tradition. Hence, the move into any new is always safe when it is "fundamentally a practice

---

169. Frestadius, *Pentecostal Rationality*, 46.
170. Alasdair C. MacIntyre, *After Virtue: A Study in Moral Theology*, 2nd ed. (Notre Dame, IN: Notre Dame University Press, 1984), 356.
171. Frestadius, *Pentecostal Rationality*, 15.
172. Ibid., 20.
173. Ibid., 32.
174. Lutz, *Tradition in the Ethics of Alasdair MacIntyre*, 7–32.
175. Frestadius, *Pentecostal Rationality*, 48.
176. Ibid.

of the community."¹⁷⁷ The Spirit of the wind is seen most clearly when we speak of "us."

In turning to MacIntyre's *Whose Justice? Which Rationality* directly, we discover that much of his work around "substantive rationality" (over against formal rationality) is about identifying and understanding one's tradition. This demands a thorough education to ensure that one understands its principles and the sense in which one recognizes the inadequacies of one's tradition and the dangers of not resolving them—including what possible remedies can emerge that do not reject the past as unfaithful in any way. MacIntyre says it this way:

> We are now in a position to contrast three stages in the initial development of a tradition: a first in which the relevant beliefs, texts, and authorities have not yet been put in question; a second in which inadequacies of various types have been identified, but not yet remedied; and a third in which response to those inadequacies has resulted in a set of reformulations, reevaluations, and new formulations and evaluations, designed to remedy inadequacies and overcome limitations.¹⁷⁸

Herein lies the tension of the prophetic. The prophets are in that second phase, where, by virtue of investigation or experience (as was the case with Peter and Cornelius), they recognize that the views of the past are no longer tenable.

Latin Catholic thinker and mystic practitioner, Richard Rohr, offers, "Normally, the way God pushes us is by disillusioning us with the present mode. Until the present falls apart, we will never look for something more. We will never discover what it is that really sustains us. That dreaded falling-apart experience is always suffering in some form."¹⁷⁹ Rohr sees these kinds of seasons of hunger as "shadowlands," writing:

> Shadowlands are good and necessary teachers. They are not to be avoided, denied, fled, or explained away. They are not even to be forgiven too quickly. First, like Ezekiel the prophet, we must eat the scroll that is "lamentation, wailing, and moaning" in our belly, and only eventually sweet as honey (see Ezek. 2:9-3:3). When we're in the shadows, there's a loss of meaning and motivation. If someone has never been able to see the shadow side, they haven't gained the right to talk the language of reconstruction ... We need to have pulled away from the idolatry of the system in order to gain the authority and the credibility to walk back in and work for reconstruction ... How can we know the light if we've never named the shadows?¹⁸⁰

---

177. Ibid., 49.
178. MacIntyre, *Whose Justice?*, 355.
179. Richard Rohr, *The Wisdom Pattern: Order, Chaos, Reorder* (Cincinnati, Ohio: Franciscan Media, 2020), 57.
180. Ibid., 143, 148, 150.

Rohr holds that prophets help God's people navigate through the shadows creatively by showing them how to let things fall apart without becoming unfaithful. He says the prophets "teach us how to lose gracefully, how to let go without fear."[181] But this is only *half* of the story. The other half is the path toward the new (or of *return*). This is where the prophets speak the new word of the Lord that is full of "union, communion, love, transcendence, connecting this world with the next world, and giving back a coherent world of meaning."[182] This is what MacIntyre refers to as the "set of reformulations, reevaluations, and new formulations and evaluations, designed to remedy inadequacies and overcome limitations."[183]

But navigating into a "new word of the Lord" is no small task. Returning to Jennings's commentary on Acts 10 and 11 we pick up on the deep, dialectic tension of this moment in the church's history:

> Peter resists the divine command. This too is extraordinary, and this too requires we slow down to capture sight of the birth pangs of the new order. Peter is not being disobedient. Indeed in Peter we have a servant who lives on the other side of betrayal, denial, repentance, and forgiveness. His obedience was refined through suffering and trial, beatings and death threats. Peter obeys, but now that obedience must take flight with the Holy Spirit into an uncharted world where the distinctions between holy and unholy, clean and unclean have been fundamentally upended. Yes, this is a moment when old word of God connects to new word of God, a moment where purity is expanded to cover what had been conceived as impure, but more crucially this is a moment of struggle for Peter to allow his vision of faithfulness to God and the covenant with Israel to expand. Is it possible to be faithful to the God of Israel in a new way? God has brought Peter inside this question and presses him toward its positive answer. This is a risky time, second only to Good Friday and Holy Saturday, in which God risks with Peter and Peter risks with God. Will Peter hear this new word from God, and will Peter believe that this is a new word from God? This is the condition of risk in which Christianity comes to exist and without which authentic Christianity does not exist. This is the risk of faith that comes to each of us, but none of us carries it alone. The risk here is found not in believing in new revelations but in new relationships.[184]

Where does one orient one's justification for the new? In the radical event of the inclusion of the Gentiles, *testimony* was where the transformation began, but theology always needs to catch up with testimony. Much of the work of the NT writings and that of the apostolic fathers helped change the imagination of the church. Thinkers like MacIntyre offer a path to aid in the process of change (and can

---

181. Ibid., 150.
182. Ibid.
183. MacIntyre, *Whose Justice?*, 355.
184. Jennings, *Acts*, 107–8.

even help discern whether a change *should* be considered) through constructing a tenable foundation; a *grounding* that is not the kind of foundationalism offered by the Enlightenment but warranted upon traditions that are socially embodied and historically contingent. MacIntyre holds:

> A tradition is an argument extended through time in which certain fundamental agreements are defined and redefined in terms of two kinds of conflict: those with critics and enemies external to the tradition who reject all or at least key parts of those fundamental agreements and those internal, interpretive debates through which the meaning and rationale of the fundamental agreements come to be expressed and by whose progress a tradition is constituted.[185]

When Frestadius discusses the ongoing crises of change within the Elim theological tradition (which, truthfully, all traditions are experiencing), he finds MacIntyre's "concept of rationality tradition-dependent and tradition-constituted"[186] a hopeful path forward. Any PTM should as well. Frestadius claims, "much of MacIntyre's work has been an argument for substantive rationality and an attempt to recover a conception of rational enquiry as embodied in a tradition."[187] This speaks of a pentecostal rationality that Frestadius claims is one of safety. MacIntyre speaks emphatically in this regard:

> The conclusion to which the argument so far has led is not only that it is out of the debates, conflicts, and enquiry of socially embodied, historically contingent traditions that contentions regarding practical rationality and justice are advanced, modified, abandoned, or replaced, but that there is no other way to engage in the formulation, elaboration, rational justification, and criticism of accounts of practical rationality and justice except from within some one particular tradition in conversation, cooperation, and conflict with those who inhabit the same tradition. There is no standing ground, no place for enquiry, no way to engage in the practice of advancing, evaluating, accepting, and rejecting reasoned argument apart from that which is provided by some particular tradition.[188]

I would argue that because MacIntyre's "substantial rationality" is deeply embedded in tradition and the *beliefs* therein, it intrinsically carries the doxastic logic discussed above. Frestadius agrees, as he bases the justification of Elim's experimental beliefs, which he draws from MacIntyre's rationality, on their doxastic practices.[189]

---

185. MacIntyre, *Whose Justice?*, 12.
186. Frestadius, *Pentecostal Rationality*, 47.
187. Ibid.
188. MacIntyre, *Whose Justice?*, 350.
189. Frestadius, *Pentecostal Rationality*, 202.

The PTM I advance here is not merely advocating for the immediate reception of the surprising new of the Spirit that is simply rooted in individual experience, testimony, or fideism. It must seek (a) to be cautious and discerning while deeply engaged in the historical pneumatological tradition; (b) to be prophetic, while always inviting the voice of the community of faith; (c) to be aware of the presence of the epistemological crises and the "shadowlands"; and (d) to be ready and willing to do the kind of philosophical work proffered by MacIntyre.

Conclusion

The goal of this chapter was to sketch out the rationale for the theological methodology (PTM) that I wish to explicate in the next chapter. Here I resourced Yong's pneumatological imagination as the foundation for a theological methodology grounded in pneumatological concerns. The use of the term "imagination," within Yong's proposal, is the human belief-forming faculty in relation to God and the world—a worldmaking capacity.

I have presented why I believe theologues should consider new theological methodologies in general, and specifically why a methodology rooted in a pneumatological imagination should be considered. We saw how there has been a renaissance concerning the doctrine and spirituality of the Holy Spirit in the context of theologizing, appearing everywhere from new theological studies in the academy to the emergence of new spiritual orientations and movements. I then shifted our attention to the concept of a pneumatological theology, highlighting four "Spirit of's" that should deeply inform any constructed PTM: (1) the *Spirit of Life*, (2) the *Spirit of Truth*, (3) the *Spirit of Love*, and (4) the *Spirit of the Wind*.

These thoughts are what I use as the foundation of a PTM I imagine. It serves as a methodology that produces a hermeneutics to help theologians respond faithfully and daringly to an everchanging world. And it is—in its own right—a kind of "worldmaking" process. Next, using the research laid out heretofore, I will construct what I believe should be the distinctives of a PTM.

Chapter 7

DOING THEOLOGY FROM A PNEUMATOLOGICAL IMAGINATION: A PNEUMATOLOGICAL THEOLOGICAL METHODOLOGY

Introduction

In Chapter 1, I asserted that the first essential to what makes pentecostalism pentecostal is *revivalism*. We saw how revival within the pentecostal tradition emerged from a primitive, a priori impulse (viz., the numinous) as it pursued an experience with the living God. The second essential of pentecostalism we explored was the constructivist form of Christian/pentecostal mysticism with its nuanced cataphatic and apophatic expressions. The third essential (which is, perhaps, the progenitor of all the essentials) is the fact that pentecostalism always privileges the pneumatic, which gives rise to a pneumatological imagination.

The theological methodology I explicate in this chapter is indebted to Yong's description of the pneumatological imagination.[1] He holds that this "imagination" is the human belief-forming faculty in relation to God and the world that discharges a kind of "worldmaking" capacity.[2] What *is* critical to my theological methodology, which I call a *Pneumatological Theological Methodology* (PTM), is how the pneumatological imagination frames our understanding of God and the world after divine encounters have been experienced, along with how those experiences create space for thought experiments in theological hermeneutics and method.

Yong suggests that this imagination becomes "an epistemological theory that proceeds from specifically thematized constructs of experiences of the Spirit."[3] This is significant. Yong contends that a pneumatological imagination occurs by "focusing on certain primordial pneumatic experiences" that "enable large-scale coherent visions of the world" as well as enabling a person to absorb and explain other "visions" that seem outside that pneumatological framework.[4]

---

1. See Yong, *Spirit-Word-Community*.
2. Ibid., 151.
3. Ibid., 123 (emphasis original).
4. Ibid., 133.

Yong's argument is situated within a pneumatological framework by which he claims is derived "from a *pneumatic* intuition."[5] It is important for Yong that this "pneumatic intuition" is seen as antecedent to the pneumatological framework and "proceeds from such pretheoretical encounters with and experiences of the Spirit of God."[6] He insists that these "encounters" and "experiences" must then be "thematized for purposes of theological reflection and communication." It is here that the pneumatic intuition gives birth to pneumatology.

Using Yong's schema to build a PTM, one could say it is a methodology that starts with a universal, essential concern to engage in the pneumatic through devotion to God's Spirit, and then proceeds to theological reflection on the meaning of that engagement (viz., pneumatology). This kind of work funds the pneumatological imagination. This pneumatological imagination, then, presses one to imagine "large-scale coherent visions of the world"—worlds where one would expect to see God's kingdom come. It is an imagination that sees the order of things (ontology) and the order of knowing (epistemology) mediated through the eternal Spirit and the God-breathed Word.[7] It is a methodology that holds in tension two questions: *What is?* over against *What if?* It is truly a "pneumatology of quest."[8]

This imaginative world-(re)making is eschatological in the sense that we see (dimly) by faith a future world that *is* and is *not yet*. But the imagination leads the Spirit-filled "imagineers" to leap into action through the work of Spirit-filled prayer and Spirit-led actions where the faithful participate in bringing that imagined world into actuality via the kingdom of God. So, by utilizing the pneumatological imagination, pentecostals attune the hope of unfolding potentialities, to miracles, that spill into existence from the depths of the Spirit. Wariboko says of this, "It is a way of instructing the self to hear, feel, and imagine the world differently."[9] Here the Spirit-filled person anticipates and places the self at the points of crossing between expected ordinariness of existence and the elemental, miraculous depths of extraordinariness graced by a life filled with the Spirit. This practice is filled with "Aha!" moments of inspiration that transform our phenomenal perceptions like the caesural moments in a poem. This pneumatological imagination dares to imagine new worlds that carry a wide range of expectations and hopes for those worlds to be made real.

Though there are many kinds of PTMs one could imagine, I have thumbnailed a particular kind here—a kind that utilizes the sensitivities and values explicated in Chapters 1 and 5—and I am limiting my imagination to the world of *theologizing*. In a sense, this PTM is a thought experiment with a set of worlds in which theology takes place in particular ways that privilege the pentecostal *qua* pentecostal I have suggested throughout this project. My attempt is to concretize this path for others

---

5. Ibid., 7 (emphasis original).
6. Ibid.
7. Cf. 2 Tim. 3:16.
8. Yong, *Spirit-Word-Community*, 8.
9. Wariboko, *The Pentecostal Principle*, loc. 1809, Kindle.

to examine and possibly employ. Though it has some novel aspects, what I offer builds upon the essences embedded in pentecostal spirituality and Christian spirituality, writ large.

Imagined Worlds

A pneumatological imagination dares to imagine new worlds. Chris Green writes of the church's ability to transcend what has been assumed as unchanging, claiming that the aim of our approach to sacred text "is not merely exegetical: it is prophetic and priestly. Ultimately, faithful readings are known by their effects, their fruit: they stir up holy love for God and love for neighbor, and draw hearers on toward higher and deeper and wider faithfulness."[10] As a result of bringing this attitude into interpretation, Green asserts, "the Spirit, after all, is infinite, and so are the possibilities of interpretation."[11] This opens up new worlds within the theological enterprise, and a PTM takes the liberty to imagine such worlds. These new worlds change our "horizons of expectation" (our *Erwartungshorizonte*) and help us to anticipate the possibilities God has for the story God is telling through the human experience.

Wariboko writes concerning this, "God (Spirit) is always active, willing, and acting wherever, whenever, and however God wills. Pentecostals do not limit the freedom of God. The freedom [always exists for] the Holy Spirit (the power of creation, the dynamic power of all of reality) to rework and advance the structures of sociality and to re-create personal lives."[12] In what follows, I suggest four imaginative theological "worlds" as descriptors for the kind of space that is optimal for theologizing within a PTM: (1) a *world of enchantment*, (2) a *world unfinished*, (3) a *world of relationality*, and (4) a *world of dialectic tension*.

World of Enchantment

A *world of enchantment* is a world that imagines the constant presence of the "Spirit of's" articulated in our last chapter (viz., the *Spirit of Life*, the *Spirit of Truth*, the *Spirit of Love*, and the *Spirit of the Wind*). It insists on the acknowledgment that Spirit is *always* present—even when there is chaos and seeming darkness and disorder (cf. Gen. 1:1-2). We have seen how interest in the Holy Spirit has not always been keen in theology. There have been moments in history where the theologians of the East accused their Western counterparts of a "forgetfulness of the Spirit."[13] A world that starts from a pneumatocentric

---

10. Chris E. W. Green, *Sanctifying Interpretation: Vocation, Holiness, and Scripture* (Cleveland, TN: CPT Press, 2020), xvii.
11. Green, *Sanctifying Interpretation*, 9.
12. Wariboko, *The Pentecostal Principle*, loc. 935–6, Kindle.
13. Kärkkäinen, *Pneumatology*, 7.

perspective seeks to right that wrong and is central to a PTM. Pinnock offers in this regard, "Far from being an incidental or isolated topic in theology, Spirit is a major theme, supplying a standpoint, in fact, for surveying the whole vista of Christian truth."[14]

A Spirit-filled world is an "enchanted" world. The secular sense of enchantment is that a forest, river, or creature is under a magic spell—you are witnessing something, *plus*. And the "plus" by definition is not explicitly seen. A good correlative to the idea of a thing being enchanted is what humans experience as the "something" behind dramatic-creative pieces of music, art, or drama. Though one may have experienced being moved by such events (e.g., a gripping piece of music or a soul-capturing story), we can only schematize that experience in a partial or fragmentary way. The real thing that touches us and evokes awe in us does not appear to be from the world of ordinary human emotions at all—it seems like something wholly *other*. It may correlate with our ordinary emotions of life, but it is from something unconceived and non-rational. Enchantment is of this ilk. It is a thing other than what can be clearly articulated—something present, but not clearly seen. Otto refers to this as a "numinous impression."[15] Enchantment is the label we give such a thing. There is *something* there. It may seem scant and imperceptible until it *presses*, but it is not imagined. On the dark end of the spectrum, one could call it a "haunting."

People in the premodern period (and still in some cultures today) were convinced that there were many spirits and/or spiritual realities in the world naturally embedded in the dynamic processes of the world. In the West, as modern thought emerged, people began to see the world in a more flat, materialistic way. This reductionism procured a disenchanted universe—one gutted of spirits. A pneumatological imagination reenchants the world by seeing Spirit everywhere and in all things. This is enchantment, not on pantheistic terms but on panentheistic ones, which is to say that Spirit is both transcendent (self-conscious and outside of creation) as well as immanent (*in* the world's processes). This imagined PTM is metamodern in the sense that it is willing to utilize perspectives that seem anachronistic or out of time. Yong writes, "Pentecostalism exhibits a pneumatology that can include the premodern, the modern and the postmodern, all in a situation that is *after* the re-enchant-ment of a globally interconnected world once thought to be on the inevitable path of complete secularization."[16]

A world of enchantment imagines life bursting out everywhere—which includes the domain of theological study. The theologue engaging in this PTM would imagine entering an enchanted theological forest filled with theological birds, trees, rivers, deer, butterflies, and chipmunks who are under the "spell" of

---

14. Pinnock, *Flame of Love*, 10.
15. Otto, *Idea of the Holy*, 69. See Chapter 1.
16. Amos Yong, "What Spirit(s), Which Public(s)? The Pneumatologies of Global Pentecostal-Charismatic Christianity," *International Journal of Public Theology* 7 (2013): 257 (emphasis original).

the Spirit. Pinnock speaks of a world enchanted by the Spirit who brings God near: "Though we speak of the Spirit as a third Person, from the standpoint of experience Spirit is first, because it is the Spirit that enables us to experience God's flying by and drawing near."[17] Theologically, the expectation for the pneumatologically oriented theologian is that rational, discursive theological thought will be supervened upon by Spirit's presence—where even the theologue experiences enchantment. It is expected within this kind of PTM that God enchants the human mind.

There is no theologizing of this kind without an active recognition of the Spirit's presence and guidance. Pinnock affirms this: "Theology done by Pentecostals will have its own qualities and characteristics. One would expect it to be dynamic not rationalistic, for example, since openness to the Spirit would be integrated in the method, so that there would be fresh contextualizations."[18] Pneumatological knowledge then is not just rational. It is not antirational (though it may be antirationalist), but rational in a way that does not petrify or absolutize its rationality. Pneumatological knowledge is more fluid and is a place where cognitivism is critiqued, and an affective understanding prioritized with the expectation of the leading of the Spirit of God. This is why discernment is central to any PTM (to which I return below). The theologian would be interested in discerning what the Spirit might be leading one to do within the theological enterprise.

This kind of theology may not provide a fully systematic theological perspective but is, what Pinnock calls, a "nondeterministic theology."[19] In other words, it is a theology that remains open to *new* discoveries, approaches, and applications of the ancient message of God amid an ever-wondrous, *world of enchantment.*

A World Unfinished

The universe continues to expand. Stars are still being born. Evolution is still happening. We are living in *a world unfinished.* This PTM holds this unfinished world in view and does not see theology as a discipline one does by *only* examining the past. One must consider what God is saying *now*, as well as recognizing that we are evolving to places we have not yet been and are going to discover things we do not yet know.

Certainly, the orthodoxy of the church's past keeps us oriented to where we are and how we got here, but we should not fear the new. It is not that truth changes, but the way truth is understood and how it is applied undergoes change. Consider Jesus' approach to the law: "Do not think that I have come to abolish the Law or the Prophets; I have not come to abolish them but to fulfill them" (Mt. 5:17). The

---

17. Pinnock, *Flame of Love*, 14.
18. Pinnock, "Divine Relationality," 4.
19. Pinnock, *Flame of Love*, 18.

understood truth of orthodoxy was not getting abolished by Jesus, but the way that truth was understood and applied changed dramatically.

In the Sermon on the Mount, Jesus does quite a bit of this kind of shifting. For example, the *lex talionis* (viz., "eye for eye, and tooth for tooth," Mt. 5:38), which helped to mitigate the escalation of violence in the First Testament, was not abolished, but nor was it allowed to continue as it was. The spirit of that truth was fulfilled in the new application offered by Jesus. The new he offers was that as one encounters evil, one should not react to it from the same place the evil struck. Jesus says, "If anyone slaps you on the right cheek, turn to them the other cheek also" (v. 39). Jesus is saying that our reaction is not to come from the sting of the slap or from the place of pain; our response is to come from the "other cheek." This implies that victims of such violence are to respond from the non-stinging, non-injured part of their souls—the part untouched by the physical evil done to us, which, arguably, is connected to the eternal. Jesus goes on to claim that this kind of move invites God into the situation. This is the new way the escalation of violence is to be mitigated—we "overcome evil with good" (Rom. 12:21).

Here are some more examples in the life of the church when past, orthodox truth did not get abolished but was understood and practiced in new ways not previously seen:

- The inclusion of the Gentiles from Acts 10 did not *abolish* the exclusive, holy aspect of the Jewish people but expanded ("fulfilled") it. The inclusion of the Gentiles fulfilled God's promise to Abraham that "all peoples on earth will be blessed through you" (Gen. 12:3). The truth of what constituted being a holy people was not abolished or cancelled; it was recast.
- The new scientific knowledge of Copernicus did not abolish the biblical view of cosmology but reordered it. Was it disorienting? Yes. Did it create deep fear and an epistemological crisis? Yes. But the church made it through. God was speaking something *new* through the crisis.
- Regarding the new social awareness in the late seventeenth century that human beings cannot own other human beings through slavery—a concept written and unchallenged in sacred text—the church's rethinking of slavery did not abolish what the Bible said. However, it recast it using a kind of "Hegelian" synthesis of NT passages like Galatians 3:28, "There is neither Jew nor Gentile, neither slave nor free, nor is there male and female, for you are all one in Christ Jesus." Texts like this provided space for the church to recalibrate the settled, orthodox view of slavery in a brand-new, never conceived of, life-giving way. This reconsideration allowed them to make revisions that brought more finishing to this *unfinished world* and helped the church to do what "seemed good to the Holy Spirit and to us" (Acts 15:28).

Holding to orthodox truth but being open to its fulfillment in some new way is precisely how early pentecostal thinkers ventured into examining truth (from reassessing the doctrine of the Trinity to integrating media into mission, receiving women in ministry leadership, being anti-war, etc.). They embraced novel views over settled issues as they discerned the voice of the Spirit—even if that meant embracing concepts that were not considered orthodox at the time. This impulse is an acknowledgment of the living nature of faith and the need for *semper reformanda* to always be at play within the Christian church. God does new things because we are part of a world unfinished.

The PTM that functions in an unfinished world will always be scanning the world for places where the Spirit is not being fully expressed. For example, the theologian utilizing a PTM must seek places where injustice and the soul-crushing biases dominate (i.e., racism, sexism, ageism, ableism, etc.). A theologue who practices this PTM will choose to speak and act prophetically to the church, peoples of all cultures, institutions, and nations in order to put to right that which is wrong. This is a cry for the fulfillment of the promise of Isaiah 45:8, "Shower, O heavens, from above, and let the skies rain down righteousness; let the earth open, that salvation may spring up, and let it cause righteousness to sprout up also; I the Lord have created it" (NRSVA).

In this more recent simulacrum, Kärkkäinen gives us a glimpse of this kind of theological work that demonstrates the passion to add finishing to the world unfinished as it is empowered by the pneumatological imagination:

> While Christian theology up until the last decades of the second millennium has been predominantly the business of white male theologians from Europe and North America, the situation is radically changing in our times. Female theologians of diverse backgrounds—feminist (white women), womanist (African American women), mujerista (Hispanic/Latina women), as well as African, Asian, and Latin American—have joined forces with other liberationists, such as sociopolitically oriented black theologians and "green" pneumatologists, in producing a more inclusive account of the Spirit. In our contemporary world, theology has the burden of showing its cultural, religious, political, and economic sensitivity. Theology can no longer be the privilege of one people. Instead, it must be context specific as it addresses the work of the Spirit of God in specific situations and in response to varying needs and challenges. [There is a] richness of pneumatology when done from multiple perspectives. Female pneumatologies—doctrines of the Spirit formulated by and from the perspective of women—attempt to interpret the Spirit experience from the vantage point of women and find feminine counterparts for addressing the divine Spirit. Liberation theologies, which evolved in the womb of the poor of Latin America, South Africa, and elsewhere, approach the Spirit from the perspective of freedom, survival, and equality. Ecological or green theologies purport to address the impending crises of the future of creation—pollution, the depletion of natural resources, and ecological disaster—by utilizing pneumatological insights and resources.[20]

20. Kärkkäinen, *Pneumatology*, 139–40.

The PTM I imagine emphasizes pentecostalism's ability to incarnate the gospel into any cultural context it encounters as it is motivated to bring more completeness to *a world unfinished*.

World of Relationality

The PTM I imagine envisages a world where all things fit together (viz., synthesis) as much as possible: methods, sources, zeitgeists, global/local concerns, communities, etc. This aspect of the PTM would appeal to a postmodern-minded individual who is, in Robert Webber's words, "more interested in broad strokes than detail, more attracted to an inclusive view of the faith than an exclusive view, more concerned with unity than diversity, more open to a dynamic, growing faith than to a static fixed system, and more visual than verbal with a high level of tolerance and ambiguity."[21] Here are a few ways this PTM works to increase relationality (drawn from my research already explicated herein):

- This PTM is a heuristic methodology deeply influenced by pentecostalism but tuned ecumenically to other methodologies in an effort to share common ground with all Christian theological camps. The dance between various methodological choices within this PTM would not be a decision to compromise for acceptance, nor should it be a loophole for personal preference and bias. The intent of this kind of theological dance within the PTM would be governed by the goal of the theologue—whether trying to interpret a particular passage of scripture, to determine a hermeneutical approach to a subject/person, to formulate a doctrinal position on an issue, to discern an appropriate ethical position, and so on.
- This PTM is open to all available sources for truth (though always privileging scripture, tradition, and reason). This theological method seeks to analyze, synthesize, and harmonize the shared themes and ideas found in theology with other outside disciplines (i.e., sociology, anthropology, psychology, philosophy, anthropology, economics, political science, etc.). Though this PTM is a theological methodology, it does not insist that God only speaks in the arena of theology or solely within the context of the local church. God speaks both inside and outside the worlds of theology and the church. I agree with Wariboko that "no a priori limitations can or should be imposed" on the Holy Spirit.[22] Moltmann's "holistic approach" is helpful here; he claims, "The operations of God's life-giving and life-affirming Spirit are universal and ... universally relevant."[23] Moltmann is making a case against limiting the working of the Spirit to *just* religious activity. The Spirit is present in *all things*—sustaining *all things* in *all people*. Moltman continues about how

---

21. Webber, *Ancient-Future Faith*, 27.
22. Wariboko, *Pentecostal Principle*, loc. 1022, Kindle.
23. Moltmann, *Spirit of Life*, loc. 81–2, Kindle.

"the possibility of perceiving God in all things, and all things in God, is grounded theologically on an understanding of the Spirit of God as the power of creation and the wellspring of life."[24] This is why the theologue utilizing a methodology like this PTM needs to be open to God speaking in everything from scripture to culture, history, and discoveries in the universe.

Because God is *in* all things, this PTM would consider all voices/evidence of truth. The inclusion of outside disciplines gives us various ways to describe reality—the language of law versus science versus anthropology versus sociology versus literary approaches—all help to generate new understanding that can be coordinated into a coherent whole. What the philosopher thinks—or the historian, the anthropologist, the sociologist, the psychologist, a young-earth creationist, an intelligent design scientist, an evolutionist, people speaking from different cultures or geographical locations—all add to the conversation and understanding of the theological enterprise. Hence, an approach open to all sources for truth affords new conceptual, theoretical, methodological, and translational innovations that can broaden the theological study and its relationality to the whole of existence. It is a unitive impulse.

- This PTM must remain aware of the historical philosophical narratives that have promoted varied metaphysical, epistemological, and hermeneutical views, which have impacted the theological enterprise. To follow the Spirit who leads us into all truth, these forces must be navigated, which is why the PTM needs to be metamodern—the relationality of times/zeitgeists and theology must be understood and resourced.
- A commitment to understanding the relationality of global and local concerns needs to be coordinated within this PTM. The term "glocalization" has been offered to combine the emphasis of both local and global concerns without biasing the moments' global pluralism against the movement's local embeddedness. Wolfgang Vondey speaks of the relationality necessary here:

> This interdependence can be described with the term "glocalization"—the elimination of "distance" between the local and the global that ultimately finds the global in the local and vice versa. Instead of proposing the globalization of local Pentecostalism and thereby effectively juxtaposing the global against the local, the understanding of Pentecostalism as a glocal phenomenon embraces the relationship between the local and the global because Pentecostalism as a whole depends on both realities.[25]

This PTM must carry a "glocalizing" impact—beyond local, but not just global. This allows for a relationality between the unique and the general.

---

24. Ibid., loc. 573-9, Kindle.
25. Vondey, *Pentecostalism*, 24-5.

- This is a PTM that imagines that a *world of relationality* involves community. The heart toward relationality must always be engaged. This means we need to welcome and seek relationality with the voices from the communion of saints—both those who currently speak and those who have spoken throughout the Christian past. Every age/place has its own unique challenges and concerns, but there is great safety in the collective wisdom of the church. We saw in Chapter 6 that theologizing is "not just an argument by individuals, but by a community of people interested in and committed to the common object of enquiry" and that the discussion "inevitably becomes socially embodied and historically extended"[26] (which draws upon MacIntyre's "substantial rationality" [see Chapter 6]).
- The need for relationality within this PTM opens the door for the embedding of what Smith calls a "storied epistemology."[27] One cannot help but think of the parables of Jesus in this regard. The shifting to the radical new was introduced through *story*. Story is the best way one can navigate through the seeming contradictions, incompleteness's, paradoxes, and complexities found in the theological enterprise (if not in all truth, generally). Story can hold us together while affording us lots of intellectual wiggle room. Story is not afraid of paradox and ambiguity but is willing to run at them to dig for more clarity. In the end, mystery may remain mystery, but it should not be so because of any intellectual laziness or overcommitment to fideism.

Interestingly, Joshua Wu points to the privileging of "relationality" in the Eastern worldview. He writes that there is an

> important worldview divide between "traditionally Western" thinking and "traditionally Eastern" thinking. Obviously Western and Eastern ways of thinking are nuanced and complex. Not to oversimplify this complexity, generally Western ways of knowing are greatly influenced by Greek philosophical systems, especially Aristotelian logic, which focuses on *abstract and categorizational thinking*, while many Eastern (and agrarian) cultures seem to focus on *concrete and relational* ways of knowing.[28]

Imaging a *world of relationality* serves to show the relational connections between things often "silo-ed" or fragmented from each other. This kind of world is suffused with doxasic logic that offers an epistemology that welcomes both the axioms and ambiguities of the Christian faith (see Chapter 6). It is a confidence rooted in more than subjective experience or fideism, but less than what is promised through Enlightenment certitude.

---

26. Frestadius, *Pentecostal Rationality*, 48.
27. Smith, *Thinking in Tongues*, 48–85.
28. Joshua Wu, "The Chinese Church and the Great Tradition," in *Shadows from Light Unapproachable: Anglican Frontier Missions 1993–2018*, ed. Tad de Bordenave (Heathsville, VA: Northumberland Historical Press, 2018), 240 (emphasis original).

World of Dialectic Tension

Most often people tend to avoid tension or conflict in their interactions. One of the central reasons this is done within the Christian ethos is because peace is often assumed to be a signifier of the *absence* of conflict. However, Nelson Mandela's description of peace in our interactions seems more appropriate:

> Peace is not just the absence of conflict; peace is the creation of an environment where all can flourish, regardless of race, color, creed, religion, gender, class, caste, or any other social markers of difference. Religion, ethnicity, language, social and cultural practices are elements which enrich human civilization, adding to the wealth of our diversity. Why should they be allowed to become a cause of division, and violence? We demean our common humanity by allowing that to happen.[29]

On Mandela's view, the tension caused by difference can "enrich human civilization" and can be seen as "adding to the wealth of our diversity" without leading to "division and violence."[30] This is precisely what is being imagined in the PTM's *world of dialectic tension*.

Jesus himself showed disagreement rather pointedly to his disciples from time to time. "How long shall I put up with you?" (Mt. 17:17) is one example. It is not accurate to think that being a loving person means one never enters confrontation. In fact, lifelong friendships and healthy families reveal that the strongest kind of intimacy is one forged in conflict. An ancient Jewish proverb asserts, "As iron sharpens iron, so one person sharpens another" (Prov. 27:17). Another says, "Rebuke the wise and they will love you" (Prov. 9:8). Obviously, to ask "How long shall I put up with you?" or to rebuke and metaphorically cross swords of iron in disagreement with another person would only be healthy if a foundation of a respectful, understanding relationship had already been built. A relationship can only withstand raw honesty like this when it is between trusted persons with whom there is a sense of safety. Proverbs 27:6 affirms this: "Wounds from a friend can be trusted."

As any theologue knows, discussions in the world of theologizing can get brutal. Some try to avoid that by constructing a unity and peace out of *sameness* and *uniformity*, where the absence of conflict is seen as evidence that the Spirit has truly brought people together. But this kind of conflict avoidance is merely a people-pleasing behavior rooted in the fear of confrontation. Most want simply to belong without the tension of disagreement. Those who believe that unity is the avoidance of conflict at any cost will feel led to isolation with a coterie of

---

29. Nelson Mandela, "Speech to the Global Convention on Peace and Non-Violence," New Delhi, India, January 31, 2004, Nelson Rolihlahla Mandela (July 18, 1918–December 5, 2013), accessed November 11, 2021, http://db.nelsonmandela.org/speeches/pub_view.asp?pg=item&ItemID=NMS914&txtstr.

30. Ibid.

folks who see and think about the world and faith the same way. This leads to groups being pedantic over their totalizing theological views, which fosters the impulse to create purity cultures, along with deeply embedded systems used for scapegoating. However, it makes people feel safe, and though it is true that conflict can be mentally and physically exhausting, avoiding it in theological work will only result in shortsighted and narrow theologizing. This *get-along-whatever-the-cost* kind of world is worlds-away from the *world of dialectic tension*. A PTM takes the completely opposite view: it expects—even welcomes conflict. Jesus accommodates this expectation with the promise that "offenses will come" (Lk. 17:1, KJV).

Ideas tossed about in an atmosphere of welcomed conflict tend to be improved upon, the superlative ego is attenuated, and the impulses for people-pleasing, protectionism, and weak intellection are blunted as the process of the dialectic continues. In such a world, positions are made, considered, challenged, countered, reconsidered, rechallenged, re-countered, and on and on. It is a clarifying and purging process that is *violent*—not to the persons involved—but to problematic or contradictory aspects of the ideas being presented. And the process leads to better thinking.

The *world of dialectic tension* is a world wherein theologians are committed to a unity that emerges by embracing the dialectic contradictions and tensions already present in every thesis of theology. Both contradiction and negation are dynamically present in all of reality—consciousness, history, philosophy, theology, art, etc. Recognizing a dialectic rhythm of thesis/antithesis to synthesis (i.e., Hegelian) allows further development until there is an appearance of *relational unity*. This kind of unity preserves contradictions as phases and sub-parts of a higher unity or understanding. No single tradition/perspective/thesis becomes the parent where all others are the child. Nor is there room for antagonism. In this world, theologues are joint heirs of how the Spirit is leading all into a greater human apprehension of God.

In a *world of dialectic tension*, we remain learners. We stay humbly aware of that which we all see through that "glass," darkly. We hold in mind the wisdom of the ancient Indian folk tale (from 500 BCE) of the blind men and the elephant (which illustrates how different perspectives afford us distinct points of view). We carry a more generous orthodoxy. We support ecumenism. And we do not think of ourselves more highly than we ought to (cf. Rom. 12:3).

These four worlds: *world of enchantment, world unfinished, world of relationality*, and *world of dialectic tension* are all important levels in the PTM I am proffering. This PTM brings the worldmaking perspectives and possible worlds articulated here to bear in the theological undertaking. It is a methodology that holds the values and perspectives of the pneumatological imagination while embracing certain ways (or attitudes) during the theological process. In the next section, I show how this PTM seeks to *be* in the theological context and how using this schema further concretizes this methodology.

The "Be's" of the PTM

Heretofore, my comments concerning a PTM have been largely descriptive. In this next section I wish to turn prescriptive and offer eight ways of "be"-ing as an example of how to reify this methodology and to prevent it from being too quixotic.[31] These guidelines could be summed up as: be converted, be prayerful, be scriptural, be historical, be philosophical, be ecumenical, be discerning, and be provisional.

Be Converted

This PTM is contextualized by the Christian story where Jesus Christ is Lord and where each theologue has a testimony of crossing the threshold of faith and being "born again" (John 3:3). Whether their story is a dramatic one, like that of St. Paul's Road to Damascus (Acts 9) story, or a seemingly more organic one, like Timothy's natural embrace of the "sincere faith," which Paul claimed, "first lived in your grandmother Lois and in your mother Eunice and … now lives in you also" (2 Tim. 1:5), the conversion must be real. O'Collins offers:

> Personal faith and moral practice affect theologians, just as regularly attending the theatre affects the work of those who teach drama at colleges or universities. How could anyone effectively educate students in the work of Shakespeare, Chekhov, Ibsen, and other great dramatists if he or she never bothered to see plays in their own city, attend drama festivals, and participate actively in the community of playwrights, producers, actors, and critics? … Unconverted theologians remain theologians who will never develop and fulfil their vocation and mission.[32]

This PTM would also insist that this conversion impacts the theologue's *way* of living, not just her or his belief system. This would include general Christian practices like church attendance, prayer, devotional study, a love for mission, etc. The PTM demands more than mental assent or academic curiosity being expressed in the arena of theologizing. It would certainly welcome conversations with theologians who are limited by mental assent or academic curiosity but would not consider such a one a practitioner within the PTM. A distinctly Christian intellectual, moral, affectional, and religious conversion is expected of theologians utilizing the PTM approach.

Additionally, though one utilizing this PTM would be open to conversations with anyone of any faith (including those outside the Christian faith—e.g., Jews, Moslems, Hindus, Taoists, atheists), one would expect a PTM theologue to lean deeply into the recognizable orthodoxy, orthopraxy, and orthopathy shared by

---

31. I draw this schema of how to "be" while executing a theological methodology drawn from O'Collins, *Rethinking Fundamental Theology*, 330–40. Reproduced with permission of Oxford Publishing Limited through PLSclear.

32. O'Collins, *Rethinking Fundamental Theology*, 340. Reproduced with permission of Oxford Publishing Limited through PLSclear.

pentecostals historically. Whatever is to be said about the way in which God is universally present and active in the Spirit in all creation, that investigation presupposes that Jesus will not be relegated to some irrelevant place. In this PTM, Jesus is always acknowledged as "the way, and the truth, and the life" (John 14:6) for all of humankind, and it insists that "Salvation is found in no one else, for there is no other name under heaven given to mankind by which we must be saved" (Acts 4:12). Being converted means that the theologue is situated within this Christian story and is convinced of its veracity. The theological work, then, is done from this admitted biased perspective. Embracing a PTM is to *be converted*.

Be Prayerful

A theologue participating in this PTM insists that the *divine encounter* remains central in her or his theological investigation and construction. This means that as any theological area is investigated, the theologian's heart begins with an intentional openness to such encounters as part of his or her theological method. Simply stated, this is the priority of *prayer*. We have seen that the emphasis of prayer has always been deeply reflected by pentecostals as they have theologized, and they have claimed that religious study/reflection should only be done within the context of prayer while looking for the leading of the Spirit. Study, then, must be a derivative of faith, versus the result of objective standards of reason. This PTM recognizes that all theologizing begins in prayer.

The kind of prayer encouraged in the PTM is not simply religious formality but prayer that carries the expectation of an encounter with God. From what was said about encounters of this sort above under the category of mysticism, and from what was covered in Chapter 1 concerning revivalism (viz., the numinous), we saw that the goal sought after in revival was the "evoking" and "awakening" to everything that comes *of the Spirit*. Revival (in this context) has the capacity to usher the human being into the pure presence of God, which results in an uncanny sense of unity with the divine, coupled with the person maintaining a deep sense of *creaturelyness*, leading to humility and an openness to the new that God brings.

Pentecostals have always associated prayer with the practice of theology, in concert with St. Augustine's advice to biblical scholars that "they should pray in order to understand."[33] Luther spoke to those who entered the field of theology to "kneel down in your little room and pray to God with real humility and earnestness, that he through his dear Son may give you his Holy Spirit, who will enlighten you, lead you, and give you understanding."[34] Embracing this PTM is to *be prayerful*.

33. Augustine's *De Doctrina Christiana*, 3.56, quoted in O'Collins, *Rethinking Fundamental Theology*, 342. Reproduced with permission of Oxford Publishing Limited through PLSclear.

34. O'Collins, *Rethinking Fundamental Theology*, 340. Reproduced with permission of Oxford Publishing Limited through PLSclear.

Be Scriptural

This PTM must be radically committed to the Bible. Theology may begin in prayer, but those prayers must be uttered with a Bible in hand. Much has already been said about the place the Bible holds in the hearts of pentecostals, but it is the *way* the Bible is thought of as God *speaking*—not just as a record of what *was* spoken—that remains the most significant here. With what was discussed concerning the value of various sources in Chapter 6, one may feel tempted to think that other disciplines, like science and history, carry the same authority as the Bible, but a theological method with a pneumatological center would not embrace that.

Since the beginning of the church, scripture has always been the treasure of each member. Returning to O'Collins:

> The words of the Scripture made a temple deep within the hearing of early Christian preachers. Not only in sermons but also in theological works, in letters, and in spiritual writings the church Fathers display an enviable verbal command of large sections of the Bible. In contrast to modern theological writings in which the Bible is cited in support of theological ideas, and hence usually relegated to the footnotes, in the early church the words of the Bible were the linguistic skeleton for the exposition of ideas. Even in the writings of the most philosophical of early Christian thinkers their thoughts are expressed in the language of the Bible, seldom above it.[35]

No other source that one uses in the discipline of theology is "inspired," as is the Bible. Chris Green gives another insightful comment in this regard:

> Here is the wonder: the depths of possibility hidden in the Scriptures open out on the depths of our spirit and our experiences of the world. And to search those depths is to share in the Spirit's searching of the deep things of God ... That is at least near the heart of what it means to say that Scripture is inspired—breathed by God. The Spirit provokes us, first, to ask God and those whom God has given us, "Why?" And then to ask, "What if?" In the process, as we are searching, we can be sure we are participating in the divine life, fighting—or playing—with God in the very conversation that is his life.[36]

However, the PTM does *not* embrace the pervading biblical hermeneutic among early American Pentecostals—the "principle of plenary relevance"[37]—where it was reasoned that the Bible "had dropped from heaven as a sacred meteor,"[38] promoting the assumption that the Bible was errorless in addressing matters of faith, history,

---

35. Wilken, *The Spirit of Early Christian Thought*, 43.
36. Green, *Sanctifying Interpretation*, 227.
37. Wacker, *Heaven Below*, 70.
38. Ibid., 73.

and science. Nor is a PTM committed to utilizing a Baconian methodology and Scottish Common Sense realism as the interpretive hermeneutics of sacred text (Chapter 3).

For the theologue utilizing this PTM, doing theology would be considered an exercise of "faith seeking understanding" over a coherent and cohesive range of topics (the study of various central Christian doctrines, like divine revelation, sin, faith, etc.) as all good Christian theology does. Other methodologies for exegesis and study common to the Christian Church would be embraced and utilized, but unlike other non-pentecostal methodologies, the PTM begins by reflecting on primary texts as one looks for how the Spirit is impacting (or has impacted) the human experience in the moment of *hearing*. As Terry Cross writes, "Clearly, our experiences with God should shape our doctrinal understanding of this God—if the experiences are truly encounters with the Living God and if we allow these experiences to inform our theological reflection. Through our experiences with God, we learn for ourselves who this God is."[39]

Augustine pens the famous story of his conversion in his *Confessions*. It was some time in the year 386 CE; Augustine was with his friend Alypius in Milan. As they were outdoors, Augustine suddenly heard the voice of a child singing a song. At first, he thought that the song related to some kind of children's game but could not place it. Then he realized that the song might be the Spirit calling him. He writes:

> I flung myself down somehow under a certain fig tree and no longer tried to check my tears, which poured forth from my eyes in a flood ... And suddenly I heard a voice from some nearby house, a boy's voice or a girl's voice, I do not know: but it was a sort of sing-song, repeated again and again, "Take and read, take and read" ... Damming back the flood of my tears I arose, interpreting the incident as quite certainly a divine command to open my book of Scripture and read the passage at which I should open ... I snatched it up, opened it and in silence read the passage upon which my eyes first fell: *Not in rioting and drunkenness, not in chambering and impurities, not in contention and envy, but put ye on the Lord Jesus Christ and make not provision for the flesh in its concupiscences.* I had no wish to read further, and no need. For in that instant, with the very ending of the sentence, it was as though a light of utter confidence shone in all my heart, and all the darkness of uncertainty vanished away.[40]

These are the kinds of stories that happen to the women and men who have open hearts to God and are near a Bible. The Bible is no ordinary book. It is not exactly "magical," but it is always used by the Spirit to do seemingly magical things. And it demands extraordinary attention. No Christian theological methodology worth a breath or pen refuses to place scripture smack in the center of the theological

---

39. Cross, "The Divine-Human Encounter," 7.
40. Augustine, *Confessions*, 159 (emphasis original).

enterprise. So, a PTM comes to sacred text *listening, expecting*. Theology emerges there.

It was the dawning of the priority on literalism within more conservative theological thought that gave the Bible a more mathematical hue, forcing the authoritative witness of the Holy Spirit to be subordinated to what amounted to be a new theological science—the perspicuity of scripture. Because this theologizing had been adapted to the Newtonian scientific expectation of the eighteenth century, it resulted in "a wooden, mechanical discipline as well as a rigorously logical one."[41] Common sense realism had afforded a moral rationale that claimed "a literal reading of Scripture implied a humble willingness to bend before the plain meaning of God's own words" and an intellectual rationale that claimed "since God's rules for the world were clear, God's Book must be equally clear. Literalism produced clarity, allegorism produced confusion."[42] Pentecostals impacted by this move to literalism and biblical inerrancy did not intentionally banish the Holy Spirit from the theologian's process of truth-discovery, but the keen awareness of the Spirit *leading* one into truth began to carry a diminishing role. Confidence in theological claims were to be found in external—not internal—cues, in the objective explication of written texts, not the subjective movement of the Spirit within the human soul. *Experience* and *witness* of the Spirit, which had played such significant roles in the early pentecostal hermeneutic, were being relegated to the background.

The PTM refuses the loss that occurs when one intellectualizes the theological process without tethering that work to human experiences with God and the witness of the Spirit. Biblical passages are seen as *that* for the pentecostal—*passages* where God "passes" through—and not just when they were uttered thousands of years ago. God still lives and passes through his Word. They are the "hiding places" where God tucks away and longs to be found by those committed to seek him there. When we encounter the passages of the Bible, we must add faith that God is actually *there* in those passages. He may not always be perceived by the senses, but God is there. This is the experimental side of theology for the pentecostal. We open up to the work of the Spirit-of's (Chapter 6) as we exegete the passages. We may not immediately discern where the Spirit will come from or where the Spirit will lead, but we cultivate an expectation of the Spirit's appearing and wait patiently to that end. We are not paralyzed here, and when we do not hear or sense anything that can be identified as Spirit, we can take that as a nod from the Spirit to proceed with normal exegesis.

Though a PTM welcomes "experimental theology," I agree with Brian Robinson who claims that "experiential theology does not need to reject Scripture as final authority, nor deny orthodox Christian reflection."[43] On the

---

41. Sandeen, *Roots of Fundamentalism*, 118.

42. Wacker, *Heaven Below*, 75.

43. Brian Robinson, "A Pentecostal Hermeneutic of Religious Experience" (paper presented at the 21st Annual Meeting of the Society for Pentecostal Studies, Springfield, MO 1992), 3.

contrary, according to Robinson, Word and Spirit are like two mirrors, which if they reflect the image in the right angle produce a glimpse of eternity. We need both objective and subjective sources in view to arrive at balanced theological conclusions.[44] It is commitment to working in that balance where the PTM commits to *be scriptural*.

Be Historical

History is important for a theologian utilizing a PTM. Being deeply familiar with the past (and with the tradition one is a part of) will communicate wisdom to the present and is a critical skill for navigating into the future. In a sense, all history is contemporary in that what has happened in the past continues to impact the present. The past is made present by what humans call tradition. Tradition fashions the bond between successive generations and through the tradition makes history our contemporary history. So, the advice to "be historical" is a call for theologians to "be traditional." O'Collins avers, "Tradition conveys to each generation the collective experience of previous generations, the cumulative experience of the history through which they have lived. To ignore or belittle tradition is to ignore or belittle history."[45] The PTM I advance must be intrinsically historical/traditional because we are to carry forward and proclaim the faith that comes to us from the apostles (cf. 2 Pet. 1:1). It is the church's story as recorded in sacred text and in a tradition stretching back to apostolic times gives the church her identity as a community.

Being historical includes several things, like understanding *how* the church has historically understood and interpreted scripture, along with the theological reflections that were offered. While exegeting the texts, a theologue utilizing the PTM would be sensitive to reading several biblical scholars across the church's history. This would be to heed O'Collins's warning.

Some theologians enlist support from biblical scholars, but limit themselves to reading only one or two authors. That practice risks taking over into theology the adventurous and even maverick opinions advanced by a particular biblical scholar or by a small group with its own special agenda—the same regrettable tendency on the part of some theologians to consult only one or two biblical scholars and naively adopt their views.[46]

Being historical also helps us see that God's people were *faithful* even when they did not get it exactly right. Consider, for example, the early view of martyrdom within the church. Though, overall, church members did not actively seek to be martyred, many of them embraced that it was the highest expression of discipleship and love of God and invited it. Perhaps they were predisposed to this view by the teachings of Christ (cf. Lk. 6:22-23; John 16:2). In the Book of Acts, the Apostles

---

44. Robinson, "A Pentecostal Hermeneutic of Religious Experience," 3.

45. O'Collins, *Rethinking Fundamental Theology*, 333. Reproduced with permission of Oxford Publishing Limited through PLSclear.

46. Ibid., 332-3.

were seen to be "rejoicing because they had been counted worthy of suffering disgrace for the Name" (Acts 5:40-41).

Early on, persecution and martyrdom became essential parts of the church's self-identity (just as any persecuted group tends to coalesce when they experience rejection and danger), and many martyr-narratives emerged during this time and were widely read (i.e., *Martyrdom of Polycarp*[47]). When these believers were condemned, they tried to imitate other martyrs by their acceptance and celebration of it, greeting their sentence with thanksgiving because they believed it was the best way to conform to the gospel and to imitate Christ. In the opening words of the *Martyrdom of Polycarp*, we read:

> We write unto you, brethren, an account of what befell those that suffered martyrdom and especially the blessed Polycarp, who stayed the persecution, having as it were set his seal upon it by his martyrdom. For nearly all the foregoing events came to pass that the Lord might show us once more an example of martyrdom which is conformable to the Gospel
>
> (Polycarp 1:1[48])

Because persecution and martyrdom were not universal, nor consistent, sexual continence became a new kind of martyrdom, which came to be known as "white martyrdom."[49] Even in marriage, self-restraint regarding the sexual impulse was seen as a mark of holiness. Athenagoras, an early second-century father of the church, wrote of the need for chastity with respect to marriage:

> Therefore, having the hope of eternal life, we despise the things of this life, even to the pleasures of the soul, each of us reckoning her his wife whom he has married according to the laws laid down by us, and that only for the purpose of having children. For as the husbandman throwing the seed into the ground awaits the harvest, not sowing more upon it, so to us the procreation of children is the measure of our indulgence in appetite.[50]

Here, there was no violent death, but a demonstration of great sacrifice and commitment on behalf of the believer in Christ. In Eusebius's *Proof of the Gospels*,

---

47. Anonymous, *The Martyrdom of Polycarp*, trans. J. B. Lightfoot, Early Christian Writings, accessed November 1, 2021, http://www.earlychristianwritings.com/text/martyrdompolycarp-lightfoot.html.

48. Ibid.

49. Clare Stancliffe, "Red, White and Blue Martyrdom," in *Ireland in Early Mediaeval Europe: Studies in Memory of Kathleen Hughes* (New York: Cambridge University Press, 1982), 21–46.

50. Athenagoras, *A Plea for the Christians by Athenagoras the Athenian: Philosopher and Christian*, trans. B. P. Pratten, Early Christian Writings, accessed November 1, 2021, http://www.earlychristianwritings.com/text/athenagoras-plea.html.

he claimed that living with sexual continence was living "above nature" and that it was a "sacrifice" not of the "destruction of bodily things, but with right principles of true holiness."[51] Mid-second century, Justin Martyr asserted the continence of Christians asserting that they do not participate in "promiscuous intercourse."[52] It was a martyrdom of a different ilk. Did they get that right? Many moderns would say no. But being aware of the historical views the church has held helps us to see that people *faithful* to God do not always get it exactly right. This needs to be our expectation as well. There is no way that a theologian from any age can get everything right. But that is not a sign of unfaithfulness, just of fallibility.

There is a provocative statement made by Jesus that should keep all theologues on alert in terms of knowledge: "I still have many things to say to you, but you cannot bear them now" (John 16:12, NKJV). What if that is true? What if there are many more things God wants to say to the church that we have not been able to bear or understand yet? In every age the Holy Spirit calls the church to examine its faithfulness to God's revelation, but the chance of being imperfect in our knowledge is exactly 100 percent. Studying theological history helps us not to be tormented by our imperfect knowledge, or to grow in pride because we now have it all. It shows us that God is still teaching his people as humanity moves toward the eschaton, always speaking when needed—not too early but just in time.

Whether through traditional theological history or through the unfolding history found in the testimony of people and cultures at this moment, the PTM must *be historical*.

Be Philosophical

To state it broadly, this PTM embraces philosophical attitudes, dispositions, and orientations through a metamodern lens—one that ranges from conservative to liberal, postliberal, postconservative, and canonical-linguistic. The PTM does not do so as a theological pastiche or because of intellectual diffidence but because this methodology recognizes the complexity of the theological enterprise and the fluidity necessary to articulate cogent theological ideas in a world of change where even the concept of truth is up for debate.

O'Collins speaks of the need for the use of philosophy in the discipline of theology. He claims that "All theology will remain low on clarity and substance unless it puts what it gleans from the Scriptures and history/tradition into dialogue

---

51. Eusebius of Caesarea, *The Proof of the Gospel*, book 1 of *Demonstratio Evangelica*, trans. W. J. Ferrar (1920), Early Christian Writings, accessed May 24, 2022, http://www.earlychristianwritings.com/fathers/eusebius_de_03_book1.html.

52. Justin Martyr, *The First Apology of Justin*, trans. Roberts-Donaldson. Early Christian Writings, accessed November 1, 2021, http://www.earlychristianwritings.com/text/justinmartyr-firstapology.html, XXIX.

with philosophy."⁵³ This openness to philosophy within theology goes back to the beginnings of the early church Fathers. Robert Wilken reports that, "Many of the best minds in the early church were philosophically astute and moved comfortably within the intellectual traditions of the ancient world. They knew the argot of philosophy, and their books and ideas were taken seriously by Greek and Roman intellectuals."⁵⁴

Indeed, scripture should be privileged over any philosophical speculations, but it was Origen who made the case that Greek philosophy should be seen as an aid in the worship of God. Presbyterian scholar, Michael J. Pereira, conveys:

> In the Exodus story, God directs the children of Israel to ask (aítéw) their neighbors (geítwn) for silver, gold and clothing. From these received materials, the Israelites were commanded to make things for the worship (latreía) of God. The spoiling of the Egyptians, according to Origen, obscurely signifies (ainíssomai) the Christian appropriation of Greek philosophy. For both, the Israelites' and Christians, the spoiling of the Egyptians or the Greeks was primarily to aid in the worship of God.⁵⁵

O'Collins conveys that theologians from the time of Justin Martyr considered that the philosophical views of God, of the world, and of divine interaction "have assisted the interpretation and appropriation of the biblical witness."⁵⁶ He speaks to how "philosophical reason sharpens the questions to be asked, helps to organize approaches to the material, partly illuminates the nature of human beings and their world, and brings conceptual clarity to bear on biblical texts,"⁵⁷ which he claims are largely pre-philosophical. O'Collins is *not* suggesting that philosophy trumps scripture in any way, or that it should be privileged over it.

Pinnock, however, offers a valid rejoinder to this position. He warns that "The Spirit-filled community expects to see surprising works of the God whom they know to be personal, dynamic, and relational. They receive these biblical metaphors not as symbols to be transcended but as reality-depicting language. And, because they read Scripture as narrative, they are less drawn to philosophically influenced interpretations."⁵⁸

---

53. O'Collins, *Rethinking Fundamental Theology*, 332–4. Reproduced with permission of Oxford Publishing Limited through PLSclear.

54. Wilken, *Spirit of Early Christian Thought*, 26.

55. Michael J. Pereira, "From the Spoils of Egypt: An Analysis of Origen's *Letter to Gregory*," *Origen as Writer*, Papers of the 10th International Origen Congress, University School of Philosophy and Education "Ignatianum," Krakow, Poland (August 31–September 4, 2009), *Bibliotheca Ephemeridum Theologicarum Lovaniesium CCXLIV* (Walpole, MA: Uitgeverij Peeters, 2011), 238.

56. O'Collins, *Rethinking Fundamental Theology*, 333. Reproduced with permission of Oxford Publishing Limited through PLSclear.

57. Ibid., 334.

58. Clark H. Pinnock, "Divine Relationality: A Pentecostal Contribution to the Doctrine of God," *JPT* 8, no. 16 (2000): 2–26, 9.

However, one could argue that the very way one reads scripture is influenced by philosophical concerns. O'Collins says that philosophy always "throws some light on what happens when we read and interpret the Scriptures. By developing insights into the nature of knowledge, meaning, and truth, philosophy elucidates to a degree that spiritual dynamism operating when we read and hear the Scriptures."[59] Bultmann insists that:

> It is an illusion to hold that any exegesis can be independent of secular conceptions. Every interpreter is inescapably dependent on conceptions which he has inherited from a tradition, consciously or unconsciously, and every tradition is dependent on some philosophy or other … It follows, then, that historical and exegetical study should not be practiced without reflection and without giving an account of the conceptions which guide the exegesis. In other words, the question of the "right" philosophy arises. At this point we must realize that there will never be a right philosophy in the sense of an absolutely perfect system, a philosophy which could give answers to all questions and clear up all riddles of human existence. Our question is simply which philosophy today offers the most adequate perspective and conceptions for understanding human existence.[60]

O'Collins explains four ways that philosophy aids the theological enterprise (which I contend need to be utilized in the PTM I am offering). First, O'Collins brings up the problem of knowledge: *How do we know what we know?* He writes: "Issues of the epistemology of theology turn up everywhere: for instance, on the question of 'evidence' for the resurrection of Christ. What counts as evidence here?"[61] Certainly philosophical epistemology comes to bear on such questions.

Second, O'Collins says that when a theologian begins to address a concept, like the "pre-existence" of Christ, how can one imagine such a thing? He declares a problem like this "cries out for dialogue with philosophers"; then adds, "What are time and eternity? How might an eternal, pre-existent person take on an existence in time?"[62] Resourcing ancient and modern philosophers gives the theologue language for such conversations.

Third, O'Collins suggests, philosophy helps us to deal with questions of *what* happens in the Bible over against *why* what happens, happens. He states that we gain insight into *what* and *why*:

> [B]y introducing the philosophical distinction between event and act: that is to say, by distinguishing between (a) the language of causality, which asks how

---

59. O'Collins, *Rethinking Fundamental Theology*, 334. Reproduced with permission of Oxford Publishing Limited through PLSclear.

60. Rudolf Bultmann, *Jesus Christ and Mythology* (New York: Charles Scribner's Sons, 1958), 54–5.

61. O'Collins, *Rethinking Fundamental Theology*, 334. Reproduced with permission of Oxford Publishing Limited through PLSclear.

62. Ibid., 334.

the central agent contributed to some occurrence and its results, and (b) the language of intention, which asks why the agent acted in the way he or she did.[63]

Fourth, O'Collins says that philosophy helps us address the complexities between language in general and religious language. He writes:

> Can literal, analogical, metaphorical, and symbolic language yield some true knowledge of God? And, in any case, what are the differences between such uses of language? In religious reflection (first style), practice (second style), and worship (third style), language is used in non-literal, extended ways ... We are guided toward ultimate realities by symbolic language, even more than by abstract concepts. Faced with analogies, metaphors, and symbols, theologians must listen to the philosophical experts on language and religious language. Contact with philosophers, who normally require precise language, can help theologians "watch their language" in the presence of God and, at least, introduce the brief qualifiers that make all the difference.[64]

Learning the language of philosophy can help soften the edges of sharp debates like whether the baptism of the Spirit always results in *glossolalia* or if the claim that "there is no other name under heaven given to mankind by which we must be saved" (Acts 4:12) is an epistemological claim or an ontological one. In being in contact with philosophers, theologians soften their discourse around truth and qualify how they think and what they write. Embracing the PTM I am advocating is to *be philosophical*.

Be Ecumenical

A properly ecumenical/inter-religious spirit calls a theologian to always be open to learning from people outside of their particular faith tradition and to be listening for how Christ and the Holy Spirit may be speaking through them. Much has already been said in this writing about the impulse toward unity and cooperation, a central value to a Spirit-filled people. The "us-ness" of faith is critical to any PTM. What is important here is to recognize that we need one another. Irrespective of what denomination or theological stream one comes from, hearing arguments less known from the historical archives of the church or from the faith life of other communities will enrich one's theological thinking.

The world of theology is vast, and there is no want for differences of opinion, but examining these differences does not mean theology will end of being too narrowly defined nor ambiguously pluralistic. Theology is generous enough to hold nuances in belief as long as the beliefs are not deeply schismatic. What has

---

63. Ibid., 335.
64. Ibid., 334.

proven to be safe through the centuries is a willingness for theologians to listen to one another and to resist the impulse to become crusaders who are willing to "kill" (viz., silence) those who disagree with them.

Another problem that arises (particularly in the American context) is that theologues become too deeply individualistic in their theological approach. The quintessential Western, modern person is the first *self-made* person. Before modernity (and this still holds true in many non-Western civilizations today), the needs of the individual were subordinated to those of the collective. But individual expression and autonomy were radicalized in the West.[65] When this becomes the prevailing wind in the arena of theology (which it often has), a person refuses to accept faith positions based on anyone else's understanding but their own. This view tends to go unchallenged when Christians are Bible-centered in their theologizing and uncritical about the novel ways they read it. A person's view becomes authoritative and the final word on issues of faith in such a milieu. Though the Bible started as a book to be heard and lived out within the context of a community of faith (from where it emerged and for whom it was written), it has been subsumed into the private study of the modern individual.[66] In discussing the implications of personal preference in biblical analysis, Henry Howorth writes that privatization of scriptural views "reduced the whole matter to a mere subjective question of personal caprice and choice, in which any good Christian might decide the most critical of all questions by internal illumination alone ... Everybody must in fact become an infallible Pope to himself."[67]

Jesus claimed that the world would know who his followers were based on their prioritization of love—their ability to connect with others, to be ecumenical. Jesus told his disciples what was to be their new focus: "A new commandment I give to you, that you love one another, just like I have loved you; that you also love one another. By this everyone will know that you are my disciples, if you have love for one another" (John 13:34-35). *Ut unum sint* ("that they may be one") was Jesus' cry

---

65. See Colin Morris, *The Discovery of the Individual: 1050–1200* (Toronto, ON: University of Toronto Press, 1987); Gurevich, *Origins of European Individualism*; and Aaron Gurevich, *The Origins of European Individualism*, trans. Katharine Judelson (Cambridge, MA: Blackwell, 1995); Charles Taylor, *Sources of the Self: The Making of the Modern Identity* (Cambridge, MA: Harvard University Press, 1989).

66. This became particularly fervent as a result of the seductive democratic impulse, particularly in America. Nathan O. Hatch (*Democratization of American Christianity* [New Haven: Yale University Press, 1989], 9) speaks of the "explosive" fervor for "indigenous expressions of faith" that "took hold among ordinary people, white and black." American life carried "a passion for equality," and this spilled into the personal faith of individuals. Hatch claims, "Christianity was reshaped by common people who molded it in their own image."

67. H. H. Howorth, "The Origin and Authority of the Biblical Canon According to the Continental Reformers: I. Luther and Karlstadt," *The Journal of Theological Studies* os-VIII, issue 31 (April 1907): 321–65. https://doi.org/10.1093/jts/os-VIII.31.321.

to the Father as he prayed in John 17:11 right before entering his Passion. In that prayer Jesus claimed that this oneness or unity would bring the greatest glory to God. Ecumenism is not a nice gesture; it is critical for our mission in the world, as well as for effective theologizing.

Ecumenism applies in the widest sense by being open to the voice of God through *anyone*—even if that voice comes through the life of those who practice a faith outside of Christianity. We share much with other faiths. Most religions have a belief in a world beyond our world (something supernatural or spiritual); most believe in a soul, have a strong sense of family, are loving and kind, meditate/pray, and care for themselves physically and emotionally—there is so much good everywhere one looks.

Finding the good within faiths outside of Christianity can help enrich the treasures of Christianity and give us fresh language for things like prayer, sacrifice, love, contentment, etc. Returning to O'Collins, "The prayer life of Muslims, for instance, could well challenge the followers of Christ and make them rethink Paul's injunction to 'pray without ceasing' (1 Thess. 5:17). A properly ecumenical spirit involves being always open to learning from all others and to hearing Christ and the Holy Spirit speaking through them."[68]

Embracing a PTM is to *be ecumenical*. It is to say, "I need others" in order to understand the truth of God and the ways in which that truth should be lived out. The goal is not to kowtow to the views of everyone else that are contrary to our own, or to confute against those views—it is an irenic enterprise that patiently and confidently listens for understanding, trusting God will speak somewhere amid the difference. O'Collins says it crisply: "In short, being ecumenical amounts to being open to God in others."[69]

Be Discerning

To be a discerning person means one can accurately judge right from wrong utilizing insight and understanding. In the Christian tradition, it implies that one examines an issue, situation, or person via spiritual guidance by the Holy Spirit. In the end for the Christian, being discerning is about deciding what is of God and what is not. A biblical worldview holds that, though creation is sustained by the Holy Spirit, good *and* evil still exists here. When K. A. Smith speaks of an enchanted cosmology, he claims that "there is a flip side this sense of the Spirit's enchantment of creation: pentecostal spirituality is also deeply attentive to what we might describe as the mis-enchantment of the world by other spirits."[70] Wouter Biesbrouck acknowledges the need to be aware of a "spirits-filled cosmology" when moving into discernment. He also argues that the process must be Spirit-led: "Whereas discernment was once understood as a judgment

---

68. O'Collins, *Rethinking Fundamental Theology*, 339. Reproduced with permission of Oxford Publishing Limited through PLSclear.

69. Ibid.

70. Smith, *Thinking in Tongues*, 41.

about Christology, it has come to be understood much more as a pneumatological process."[71]

A PTM insists that all theologizing must take into account how spirits work behind things in good and evil ways. Yong says, "Properly understood, spiritual discernment is much more than the charismatic gift of Discernment of spirits. Rather, in its broadest sense, it should be understood as both a divine gift and a human activity aimed at reading correctly the inner processes of all things—persons, institutions, events, rites, experiences, and so on."[72] This is a claim that God is at work in the world, but the influence of God is not the only influence at work.

Discerning the Evil By the fact that a PTM is interested in what God is *saying* (which may involve something perceived as new), special caution must be taken to discern *who* is speaking. St. Paul warns that Satan can reveal himself as an "angel of light" to deceive the elect (2 Cor. 11:14). This means that not every seeming insight/voice is of God. When a special message comes to the people of God through those deemed to be prophets, Paul urges the church to examine what has been said and to "let the others [prophets] judge" (1 Cor. 14:29, NKJV). We may not like to admit it, but the saints sometimes "give place to the devil" (Eph. 4:27, NKJV). That does not mean that we become demon possessed or lose our salvation—it simply means we do not always get it right, and sometimes we are influenced by forces of darkness. In another place, Paul exclaims, "But I am afraid that just as Eve was deceived by the serpent's cunning, your minds may somehow be led astray from your sincere and pure devotion to Christ" (2 Cor. 11:3). Peter adds warning as well, "Be alert and of sober mind. Your enemy the devil prowls around like a roaring lion looking for someone to devour" (1 Pet. 5:8).

This does not suggest that we *sometimes* encounter dark forces, it suggests we should assume that we are *always* being influenced by the demonic on some level—which is why we should humbly and consistently go to God in prayer and stay actively involved in a faith community. O'Collins urges that theologians need to adapt the classical axiom, "the law of praying" (*lex orandi*) is "the law of discerning" (*lex discernendi*).[73] Whenever we come to light, darkness is exposed and dispelled. Understanding this gives warrant for the cry embedded in the Our Father, "deliver us from evil" (Mt. 6:13). The relentless encroachment of evil is the point Paul is making in Ephesians 6:10: "For our struggle is not against flesh and blood, but against the rulers, against the authorities, against the powers of this

---

71. Wouter Biesbrouck, "Discerning the Divine and the Demonic through Dialogue: Recent Evangelical Theology of Religions," in *The Past, Present, and Future of Theologies of Interreligious Dialogue*, 1st ed., Terrence Merrigan and John Friday (Oxford, UK: Oxford University Press, 2017), 122.

72. Yong, *Beyond the Impasse*, 129.

73. O'Collins, *Rethinking*, 211.

dark world and against the spiritual forces of evil in the heavenly realms." Walter Wink claimed that the powers that act in the world "are both heavenly and earthly, divine and human, spiritual and political, invisible and structural."[74] He further insists that, "These Powers are also good and evil."[75]

It is critical to note that the discernment of evil is not a thought experiment. To speak of evil in some non-incarnate, ambiguous way carries no relevance. Wink points to how the powers always manifest in incarnate ways through social, institutional, structural, and political ways.[76] Yong makes the case that central to the discernment of evil (or good, for that matter) is searching for its *concreteness*. He reports, "We can therefore talk meaningfully of the spirit of lust, or the spirit of murder, or the spirit of alcoholism, only because we see its effects in ruined relationships, tragic homicides, civil wars, malfunctional kidneys, or successive generations of families inflicted by habitually destructive patterns of activity."[77] Yong further claims that "the inner spirit of any entity is what determines its shape, personality, and activity vis-à-vis its relationship with other things and entities."[78] He goes on to assert that the demonic "is a destructive reality that opposes the goodness and purposes of God" and that it manifests itself "in concrete forms and particular actualities [that are] sustained as fields of force with destructive capacities."[79]

But evil is not only concretized through individual behavior; it can also show up in corporate forms like communities, agencies, institutions, businesses, churches, social groups, political and national entities, and so forth. At the close of the nineteenth century, George Gordon speaks of the ways evil goes from the heart to the community: "The evil in men's hearts has gained immense influence through expression in custom, law, government. Inhumanity has fortified itself in the institutions of trade, society, politics, and religion."[80] Yong points out how evil was seen corporately through the "concrete events of 'holy war,' taking the form of knights, swords, the putrid gas chambers of Auschwitz, Boeing 747s used as

---

74. Walter Wink (*Naming the Powers: The Language of Power in the New Testament, The Powers 1* [Philadelphia, PA: Fortress, 1984], 11) claims that "These Powers are both heavenly and earthly, divine and human, spiritual and political, invisible and structural." He further insists that "These Powers are also good and evil" (Wink, *Naming the Powers*,12).

75. Ibid.

76. Walter Wink published a trilogy on "the powers" to capture Paul's concept of spiritual warfare: Wink, *Naming the Powers 1*; Wink, *Unmasking the Powers: The Invisible Forces that Determine Human Existence, The Powers 2* (Philadelphia, PA: Fortress, 1986); and Wink, *Engaging the Powers: Discernment and Resistance in a World of Domination, The Powers 3* (Philadelphia, PA: Fortress, 1992).

77. Yong, *Beyond the Impasse*, 138.

78. Ibid., 137.

79. Ibid.

80. George A. Gordon, *New Epoch for Faith* (New York: Houghton, Mifflin and Company, 1901), 40.

missiles of mass destruction, and the socio-economic and political segregation and discrimination of people based on the color of their skin."[81] To discern evil then, one must look for the result or "fruit" of an action, a person, an institution, an event, an experience, etc. This echoes Jesus' words from Mathew 7:16 as he spoke about discerning false prophets: "You will know them by their fruits." Discernment is a lot about the inspection of concrete fruit. Pinnock speaks of the need for discernment in the work of theology:

> There are things in the world that cannot be attributed to God. God reigns over the world, but warfare and resistance are also real. God is not the only power there is, and God does not control everything unilaterally. There is a struggle between good and evil in history, and divine victory waits for the future. Though present everywhere, Spirit is not identical with everything, and certainly is not related to that which deceives and destroys. Powers hostile to truth and threatening to life must be discerned and resisted.[82]

Yong gives a general schema for unveiling the demonic by suggesting three characteristics that feature in the demonic.[83] First, the demonic is bent on causing destruction and "attempts to influence the course of things and events so that destructive outcomes ensue."[84] Second, evil things try to make connections in inappropriate ways. "Rather than harmoniously connecting with others, demonic entities reject the divinely constituted relationality of things, resulting in strife, violence, isolation, and desolation."[85] This is reminiscent of St. Maximus's claim that "The devil, man's tempter from the beginning, had separated him in his will from God, and had separated men from each other."[86] Third, the demonic promotes a violation of the principle of subsidiarity. It carries an impulse toward hegemony. Yong claims "[The demonic] inspires any thing to overreach its divinely appointed reason for being."[87]

Discerning the Good Though evil may persist in our lives in various forms and degrees, the same is also true about the good. There may be something wrong with us all the time, but there is also something right about us. In the Christian theological tradition, we do not just have original sin; we have original blessing. Human beings were made in the *imago Dei*—we bear the image of God. That means there is always good present in us. This is true about Christians and non-Christians alike. The PTM theologue should look for the good and for the

---

81. Yong, *Beyond the Impasse*, 137.
82. Pinnock, *Flame of Love*, 208–9.
83. Yong, *Beyond the Impasse*, 137.
84. Ibid.
85. Ibid.
86. St. Maximus the Confessor, quoted in de Lubac, *Catholicism*, 35.
87. Yong, *Beyond the Impasse*, 138.

testimony of God embedded in the lives of every culture and person encountered (looking past what is not good). By carrying an expectation of the good that God is working in every person everywhere, we can *look* and *listen* in order to name that good and to give God thanks for it.

The Complexity of Discernment Because of the presence of both good and evil in the human experience, the process of discernment is not always simple. Kärkkäinen remarks in this regard:

> If we discern the Spirit using Christian (for example, biblical) criteria, we end up either "christianizing" the other insofar as we find the Spirit is present, or "demonizing" the other insofar as we find the Spirit absent. These dangers should be kept in mind but they should lead neither to the uncritical affirmation of the Spirit's work everywhere nor to the idea of the incommensurability of Christian pneumatology with other traditions; the latter conclusion would mean leaving behind the dialogue.[88]

The following examples indicate how this complexity presents itself. There is an incident in Acts 16 where the Apostle Paul and his team were going to "a place of prayer," and "a slave woman who had a spirit of divination" and who had brought "great profit to her masters by fortune-telling" (v. 16) started following Paul around crying out repeatedly, "These men are bond-servants of the Most High God, who are proclaiming to you a way of salvation" (v. 17). Notice what she asserts as the truth. It *seems* like a positive endorsement—like good news. But it was the demonic, and the demonic can use truth to bring about destructive ends (cf. Mt. 4:1-11). Paul eventually deals with this demonic possession, but not immediately. The text says "she continued doing this for many days" (v. 18) before Paul discerns what exactly was going on and how to take action.

In discernment, one should be deeply aware of the power of their personal opinion. Opinion is not only potentially problematic in theology, it is also problematic in any field of inquiry. Stanley Fish speaks of a "contradictory caution" that all thinkers carry "personal convictions" that function from our "historical situation."[89] He asserts that we must clearly recognize and name those convictions to keep them from controlling our judgments/interpretations. Fish says there is an "inescapable interest" that everyone carries as they "read" what they read. He insists that "there are no unmediated facts," and "no such thing as a neutral observation language," claiming that "all descriptions are from a perspective."[90] The hope he gives is that *if* we become aware of our own biased

---

88. Veli-Matti Kärkkäinen, *Spirit and Salvation: A Constructive Christian Theology for the Pluralistic World* (Grand Rapids, MI: Eerdmans, 2016), 160.

89. Stanley Fish, *Doing What Comes Naturally: Change, Rhetoric, and the Practice of Literary and Legal Studies* (Durham: Duke University Press, 1989), 436.

90. Ibid., 437.

interests, then we can "bracket" those interests to the side, which gives us a kind of objective view that is free (as much as it is possible) of "any resulting biases and/or prejudices."[91]

Discernment Requires Time Because of the complexity, it often takes time to discern the good or evil present in a situation. Theologically speaking, caution is particularly important when trying to discern whether or not a belief or practice needs to be readdressed or reframed. There are questions that need to be answered: *Is the old way of looking at this creating some injustice or cognitive dissonance* (e.g., slavery; roles of women)? *Is there new truth or evidence that demands an idea or position be reexamined* (e.g., the new cosmology of Copernicus; evidence of evolution)? *Are there questions that are not fully addressed in our current theological position* (e.g., the debate over Christology and Trinitarian thought, over soteriology [who is "saved"], over questions surrounding human sexuality, etc.)?

One must consider other kinds of questions as well: *What proposals are being offered to resolve the theological problem(s), and will it help or hurt persons and/or institutions—or maybe do a little of both? What do other theologues in my tradition say about this? What do theologians from other traditions say about it? How dramatic are the shifts being considered? Can we expect speedy wide adoption of these shifts or is it a shift that may take longer than the work of one generation?* This last question speaks to the issue of capacity. As Jesus said, "I have much more to say to you, more than you can now bear" (John 16:12). This leads to the legitimate question about those who will be affected by change. Are they in a place where they can "bear" the change?

In 1999, as a result of extensive ecumenical dialogue, the Roman Catholic Church and the Lutheran World Federation signed "The Joint Declaration on Doctrine of Justification" (JDDJ), which said in effect that the Reformation was over.[92] In the fall of 2007, I was visiting the Vatican in Rome at a gathering led by the Pontifical Council for Promoting Christian Unity. This was the first time I had heard of the JDDJ. The smiling priest giving the presentation exclaimed, "The Reformation is over! Luther was right!" I immediately made my way to him after the session and asked him, "Father, I had not heard of this agreement. I am so intrigued. May I ask you what the next steps are to see this become more than words in a document?"

He responded, "What do you mean?"

I answered, "What are the practical steps you'll be taking to make this tangible, and what is your timetable?"

He looked at me quizzically and asked, "You *do* realize that we have been through centuries of trauma and division where parishes and families around

---

91. Ibid., 437.

92. The text for this declaration is found in the *Joint Declaration on the Doctrine of Justification* (Grand Rapids, MI: William B. Eerdmans Publishing Company, 2000).

the world have been torn over a Catholic marrying a Lutheran and leaving the Catholic Church and vice versa?"

I nodded yes.

He said, "Practical unity will not be easy. It has to start on paper."

Then I pressed, "But what is your guess as to how long before any of this is seen concretely in the lives of Catholics and Lutherans?"

"Oh," he said, with brightening eyes, "we are so hopeful that within the next three to five hundred years there will be tangible results from this declaration of unity."

My American pragmatic mind was shocked. *Three to five hundred years?* I was hoping for something tangible within the next *ten to fifteen*.

But sometimes shifts being considered are so great that they require the work of more than one generation. I feel suspicious that the changes in our world that have appeared in just the last one hundred years will only grow exponentially over the next five hundred. If these changes are as iconoclastic or seemingly insuperable for theology or science or society (i.e., what if we discover life on other worlds, or there is evidence of an emerging new *homo* species, or medical breakthroughs increase life spans to 200 years, or 100,000 years pass and the Second Advent has not come), then future theologians will need to be ready to patiently consider and discern appropriate responses. A PTM affords the theologue the necessary tools to *be discerning* in any scenario.

Again, discernment, in Yong's words from above, is "both a divine gift and a human activity aimed at reading correctly the inner processes of all things—persons, institutions, events, rites, experiences, and so on."[93] Because it is an admixture of both divine and human activity, we must not panic in spaces that are hard to discern and refuse to rush to judgment (resting our minds in the One who is beyond time), while we work tirelessly to judge well and correctly read what is going on around us to assess as accurately as possible what is of God and what is not. The PTM theologue must *be discerning*.

Be Provisional

To say that the PTM needs to *be provisional* is to say that all theological decisions and positions should be considered as serving for the time-being only. They may be *right enough* at this historical moment but may need to be adjusted in the future with nuanced clarifications or new understandings. This does not imply that our beliefs are invalid or untrustworthy, but rather acknowledges that our attempts to articulate the truth fall short due to our inherent limitations. The truth, being rooted in God, surpasses our ability to fully comprehend and describe truth accurately. O'Collins sums it up well:

> Short of the final vision of God, we "see only dimly" and not yet "face to face" (1 Cor. 13:12). Insofar as they deal with the mystery of God, theologians cannot be

---

93. Yong, *Beyond the Impasse*, 129.

too "knowing" but must remain provisional, modest, and apophatic in what they say and claim. This involves restraining the desire for a closure that works in the spirit of "that's it," and remembering constantly the restless "seeking" (*quaerens*) that should distinguish any style of theology. Far from ever reaching definitive solutions, an apophatic awareness always experiences a sense of incompleteness, a feeling that there is "something more," and never loses its sense that what it does not know far surpasses the little truth it may have glimpsed.[94]

All our affirmations of truth must be qualified by a corresponding negation that recognizes that God and God's truth infinitely transcend our human categories and capacities. We heard the ancient voice of Lactantius in Chapter 2 arguing for the ineffable aspects of God—aspects that can only be appreciated and responded to from the heart, versus apprehended by the mind. He wrote, "[God] whom the human mind has no power to appraise, nor tongue of mortals to utter. For he is too sublime and too great to be grasped in the thought or the speech of man."[95] God's-self and all truth that has been revealed to us from God is always provisional. Yong claims that we must carry a "contrite fallibilism, wherein all knowledge is provisional, relative to the questions posed by the community of inquirers, and subject to the ongoing process of conversation and discovery."[96]

In the PTM I proffer here, Enlightenment certitude is not on the table, not even as a desideratum. Therefore, a theologue embracing this methodology must *be provisional*. We can know things with enough certainty that we can say we believe thusly (e.g., The Apostles' Creed, the plain reading of scripture, tradition, reason, etc.), but we cannot know things absolutely, and we must remain prayerfully open to the new or *adapted* understanding that the Spirit may bring through theological inquiry and process. We are told, "do not refuse him who speaks" (Heb. 12:25, ESV) because God continues to speak.

Conclusion

The foundational pneumatology and a pneumatological imagination explicated throughout this project are central to the question of hermeneutics and theological method. I believe a PTM is a sure way of getting to the purest kind of theologizing. The four imagined worlds: a *world of enchantment*, a *world unfinished*, a *world of relationality*, and a *world of dialectic tension*—along with these eight ways of "be"-ing: *be converted, be prayerful, be scriptural, be historical, be philosophical, be ecumenical, be discerning,* and *be provisional*—are pragmatic guides for reifying a PTM, turning this methodology into a kind of *cheesecloth* that strains out what is unhelpful,

---

94. O'Collins, *Rethinking Fundamental Theology*, 336–7. Reproduced with permission of Oxford Publishing Limited through PLSclear.

95. Lactantius, quoted in Otto, *Idea of the Holy*, 96.

96. Yong, *Beyond the Impasse*, 58–9.

while securing what is best in the theological enterprise. As a kid, my family had a raspberry patch in the backyard, which we harvested each year. I watched as my mom washed and separated the berries and put them into a cheesecloth. She would twist the cloth until all the juice from the berries had been squeezed out into a bowl—devoid of most of the pulp, leaf fragments, or bugs from the patch. The result was *mostly* berry. A PTM is like the cheesecloth. It separates the good of theology from most of the unwanted pulp, leaf fragments, and bugs—though not all.

I wish to encourage theologians everywhere and from all traditions to carefully consider a PTM like what I have offered here as a global, pneumatologically contextualizing lens (a kind of *gestalt*) that should imbue and energize their systematic theology. My contribution is not really an entirely new methodology as much as it is a heuristic methodology that seeks a Spirit-led synthesis of the many respected methodologies within the Christian tradition. It is this synthesis that is most hopeful about a PTM. It affords space for the *ecclesia semper reformanda* as well as room for the theological processing of new discoveries being made in the modern world. This PTM carries no fear of contradiction, nor is it driven by the impulse to an exacting perspicuity. In fact, a recognition of the ambiguities, contradictions, and uncertainties germane to theology (and, arguably, to human knowledge, broadly) is believed to be the way to remain faithful to the Eternal God and God's work in the world. As the Apostle Paul asserts, "And without controversy great is the mystery of godliness" (1 Tim. 3:16, KJV). All theology dares to reflect rationally on the mysteries of the faith. It is a tautology to say that any rational reflection on any pre-rational and pre-theological Reality must carry ambiguity and inconsistency on some level. We must work hard to eliminate those insufficiencies, trusting that the Spirit will help us grow in knowledge "until we all reach unity in the faith and in the knowledge of the Son of God and become mature, attaining to the whole measure of the fullness of Christ" (Eph. 4:13). But such insufficiencies will not be fully resolved until the eschaton. The PTM theologian is comfortable with the apophatic nature of theology and dares to wander in and out of the "Door" (who is Jesus, cf. John 10:9) as she or he explores the boundaries of Christian theology and how they may or may not expand or contract.

Chapter 8

EPILOGUE

Summary and Contributions

This writing has sought to put forward a methodology grounded in a foundational pneumatology (viz., pentecostal *qua* pentecostal) that has been constructed from a pneumatological imagination. It is in line with a call from Cheryl Bridges Johns for pentecostal theologians to offer a theological approach that embodies a "systemic, open, and highly interdisciplinary worldview."[1] She goes on to explain what this kind of approach would look like:

> Under the auspices of Azusa, education would by its very nature be deconstructive. It would not allow for a tight "systematic" theological paradigm. Rather, it would call for a systemic paradigm that is at the same time closed by the limits of the canon and open by the parameters of ongoing revelation. It would be a paradigm that would not take itself too seriously, thereby creating a culture in which the educated are open to the surprising knowledge of the uneducated. Its *paideia* would enculturate students into an inviting and yet dangerous landscape of education where the disciplines of science and the humanities interact to formulate new paradigms. At the core of the curriculum would be an all-consuming passion for God and the kingdom. Visions and dreams would be honored as well as highly technical scholarship.[2]

This writing and the imagined PTM I proffer here is my attempt at this kind of work. Here are some of the highlights of this writing that I think contribute to this approach.

First, Chapter 2 offers a description of pentecostalism that is more primal than the traits often cited to describe pentecostal spirituality (e.g., "initial evidence" of glossolalia, miracles, gifts of the Spirit, a shared set of idiosyncratic dogmas, priorities, hermeneutics, etc.). This insight acknowledges the validity of the many "pentecostalisms" that have emerged around the world without privileging the particular expression of the pentecostalism that emerged in North America. Global pentecostalism carries the unique capacity to be expressed, differentiated, and

1. Johns, "Athens, Berlin, and Azusa," 145.
2. Ibid., 146.

specialized in various local contexts, while carrying a universal set of essentials. The term "glocalization" is in use to acknowledge the commonalities of the global expression of pentecostalism without restricting it in how it is expressed in varied ways locally.[3] This prevents biasing one kind of cultural expression against other cultural/national/local expressions.

Second (and perhaps the most important contribution of this study) is how pentecostalism is vulnerable to the theological and philosophical contexts in which it arises (Chapters 3). My research indicated that the mystical, non-rational aspect of the pentecostalism cannot be separated entirely from rational or theological contexts. In other words, some preconceptions about religion are carried into any divine/human encounter, which is to say that cultural/religious boundaries superintend any pentecostal experience to a degree. It turns out that rational reflection on prerational experiences is a natural, instant reflex that is informed or evoked by some previous understanding. Though the actual experience may feel complicated and experimental, the person will bring other experiences and understandings already known and familiar to make sense of it. This means that once rational reflection begins (viz., theologizing), pentecostals are not *only* "following the Lord" but are influenced by the religious, philosophical, and cultural currents swirling all around them as well. This observation is not made as an attack on pentecostalism's divine origins but as an acknowledgment that though pentecostals may be a "Spirit-filled" people, they are also regular people, influenced by the same ideological and social forces as everyone else.

Third, the entanglement of pentecostalism with outside rational influences (e.g., religious, philosophical, and cultural) in the North American context strengthened pentecostals in some ways but weakened them too (as they are not native to pentecostalism). We showed how these religious/philosophical leanings limited the open and generous impulse within nascent pentecostalism, and how the movement was unwittingly taken captive by the restraints of rational thought (Chapter 4), which weakened its "essentials" and "evidences" described in Chapter 2.

Fourth, drawing on the work of the previous sections, Chapter 5 gives us a sustained, coherent, and robust account of how pentecostals began to recapitulate the orthodoxic, orthopraxic, and orthopathic priorities (and thought) that is critical to what is pentecostal. To that end, the chapter shows how pentecostals quite naturally engage with and embrace the best from the various zeitgeists: premodernism, modernism, and postmodernism—demonstrating that philosophical constructs do not have to dominate pentecostalism in deleterious ways. This penchant shows that the pentecostal movement is one born "out of time" (viz., metamodern) and is well suited to always contend for *ecclesia semper reformanda*.

Fifth, Chapter 6 proposes the rationale behind a pneumatological theological methodology (PTM) that emerges from that which is pentecostal. Like other

---

3. Vondey, *Pentecostalism*, 24–5.

pentecostal works, it iterates the place of the Holy Spirit in the mind of the theologue as they do theology. However, it goes beyond other work of its kind in that it self-consciously attempts to position a pneumatological imagination as the foundation for a theological methodology grounded in pneumatological concerns. These concerns are calibrated to produce a hermeneutics that help theologians respond faithfully and daringly to an everchanging world in ways that are biblical, pentecostal, and catholic all-at-once.

Sixth, this study culminates by offering a model for the pentecostal theological constructive task (Chapter 7). While it remains deeply indebted to other pentecostal theological models, this model is nonetheless unique in certain key respects. Like other pentecostal theological works, it draws heavily on how the pneumatological frames our understanding of God and the world but shifts its focus to create space for thought experiments in theological hermeneutics and method. The pneumatological imagination works from primordial pneumatic experiences that afford the potential of seeing large-scale coherent visions of the world—to imagine *What if?* as one juxtaposes *What is?* over against the purposes of the kingdom of God. This methodology also enables a theologian to absorb and explain other inter-faith "visions" that may seem outside Christian constructs but explicable within a pneumatological framework.

Further Tasks

In the light of the contributions made through this study, the following suggestions present themselves as points of entry into areas for further research.

First, my definition of pentecostal *qua* pentecostal was approached through the limited lens of the North American context. I contend that if one would examine any pentecostalism emerging in any context around the globe, one would find (and be able to trace) its primal essences of revivalism, mysticism, and the pneumatological imagination outlined herein. A study comparing two or three different pentecostalisms within various cultures and denominations outside the hegemony of the Christian West (i.e., South American, African, Asian), which carry different social imaginaries, would either confirm, enhance, or refute aspects of the morphological claims I make.

Second, this project could not exhaust the variety of theological, philosophical, cultural, and social themes that require attention. Many issues remain unresolved, including the debate about rational and non-rational aspects of the foundational pneumatology, the ethical complexities of the pneumatological imagination and power, and the methodological challenges regarding the epistemic claims of a pneumatological epistemology. This writing was not meant to treat all these issues systematically. Its value lies in the juxtaposition of what is pentecostal, along with the second-level theologizing done in conversation with the variety of disciplines and cultural claims—which reveal promising common ground as well as fundamental issues of conflict for further debate.

Third, pentecostal scholarship has given comparatively little attention to the vulnerability of pentecostalism to the theological and philosophical contexts in which it arises. What are the long-term theological and practical outcomes of this claim? Are there particular cultures that hoist up more resistance to pentecostal thought than others? Why? As Christianity expanded historically, it invested in the idioms and cultures it encountered. The pneumatological imagination carries the unusual capacity to continue that tradition and to highlight aspects of Christian teaching in ways that can be readily understood within other cultural milieus. What if this enables those engaged in mission to reach those living in conceptually different worlds in non-imperialistic ways? Perhaps engaging in ministry in this way will make it easier to frame the Christian message in terms of its host culture and to feed off the diverse cultural streams encountered there using the local idiom as the chosen vessel.

Fourth, the methodology proffered here privileges divine encounter over rational theological endeavor. As one does theology from a pneumatological imagination, the rational theological enterprise is couched in wonder, openness, and humility—essential for theologizing in twenty-first century, and beyond. The focus of much of North American pentecostalism has been on a naïve realism rooted in a restorationist paradigm of the early church, along with an immediate expectation of eschatological events. But the world has changed. From the Copernican Revolution to the theory of evolution, modern technology, quantum physics, and the discovery of the universe—these changes are nothing short of dizzying. In some ways, at the dawn of the third millennium, pentecostal theologues are waking up, stretching their limbs, and rubbing their eyes. What are the implications of these changes on our theologizing or on our understanding of the axiomatic claims of the Christian faith? How could a PTM help to navigate those conversations? Changes in the world of medicine, with its resulting increase in longevity, represents just one of the tsunamis of change that have emerged since the pages of sacred text were penned.

What if Jesus does not return for another fifty thousand years (or more!)? Certainly, dramatic change and discovery will continue. What if we find intelligent life from outside our solar system? What would be the theological implications of that? What if our increasing knowledge of human biology opens the way to create humans without defect (a kind of superhuman)? What should the theological/ethical responses be? The new questions that arise in any metamorphosed age need to be answered with fresh thought and theological/philosophical analysis. Theologians need new methodologies that can suggest plausible responses to these changes, while being honest about their own presuppositions and "come-froms." This endeavor must negotiate the gospel in conversation with the new expectations of those asking new questions—in tenable, yet faithful ways. Otherwise, theologians will eventually become inapposite in cultural and intellectual affairs. The truth is (as was the case in the eighteenth century), today's theological voice is in constant danger of being lost at the *sea of change*. If that happens, then Jesus' question, "When the Son of Man comes, will He find faith on the earth?" (Lk. 18:8), will not simply be a rhetorical one.

Fifth, a PTM has the great potential to foster ecumenism between the many pentecostalisms globally—with other Christian denominations, and even within interfaith conversations. But further research is needed to explicate the boundaries of such conversations, along with what the non-negotiables should be in such conversations. The long-term theological and practical implications of such work should also be carefully considered. Furthermore, how can one keep one's idiosyncratic convictions/practices while seeking the *ecclesia catholica*?[4]

Finally, the impress of that which is pentecostal (e.g., revivalism, mysticism, and the pneumatological imagination/impulse) fades; it is not static. Pentecostal experiences carry profound transcendental elements empowered and informed in a way characterized by paradox: they are personal yet self-transcending, noetic while in some sense ineffable, striven after but also recognized as independent of human effort. Just as food quickly loses its freshness, so too does pentecostal spirituality. The very nature of pentecostal spirituality eventuates spiritual deserts. This leads to a potentially untidy and bumpy spirituality if one expects to be in some kind of perpetual spiritual bliss. The promise of scripture is that there will be "times of refreshing" (Acts 3:19), not a life of unending refreshing. Too little work (at least in the North American pentecostal context) has been done by pentecostal academicians and practitioners regarding what to do in the loss of revival "fire." Often pentecostals replace the quest for the spiritual with reasoned principles and beliefs that give a sense of stability. But the stability grounded in a pneumatic epistemology does not begin with arguments or proofs; it is grounded in events that seize the human heart. In Chapter 3 we saw how Wesley claimed it was much easier to hold on the "form of religion" (practices and knowledge) than to hold on to its "spirit" (affections). It is not possible to maintain a revival "fire" because our hearts are always "prone to wander."[5] I recommend two lines of inquiry from theologues within the pentecostal ethos concerning this: (1) *remembrance* and (2) resourcing historical *liturgical worship practices.*

We briefly looked at the role *memory* has when human beings cannot produce metaphysical experiences but can access past ones via remembrance (Chapter 2). To "remember" is the idea of bringing to one's mind some experience of the past—to make it present. Christian Wiman reminded us of Abraham Heschel's definition of faith as "primarily faithfulness to a time when we had faith."[6] In a word, we must remember those places where God seemed most real and thereby "access" those revival moments—to keep them alive. What are the pragmatic

---

4. Here are a few works that would be helpful in this regard: Anderson, *An Introduction to Pentecostalism*; Wolfgang Vondey, ed., *The Routledge Handbook of Pentecostal Theology* (New York, NY: Routledge, 2020); Alexander Estrelda Y. and Amos Yong, eds., *Afro-Pentcostalism: Black Pentecostal and Charismatic Christianity in History and Culture* (New York: New York University Press, 2011); and Kärkkäinen, *Pneumatology*.

5. A lyric from the Christian hymn, "Come Thou Fount of Every Blessing," written by the pastor and hymnodist Robert Robinson in 1758.

6. Wiman, *He Held Radical Light*, 33.

aspects of this kind of "remembrance" for the pentecostal? Could the celebration of the Eucharist (the Great Thanksgiving), which is rooted in a "remembrance" tradition, carry an ongoing impact into one's spiritual vitality in times of perceived spiritual deserts?[7]

And what if pentecostals resourced the remembrance tradition rooted in historical liturgical worship? Could that help pentecostals live in the light and energy of past revival? In recent years, some pentecostal scholars have been exploring the role of the liturgical worship within the pentecostal context.[8] At first blush, this may seem counterintuitive because of the restrictive nature of liturgy, but liturgical worship is filled with the use of scripture and spaces that engender reverence and holiness. Liturgy also carries space to process loss and "the dark night of the soul" experienced by all followers of Jesus. To be sure, apophatic, mystical, and reflective approaches to worship appeal to the postmodern mind and sensibilities, but how can these approaches—not rooted in spontaneity or American philosophical positivism (in the North American context)—be implemented in pentecostal worship?

These six further tasks flow out of the arguments I have set forth in this work. The future might be uncertain for theologians in our fast-changing and helter-skelter world but there is hope because our God is never taken by surprise.

A prayer from the New Zealand Prayer Book (Anglican) comes to mind as I finish my thoughts here:

What has been done has been done;
what has not been done has not been done;
let it be.
Let us look expectantly to a new day,
new joys,
new possibilities.
In your name we pray.
    Amen.[9]

---

7. Green's *Toward a Pentecostal Theology of the Lord's Supper* is a hopeful resource to this end.

8. A great example of this is Chan, *Liturgical Theology*. See also, Webber, *Ancient-Future Faith*; and D. H. Williams, *Evangelicals and Tradition: The Formative Influence of the Early Church*. Evangelical Resourcement, Ancient Sources for the Church's Future (Grand Rapids, MI: Baker Academic, 2005).

9. The Anglican Church in Aotearoa, New Zealand and Polynesia, *A New Zealand Prayer Book* (New York: HarperOne, 1989), 184.

BIBLIOGRAPHY

Ackland, Randal H. *Towards a Pentecostal Theology of Glossolalia*. Cleveland, TN: CPT Press, 2020.

Ackrill, J. L. "Change and Aristotle's Theological Argument." In *Oxford Studies in Ancient Philosophy*, edited by H. Blumenthal and H. Robinson. Oxford: Clarendon Press,1991.

Aichele, George. *The Limits of Story*. Philadelphia, PA: Fortress Press, 1986.

Alexander Estrelda Y. and Amos Yong, eds. *Afro-Pentcostalism: Black Pentecostal and Charismatic Christianity in History and Culture*. New York: New York University Press, 2011.

Allen, Paul L. *Theological Method: A Guide for the Perplexed*. London: T&T Clark International, 2012.

Alston, William P. *Epistemic Justification: Essays in the Theory of Knowledge*. Ithaca, NY: Cornell University Press, 1989.

Alston, William P. *Perceiving God: The Epistemology of Religious Experience*. Ithaca, NY: Cornell University Press, 2014.

Anderson, Allan Heaton. *An Introduction to Pentecostalism*. 2nd ed. Cambridge, UK: Cambridge University Press, 2014.

Anderson, Allan Heaton. *To the Ends of the Earth: Pentecostalism and the Transformation of World Christianity*. Oxford: Oxford University Press, 2013.

Aquinas, Thomas. *Summa Theologica*.

Archer, Kenneth J. "A Global Pentecostal Theological Methodology: Worship, Witness, and Work." A Paper presented to the III International Seminar on Pentecostals, Theology and the Sciences of Religion at the Methodist University of Sao Paulo (UMESP), Sao Paulo, Brazil, August 17–19, 2016.

Archer, Kenneth J. *A Pentecostal Hermeneutic: Spirit, Scripture and Community*. Cleveland, TN: CPT Press, 2009.

Archer, Kenneth J. "Pentecostal Story: The Hermeneutical Filter for the Making of Meaning." *Pneuma* 26, no. 1 (Spring 2004): 36–59.

Aristotle, *Metaphysics*. Translated by C. D. C. Reeve. Indianapolis, IN: Hackett Publishing Company, 2016.

Arrington, French. "Hermeneutics." In *DPCM*, edited by Stanley M. Burgess, Gary B. McGee, and Patrick H. Alexander, 376–89. Grand Rapids, MI: Zondervan Publishing House, 1988.

Athenagoras. *A Plea for the Christians by Athenagoras the Athenian: Philosopher and Christian*. Translated by B. P. Pratten. Early Christian Writings. Accessed November 1, 2021. http://www.earlychristianwritings.com/text/athenagoras-plea.html.

Augustine. *City of God*. Translated by Marcus Dods. New York, NY: Random House, Inc., 1993.

Augustine. *Confessions*. 2nd ed. Translated by F. J. Sheed. Indianapolis, IN: Hackett Publishing Company, 2006.

Augustine. *De Doctrina Christiana*.

Balswick, Jack O., Pamela Ebstyne King, and Kevin S. Reimer. *The Reciprocating Self: Human Development in Theological Perspective*. Downers Grove, IL: InterVarsity Press, 2005.

Barrow, John D. *The World within the World*. Oxford: Clarendon Press, 1988.

Barth, Karl. *Church Dogmatics*. Vols I–V. Translated by G. W. Bromiley. Edinburgh: T&T Clark, 1936.

Barth, Karl. *Evangelical Theology: An Introduction*. Translated by Grover Foley. Grand Rapids, MI: Eerdmans, 1963.

Behrens, Georg. "Feeling of Absolute Dependence or Absolute Feeling of Dependence? (What Schleiermacher Really Said and Why It Matters)." *Religious Studies* 34, no. 4 (1998): 471–81.

Best, Steven, and Douglas Kellner. *Postmodern Theory: Critical Interrogations*. New York: The Guilford Press, 1991.

Biesbrouck, Wouter. "Discerning the Divine and the Demonic through Dialogue: Recent Evangelical Theology of Religions." In *The Past, Present, and Future of Theologies of Interreligious Dialogue*. 1st ed., edited by Terrence Merrigan and John Friday, 111–23. Oxford, UK: Oxford University Press, 2017.

Bitel, Lisa M. *Women in Early Medieval Europe, 400–1100*. New York: Cambridge University Press, 2002.

Bouyer, Louis. *Eucharist: Theology and Spirituality of the Eucharistic Prayer*. Translated by Charles Underhill Quinn. Notre Dame, IN: University of Notre Dame Press, 2006.

Brown, Peter. *The World of Late Antiquity: AD 150–750*. New York: W. W. Norton & Company, 1989.

Brueggemann, Walter. *The Message of the Psalms: A Theological Commentary*. Minneapolis, MN: Augsburg Publishing House, 1984.

Buber, Martin. *I and Thou*. Translated by Walter Kaufmann. New York: Touchstone, 1970.

Bultmann, Rudolf. *Essays Philosophical and Theological*. London: SCM Press, 1955.

Bultmann, Rudolf. *Jesus Christ and Mythology*. New York: Charles Scribner's Sons, 1958.

Cameron, Euan. *Interpreting Christian History: The Challenge of the Churches' Past*. Malden, MA: Blackwell Publishing, 2005.

Caseau, Beatrice. "Sacred Landscapes." In *Late Antiquity: A Guide to the Postclassical World*, edited by G. W. Bowersock, Peter Brown, and Oleg Grabar, 21–59. Cambridge, MA: Belknap Press of Harvard University Press, 1999.

Castelo, Daniel. *Pentecostalism as a Christian Mystical Tradition*. Grand Rapids, MI: William B. Eerdmans Publishing Company, 2017.

Cauthen, Kenneth. *The Impact of American Religious Liberalism*. New York: Harper & Row Publishers, 1962.

Chan, Simon. *Liturgical Theology: The Church as Worshipping Community*. Downers Grove, IL: IVP Academic, 2006.

Chenu, Marie-Dominique. "Une theologie de la vie mystique." *La vie spirituelle* 50 (1937).

Chrysostom, John. "On the Inconceivable in God." Accessed February 15, 2019. https://www.wilmingtonfavs.com/religious-experience-2/appendix-i.html.

Clark, Elizabeth. *History, Theory, Text: Historians and the Linguistic Turn*. Cambridge, Massachusetts: Harvard University Press, 2004.

Clarke, Clifton, and Marcia Clarke. "Church Unity and the Spirit of Ubuntu: Insights from the Global South." In *Pentecostal Theology and Ecumenical Theology*, 333–58. Leiden, The Netherlands: Brill, 2019.

Comstock, Gary L. "Two Types of Narrative Theology." *Journal of the American Academy of Religion* 55, no. 4 (1987): 687–717.

Coulter, Dale M., "Introduction: The Language of Affectivity and the Christian Life." In *The Spirit, the Affections, and the Christian Tradition*, edited by Dale M. Coulter and Amos Yong, 1–27. Notre Dame, ID: University of Notre Dame Press, 2016.
Coulter, Dale M., and Amos Yong. "Preface." In *The Spirit, the Affections, and the Christian Tradition*, edited by Dale M. Coulter and Amos Yong, ix–xi. Notre Dame, ID: University of Notre Dame Press, 2016.
Cox, Harvey. *Fire from Heaven: The Rise of Pentecostal Spirituality and the Reshaping of Religion in the Twenty-First Century*. Cambridge, MA: De Capo Press, 1995.
Crites, Stephen. "The Narrative Quality of Experience." *Journal of the American Academy of Religion* 39, no. 3 (September 1971): 291–311.
Cross, Terry L. "The Divine-Human Encounter: Towards a Pentecostal Theology of Experience." *Pneuma* 31, no. 1 (January 2009): 3–34.
Cross, Terry L. "The Rich Feast of Theology: Can Pentecostals Bring the Main Course or Only the Relish?" *JPT* 8, no. 16 (2000): 34–5.
Cross, Terry L. *Serving the People of God's Presence: A Theology of Ministry*. Grand Rapids, MI: Baker Academic, 2020.
Dayton, Donald W. *Theological Roots of Pentecostalism*. Grand Rapids, MI: Baker Academic, 1987.
de Lubac, Henri. *Catholicism, Christ and the Common Destiny of Man*. San Francisco, CA: Ignatius Press, 1988.
Di Berardino, Angelo, ed. *Encyclopedia of Ancient Christianity: Ancient Christian Doctrine, Ancient Christian Commentary*, and *Ancient Christian Texts*. 3 vols. Downers Grove, IL: IVP Academic, 2014.
Diogenes, Allen and Eric O. Springsted. *Philosophy for Understanding Theology*. 2nd ed. Louisville, KY: Westminster John Knox Press, 2007. Kindle.
Dreyer, Elizabeth A. "An Advent of the Spirit: Medieval Mystics and Saints." In *Advents of the Spirit: An Introduction to the Current Study of Pneumatology*, edited by Bradford E. Hinze and D. Lyle Dabney. Milwaukee: Marquette University Press, 2001.
Dreyer, Elizabeth A. "The Transformative Role of Emotion in the Middle Ages: Deliverance from Lukewarm Affections." In *The Spirit, the Affections, and the Christian Tradition*, edited by Dale M. Coulter and Amos Yong, 113–42. Notre Dame, ID: University of Notre Dame Press, 2016.
Dunne, John S. *The City of the Gods*. New York: Macmillan, 1965.
Dunne, John S. *The Way of All the Earth*. New York: Macmillan, 1972.
Dunne, John S. *Time and Myth: A Meditation on Story Telling as an Exploration of Life and Death*. Notre Dame, ID: University of Notre Dame Press, 1973.
Dupré, Louis. "Mysticism." In *Encyclopedia of Religion*, edited by Lindsay Jones, 9:6341–55. Detroit, MI: Macmillan Reference USA, 2005.
Eliade, Mircea. *Patterns in Comparative Religion*. New York: Sheed & Ward, 1958.
Erickson, Millard J. *Christian Theology*. 2nd ed. Grand Rapids, MI: Baker Academic, 1998.
Ervin, H. M. "Hermeneutics: A Pentecostal Option." *Pneuma* 3, no. 1 (1981): 11–25.
Eusebius of Caesarea. *The Proof of the Gospel*. Book 1 of *Demonstratio Evangelica*. Translated by W. J. Ferrar (1920). Early Christian Writings. Accessed May 24, 2022. http://www.earlychristianwritings.com/fathers/eusebius_de_03_book1.html.
Faupel, D. William. "The Function of 'Models' in the Interpretation of Pentecostal Thought." *Pneuma* 2, no. 1 (1980): 51–71.
Feuerbach, Ludwig. *The Essence of Christianity*. Translated by George Eliot. Amherst, NY: Prometheus Books, 1989.

Fish, Stanley. *Doing What Comes Naturally: Change, Rhetoric, and the Practice of Literary and Legal Studies*. Durham: Duke University Press, 1989.

Forman, Robert K. "Introduction: Mysticism, Constructivism, and Forgetting." In *The Problem of Pure Consciousness: Mysticism and Philosophy*, edited by Robert K. Forman. Oxford: Oxford University Press, 1997.

Frestadius, Simo. *Pentecostal Rationality: Epistemology and Theological Hermeneutics in the Foursquare Tradition*. New York: T&T Clark, 2021.

Ganzevoort, R. Ruard, Maaike de Haardt, and Michael Scherer-Rath, eds. *Religious Stories We Live By*. Leiden, The Netherlands: Brill, 2013.

Garb, Jonathan. "Mystics' Critiques of Mystical Experience." *Revue de l'histoire des religions* 221, no. 3 (2004): 293–325.

Gimello, Robert. "Mysticism in Its Contexts." In *Mysticism and Religious Traditions*, edited by Steven T. Katz, 61–88. Oxford: Oxford University Press, 1983.

Gingerich, Owen. "From Copernicus to Kepler: Heliocentrism as Model and as Reality." *Proceedings of the American Philosophical Society* 117, no. 6 (December 31, 1973): 513–22.

Gordon, George A. *New Epoch for Faith*. New York: Houghton, Mifflin and Company, 1901.

Gossman, Lionel. "Augustin Thierry and Liberal Historiography." *History and Theory* 15, no. 4 (December 1976): 3–6.

Grave, S. A. *The Scottish Philosophy of Common Sense*. Oxford: Oxford Clarendon Press, 1960.

Gray, Jeremy. *Ideas of Space: Euclidean, Non-Euclidean, and Relativistic*. 2nd ed. Oxford: Clarendon Press, 1989.

Green, Chris E. W. "Pentecostalism." In *The Cambridge Companion to American Protestantism*, edited by Jason Vickers and Jennifer Woodruff, 461–78. New York: Cambridge University Press, 2022.

Green, Chris E. W. *Sanctifying Interpretation: Vocation, Holiness, and Scripture*. Cleveland, TN: CPT Press, 2020.

Grenz, Stanley J. and John R. Franke. *Beyond Foundationalism: Shaping Theology in a Postmodern Context*. Louisville: Westminster John Knox Press, 2001.

Gribben, John R. *The Scientists: A History of Science Told through the Lives of Its Greatest Inventors*. New York: Random House, 2002.

Grimes, Ronald L. "Of Words the Speaker, Of Deeds the Doer." *Journal of Religion* 66, no. 1 (January 1986): 1–17.

Gurevich, Aaron. *The Origins of European Individualism*. Translated by Katharine Judelson. Cambridge, MA: Blackwell, 1995.

Hacking, Ian. *Representing and Intervening: Introductory Topics in the Philosophy of Natural Science*. New York, NY: Cambridge University Press, 1983.

Hamer, Dean. *The God Gene: How Faith Is Hardwired into Our Genes*. New York: Random House, 2005.

Harari, Yuval Noah. *Sapiens: A Brief History of Humankind*. New York: Harper Perennial, 2015.

Harmless, William. *Mystics*. Oxford: Oxford University Press, 2008.

Hassan, Isab. *The Postmodern Turn: Essays in Postmodern Theory and Culture*. Columbus, Ohio: Ohio State University Press, 1987.

Hatch, Nathan O. *The Democratization of American Christianity*. New Haven: Yale University Press, 1989.

Heschel, Abraham Joshua. *God in Search of Man*. New York: Farrar, Straus, and Giroux, 1955.

Hocken, Peter D. "Charismatic Movement." In *The New International Dictionary of Pentecostal and Charismatic Movements*, edited by Stanley Burgess and Eduard M. Van Der Maas, 477–519. Grand Rapids, MI: Zondervan, 2002.

Hodge, Charles. *Systematic Theology*. Vol. 1. New York: Scribner, Armstrong, and Co., 1877.

Hollenback, Jesse Byron. *Mysticism: Experience, Response and Empowerment*. Philadelphia, PA: Pennsylvania University Press, 1996.

Hollenweger, Walter J. *The Pentecostals: The Charismatic Movement in the Churches*. Peabody, MA: Hendrickson, 1988.

Howard, Don A. and Marco Giovanelli. "Einstein's Philosophy of Science." In *The Stanford Encyclopedia of Philosophy*, edited by Edward N. Zalta (Fall 2019).

Howorth, H. H. "The Origin and Authority of the Biblical Canon According to the Continental Reformers: I. Luther and Karlstadt." *The Journal of Theological Studies* os-VIII, no. 31 (April 1907): 321–65. https://doi.org/10.1093/jts/os-VIII.31.321

Hughes, Kevin L. "The Crossing of Hope, or Apophatic Eschatology." In *The Future of Hope: Christian Tradition amid Modernity and Postmodernity*, edited by Miroslav Volf and William Katerberg, 101–24. Grand Rapids, MI: William B. Eerdmans Publishing Company, 2004.

Hutchison, William R. *The Modernist Impulse in American Protestantism*. Durham, NC: Duke University Press, 1992.

Huxley, Aldous. *The Perennial Philosophy*. New York: Harper, 1970.

Jacobsen, T., J. E. Jacobsen, and L. Ahonen. "Denmark." In *NIDPCM*, edited by Stanley M. Burgess and Eduard M. Van Der Maas, 273–8. Grand Rapids, MI: Zondervan, 2002.

Jacobsen, Douglas. "Pentecostal Hermeneutics in Comparative Perspective." Paper presented at the Annual Meeting of the Society for Pentecostal Studies. Patten College, Oakland, CA. March 13–15, 1997.

Jacobsen, Douglas. *A Reader in Pentecostal Theology: Voices from the First Generation*. Bloomington, IN: Indiana University Press, 2006.

Jacobsen, Douglas. *Thinking in the Spirit: Theologies of the Early Pentecostal Movement*. Bloomington, IN: University of Indiana Press, 2001.

James, William. *The Varieties of Religious Experience: A Study in Human Nature, Being the Gifford Lectures on Natural Religion Delivered at Edinburgh in 1901–1902*. New York: Longmans, Green, and Co., 1902.

Jennings, Willie James. *Acts*. Louisville, KY: Westminster John Knox Press, 2017.

Jenson, Robert W. *A Theology in Outline: Can These Bones Live*. New York: Oxford University Press, 2016.

Jinkins, Michael. *Invitation to Theology*. Downers, Grove, IL: InterVarsity Press, 2001.

Johns, Cheryl Bridges. "The Adolescence of Pentecostalism: In Search of a Legitimate Sectarian Identity." *Pneuma* 17, no. 1 (Spring 1993): 3–17.

Johns, Cheryl Bridges. "Athens, Berlin, and Azusa: A Pentecostal Reflection on Scholarship and the Christian Faith." *Pneuma* 27, no. 1 (Spring 2005): 136–47.

Johnson, Andrew. "The Evolution Articles." *Pentecostal Herald* 38 (September 29, 1926).

Kant, Immanuel. *Critique of Pure Reason*. Translated and edited by Paul Guyer and Allen W. Wood. New York: Cambridge University Press, 1998.

Kant, Immanuel. *Groundwork of the Metaphysics of Morals*. Translated and edited by Mary Gregor and Jens Timmerann. Cambridge, MA: Cambridge University Press, 2012.

Kärkkäinen, Veli-Matti. "Hermeneutics: From Fundamentalism to Postmodernism." In *Toward a Pneumatological Theology: Pentecostal and Ecumenical Perspectives on Ecclesiology, Soteriology, and Theology of Mission*, edited by Amos Yong, 3–21. Lanham, MD: University Press of America, 2002.
Kärkkäinen, Veli-Matti. *One with God: Salvation as Deification and Justification.* Collegeville, MN: Liturgical Press, 2004.
Kärkkäinen, Veli-Matti. *Pneumatology: The Holy Spirit in Ecumenical, International, and Contextual Perspective.* Grand Rapids, MI: Baker Publishing Group, 2018.
Kärkkäinen, Veli-Matti. *Spirit and Salvation: A Constructive Christian Theology for the Pluralistic World.* Grand Rapids, MI: Eerdmans, 2016.
Kärkkäinen, Veli-Matti. *Toward a Pneumatological Theology: Pentecostal and Ecumenical Perspectives on Ecclesiology, Soteriology, and Theology of Mission.* Edited by Amos Yong. Lanham, MD: University Press of America, 2002.
Kärkkäinen, Veli-Matti, ed. *The Spirit in the World: Emerging Pentecostal Theologies in Global Contexts.* Grand Rapids, MI: William B. Eerdmans Publishing Company, 2009.
Katz, Steven T. "The Conservative Character of Mystical Experience." In *Mysticism and Religious Traditions*, edited by Steven T. Katz, 3–60. Oxford: Oxford University Press, 1983.
Kennedy, David S. "Christianity and the Social Order." *The Presbyterian* XC, January 8, 1920, 3.
Kennedy, David S. "The Practice of the Presence of God." *The Pentecostal Evangel* (February 14, 1925): 3.
Knight, Kelvin. "Introduction." In *The MacIntyre Reader*, edited by Kelvin Knight, 1–27. Cambridge, MA: Polity Press, 1998.
Krüger, Gustav. "Theology of Crisis: Remarks on a Recent Movement in German Theology." *Harvard Theological Review*, 19, no. 3 (July 1926): 227–58.
Kruschwitz, Robery B. "The Wild Goose." In *Prophetic Ethics.* Vol. 6 of *Christian Reflection, A Series in Faith and Ethics*, edited by Robert B. Kruschwitz, 40–4. Waco, TX: Baylor University Press, 2003.
Land, Steven Jack. *Pentecostal Spirituality: A Passion for the Kingdom.* Cleveland, TN: CPT Press, 2010.
Land, Steven Jack, Rick D. Moore, and John Christopher Thomas. "Editorial." *JPT* 1, no. 1 (1992): 3–5.
Lane, Belden C. *The Solace of Fierce Landscapes: Exploring Desert and Mountain Spirituality.* New York: Oxford University Press, 1998.
Lash, Nicholas. *The Beginning and the End of "Religion."* Cambridge, MA: Cambridge University Press, 1996.
Lauritzen, Paul. "Is 'Narrative' Really a Panacea? The Use of 'Narrative' in the Work of Metz and Hauerwas." *Journal of Religion* 67, no. 3 (July 1987): 332–9.
Lecky, William Edward Hartpole. *History of England in the Eighteenth Century, Vol. III.* London: Longmans, Green, and Co., 1913.
Lewis, Gordon R. and Bruce A. Demarest. *Integrative Theology.* Grand Rapids, MI: Zondervan, 1996.
Lindberg, David C. and Ronald L. Numbers, eds. *God and Nature: Historical Essays on the Encounter between Christianity and Science.* Berkeley: University of California Press, 1986.
Lindley, David. *Uncertainty: Einstein, Heisenberg, Bohr, and the Struggle for the Soul of Science.* New York, NY: Anchor Books, 2007.
Lints, Richard. "The Postpositivist Choice Tracy or Lindbeck?" *Journal of the American Academy of Religion* 61, no. 4 (1993): 655–77.
Lippman, Walter. *A Preface to Morals.* New York: Macmillan, 1929.

Lonergan, Bernard. *Method in Theology.* New York: Seabury Press, 1972.
Lossl, Josef. *The Early Church: History and Memory.* New York: T&T Clark, 2010.
Lowenthal, David. *The Past Is a Foreign Country.* Cambridge: Cambridge University Press, 1985.
Luther. *Table-Talk* (Wei. V. 5820).
Lutz, Christopher Stephen. *Tradition in the Ethics of Alasdair MacIntyre: Relativism, Thomism, and Philosophy.* New York: Lexington Books, 2009.
MacIntyre, Alasdair C. *After Virtue: A Study in Moral Theology.* 2nd ed. Notre Dame, IN: Notre Dame University Press, 1984.
MacIntyre, Alasdair C. "First Principles, Final Ends, and Contemporary Philosophical Issues." In *The Tasks of Philosophy: Selected Essays, Volume 1*, edited by Alasdair MacIntyre, 143–78. Cambridge: Cambridge University Press, 2007.
MacIntyre, Alasdair C. *Whose Justice? Whose Rationality.* Notre Dame, IN: University of Notre Dame Press, 1988.
Mandela, Nelson. "Speech to the Global Convention on Peace and Non-Violence." New Delhi, India. January 31, 2004. Nelson Rolihlahla Mandela (July 18, 1918–December 5, 2013). Accessed November 11, 2021. http://db.nelsonmandela.org/speeches/pub_view.asp?pg=item&ItemID=NMS914&txtstr.
Manly, William F. "A Sanctified Heart." *The Household of God* 2, no. 9 (September 1906).
Maréchal, Joseph. *The Psychology of the Mystics.* Mineola, NY: Dover Publications, 2004.
Marsden, George M. *Fundamentalism and American Culture.* 2nd ed. New York: Oxford University Press, 2006.
Martyr, Justin. *The First Apology of Justin.* Translated by Roberts Donaldson. Early Christian Writings. Accessed November 1, 2021. http://www.earlychristianwritings.com/text/justinmartyr-firstapology.html, XXIX.
The Martyrdom of Polycarp. Translated by J. B. Lightfoot. Early Christian Writings. Accessed November 1, 2021. http://www.earlychristianwritings.com/text/martyrdompolycarp-lightfoot.html.
Mathews, Shailer. *The Faith of Modernism.* New York: The Macmillan Co., 1924.
McClymond, Michael J. "Holy Tears: A Neglected Aspect of Early Christian Spirituality in Contemporary Context." In *The Spirit, the Affections, and the Christian Tradition*, edited by Dale M. Coulter and Amos Yong, 87–111. Notre Dame, IN: University of Notre Dame Press, 2016.
McDonald, Lee Martin. *The Biblical Canon: Its Origin, Transmission, and Authority.* Grand Rapids, MI: Baker Academic, 2007.
McDonnell, Killian. "The Determinative Doctrine of the Holy Spirit." *Theology Today* 39, no. 2 (1982): 142–61.
McDonnell, Killian. "A Trinitarian Theology of the Holy Spirit?" *Theological Studies* 46, no. 2 (1985): 191–227.
McGinn, Bernard. *The Flowering of Mysticism: Men and Women in the New Mysticism (1200–1350).* Vol. III. New York: Crossroad Publishing, 1998.
McGinn, Bernard. "Mysticism and the Reformation: A Brief Survey." *Acta Theologica* 35, no. 2 (2015): 50–65.
McGrath, Alister E. *Christian Theology: An Introduction.* 5th ed. Oxford: John Wiley & Sons, 2011.
McMahan, David L. *The Making of Buddhist Modernism.* Oxford: Oxford University Press, 2008.
Menzies, Robert. "Jumping off the Postmodern Bandwagon." *Pneuma* 16, no. 1 (Spring 1994): 115–20.

Merkur, Dan. "Mysticism." *Encyclopedia Britannica*. Accessed May 22, 2021. https://www.britannica.com/topic/mysticism.
Milbank, John. "The Gospel of Affinity," In *The Future of Hope: Christian Tradition amid Modernity and Postmodernity*. Edited by Miroslav Volf and William Katerberg. Cambridge, UK: William B. Eerdmans Publishing Company, 2004.
Milbank, John. "'Postmodern Critical Augustinianism': A Short Summa in Forty-Two Responses to Unasked Questions." *Modern Theology* 7, no. 3 (1991): 225–37.
Moltmann, Jürgen. "Preface." In *The Spirit in the World: Emerging Pentecostal Theologies in Global Contexts*, edited by Veli-Matti Kärkkäinen, viii–xii. Grand Rapids, MI: William B. Eerdmans Publishing Cmpany, 2009.
Moltmann, Jürgen. "Progress and Abyss: Remembrances of the Future of the Modern World." In *The Future of Hope: Christian Tradition amid Modernity and Postmodernity*. Edited by Miroslav Volf and William Katerberg. Cambridge, UK: William B. Eerdmans Publishing Company, 2004.
Moltmann, Jürgen. *The Spirit of Life: A Universal Affirmation*. Minneapolis, MN: Fortress Press, 2001. Kindle.
Moody, D. L., Harriet Beecher Stowe, J. C. Ryle, George Müller, D. W. Whittle, Geo C. Needham, and Charles H. Spurgeon. *The Second Coming of Christ*. Lawton, OK: Trumpet Press, 2019.
Moore, Rickie D. "Revelation: The Light and Fire of Pentecost." In *The Routledge Handbook of Pentecostal Theology*, edited by Wolfgang Vondey, 53–62. New York: Taylor & Francis Group, 2020.
Morris, Colin. *The Discovery of the Individual: 1050–1200*. Toronto, ON: University of Toronto Press, 1987.
Murphy, Nancey. *Beyond Liberalism & Fundamentalism: How Modern and Postmodern Philosophy Set the Theological Agenda*. Harrisburg, PA: Trinity Press International, 1996.
Murphy, Nancey. "MacIntyre, Tradition-Dependent Rationality and the End of Philosophy of Religion." In *Contemporary Practice and Method in the Philosophy of Religion: New Essays*, edited by David Cheetham and Rolfe King, 32–44. New York: Bloomsbury Academic, 2008.
Murphy, Nancey and James Wm. McClendon. "Distinguishing Modern and Postmodern Theologies." *Modern Theology* 5, no. 3 (April 1989): 191–214.
Nel, Marius. "A Distinctive Pentecostal Hermeneutic: Possible and/or Necessary?" *Acta Theologica* 37, no. 2 (2017): 86–103.
Neumann, Peter D. *Pentecostal Experience: An Ecumenical Encounter*. Eugene, OR: Pickwick Publications, 2012.
Niebuhr, H. Richard, *The Social Sources of Denominationalism*. New York: World Publishing, 1972.
Noll, Mark A. *The Scandal of the Evangelical Mind*. Grand Rapids, MI: William B. Eerdmans Publishing Company, 1994.
Novak, Michael. *Ascent of the Mountain, Flight of the Dove: An Invitation to Religious Studies*. New York: Harper and Row, 1971.
O'Collins, Gerald. *Rethinking Fundamental Theology: Toward a New Fundamental Theology*. Oxford: Oxford University Press, 2011.
Oden, Thomas C. *Life in the Spirit*. San Francisco, CA: HarperSanFrancisco, 1992.
Oden, Thomas C. *The Living God*. San Francisco, CA: HarperSanFrancisco, 1987.
Oden, Thomas C. *The Living Word*. San Francisco, CA: HarperSanFrancisco, 1989.

Oesterdiekhoff, Georg W. "The Nature of 'Premodern' Mind: Tylor, Frazer, Lévy-Bruhl, Evans-Pritchard, Piaget, and Beyond." *Anthropos: International Review of Anthropology and Linguistics* 110, no. 1 (January 2015): 15–25.

"The Old-Time Pentecost." *The Apostolic Faith* 1, no. 1 (June–September 1907): 2.

Oliverio, L. William Jr. *Theological Hermeneutics in the Classical Pentecostal Tradition: A Typological Account*. Boston: Brill, 2012.

Olson, Roger E. *The Mosaic of Christian Belief: Twenty Centuries of Tradition and Reform*. Downers Grove, IL: InterVarsity Press, 1999.

Otto, Rudolf. *The Idea of the Holy: An Inquiry into the Non-Rational Factor in the Idea of the Divine and Its Relation to the Rational*. Translated by John W. Harvey. London: Oxford University Press, 1958.

Otto, Rudolf. *Mysticism East and West: A Comparative Analysis of the Nature of Mysticism*. Wheaton, IL: Theosophical Publishing House, 1987.

Oubré, Alondra Yvette. *Instinct and Revelation: Reflections on the Origins of Numinous Perception*. London: Taylor & Francis, 2007.

Palamas, Gregory. *Defense of the Hesychasts*.

Parsons, William B. "Teaching Mysticism: Frame and Content." In *Teaching Mysticism*, edited by William B. Parsons, 3–10. Oxford: Oxford University Press, 2011.

Pascal, Blaise. *Pensées*. Translated by W. F. Trotter. New York: E. P. Dutton & Co., 1958.

Penner, Hans H. "The Mystical Illusion." In *Mysticism and Religious Traditions*, edited by Steven T. Katz, 89–116. Oxford: Oxford University Press, 1983.

"Pentecost Has Come." *The Apostolic Faith* 1, no. 1 (September 1906): 1.

Pereira, Michael J. "From the Spoils of Egypt: An Analysis of Origen's *Letter to Gregory*." *Origen as Writer*. Papers of the 10th International Origen Congress, University School of Philosophy and Education "Ignatianum," Krakow, Poland (August 31–September 4, 2009). *Bibliotheca Ephemeridum Theologicarum Lovaniesium CCXLIV*. Walpole, MA: Uitgeverij Peeters, 2011.

Peters, Ted. "Truth in History: Gadamer's Hermeneutics and Pannenberg's Apologetic Method." *The Journal of Religion* 55, no. 1 (1975): 36–56.

Pinnock, Clark H. "Divine Relationality: A Pentecostal Contribution to the Doctrine of God." *JPT* 8, no. 16 (2000): 2–26.

Pinnock, Clark H. *Flame of Love: A Theology of the Holy Spirit*. Downers Grove, IL: IV Press, 1996.

Pohoata, Gabriela. "Leibniz Universalism." *Cogito: Multidisciplinary Research Journal* 4, no. 1 (2012): 1–13.

Poirier, John C. "Narrative Theology and Pentecostal Commitments." *JPT* 16, no. 2 (2008): 69–85.

Poirier, John C., and B. Scott Lewis. "Pentecostal and Postmodernist Hermeneutics: A Critique of Three Conceits." *JPT* 15, no. 1 (October 2006): 3–21.

Popper, Karl. *The Logic of Scientific Discovery*. New York: Harper, 1965.

Pratt, James Bissett. *The Religious Consciousness: A Psychological Study*. New York: Macmillan, 1920.

Quine, W. V. O. "Two Dogmas of Empiricism." In *From a Logical Point of View*, 42–3. Cambridge, MA: Harvard University Press, 1953.

Rahner, Karl. *Theological Investigations XI*. New York: Crossroad, 1960.

Ratzinger, Joseph. "The Holy Spirit as *Communio*: Concerning the Relationship of Pneumatology and Spirituality in Augustine." *Communio* 25 (Summer 1998): 324. Accessed May 17, 2022. http://www.communio-icr.com/files/ratzinger25-2.pdf.

Richie, Tony. "Pentecostalism's Wesleyan Roots and Fruit." *Seedbed*. Asbury University, March 2014. Accessed May 11, 2022. http://www.seedbed.com/pentecostalisms-wesleyan-roots-fruit/.

Robbins, Wesley J. "Narrative, Morality and Religion." *The Journal of Religious Ethics* 8, no. 1 (Spring 1980): 161–76.

Robeck, Jr., Cecil M. "William J. Seymour and 'The Bible Evidence.'" In *Initial Evidence: Historical and Biblical Perspectives on the Pentecostal Doctrine of Spirit Baptism*, edited by Gary B. McGee. Grand Rapids, MI: Zondervan, 1988.

Robeck, Jr., Cecil M. "Azusa Street Revival." In *The New International Dictionary of Pentecostal and Charismatic Movements (NIDPCM)*, edited by Stanley M. Burgess and Eduard M. Van Der Maas, 344–5. Grand Rapids, MI: Zondervan, 2002.

Robinson, Brian. "A Pentecostal Hermeneutic of Religious Experience." Paper presented at the 21st Annual Meeting of the Society for Pentecostal Studies, Springfield, MO, 1992.

Robinson, Marilynne. "Happiness." A paper presented at the Yale Center for Faith and Culture Consultation on Happiness and Human Flourishing, sponsored by the McDonald Agape Foundation. Accessed June 7, 2018. https://faith.yale.edu/sites/default/files/robinson_1.pdf.

Rohr, Richard. *The Wisdom Pattern: Order, Chaos, Reorder*. Cincinnati, OH: Franciscan Media, 2020.

Roman Catholic Church and the Lutheran World Federation. *Joint Declaration on the Doctrine of Justification*. Grand Rapids, MI: William B. Eerdmans Publishing Company, 2000.

Rose, H. J. *Primitive Culture In Italy*. London, UK: Methuen & Co. Ltd., 1926

St. John of the Cross. *Dark Night of the Soul*. Translated by E. Allison Peers. Mineola, NY: Dover Publications, 2003.

Sachs, John R. "'Do Not Stifle the Spirit': Karl Rahner, the Legacy of Vatican II, and Its Urgency for Theology Today." *Catholic Theological Society of America Proceedings* 51 (1996): 15–38.

Sandeen, Ernest R. *The Roots of Fundamentalism: British & American Millenarianism 1800–1930*. Chicago: The University of Chicago Press, 1970.

Sauvage, George. "Aseity." In *The Catholic Encyclopedia*. Vol. 1. New York: Robert Appleton Company, 1907.

Schilling, S. Paul. "Revelation and Reason." *Journal of Bible and Religion* 16, no. 1 (1948): 13–72.

Schleiermacher, Friedrich. *Brief Outline of the Study of Theology*. Translated by Terrence N. Tice. Richmond, VA: John Knox Press, 1966.

Screech, Michael A. *The Anatomy of Madness: Essays in the History of Psychiatry*, edited by William F. Bynum et al. London UK: Routledge, 2004.

Seymour, William Joseph. *The Apostolic Faith* 2, no. 13 (May 1908): 3.

Seymour, William Joseph. "The Apostolic Faith Movement." *The Apostolic Faith* 1, no. 1 (September 1906).

Seymour, William Joseph. "To the Baptized Saints." *The Apostolic Faith* 1, no. 9 (September 1906): 2.

Shults, F. LeRon and J. Sandage Steven. *The Faces of Forgiveness: Searching for Wholeness and Salvation*. Grand Rapids, MI: Baker Academic, 2003.

Smith, Huston. *Beyond the Postmodern Mind: The Place of Meaning in a Global Civilization*. 3rd ed. Wheaton, IL: Quest Books Theosophical Publishing House, 2003.

Smith, James K. A. *The Fall of Interpretation: Philosophical Foundations for a Creationist Hermeneutic*. Grand Rapids, MI: Baker Academic, 2012.

Smith, James K. A. "The Logic of Incarnation: Towards a Catholic Postmodernism." In *The Logic of Incarnation: James K. A. Smith's Critique of Postmodern Religion* (with Contribution and Response by James K. A. Smith), edited by Neal DeRoo and Brian Lightbody, 3–40. Eugene, OR: Pickwick Publications, 2009.

Smith, James K. A. "Scandalizing Theology: A Pentecostal Response to Noll's *Scandal*." *Pneuma* 19, no. 2 (Fall 1997): 225–38.

Smith, James K. A. *Thinking in Tongues: Pentecostal Contributions to Christian Philosophy*. Grand Rapids, MI: William B. Eerdmans Publishing Company, 2010.

Smith, James K. A. "What Hath Cambridge to Do with Azusa Street? Radical Orthodoxy and Pentecostal Theology in Conversation." *Pneuma* 25, no. 1 (Spring 2003): 97–114.

Smith, James K. A. *Who's Afraid of Postmodernism? Taking Derrida, Lyotard, and Foucault to Church*. Grand Rapids, MI: Baker Academic, 2006.

Snyder, Howard A. "Wesleyanism, Wesleyan Theology." In *Global Dictionary of Theology*, edited by William A. Dryness, and Veli-Matti Kärkkäinen, et al. Downers Grove, IL: IVP Academic, 2008.

Sölle, Dorothy. *The Window of Vulnerability*. Minneapolis: Fortress Press, 1990.

Sokolowski, Robert. *Phenomenology of the Human Person*. Cambridge: Cambridge University Press, 2008.

Stace, Walter. "The Nature of Mysticism." In *Philosophy of Religion: Selected Readings*, edited by William L. Rowe and William J. Wainwright. Oxford: Oxford University Press, 1998.

Stace, William T. *Mysticism and Philosophy*. London: Macmillan, 1960.

Stancliffe, Clare. "Red, White and Blue Martyrdom." In *Ireland in Early Mediaeval Europe: Studies in Memory of Kathleen Hughes*, 21–46. New York: Cambridge University Press, 1982.

Stephenson, Christopher A. *Types of Pentecostal Theology: Method, System, Spirit*. Oxford: Oxford University Press, 2016.

Stone, Lawrence. "The Revival of Narrative: Reflections on a New Old History." *Past & Present* 85, no. 4 (November 1979): 3–24.

Storm, Jason, and Ananda Josephson. *Metamodernism*. Chicago: University of Chicago Press, 2021.

Sweet, Leonard. *Soul Tsunami: Sink or Swim in New Millennium Culture*. Grand Rapids, MI: Zondervan, 1999.

Taylor, Charles. *Sources of the Self: The Making of the Modern Identity*. Cambridge, MA: Harvard University Press, 1989.

Taylor-Perry, Rosemarie. *The God Who Comes: Dionysian Mysteries Revisited*. New York: Algora Publishing, 2003.

Theissen, Gerd. *A Theory of Primitive Christian Religion*. Translated by John Bowden. London: SCM Press, 1999.

Thiemann, Ronald F. *Revelation and Theology: The Gospel as Narrated Promise*. Eugene, OR: Wipf & Stock Publishers, 2005.

Tillich, Paul. *Shaking of the Foundations*. Eugene, OR: Wipf & Stock Publishers, 1948.

Tillich, Paul. "Theology and Symbolism." In *Religious Symbols*, edited by F. Ernest Johnson. New York: Harper and Row, 1955.

Toulmin, Stephen. *Cosmopolis: The Hidden Agenda of Modernity*. New York: The Free Press, 1990.

Tracey, David. *The Analogical Imagination: Christian Theology and the Culture of Pluralism*. New York: Crossroad, 1981.

Trenery, David. *Alasdair MacIntyre, George Lindbeck, and the Nature of Tradition*. Eugene, OR: Pickwick Publications, 2014.

Trevett, Christine. *Montanism: Gender, Authority and the New Prophecy*. Cambridge: Cambridge University Press, 1996.

Turner, Denys. *The Darkness of God: Negativity in Christian Mysticism*. Cambridge: Cambridge University Press, 1995.

Tutu, Desmond. *No Future without Forgiveness*. New York: Doubleday, 1999.

Tyson, Adam. "The Mystical Debate: Constructivism and the Resurgence of Perennialism." *Intermountain West Journal of Religious Studies* 4, no. 1 (2012): 77–92.

Underhill, Evelyn. *Mysticism: The Development of Humankind's Spiritual Consciousness*. London: Bracken Books, 1995.

van der Leeuw, Gerard. *Religion in Essence and Manifestation: A Study in Phenomenology*. New York: Harper & Row, 1963.

van Huyssteen, J. Wentzel. *Alone in the World? Human Uniqueness in Science and Theology*. Grand Rapids, MI: William B. Eerdmans Publishing Company, 2006.

Volf, Mirslav and William Katerberg. "Introduction: Retrieving Hope." In *The Future of Hope: Christian Tradition amid Modernity and Postmodernity*, edited by Miroslav Volf and William Katerberg. Cambridge, UK: William B. Eerdmans Publishing Company, 2004.

Vondey, Wolfgang. *Pentecostalism: A Guide for the Perplexed*. New York: T&T Clark, 2012.

Vondey, Wolfgang. "Religion as Play: Pentecostalism as a Theological Type." *Religions* 9, no. 80 (2018): 1–16.

Vondey, Wolfgang, ed. *The Routledge Handbook of Pentecostal Theology*. London: Routledge, Taylor and Francis, 2020.

Wacker, Grant. *Heaven Below: Early Pentecostals and American Culture*. Cambridge, MA: Harvard University Press, 2001.

Wallace, Anthony F. C. *Religion: An Anthropological View*. New York: Random House, 1966. Kindle.

Wariboko, Nimi. *The Pentecostal Principle: Ethical Methodology in New Spirit*. Grand Rapids, MI: William B. Eerdmans Publishing Company, 2012. Kindle.

Webber, Robert E. *Ancient-Future Faith: Rethinking Evangelicalism for a Postmodern World*. Grand Rapids, MI: Baker Academic.

Welker, Michael. *God the Spirit*. Translated by John Hoffmeyer. Minneapolis: Fortress, 1994.

Wesley, John. *The Manners of the Ancient Christians Extracted from a French Author*. 2nd ed. Bristol: Felix Farley, 1749.

West, Cornel. *The Cornel West Reader*. New York: Basic Civitas Book, 1999.

White, Haydon. *Metahistory: The Historical Imagination in the Nineteenth Century*. Baltimore: John Hopkins University Press, 1973.

Wilken, Robert Louis. *The Spirit of Early Christian Thought: Seeking the Face of God*. New Haven, CT: Yale University Press, 2003.

Williams, D. H. *Evangelicals and Tradition: The Formative Influence of the Early Church*. Evangelical Resourcement, Ancient Sources for the Church's Future. Grand Rapids, MI: Baker Academic, 2005.

Williams, Rowan. *The Wound of Knowledge*. Cambridge, MA: Cowley Publications, 1990.

Williams, Rowan. *Why Study the Past? The Quest for the Historical Church*. Grand Rapids, MI: Wmilliam B. Eerdmans Publishing Company, 2005.

Wiman, Christian. *He Held Radical Light: The Art of Faith, The Faith of Art*. New York: Farrar, Straus and Giroux, 2018.

Wink, Walter. *Naming the Powers: The Language of Power in the New Testament, The Powers 1*. Philadelphia, PA: Fortress, 1984.
Wink, Walter. *Unmasking the Powers: The Invisible Forces that Determine Human Existence, The Powers 2*. Philadelphia, PA: Fortress, 1986.
Wink, Walter. *Engaging the Powers: Discernment and Resistance in a World of Domination, The Powers 3*. Philadelphia, PA: Fortress, 1992.
Wu, Joshua. "The Chinese Church and the Great Tradition." In *Shadows from Light Unapproachable: Anglican Frontier Missions 1993–2018*, edited by Tad de Bordenave, 233–52. Heathsville, VA: Northumberland Historical Press, 2018.
Yong, Amos. *Beyond the Impasse: Toward a Pneumatological Theology of Religions*. Ada, MI: Baker Academic, 2003.
Yong, Amos. "The Demise of Foundationalism and the Retention of Truth: What Evangelicals Can Learn from C. S. Peirce." *Christian Scholar's Review* 29, no. 3 (Spring 2000): 563–88.
Yong, Amos. *Spirit-Word-Community: Theological Hermeneutics in Trinitarian Perspective*. Eugene, OR: Wipf & Stock Publishers, 2002.
Yong, Amos. "What Spirit(s), Which Public(s)? The Pneumatologies of Global Pentecostal-Charismatic Christianity." *International Journal of Public Theology* 7, no. 3 (2013): 241–59.
Yong, Amos. "Whither Systematic Theology? A Systematician Chimes in on a Scandalous Conversation." *Pneuma* 20, no. 1 (Spring 1998): 85–93.
Zaehner, Robert C. *Mysticism Sacred and Profane: An Inquiry into Some Varieties of Praeternatural Experience*. Oxford: Oxford University Press, 1961.

INDEX

Adam and Eve 15
affection 46–51, 64, 132. *See also* love
   difficulty with 50–1
   as motivation 49
   right affection 46–7, 46 n.169, 50
Africa/African 68–9, 183
agnostic/agnosticism 33, 134
Allen, Paul 127, 130, 134, 147, 154
Alston, William 150–1
   minimal foundationalism 150, 150 n.78
   Perceiving God 152
Anderson, Allan 10, 63
antecedent 2, 16, 23, 29–30, 39, 70, 84, 105, 151, 178
anthropology/anthropological 12, 15, 17, 36, 45, 72, 85, 145, 147, 149, 184–5
anti-revival 26. *See also* revival/revivalism
apatheia, Stoic 27
apostles 21, 40–1, 52–3, 77–8, 161, 170, 194–5, 205, 208–9
   apostolicity 73, 77–9
Aquinas, Thomas 129, 129 n.15
Archer, Kenneth J. 103–4, 120, 155
   Bible Reading Method 56–7, 74–5
   proof-texting system 74–5
Aristotle/Aristotelian 12 n.11, 23 n.53, 86, 88, 110, 186
   Aristotelian scholasticism 86 n.5, 88–9
   notion of science 129
Arrington, French 73, 76, 144
atheism/atheistic 96 n.26, 134, 189
Athenagoras 195
Athens 26
Augustine, St. 1, 53, 131, 137, 143
   The Confessions 18, 192
   De Musica 162
awakening 21, 29, 72, 190
axiomatic truth 151, 154
Azusa Street Revival, Los Angeles 9, 51, 77, 211

Bacon, Francis 92, 150
   Baconian methodology 75, 92, 95, 106, 192
baptism 35, 37, 41, 51–3, 55–6, 61–2, 70, 138, 199
Barth, Karl 45, 61, 167
beliefs and practices 4, 9, 12, 14, 23, 28, 31–2, 42, 46 n.169, 53, 59, 63 n.229, 70, 72–3, 75–80, 85, 87, 89–90, 94–5, 102, 105, 111–12, 117–18, 120, 131–3, 148, 150–2, 157, 159, 168–71, 175, 189, 199, 201, 206–7, 215
The Bible (biblical) 2, 9, 15, 20, 39, 42–4, 57–60, 68, 74–5, 74 n.41, 78, 84–6, 92, 94–6, 98, 100, 105, 132, 134, 139–40, 145–6, 148, 155–8, 160, 163–4, 167, 169, 182, 191–4, 197–8, 200–1, 205
Bible Reading Method 56–7, 74–5
Book of Acts 35, 40, 76 n.49, 78–9, 158, 166–7, 194
Bryan, William Jennings 101, 101 n.41
Buber, Martin 116, 141

Carroll, Lewis, *Alice in Wonderland* 110
Castelo, Daniel 3 n.13, 35–8
Celsus 43
certain knowledge 89–91, 111, 129
charismatic movement 2, 4, 10, 39, 41, 44–5, 136, 138
Christ 1, 10, 19, 21, 40, 43, 53–4, 123, 137, 142–3, 162, 195, 199, 201, 209
   pre-existence of 198
   resurrection of Christ 68, 78, 198
Christian/Christianity 2, 13, 18–19, 24, 26, 28–31, 33, 41–4, 46–7, 49, 54–5, 58–9, 63 n.229, 70, 73, 74 n.41, 77, 79, 88, 96–7, 99, 102–3, 105–6, 118–22, 127, 131, 133, 135, 139, 146–7, 151–2, 154, 156–8, 160–3, 168, 174, 196, 200–1, 200 n.66, 205, 209, 214
   African-American 71, 125

Christian mysticism 34–8, 34 n.111, 177
  conversion to 14, 42
  Eastern Orthodoxy 56, 127
  evangelicals 96 n.26, 99, 102–5, 132, 148, 157
  general practices of 189
  orthodox Christians 2, 4, 24, 26, 37–8, 57, 70, 72, 97, 193
  Protestant Christian 59, 75, 80, 93, 99, 105
  Roman Catholics 67, 206
Christology 70, 80, 202, 206
church-catholic 2, 5, 38–9, 44, 70, 72 n.23, 119, 132, 137–8
church Fathers 26, 34–5, 43, 53, 191, 197
Clarke (Clifton and Marcia) 68–9, 69 n.7
classical Pentecostals of North America 2 n.7, 6, 10, 13, 58, 63, 67, 70–4, 78, 93, 105
cognitive dissonance 146, 161–2, 206
cognitive fundamentalism 102
Comstock, Gary 155, 157
consciousness 16–17, 19–20, 51, 54, 116, 132, 188
constructivist mysticism 32–4
Copernican Revolution 89, 107, 109–14, 116 n.32, 214
Copernicus 89, 107, 182, 206
cosmology 88, 145, 182, 201, 206
Coulter, Dale 46–7
counterculture 4, 121
Cox, Harvey 21, 36–7, 122
creature-consciousness 1, 20, 28, 132
Cross, Terry L. 35, 76, 129, 192
  Serving the People of God's Presence: A Theology of Ministry 38 n.131

Darwin, Charles 98, 101–2
Day of Pentecost 5, 23, 35, 40, 77, 166
Dayton, Donald 72–3
  Theological Roots of Pentecostalism 70
deconstruction 169, 169 n.160
denominations, pentecostal 2 n.7, 4, 9–10, 101, 213
destructive rationalism 44
Dionysian impulse 19, 19 n.41
discernment 59, 128, 131, 137, 170, 181, 201–7
  complexity of 205–6
  discerning the evil 202–4
  discerning the good 204–5
  and time 206–7
disciples of Jesus 35 n.112, 36, 40, 54, 141, 157–8, 165–6, 187, 200
diversity 3 n.13, 9–11, 69 n.7, 110, 134, 155, 166, 184, 187
divine 1, 9, 15, 17–20, 22, 24, 27, 30–1, 35 n.112, 41, 47–8, 63, 167
  divine aseity 26
  divine-human encounter 38, 41, 54, 69, 81, 190, 212, 214
  divine impassibility 26
  divine nature 18, 139
  divine touch 165, 167
doctrines 24, 26, 30, 35, 49, 55–8, 72, 74–5, 80, 96–8, 102, 118–19, 121, 133, 135–6, 141, 146, 151, 154, 159, 176, 182–3, 192
dogmas/dogmatism 24, 26–7, 37, 55, 60, 62, 72, 80, 88, 122, 125, 131, 141, 152, 160, 162, 211
doxastic logic 145, 149–52, 154, 157, 160, 175, 186
Dreyer, Elizabeth A. 135, 139

Eastern Orthodoxy 56, 127
ecclesia semper reformanda 209, 212
ecclesiastical/ecclesiasticism 14, 29–30, 104, 136, 138, 168
economic Trinity 147
ecumenism/ecumenical 4, 31, 104, 132, 135, 135 n.30, 188–9, 199–201, 206, 215
Edwards, Jonathan 24, 46
Einstein, Albert 110, 110 n.8
Elim theological tradition 172, 175
emotion/emotionalism 20, 36, 46–8, 47 n.173, 48 n.179, 180, 201
empiricism 90–7, 105, 107, 109, 111, 115, 126 n.7, 134
enchantment 179–81, 201
Enlightenment 42, 44, 46, 84, 92 n.21, 148, 153, 158, 163, 171–2, 175, 186, 208
enthusiasm (ενθουσιασμός) 19, 49, 135
epistemology 3, 20 n.46, 39–42, 84–5, 89–90, 94, 106, 115, 126, 178, 186, 198
  epistemic foundationalism 90, 109
  epistemic justification 150, 172

epistemic reality 41, 43, 152
epistemological crises 89, 171–6
epistemological holism 117–18
pneumatological 41–2, 41 n.142, 44, 59, 149–50, 152, 160, 213, 215
storied 186
Ervin, Howard M. 42, 44, 111
eschatology/eschatological 23, 36 n.119, 71, 78–9, 100, 103, 145, 178, 214
essentials of pentecostalism 12–13, 15, 64, 120, 123, 125, 164, 177. *See also* mysticism; pneumatological imagination; revival/revivalism
eternity 18–19, 25, 163, 194, 198
Eucharist (the Great Thanksgiving) 35, 51, 216
Europe/Europeans 69, 87, 148, 183
mortality rate of children 88 n.8
Eusebius of Caesarea, *The Proof of the Gospel* 195–6
Evangelicalism/evangelical Christians 55, 96 n.26, 99, 102–5, 132, 148, 150, 157
evangelical liberals 97
Evangelical Unitarianism 56, 70 n.13
evidences of pentecostalism 45–62, 125
affection (*see* affection)
Jesus-centered and missional 61–2, 64
priority of love 51–6, 64
theological openness 56–61, 64
evolution 84, 101, 181, 206, 214
exegesis 44, 192–3, 198
Exodus 197
experimental theology 193

faith 4, 6, 14–17, 23–6, 28, 43–4, 50–1, 60, 70, 72, 78, 84, 86, 95, 97–8, 102, 106, 119–21, 123, 131, 144, 146, 151–2, 160, 163, 168, 176, 183, 186, 188–90, 193, 199–200, 200 n.66, 202, 209, 215
feminists 69, 183
fideism 90, 96, 160, 171, 176, 186
First Book of God 110–11
First Testament 140, 164, 182
Fish, Stanley 205
forgetfulness of the Spirit 4, 136, 179

foundationalism 84, 84 n.3, 90–1, 95–6, 106, 108–9, 111–12, 116–18, 150, 175
Enlightenment foundationalism 148, 172
epistemic foundationalism 90, 109
foundational pneumatology 29, 69, 123, 126, 208, 211, 213
minimal 150, 150 n.78
Murphy on 90–1
Franke, John 90, 148 n.76
Frestadius, Simo 126, 171–2, 175
full gospel 37, 58, 70, 80, 105. *See also* Gospels
fundamentalism/fundamentalists 97–105
cognitive 102
Marsden on (*see* Marsden, George M.)

Ganzevoort, R. Ruard 158–9
Genesis 20, 38, 41, 140
Gentiles 167, 170, 174, 182
gestalt 5, 70, 209
global pentecostalism 3 n.13, 10–11, 21, 36, 63, 211–12
Global South, pentecostals of 69
glocalization 7 n.25, 185, 212
glossolalia 20 n.47, 37, 40, 56, 62, 125, 199
God 1, 16, 18–19, 22, 26–30, 34–5, 38, 42–3, 48–9, 53–4, 57–60, 62, 64–5, 69–70, 75–7, 84, 87, 89, 92, 94–6, 100, 121, 126, 129–35, 139, 145–6, 151, 161–2, 167–8, 177, 179, 181–2, 184–5, 190–1, 193, 196–7, 201, 204, 208–9. *See also* Satan/demons
breath of God (*ruach*) 140–1, 144, 164–5
experience of God 1, 14, 22, 67, 129–30
incomprehensibility 26–7
interaction with human beings 15
knowledge of God 18, 38, 43
living God 12 n.10, 16, 26–8, 35, 43, 130–1, 168, 177, 192
personal identity 139
Person of God 28, 54, 130, 132, 134
presence of God 22, 35, 37, 103, 144, 160, 190, 199
self-revelation/revelation of 29, 38, 58, 96 n.26, 130, 143, 147, 164–5, 196

word of God 27, 43–4, 99–100, 140, 163, 168, 174
work of God 12, 19, 45, 62, 77, 158
Gospels 19, 21, 35, 37, 40, 43, 70, 103, 105, 128, 143, 146, 153, 157, 166, 184, 195, 214
Greco-Roman Roman culture 83, 122
Greek philosophy 26, 88, 186, 197
Green, Chris 10–11, 36, 41, 179, 191
Grenz, Stanley 90, 148 n.76

Hatch, Nathan O., *Democratization of American Christianity* 200 n.66
Hebrew 27, 130, 140 n.53
Hegel/Hegelian 119 n.41, 121, 182, 188
Heisenberg, Werner, uncertainty principle 110
hermeneutics/hermeneutical 6, 10, 12, 16, 38, 56–9, 62, 70–7, 70 n.9, 76 n.49, 78, 80, 84–5, 94–5, 104–6, 108, 118–19, 123, 125–6, 132, 148, 152, 155–6, 177, 184, 191, 193, 208, 213
Heschel, Abraham Joshua 51, 58, 215
Hodge, Charles 94
Holiness 17, 46–7, 57, 67, 72, 79–80, 95, 101–3, 141–2, 195–6, 216
Holiness-Revivalism 71, 125
holism 151
holistic pneumatology 138, 142, 144, 184
Hollenweger, Walter 3, 36
  blood and wounds mysticism 36 n.119
holy fools 25
Holy Ghost 35, 52, 62, 71, 77, 102
holy pagans 15, 15 n.19
Holy Spirit 1–2, 9, 19, 29, 36–8, 40–1, 44–5, 52, 54–6, 58 n.213, 68, 70–2, 74, 120, 126 n.7, 135–41, 152, 156–7, 160, 164, 169–70, 174, 179, 184, 190, 193, 196, 199, 201, 213
humanism 96–7
humanity 45, 53–4, 87–9, 91, 100, 109, 111, 113, 122, 140–1, 144, 147, 162, 187, 196

I-It schema 116, 130–1
imaginative theological worlds. *See* pneumatological imagination

imago Dei 204
inductive reasoning 92, 120
intellectual history 84–92, 116 n.32
interdisciplinary approach 4, 145–9, 148 n.75
Isaiah 5, 20, 164 n.138, 183
I-Thou orientation 116–17, 141

Jacobsen, Douglas, *Thinking in the Spirit: Theologies of the Early Pentecostal Movement* 80 n.70
James, William 18, 33
Jennings, Wille James 166–9, 174
Jenson, Robert 139, 153, 165
Jerusalem 26, 141, 170
Jesus Christ 29, 36–7, 53, 61–2, 72, 96 n.26, 141, 143–5, 163, 165–7, 169, 181–2, 187–90, 196, 200–1, 204, 206, 214, 216
Jesus of Nazareth 40, 139
Jews/Jewish 15 n.19, 27, 53, 162, 167, 182, 187, 189
Jinkins, Michael 134–5
Johns, Cheryl Bridges 5, 121–2, 211
The Joint Declaration on Doctrine of Justification (JDDJ) 206, 206 n.92
Judaism 162

kanon 148
Kant, Immanuel 17, 116 n.32
Kärkkäinen, Veli-Matti 39–40, 44, 56, 71, 76, 102, 104, 138, 140, 164, 183, 205
  Pneumatology: The Holy Spirit in Ecumenical, International, and Contextual Perspective 135–6
Katerberg, William 114
Kerr, Daniel Warren 74
Keswick tradition 6, 34, 67, 75
Kruschwitz, Robert, "The Wild Goose" 169–70
Ku Klux Klan 101

Lactantius 208
  De Ira Dei 26–7
Land, Steven Jack 16, 71, 77–9, 132
  Pentecostal Spirituality 156 n.112
Latter Rain Covenant 77–8

Lecky, William 49
  *History of England in the Eighteenth
    Century* 47–8
lex talionis 182
Lindbeck, George 152 n.90
Lints, Richard 152, 152 n.90
literalism 75, 76 n.50, 97–8, 193
  theological (*see* theological liberalism)
liturgy 216
lived certainty 42
Lonergan, Bernard, *Method in Theology*
  133 n.23
love 42, 49, 51–6, 64, 70, 100, 142, 151,
  159, 163–4, 166 n.147, 174, 179,
  194, 200–1. *See also* affection
  spirit of love 160–1
Lowenthal, David, *The Past Is a Foreign
  Country* 79
Luke 21, 76 n.49, 166–7
Lutherans 68, 207
Lutheran World Federation 206
Luther, Martin 18, 54, 140, 190

MacIntyre, Alister 171–2, 174–6, 186
  Whose Justice? Which Rationality 173
mainstream church 2, 45, 136
Mandela, Nelson 187
manifestation 41, 46, 49–50, 103, 151, 164
Marsden, George M. 97
  Fundamentalism and American Culture
    98 nn.35–6
  on fundamentalism/fundamentalist
    movement 100–3
Martyrdom of Polycarp 195
Martyr, Justin 42–3, 196–7
M-beliefs 151
McCown, Wayne 73
McDonald, Lee Martin 59–60
McGrath, Alister E. 2, 136
McMahan, David L. 30–2
memory 51, 168, 215
metamodern/metamodernism 7 n.23,
  120–3, 180, 185, 196, 212
metaphysics/metaphysical 23, 26, 51,
  84–5, 90, 106, 111, 115, 126, 160,
  185, 215
Methodism 49–50, 72–3, 79
Methodist revivalism 48, 72
Michelson, Albert A. 109

Milbank, John 115, 162–3
minimal foundationalism 150, 150 n.78
modernism 7, 101, 107 n.1, 108, 113–14,
  116, 118–19, 121–2, 125, 212
modernist liberals/liberalism 96 n.26, 97
modernity 26 n.69, 85, 87, 89, 107–8, 111,
  113–14, 116, 118–21, 145, 200
modernization 113
Moltmann, Jürgen 1, 45, 61, 113, 137–8,
  140–2, 165
  holistic pneumatology 138, 142, 144,
    184
  movement metaphors 165
Montanism 136
Moody, D. L. 100
Moses 5
movement metaphors 165
Murphy, Nancey 111, 116–17, 151
  on foundationalism 90–1
mystery 1, 20, 23, 41–2, 53, 95, 116–20,
  137, 164–5, 186, 207, 209
mysticism 13, 30–8, 30 n.85, 60, 62–4, 69,
  83, 95, 107, 125–6, 190, 215
  Christian/Pentecostal 34–8, 34 n.111,
    177
  constructivist 32–4
  mystical experiences 14, 30, 32–3, 37,
    44, 64
  perennial 31
  pure mysticism 33

narrative theology 152–60, 156 n.112,
  159 n.122
National Association of Evangelicals 104
Nel, Marius 38, 44
neo-pentecostalism/neo-charismatic 10
neo-realism 93–4
neshamah (breath) 140 n.53
new creation 166–7
New Testament 34, 44, 53, 57, 77, 164
new theological methodology 96–7, 105,
  127–9, 132, 176, 193
Newton/Newtonian 91, 110–11, 115, 193
New Zealand Prayer Book (Anglican) 216
nondeterministic theology 181
non-Euclidean geometries 110 n.12
non-rational 1, 12, 16, 20, 22, 24, 26–9, 33,
  41, 44, 52, 56, 120, 125–6, 131–2,
  212

North America 3, 6, 9–10, 23 n.53, 67, 69, 72, 80, 84, 107, 153, 183, 211–12, 214–15. *See also* classical Pentecostals of North America
numinous 15–17, 22–5, 28–9, 32–4, 38–9, 50, 63, 67, 69, 190
  co-witnessing spirit 21
  numinous awe/wonder 19–22
  numinous impression 180
  predispositions of 17–19, 21

O'Collins, Gerald 4, 189, 194, 197–9, 201–2, 207
Oden, Thomas C. 148–9
Old Testament 27, 165
Oliverio, L. William 58–60, 78, 103, 105, 172
  Theological Hermeneutics 75 n.43
Oneness/Jesus Only group 30–1, 56–62, 70 n.13
ontology 3, 40, 115, 126, 160, 178, 199
optimism 114
order of knowing (epistemology) 3, 40, 178
order of things (ontology) 3, 40, 126, 178
Origen 34, 43, 146, 197
orthodox Christians/Christianity 2, 4, 24, 26, 37–8, 57, 70, 72, 97, 193
orthodox truth 182
orthopathy/orthopathic 46–7, 46 n.169, 50, 55, 70, 119, 131–2, 138, 189, 212
Otto, Rudolf 15–18, 15 n.16, 22–5, 28–30, 33–4, 63, 67, 132, 180
  The Idea of the Holy 15, 20 n.43
  mysterium tremendum (awe inspiring mystery) 20–1
  numinous (*see* numinous)
  profounder in religion 17

pagan 27, 36, 43, 146
paideia 6, 211
paleo-orthodoxy 148 n.76
Parham, Charles Fox 53, 57
Pascal, Blaise 24, 91
Patristic period 26, 128
peace 18, 187
perennialism 30–2
  perennial mysticism 31
  perennial philosophy (*philosophia perennis*) 31–2

pessimism 47, 116
physical science 109, 139
physics 109–13. *See also* metaphysics/metaphysical; quantum physics
Pietism 71, 125
Pinnock, Clark 106, 121, 141, 160, 180–1, 197
  "Divine Relationality: A Pentecostal Contribution to the Doctrine of God" 71 n.17
  Flame of Love: A Theology of the Holy Spirit 6, 135 n.36
  nondeterministic theology 181
Plato 34, 54, 88, 116 n.32
pluralism 32, 118, 142, 185
pneuma 140–1, 164
pneumatic intuition 39, 41, 178
pneumatocentric/pneumatocentricity 7, 12, 40, 45, 153, 163, 166, 179–80
pneumatological epistemology 41–2, 41 n.142, 44, 59, 149–50, 152, 160, 213, 215
pneumatological imagination 2, 4, 7, 13, 38–45, 62, 64, 69, 83, 95, 105, 107, 125–9, 126 n.7, 131, 135, 176–8, 188, 208, 211, 213–15
  world of dialectic tension 187–8
  world of enchantment 179–81
  world of relationality 184–6
  world unfinished 181–4
pneumatological knowledge 181
pneumatological renaissance 4, 7, 44
pneumatological theological methodology (PTM) 2, 4, 7, 127, 129, 132, 134, 139, 143–5, 151, 154, 159–61, 164, 175–81, 183–8, 209, 212, 214–15
  be converted 189–90
  be discerning (*see* discernment)
  be ecumenical 199–201 (*see also* ecumenism/ecumenical)
  be historical 194–6
  be philosophical 196–9
  be prayerful 190
  be provisional 207–8
  be scriptural 191–4
pneumatology of quest 3, 84, 123, 127, 178
Poirier, John, "Narrative Theology and Pentecostal Commitments" 159 n.122

Pontifical Council for Promoting Christian Unity 206
Pope Francis 135, 136 n.30
Popper, Karl, *Logik der Forschung* 111
postmodern 108, 108 n.5, 114–20, 133, 150, 155, 180, 216
postmodernism/postmodernity 7, 107–8, 107 n.1, 114–22, 114 n.23, 125, 154, 212
pragmatism 68, 106
premodernism/premodernity 7, 86 n.5, 87, 106, 108, 113–14, 116, 119–22, 125, 155, 212
prerational 15–16, 21, 23, 26, 34, 57, 67, 132, 212
pretheological 15–16, 57, 67, 70, 76, 84, 120, 125–6
pretheoretical 16, 23–4, 26, 39, 41, 44, 69, 70, 76
primal spirituality 122
Prime Mover (God) 26
proof-texting system 74–5
prophets/prophetic 4, 15, 43, 53, 61, 106, 121–2, 136, 146–7, 166, 168–70, 173–4, 176, 179, 181, 202, 204
Protestant Christian/Christianity 59, 75, 80
psychology 4–5, 145, 147–8, 184
Puritanism 71, 125

quantum mechanics 110–11
quantum physics 115, 214
Quine, W. V. O.
    on ordinary knowledge 112
    "Two Dogmas of Empiricism" 112

radical countercultural identity 4
rational/rationalism/rationality 16–17, 22, 24–6, 28–9, 33–4, 44, 64, 67, 93, 96, 120, 125–6, 131, 150, 154, 171, 175, 209
    formal 172–3
    rational reflection 22–3, 34, 67, 131, 209, 212
    rational theological gestalt 71–9
    substantive/substantial 172–3, 175, 186
realism 90–1, 93–4, 107, 109, 118, 134, 172, 192–3, 214

reality 20, 22–4, 27, 30–1, 33, 41–3, 62, 76, 88, 93, 96, 113–14, 116–17, 126, 136, 138, 145, 149, 152, 155, 158, 166, 185, 188, 203, 209
reconstruction 169
reductionism 102, 180
Reformation 147, 162, 206
Reid, Thomas 93
relationality 160, 172, 184–6, 188, 204, 208
relational unity 6, 188
relativism 108, 154–5, 171
relativity 111, 113, 117–18
religion(s) 14–15, 17, 19 n.41, 28, 31, 33, 67, 96, 102, 132, 212, 215
    characteristics of 14
    rational 22, 24, 29, 64, 69, 107 (*see also* Christian/Christianity)
    religious experiences 9, 14, 19–21, 24, 30–2, 34, 39, 64, 67–8, 81, 95, 130, 142, 152, 156
    religious language 25, 68, 71, 199
    religious pluralism 32
    and science 96, 96 n.28
remembrance tradition 51, 215–16
resolute optimism 114
restorationism 77–8
revival/revivalism 12–13, 12 n.10, 14–16, 18, 21–6, 23 n.53, 38, 46, 48, 50–1, 60, 62, 64, 67–70, 79, 83, 95, 107, 125–6, 132, 177, 190, 215
    and incomprehensibility 26–7
    and theological reflection 28–9
Riemann, Bernhard, non-Euclidean geometries 110
Robeck, Cecil (Mel) 54, 77
Robinson, Brian, experiential theology 193
Robinson, Robert, "Come Thou Fount of Every Blessing" 50 n.184, 215 n.5
Rohr, Richard 173–4
Roman Catholics 67, 206
Romans 17
Romanticism 119, 148
Runyon, Theodore, orthopathy 46–7, 46 n.169

Sachs, John 137–8
sacred text 4, 16, 27, 50, 58–60, 76, 95, 105, 133, 146, 158, 159 n.126, 163, 179, 182, 193–4, 214

salvation 15 n.19, 36, 52–3, 55, 62, 70, 72, 88, 98, 136, 143, 183, 190, 202, 205
Satan/demons 97–8, 100, 202–5. *See also* God
schism/schismatic 55, 136, 161, 164, 199
Schleiermacher, Friedrich D. E. 20, 20 n.43
scientific knowledge 90, 109, 182
scientific method 92
Scopes Trial (1925) 101 n.41, 104
Scottish Common Sense Realism 75, 92–5, 92 n.21, 105, 192–3
Scriptures 4, 9, 15 n.19, 26–8, 37, 45, 54, 57–60, 73–8, 95, 98, 102, 135, 144–7, 156, 164, 191–4, 196–8, 215–16
The Second Vatican Council, reports of 128
semper reformanda 107, 169 n.160, 183
Seymour, William Joseph 53–5
  The Apostolic Faith 51–2
shadowlands 173, 176
slavery 182, 206
Smith, Huston 85, 88, 110
Smith, James K. A. 16, 24, 36, 58, 102, 105, 108, 115, 117, 156–7, 172, 201
Social Deprivation theory 103
sociology 128, 148–9, 184–5
Sokolowski, Robert, *The Phenomenology of the Human Person* 25
Sölle, Dorothy, *The Window of Vulnerability* 8 n.26
soteriology 61, 72, 80, 134, 136, 142, 206
Spirit of God 19, 28–9, 39–40, 54, 132, 142–3, 178, 181, 185
spirit of life 140–3, 179
spirit of love 160–1, 179
spirit of truth 144–9, 179
spirit of wind 164–76, 179
spiritual/spirituality 3, 9, 19 n.41, 24, 28, 31–2, 36–7, 39, 50, 64, 128, 131–2, 135, 138–9, 141, 156–7, 179–80, 201, 211
  Christian spirituality 37, 128, 131, 179
  elemental 37
  primal 122
Stephenson, Christopher 154
St. John of the Cross, *The Dark Night of the Soul* 64, 64 n.233
St. Maximus 53, 204

Stone, Lawrence, "The Revival of Narrative: Reflections on a New Old History" 153, 153 n.93
storied epistemology 186
Storm, Jason 121
Storm, Josephson, *Metamodernism* 7 n.23
supernatural/supernaturalism 14, 16, 24, 41, 44, 49, 60, 97, 102–3, 119, 125, 201

testimony(ies) 15, 18, 38, 59, 76, 156–8, 166, 174, 176, 189, 196, 205
theism 118, 160
Theissen, Gerd, *A Theory of Primitive Christian Religion* 71 n.15
theological academy 84, 130, 134
theological conservatism 92, 99, 106–7
theological enterprise 2, 5, 28, 60, 125, 131–3, 147–8, 159, 179, 181, 185–6, 198, 209, 214
theological knowledge 70, 92, 105, 126
theological liberalism 92, 107
  challenge of 95–7
theological methodology 1–2, 4–5, 7–9, 14, 125, 125 n.1, 127–9, 132–5, 133 n.23, 144–5, 148–9, 176–7, 184, 189 n.31, 192, 213
theological openness 56–61, 64, 159, 164, 190, 197
theological pluralism 55, 161–4
theological reflections 1–3, 10, 22, 28–9, 39–40, 56, 62, 69–70, 130–1, 138, 154, 192, 194
Thiemann, Ronald 151–2
Tillich, Paul, *The Shaking of the Foundations* 143
Toulmin, Stephen 114
transcendent/transcendental 20, 30–1, 35, 149, 152, 155, 180, 197, 208, 215
Trinity/Trinitarian 29, 35, 56–7, 70, 146, 154, 182, 206
true knowledge 44, 89–90, 92
truth 43, 64, 74–5, 77, 85, 87, 89–90, 92, 96, 99, 109, 115, 118, 150, 159, 161–3, 169 n.160, 179, 196, 201, 207–8, 214
  axiomatic truth 151, 154
  orthodox truth 26, 182
  perennial truth 30

spirit of truth 144–5, 149
theological truth 154
Tutu, Desmond, *No Future without Forgiveness* 68 n.3

Ubuntu philosophy 68–9, 68 n.3
the United States 10, 63 n.229, 70–1, 112
  social change in 98, 98 n.35
unity 4–6, 31, 35 n.112, 52–5, 60, 69, 104, 161–4, 184, 187–8, 190, 199, 201, 209
Universal Religion 30

violence, escalation of 182
Volf, Miroslav 114

Wacker, Grant 46, 48 n.179, 55, 74, 74 n.41, 78, 156, 161
Wallace, Anthony 14
Wariboko, Nimi 140–1, 165, 178–9
  Pentecostal Principle 166 n.147
Webber, Robert 112, 117, 184
Wesleyan-Holiness 6, 10, 34, 47–8, 67, 71, 73, 75, 79–80

Wesleyanism 71, 80, 125, 132
Wesley, John 46, 50, 56, 72–3, 77, 215
white martyrdom 195
Wilken, Robert Louis 42–3, 83, 122, 146–7, 197
Wiman, Christian 51, 215
Wink, Walter
  Naming the Powers: The Language of Power in the New Testament, The Powers 1 203
  trilogy on the powers 203 n.76
World Christian Database 9
worldmaking capacity/process 126, 176–7, 188

Yong, Amos 3, 7, 16, 19, 23–4, 29, 39–42, 123, 126, 150, 161, 165, 172, 176–8, 180, 202–4, 207–8
  imagination 126
  pneumatological imagination of (*see* pneumatological imagination)

zeitgeists 7, 7 n.23, 69, 108, 119–22, 125, 133, 160, 185, 212

www.ingramcontent.com/pod-product-compliance
Lightning Source LLC
Chambersburg PA
CBHW071934240426
43668CB00038B/1679